*State Secularism and Lived Religion
in Soviet Russia and Ukraine*

# State Secularism and Lived Religion in Soviet Russia and Ukraine

Edited by
Catherine Wanner

Woodrow Wilson Center Press
Washington, D.C.

Oxford University Press
New York

# OXFORD
UNIVERSITY PRESS

Oxford University Press, Inc., publishes works that further
Oxford University's objective of excellence
in research, scholarship, and education.

Oxford   New York
Auckland   Cape Town   Dar es Salaam   Hong Kong   Karachi
Kuala Lumpur   Madrid   Melbourne   Mexico City   Nairobi
New Delhi   Shanghai   Taipei   Toronto

With offices in
Argentina   Austria   Brazil   Chile   Czech Republic   France   Greece
Guatemala   Hungary   Italy   Japan   Poland   Portugal   Singapore
South Korea   Switzerland   Thailand   Turkey   Ukraine   Vietnam

Published by Oxford University Press, Inc.
198 Madison Avenue, New York, New York 10016
www.oup.com

Oxford is a registered trademark of Oxford University Press

All rights reserved. No part of this publication may be reproduced,
stored in a retrieval system, or transmitted, in any form or by any means,
electronic, mechanical, photocopying, recording, or otherwise,
without the prior permission of Oxford University Press.

Woodrow Wilson Center Press
One Woodrow Wilson Plaza
1300 Pennsylvania Avenue, N.W.
Washington, DC 20004-3027
Telephone: 202-691-4029
www.wilsoncenter.org

ISBN: 978-0-19-993763-9

© 2012 the Woodrow Wilson International Center for Scholars
All rights reserved
Printed in the United States of America on acid-free paper
2 4 6 8 9 7 5 3 1

*Library of Congress Cataloging-in-Publication Data*

State secularism and lived religion in Soviet Russia and Ukraine / edited by Catherine Wanner.
    pages ; cm
    Includes papers of two conferences: "New Religious Histories: Rethinking Religion and Secularization in Twentieth-Century Russia and Ukraine," held at Pennsylvania State University from March 25 to 27, 2010 and "Religion and the State in Desecularizing Russia," held at the Kennan Institute of the Woodrow Wilson International Center, October 2010.
    Includes index.
    1. Secularism—Soviet Union—Congresses. 2. Secularism—Ukraine—Congresses. 3. Religious awakening—Soviet Union—Congresses. 4. Religious awakening—Ukraine—Congresses. 5. Soviet Union—Religion—Congresses. 6. Ukraine—Religion—Congresses. I. Wanner, Catherine, 1960–
    BL2765.S65S73 2012
    200.947'0904—dc23
                                                                          2012038260

The Woodrow Wilson International Center for Scholars is the national, living U.S. memorial honoring President Woodrow Wilson. In providing an essential link between the worlds of ideas and public policy, the Center addresses current and emerging challenges confronting the United States and the world. The Center promotes policy-relevant research and dialogue to increase understanding and enhance the capabilities and knowledge of leaders, citizens, and institutions worldwide. Created by an act of Congress in 1968, the Center is a nonpartisan institution headquartered in Washington, D.C., and supported by both public and private funds.

Conclusions or opinions expressed in Center publications and programs are those of the authors and speakers and do not necessarily reflect the views of the Center staff, fellows, trustees, advisory groups, or any individuals or organizations that provide financial support to the Center.

The Center is the publisher of *The Wilson Quarterly* and home of Woodrow Wilson Center Press and *dialogue* television and radio. For more information about the Center's activities and publications, please visit us on the Web at www.wilsoncenter.org.

Board of Trustees

Jane Harman, Director, President, and CEO

Joseph B. Gildenhorn, Chairman of the Board
Sander R. Gerber, Vice Chairman

Public Board Members:
James H. Billington, Librarian of Congress; Hillary R. Clinton, Secretary, U.S. Department of State; G. Wayne Clough, Secretary, Smithsonian Institution; Arne Duncan, Secretary, U.S. Department of Education; David Ferriero, Archivist of the United States; James Leach, Chairman, National Endowment for the Humanities; Kathleen Sebelius, Secretary, U.S. Department of Health and Human Services; Designated Appointee of the President from within the Federal Government: Fred P. Hochberg, Chairman and President, Export-Import Bank

Private Board Members:
Timothy Broas, John T. Casteen III, Charles E. Cobb Jr., Thelma Duggin, Carlos M. Gutierrez, Susan Hutchison, Barry S. Jackson

Wilson National Cabinet:
Eddie and Sylvia Brown, Melva Bucksbaum and Raymond Learsy, Ambassadors Sue and Chuck Cobb, Lester Crown, Thelma Duggin, Judi Flom, Sander R. Gerber, Ambassador Joseph B. Gildenhorn and Alma Gildenhorn, Harman Family Foundation, Susan Hutchison, Frank F. Islam, Willem Kooyker, Linda B. and Tobia G. Mercuro, Dr. Alexander V. Mirtchev, Wayne Rogers, Leo Zickler

# Contents

Acknowledgments ix

Introduction 1
*Catherine Wanner*

1 Subversive Atheism: Soviet Antireligious Campaigns
 and the Religious Revival in Ukraine in the 1920s 27
 *Gregory L. Freeze*

2 From the Red Cradle: Memories of Jewish Family Life
 in the Soviet Union 63
 *Anna Shternshis*

3 Christianity and Radical Nationalism: Metropolitan
 Andrei Sheptytsky and the Bandera Movement 93
 *John-Paul Himka*

4   The Revival of Monastic Life in the Trinity-Sergius Lavra
    after World War II                                                    117
    *Scott Kenworthy*

5   "They Burned the Pine, but the Place Remains All the Same":
    Pilgrimage in the Changing Landscape of Soviet Russia                 159
    *Stella Rock*

6   Sacramental Confession in Modern Russia and Ukraine                   190
    *Nadieszda Kizenko*

7   A Time and Space of Suffering: Reflections of the Soviet
    Past in the Memoirs and Narratives of the Evangelical
    Christians–Baptists                                                   218
    *Olena Panych*

8   Preaching the Kingdom Message: The Jehovah's Witnesses
    and Soviet Secularization                                             244
    *Zoe Knox*

9   A Multireligious Region in an Atheist State: Unionwide
    Policies Meet Communal Distinctions in the Postwar
    Mari Republic                                                         272
    *Sonja Luehrmann*

10  The Revival before the Revival: Popular and Institutionalized
    Religion in Ukraine on the Eve of the Collapse of Communism           302
    *Viktor Yelensky*

Contributors                                                              331

Index                                                                     335

# Acknowledgments

Many people and institutions contributed to this collection of essays seeing the light of day. Most of this book's ten chapters began as presentations at the conference "New Religious Histories: Rethinking Religion and Secularization in Twentieth-Century Russia and Ukraine," which was held at Pennsylvania State University from March 25 to 27, 2010. This conference was made possible thanks to support from the Woskob Family Fund for Ukrainian Studies at Pennsylvania State University. The editor wishes to thank the Woskob family as well as other participants in the conference, including Olga Bertelsen, Greg Eghighian, Roger Finke, Linda Ivanits, Philip Jenkins, Judy Maltz, Michael Naydan, Serhii Plokhy, Gregg Roebber, Vera Shevzov, Olha Tytarenko, and Slava Yastremski, who presented papers, offered valuable comments, and raised challenging issues for discussion.

Another event at the Kennan Institute of the Woodrow Wilson International Center for Scholars in October 2010 continued the discussion of religion in the USSR. This conference, "Religion and the State in

Desecularizing Russia," was sponsored by the Keston Institute of Baylor University and the Kennan Institute. Here thanks go to the organizer, Christopher Marsh, as well as Peter Berger, Vyacheslav Karpov, and Elena Lisovskaya.

The editor and contributors express their gratitude to Blair Ruble, the director of the Kennan Institute, for his ongoing support of innovative scholarship in the humanities of the former Soviet Union. Joe Brinley, the director of the Woodrow Wilson Center Press, was supportive of this volume from its inception. Robert H. Greene and another anonymous reader provided very engaged and insightful comments, from which all of us have benefited. Alfred Imhoff ably managed the book's editorial-production process, and Barbara Kohl likewise copyedited the book.

Last, just as with all other things I undertake to accomplish in life, I express heartfelt thanks and gratitude to Adrian Wanner, for his patience, encouragement, and sharp critical eye.

*State Secularism and Lived Religion in Soviet Russia and Ukraine*

# Introduction
## Catherine Wanner

Secularization was an integral element to socialist modernity and state building in the USSR. The Soviet state sought to distinguish itself from its Imperial predecessor as well as from the surrounding bourgeois alternatives to social and political organization by creating secular forms of governance with a public sphere in which the power, and even the presence, of religious institutions would be confined to a silent, privatized sphere that was ostensibly divorced from politics. Yet over time, the Soviet experience of modernity, with its advancing secularization, ultimately led to a crisis of meaning and became one factor in the dramatic and rapid collapse of communism in 1991. Much to the surprise of many, the final years of Soviet rule coincided with a religious revival that quickly took root in the USSR's fifteen republics. Religion rapidly emerged as a rallying force for change and blended with nationalism to effectively galvanize large groups in protest against Soviet rule.

How can these seemingly contradictory trends of antireligious campaigns and pervasive, deepening secularization be followed in quick succession by a religious revival? This collection of essays, written by scholars trained in a variety of disciplines from around the world, begins to answer this question by arguing that Soviet efforts to promote atheism via waves of antireligious campaigns that suppressed public expression of religion, especially in its institutional forms, did not, as they were intended, eliminate belief in and appeals to the supernatural. Rather, the Soviet state's efforts to secularize Soviet society yielded substantial momentum that fueled religious change by shifting the objects and loci of religious expression. The following essays analyze the myriad forms of religious practice and belief that emerged in Soviet society in conjunction with the Soviet government's commitment to secularization. By considering lived religious experiences in tandem with efforts to promote nonbelief, these essays make a unique contribution to the growing interest in the late Soviet period by showing how religious practice in the USSR and efforts to secularize Soviet society were mutually constituting and shaped the ongoing possibilities for individual and collective self-definition throughout the Soviet period.

The Soviet project, radical for its time, to eliminate manifestations in the public sphere of religious practice and religious belief, was at best a mixed success. The following essays detail the variety of ways in which successive efforts to purge the Soviet public sphere of religious content were compromised by competing efforts on the part of certain groups to create alternatives to a Soviet worldview that involved evocations of the sacred and the supernatural. By examining the enchanted nature of everyday life in the USSR as many Russians and Ukrainians experienced it, and the vibrant, albeit often clandestine, religious practices that communities undertook, we gain a fuller picture of the role of the sacred and the profane in shaping the possibilities for protest, compliance, and acquiescence to the Soviet understandings of progress, and especially the project to create a "new Soviet man." Until now, the role of religion as a means of forging an adaptive response to Soviet-styled modernity, along with how these responses—meaning religiosity itself—were shaped by state-led and other social processes of secularization in the USSR, has received surprisingly little scrutiny.

Most studies of religion during the Soviet period have focused on either the repression of specific denominations,[1] or on Soviet antireligious policies.[2] This is in part attributable to the propensity in scholarship during much of the twentieth century to consider religion and politics as different spheres, and therefore in different disciplines, and to frame religious history largely in terms of institutional accounts of change and continuity within specific denominations.

Furthermore, during the Soviet period, Cold War agendas restricted access to some archival materials, which hindered the analysis of certain topics, such as clandestine religious communities and their practices, and favored the selection of others, such as the repressive tactics of the Soviet state, especially during the Stalinist period. These are valid themes that deserve to be pursued, but a one-sided focus on either religion or politics has the potential to introduce blinders, compromising our ability to fully understand the role and function of religion in Soviet society and the meaning of religious beliefs in the lives of individual Soviet citizens.

Soviet antireligious policies, especially initially, went to the heart of reducing the institutional infrastructure of the Russian Orthodox Church and dismantling its authority. Subsequent efforts were made to crush and even outlaw other denominational structures, such as the Ukrainian Greek Catholic Church, and forcefully control others, such as the Baptists, the Pentecostals, and the Jehovah's Witnesses. Additional efforts to secularize Soviet society focused on fundamentally remaking experiences of space and time. A multitude of religious buildings and sacred sites across the USSR were simply destroyed or otherwise made inaccessible. New state-designed means of organizing and marking time, purged of overt religious content, emerged in the form of secular commemorations, Sovietized life-cycle rituals, and work schedules that did not yield to holy days, the Sabbath, Ramadan and so on. The state fostered experiences of time and space that reaffirmed the values and practices that underpinned Soviet culture and a sense of being Soviet that was firmly anchored in progress and change. The combination of these factors over time led to a tendency among scholars to dismiss the importance, sometimes even the viable existence, of religious communities and to the widespread assumption that Soviet society had become secular, if not atheist. The tendency to conflate processes of state-led modernization to include successful secularization not only shaped the scholarship of religion in the USSR, but also studies of religion in other communist societies as well.[3]

Dimitry Pospielovsky went against the inherent assumptions in modernization and secularization theories and became one of the earliest and most ardent analysts of religion and secularization in the USSR.[4] Following the common conventions of the times of considering religion and politics in different spheres, he addressed religious history and Soviet atheist policies in separate monographs. Other early studies of secularization, such as those by David Powell, analyzed the strategies and tactics of persuasion employed by the state in the latter half of the Soviet period to drive the processes of secularization and foster atheism. More recent institutional histories, such as those written by Daniel Peris and William Husband, are more critical of the state's efforts and point to shortcomings and failures. Husband, for example, argues that the techniques of promoting atheism used through the end of the Cultural Revolution did not convince many Soviet citizens to abandon their religious convictions, but they did alter traditional forms of piety. Beyond being a very significant agent for religious change, Husband argues that the primary success of these antireligious campaigns was the legitimation of nonbelief, which is quite notable in and of itself, but that this success was primarily attributable to the indifference of a great many Russians who neither resisted nor participated in antireligious campaigns.[5]

Peris's study makes the argument that the League of the Militant Godless, in many ways the early centerpiece of antireligious efforts, contributed very little to Soviet secularization. Soviet political culture, Peris argues, rendered the league's work all but useless. To the extent that secularization was achieved and the authority of clergy and religious institutions receded in Soviet society, it was mostly thanks to rapid industrialization, urbanization, and culture change—in other words, generalized dynamics of modernization experienced by a number of societies in the twentieth century—and not as a result of antireligious agitation. In sum, all of these studies share the assessment that even when secularizing goals were reached in the USSR, it was not through intended means and, as a result, antireligious policies often produced unintended consequences.

As Glennys Young has written, "We can learn much from these studies about how the Soviet regime mobilized against religion. But almost invariably these studies treat religion as an object of Soviet political mobilization. Consequently, it is easy to overemphasize the active role played by the state in a process that was necessarily two-sided."[6] I think Young is articulating an important point here. Individuals, whether they were believers or not, were not passive in this process. Indeed, it is their very reactions to secularizing policies that prompted the state to respond in particular ways, thereby triggering new reactions and setting up a dynamic of interaction that obliged the state over time to become far more pragmatic and calculating of possibilities in dealing with religious communities and individual believers than the dominant image of a powerful and monolithic Soviet state bent on crushing religion would suggest.[7] A more regional and comparative examination among a variety of denominations of the dynamics of secularization within the USSR shows the Soviet state at times to be more informed, flexible, and willing to tailor policies to the specific practices and beliefs of individual communities and local circumstances to a greater degree than is usually advanced.[8]

There is a twofold explanation as to why we have bypassed consideration of or otherwise underestimated the transformative impact of processes of secularization for religion in the USSR, preferring instead to see secularization in terms of a "loss" of religion. First, many of the key Bolshevik leaders were influenced by Marx's understanding of the role of religion in social change. Marx saw religion as a form of superstition born of ignorance and a misguided response to suffering that was entirely reactive and derivative. Such a view denied religion properties of agency and implied that it merely mediated between individuals and their social surroundings.[9] Although Marx never advocated the state-led coercive attempts to drastically limit the presence and influence of religious institutions that were undertaken in the USSR, he clearly understood religion to be an impediment to progressive economic and social change. As an "opiate of the people," religion served to accommodate the sources of oppression, rather than assist in overturning them. Such a view conceptualizes religion as a bounded cultural form, an engine that generates false sources of authoritative knowledge, and one that is an epiphenomenon of economic relations. These factors combined to suggest that religion was not relevant, except in terms of its potential to slow the building of socialism, for, as Lenin wrote, it was rapidly being "swept out as rubbish by the very course of economic development."[10]

In addition to Marxist philosophy and Bolshevik policies that embodied it, a second reason that scholars were prompted to dismiss consideration of religion during the Soviet period was the influence of a Weberian view of secularization, which took Europe as a normative model for social and cultural development. This thesis posited that secularization was an inevitable outcome of modernization, that is, a byproduct of increased urbanization, education, and bureaucratization. As these developments intensified, the thinking went, an inevitable shift from religious myth to rational scientific thinking would evolve, prompting new understandings as to what constitutes authoritative knowledge, which would lead to the privatization of religious belief and eventual withering away of the role of religion in social institutions and in the public sphere.[11]

In other words, the conditions generated by modernity would yield new sensibilities and new forms of knowing that would contribute to the secularization of individual consciousness. This, the thinking went, would in turn fuel the secularization of social institutions, which would accelerate the secularization of individual consciousness, ultimately closing the circle and putting in place a self-reinforcing dynamic. As the authority and power of religion were removed from public life and individuals' commitments to religious beliefs and practices weakened, societies would become secularized. Politically, this trajectory translated into the conviction that the most stable and democratic form of government in modern societies would be one where religious values, practices, and identities would not be allowed to impose themselves on the rule of law and would be sequestered in private life. The public sphere was to be created and maintained as a secular domain, thereby negating the possibility of a particular religious group or groups becoming privileged as others were discriminated against and disempowered.

The Soviet Union, as the quintessential example of accelerated modernization, had policies in place to speed up secularization and the sequestration and renunciation of religion, which included coercion, agitation, and persuasion through propaganda. The rejection of all things religious, in favor of science and progress, became a sustaining national ideal. Over time, secularization, as evidenced by such standard indicators as falling church attendance, decreasing performance of religious rituals, and diminishing consultation with clergy, proceeded steadily in the USSR. Yet it is erroneous to equate this broad and pervasive secularizing trend, which greatly affected formalized religious practice, with an equally broad and pervasive presence of accepted atheism.

I do not mean to deny the achieved degree of secularity in Soviet society, which has hardly vanished in Russian and Ukrainian society today. Nor do I mean to suggest that religiosity is inevitable, an inherent part of human nature, and therefore cannot be eradicated. Rather, my point is that it would be a mistake to equate diminished formal religious practice with an absence of belief and disregard for religious institutions because these two are not mutually determinative.

Similar degrees of secularity might have been produced in parts of the former Soviet Union and in Europe, which are well in excess of other regions in the world, yet key differences in the processes by which this was accomplished remain. State-led initiatives to secularize the public sphere in the USSR by radically limiting the authority and even presence of religious institutions unleashed processes that were very different from the secularizing dynamics that were propelled in twentieth-century Europe by the recognition of European state churches and the emergence of welfare state policies. These differences suggest that using a normative European model to understand secularization in the USSR, which has been accepted practice up until recently, is not helpful. In discussing secularization, many scholars now refer to "European exceptionalism," meaning that the Weberian thesis of modernization and secularization rather accurately depicts secularizing dynamics that have evolved across much of Europe, but it fails to account for ongoing religiosity in other parts of the world, including the former Soviet Union.

Most theories of secularization have focused on analyses of Catholic and Protestant Europe, inexcusably casting aside consideration of secularization among Orthodox believers.[12] The predominance of Orthodoxy in Russia and Ukraine has yielded key differences in how the secular was forged and in how attitudes toward religion were shaped given the different nature of secularizing pressures over the course of the twentieth century in the USSR, especially when compared with European Protestant and Catholic communities. Among other attributes, Orthodoxy differs from Protestantism and Catholicism in its nation-state denominational structure (i.e., the Bulgarian Orthodox Church, Romanian Orthodox Church, Serbian Orthodox Church, and so on), which fuses religion with nationality and yields a sense of religiosity as something inherited and inalienable. Moreover, Orthodox practice places a distinct emphasis on the sacred and mysticism, which fosters extrainstitutional forms of religious practice. All this contributes to vibrant forms of lived religiosity, sometimes referred to as popular religion, which until now have been largely overlooked. This presents an opportunity for scholars of Russia and Ukraine to make insightful contributions to theories of secularization as well as to examine the responses of a variety of religious communities, not just Protestant and Catholic, to secularizing dynamics and policies.

## Rethinking Secularization

To understand how religious practice was experienced in the USSR, and therefore the meanings it held for individuals and the society alike, we must move beyond conceptualizing religion and secularization in terms of a dialectics of enchantment. That is to say, rather than accepting that it was disenchantment itself that triggered reenchantment, or secularization that triggered revival, we need to consider how belief and its expression over time were altered during the Soviet period, including how they often combined with colonialism and nationalism for mutually reinforcing effect, and to finally abandon the assumption that they disappeared. As these essays make clear, the outcome of processes of secularization in the USSR was not a loss of religion, but religious change. Therefore, the task at hand is to explore the forms of religious change that unfolded during the Soviet period, analyze how and why these changes came about, and assess what the consequences have been.[13]

So what should we make of Soviet secularism? To move beyond the view of secularism that the European historical experience offers, we must also jettison the binaries that pit "the secular" against "religion." It is perhaps more insightful to think of Soviet secularism as a historically shifting category with its own genealogy that contributed, above all, to religious change, and indeed change that has moved in multiple directions. Secularization, therefore, should be seen as an ongoing process that is manifested in relaxations and intensifications of religious sentiment and expression that in the long run yield change, rather than negation.[14] This is a dynamic that is vividly depicted in the final essay in this volume by Viktor Yelensky on the "revival before the revival," in which he argues that in advance of the galvanization of religion with nationalist politics in the late 1980s that ultimately helped bring down the Soviet state, a renewed interest in religion and spiritual questions was embraced by the intelligentsia beginning in the 1960s that was in part also driven by disillusionment with Soviet ideology.

However, even if we think of secularization as a process of intensifying and relaxing religious expression, a question still remains: What drives the crafting of these peaks and troughs that cast and recast the prominence of religion and the experience of the sacred more broadly? Talal Asad argues that secularism as a political project is essentially about reshaping the form religion takes by endorsing certain religious subjectivities and condemning others.[15] Asad has argued that in the modern period, governance has become inextricably entwined with religion because "only by compelling religion, as concept and practice, to remain within prescribed limits can the transcendent power of the secular state secure liberty of belief and expression."[16] In other words, religion becomes enmeshed with power, and in particular state power, because the state always has a vested interest in limiting, administering, or harnessing for itself the power of religious institutions, of the sacred, and even of the supernatural.[17] Yet, in order for secularization to occur, the sovereign power of the state must retain the authority and ability to impose decisions affecting religious life and practice, as it did in the

USSR and Europe in the twentieth century. Without an independent quality to political power, secularization is much less likely to occur.

Taking inspiration from Talal Asad, I suggest that secularism is inextricably tied up with governance and should be considered more in such terms, rather than purely in conjunction with religion. Asad's governmentalist view of secularization draws our attention to the forces affecting religious change, what constitutes the sacred, and how this works in tandem with the needs of the state to generate compliance at a particular time. Both religion and politics are concerned with the nature and practice of power and authority and with regulating moral conduct. Modern government requires new links to be forged among governance, space, and power, and this was especially true for the Bolsheviks given the ambitious plans they had for massively remaking social and political life as well as individual consciousness.

So, if we depart from the understanding that secularizing policies affecting religious change are intensified or relaxed in tandem with the needs of a state and the necessity of generating compliance, obedience, and at times even mobilization, either through arguments based on science or the prompting of emotions that evoke the supernatural, we see that it is the historically shifting needs of governance that provoke the ups and downs of intensity of religious sentiment and shifting understandings as to what constitutes belief and appropriate practice. By using a governmentalist approach to secularism when studying Soviet history, we can trace how the operation of power creates subjects, discourses, and institutions over time, which evoke religion to varying degrees. Therefore, I would argue that processes of secularization over the course of the Soviet period essentially reflect the state using religion to more effectively govern given the challenges it faced at a particular moment in time. This is true of states in general, and the Soviet state is no exception.

What is distinct, however, about the Soviet Union is that the dynamics of secularization, which have yielded relaxations and intensifications of religious sentiment, seem above all to have provoked religious change in terms of new understandings as to what constitutes the sacred and who has the authority to declare it so. As the Soviet state set out to secularize Soviet society by altering the power and ability of religious institutions to affect governance, new objects, places, practices, and symbols became revered as sacred and were integrated into noninstitutional, often improvised, experiences of everyday religiosity. This is one of the key consequences of Soviet policies of secularization.

## Rethinking Religion in the USSR

With such a theoretical framework in mind, we now turn our attention to how such dynamics of secularization might have engendered religious change at specific historical moments and for specific religious communities. The essays in this volume address the histories of a number of religious communities in twentieth-century Russia and Ukraine—Orthodoxy, Judaism, Greek Catholicism, Protestantism, Islam, indigenous faith traditions, and groups that were considered "cults"—and there are considerably more religious communities that could have been included. Although comparing the experiences of different groups under Soviet rule is quite revealing, no attempts have been made to paint a comprehensive portrait of religious life in the USSR. Rather, the goal of this collection is to give a sense of the interplay over time between the spectrum of secularizing dynamics and the range of religious responses. The essays are arranged in a loose chronological order. This serves to simultaneously narrate how antireligious policies unfolded and evolved over time, and how various religious groups adjusted their practices to render them meaningful and compatible with the new conditions set by the Soviet government.

A comparative view of religious groups also shows the extent to which state authorities, in turn, were highly selective in modifying their own goals of achieving atheism and purging the public sphere of religious content, depending on how they assessed the strengths of the challenges communities and religious believers could mount in certain regions at particular times. When taken together, this collection of essays illustrates how the lived religious experiences of Soviet believers were constituted, not only by religious communities (their doctrines, hierarchies, practices, and so on), but also by the demands of the ways in which Soviet ideology was interpreted and used to redirect attitudes as to what was considered sacred, meaningful, and authoritative in the name of realizing atheism in the USSR.

This process was highly variable over time, and given that the essays by Gregory Freeze and Anna Shternshis address the prewar period, it is worth considering the historical context in which these early efforts at secularization unfolded. Overall, the unprecedented nature and grandiosity of the project to forge a "New Soviet Man" perhaps explains the unintended and often paradoxical consequences these secularizing efforts produced. The motivation for enacting secularizing antireligious policies was twofold. First, the Bolsheviks had to contend with the Russian Orthodox Church as a competing institution that commanded the allegiance of much of the Russian

Empire's populace and, even more significantly, was an institution that was closely allied with the absolute Tsarist monarchy. For the Bolsheviks to secure political power, they had to compound the internal difficulties that the Church was already experiencing in the early twentieth century by weakening its standing among the faithful during this tumultuous period. Second, following Marxist ideology, the Bolsheviks reasoned that religious beliefs fostered false consciousness and impeded the masses' ability to address social problems and the sources of poverty-related suffering in the here and now. They sought to shift understandings as to how one understood assertions to be "true" away from sacred, visceral sensations to cognitively understood ideological proclamations buttressed by scientific forms of proof.

Secularism, as a set of political ideals, informed the very state-remaking process and tactics of governance that the Bolsheviks embarked upon after 1917. Initially, the Bolsheviks sought to secularize society by removing religion from governance—that is, from the workings of the state—and then to reduce the authority that religious beliefs had over governing individual lives. The means they used to achieve these goals centered on destroying the infrastructure of the Russian Orthodox Church, which they hoped would disrupt the functioning of the Church and break the ability of one generation to transfer to the next the knowledge of religious doctrine, symbolism and practice.

Early efforts to secularize Soviet society were successful to a remarkable degree because they involved altering the place of the Russian Orthodox Church in society. Already in 1918, the Bolsheviks issued the Separation Decree, which stated, "Every citizen may confess any religion or profess none at all. Every legal restriction connected with the profession of certain faiths or with the profession of no faith is now revoked."[18] This was an important step in altering how populations were governed, shifting the social and administrative functions of the Church to the state and, importantly, making nonbelief and nonaffiliation real options. Far beyond simply advocating a separation of church and state, Lenin revealed the complexity of the relationship he envisioned between religion and state power when he wrote:

> We demand that religion be held a private affair so far as the state is concerned. But by no means can we consider religion a private affair so far as our Party is concerned. Religion must be of no concern to the state, and religious societies must have no connection with governmental authority. . . . Our Party is an association of class-conscious, advanced fighters for the emancipation

of the working class. Such an association cannot and must not be indifferent to lack of class-consciousness, ignorance or obscurantism in the shape of religious beliefs.[19]

So though the state was to take a fairly neutral position toward religious organizations and practice, the Communist Party was to take a decidedly adversarial stance. It is critical to note that, in essence, Lenin was proposing a radical disruption of the historic linkages between religion and state politics, between the sacred transcendent and political orders, all of which had long characterized governance in this part of the world.

This legislation was followed by brutal campaigns that involved destruction of church property and the physical harassment, imprisonment, and execution of clergy and some of the most active believers. Coercive measures such as these were reinforced by antireligious propaganda in the media, in public debates and lectures, in the curricula of educational institutions, and the promotion of secular celebrations during periods of religious ritual. All these measures were part of an effort to divest religious institutions of political power—what scholars have called "functional differentiation"—and to eliminate the role of clergy in key spheres of public and private life.

During this first phase of secularization, the state willfully instigated processes to secularize the public sphere and public life, during which the infrastructure and leadership of formal religious institutions, mostly the Russian Orthodox Church, became the target of the Soviet state's repressive policies. As Gregory Freeze argues in chapter 1 of this volume, reactions to the repression of clergy in the 1920s yielded two key consequences immediately. First, though the attack on the institutional structure of the Russian Orthodox Church left the institution in disarray, parish life led by local clergy by and large remained intact. Moreover, the *tserkovniki*, or lay activists at the parish level, were galvanized after the frontal assault on the Church from 1921 to 1923. Indeed, Freeze argues, state officials quickly realized that the *tserkovniki*, given the support they received from kulaks, nationalists, and others opposed to a Bolshevik remake of society, were ultimately more of an oppositional force to their policies than the clergy were. There were more of them and they were harder to delineate from the population at large. The effective challenges that lay activists were able to mount at this time to Bolshevik policies regarding religion became a contributing factor to measures adopted later to repress lay activists, not just clergy, as churches were closed after 1929. Repressing laity, especially those who rose to leadership roles after clerical ranks were reduced, served the state's needs by facilitating governance and securing a monopolization of power by weakening the ability of lay activists to form or join coalitions of oppositional groups.

Freeze also illustrates the multiple ways in which antireligious policies had to be softened and modified in Ukraine, not least because the Orthodox Church as well as the Soviet state had to contend with a nationalist movement that not only sought its own state but its own Orthodox church as well. This is one of the many reasons that explain why, especially in Ukraine, various minority faith groups thrived in the 1920s. This decade is often referred to as the "golden period" of Soviet rule for minority faith groups because before antireligious policies accelerated after 1929, they were able to grow relatively unfettered, providing a critically important opportunity to either strengthen or create communities of believers in the USSR. Baptists are an example of a group that significantly bolstered its ranks in the 1920s, whereas the Jehovah's Witnesses created a significant base of believers during this pivotal decade. As is illustrated in chapters 7 and 8 of this volume—by, respectively, Olena Panych and Zoe Knox—the Soviet state would have to contend with the members of these religious communities as political dissidents and the incessant challenges they mounted to Soviet governance for decades to come. Over time, repressive policies toward the Orthodox clergy not only served to mobilize its laity and trigger the growth of minority faiths; these actions also redirected personal piety, professed belief, and manifest religious practices toward nonreligious spheres of social life.

In chapter 2, Anna Shternshis illustrates the extent to which the family was charged with transmitting religious beliefs and culturally crafted manifestations of religious practice when formal religious institutions no longer could to the same degree. In the same breath, however, Shternshis argues that the family itself became an embodiment, and even carrier, of secularizing dynamics in Soviet society. Even for the first generation of Yiddish-speaking Soviet Jews, fundamental rites of passage—such as weddings, the cornerstone ritual to create a family—readily took on new forms that were entirely devoid of religious content and clerical or religious group participation.

Just as lay activists took on more responsibility in the face of clerical shortages, which altered who had authority, the attack on the infrastructure of religious communities—in this instance, not just synagogues but also the *yeshivas* where boys were given formal religious instruction—also shifted the site of where religious knowledge was transmitted (when it was transmitted at all) from formal religious institutions to individual homes. This "privatization" and "domestication" of Judaism to the family sphere, beginning in the 1920s but accelerating during the 1930s, meant that attempts to promote atheism and further the secularization of Soviet society had important gender implications. The feminization of piety is a thread that runs through many of these chapters. Shternshis shows that even as some Jewish women took on a greater role as the purveyors of religious knowledge, others understood the Soviet repression of religious institutions as a means to "emancipate" women from religious law, meaning that gender played crosscutting roles in forging religious change and religion played mixed roles in either spurring or slowing the remake of gender-based conceptions of self in the early Soviet period. Ultimately, Shternshis argues that by gutting Jewish identity of its religious content and religious cultural practices—and yet designating it as a nationality—Soviet policies heightened the importance of the more secular, cultural components of Jewish identity. This is why, she explains, the first generation of Soviet Jews simultaneously and unproblematically saw themselves as Soviet and as kosher—that is, as following Jewish dietary and other ceremonial laws. Familial cultural practices that were seen as distinctly Jewish continued to persist. Although shorn of their religious content, these everyday practices remained meaningful for individual and collective identities just the same. Together, the chapters by Freeze and Shternshis begin to illustrate how and why authority in religious matters shifted away from formal institutions and formally sanctioned leaders to more informal, improvised domains where it took on new forms and became less visible, but often remained palpable just the same.

Antireligious policies continued to broaden and intensify throughout the 1930s. Not only the Russian Orthodox Church but also a broad spectrum of religious groups were now targeted. Their buildings were slated for closure or destruction. Coercive and violent means were swiftly used to silence believers of all ranks. A turning point in religious policy came with the outbreak of World War II. Dire wartime conditions prompted the redefinition of the public role of religious institutions and clergy and the political implications of the religious identities they inspired. The war ushered in massive suffering and widespread dislocation, which, of course, followed on the heels of the Great Terror, with its enormously destabilizing, even traumatizing, effects. The state was obliged to issue urgent appeals for soldiers willing to fight and civilians willing to sacrifice. At such a critical juncture, religion was harnessed to the cause. National allegiance and religion blended for mutually reinforcing effects. The ability of the clergy to mobilize the population for war was unparalleled, and, conversely, their power to quell interethnic violence in the USSR was also formidable. As the state capitalized on these advantages, it accepted the inevitable rebounding effects on religious life. As Daniel Peris notes:

> For many Soviet citizens during the war—particularly its early stages—the regime's claim to permanence paled in comparison with Orthodoxy's claim, and the invocation of God proved necessary when the reliance on Soviet power seemed insufficient. With the regime under siege, the community of the Orthodox seemed more solid than the community of the Soviets. While many Orthodox saw little contradiction in placing faith in a combination of the Soviet state and Orthodoxy, this solace counted as an undeniable failure for a regime that originally demanded exclusive ideological allegiance.[20]

Beginning in 1941, antireligious policies began to wane. The Union of Militant Atheists was disbanded in 1942, the patriarchal administration of the Russian Orthodox Church was officially reestablished in 1943, Easter and Christmas were reinstated as official holidays, and the westward expansion of the Soviet border added thousands of religious communities to the Soviet Union. For individuals, it became possible to disregard previous assertions that loyalty to the Soviet state and loyalty to certain faith groups constituted a contradiction, and they were able to actively and openly express their support for both during the wartime years.

For the leaders of the Greek Catholic Church, who supported a nationalist project to achieve an independent Ukrainian state, the outbreak of war held out other possibilities as religious and political goals fused ever more tightly together in pursuit of statehood. The Ukrainian Greek Catholic Church is a particularly dramatic example of how religion and nationalism blended for mutually reinforcing effect over issues of governance and, as a result, yielded forces that were particularly resistant to secularizing pressures. Especially during the war, clergy became more than just moral leaders and increasingly took on active roles in shaping political positions. In chapter 3, John-Paul Himka explores the dilemmas these religious leaders and believers faced when they used religion to actively endorse and pursue a secular political ideal, such as nationalism with its promises of a restoration of dignity via political independence. Himka depicts the influence and power that the Ukrainian Greek Catholic clergy, and particularly Metropolitan Andrei Sheptytsky, held during the wartime period. Such power only heightened the ethical dilemmas that Metropolitan Sheptytsky confronted during the war as he tried to balance competing moral claims of loyalty to a people and a commitment to statehood as the preferred means to ensure their well-being on one hand, and his own religiously inspired moral values that condemned the use of violence to achieve these goals on the other hand. As Himka succinctly explains, such historical inquiry reveals a history of conscience and how the very morality and moral authority underpinning personal and political goals is forged by local conditions.

The wartime reprieve from antireligious policies was not to last. After the war ended, and later, especially after the death of Stalin, levels of religious tolerance shifted again. However, subsequent vacillations in repressive tactics never again matched the policies of raw coercion experienced in the 1920s and 1930s. For the Russian Orthodox Church, church-state relations entered a new phase of accommodation. The same cannot be said of other minority religious groups within Ukraine and Russia. After 1945, religious groups were evaluated individually in terms of their potential to pose a challenge to the Soviet state and its official ideology, and these were the considerations that shaped the state's postwar response to religious revitalization. For some faith groups, the war's conclusion brought forth unprecedented levels of coercion. The support for certain secular political projects that the Ukrainian Greek Catholic Church advocated was a justification Soviet authorities used to outlaw the Church in 1946. The Ukrainian Greek Catholic Church became the largest faith group in the world to be denied the right to exist, a distinction it held until the Soviet Union collapsed. The swift and sharp repression of the Greek Catholic Church, its clergy, and its laity was motivated by two key concerns: the Vatican's potential intervention in the Eastern European countries newly annexed into the Soviet Bloc, many of which, such as Poland, had large Catholic populations; and the Catholic Church's support for Ukrainian statehood and other secular, nationalist projects, which was of special concern given the authority that the Church and its clergy had over believers.[21]

The early postwar years also saw an assault on Yiddish culture as numerous cultural figures were arrested on charges of "bourgeois nationalism" and many cultural institutions were shut down. In 1948, the last Yiddish publishing house was closed down and the Jewish section of the Soviet Writers Union was dissolved. Then came the Anticosmopolitan Campaign, which initially targeted writers, musicians, and other artists, the overwhelming majority of whom were Jewish, and accused them of "rootless cosmopolitanism," which was deemed antithetical to the new Soviet man. This was followed in quick succession by a domestic campaign against

Zionism shortly after the state of Israel was founded. It became increasingly clear that, although a Jewish identity had been purged of much of its religious content, having designated Jews as a separate nationality—as the Soviet system had categorized other ethnoreligious groups—the state could always question their loyalty. Jewish Soviet citizens knew this meant that they could always potentially encounter discrimination and even repression as new campaigns emerged. In the postwar period, Jews ultimately faced a choice that Zvi Gitelman encapsulated as "conform, reform or leave," which explains why so many did indeed emigrate.[22]

In contrast, hostilities to the Russian Orthodox Church softened in the postwar years. Especially after the disappointments and failures of Khrushchev's antireligious campaign, which was a final vigorous effort to use propaganda and administrative means to promote atheism from 1958 to 1964, antireligious policies were reoriented to manage the Church's power and visibility, rather than attempting to eradicate them. Repressive tactics shifted from raw coercion and violence to propaganda and agitation as the main means to suppress religious practice and belief in the public sphere. In chapter 4, Scott Kenworthy analyzes why this shift occurred and specifically what it meant for the negotiated revival of monastic life in Russia. This new stance toward the Russian Orthodox Church, he suggests, was supposed to deliver greater acquiescence in the Eastern European countries, which were now part of the Soviet Bloc, and to allow Soviet influence in postwar Eastern Europe to be extended and strengthened via the Russian Orthodox Church. Accommodating the Russian Orthodox Church to a greater degree could also serve as a platform to rebuke Western charges of religious repression and violation of human rights in the USSR. To this end, visiting Western dignitaries in the postwar period were often taken to reopened monasteries and churches as evidence of the freedom of religious life in the Soviet Union. Thus, allowing a limited religious presence offered numerous advantages domestically and improved the image of the USSR abroad.

Kenworthy's study of the Trinity-Sergius Lavra, the central monastery of the Russian Orthodox Church located outside Moscow, shows that the promise of these potential benefits to the state accorded the monastery a surprising amount of leverage in negotiating with the state over the conditions in which the monastery would be allowed to function immediately after the war. The wartime reprieve had already allowed the monastery to not only reopen but also to re-create a strong brotherhood of experienced monks as well as to recruit many new monks.

Monasteries were of considerable importance to individual believers. As sites of historic, artistic, and, of course, religious significance, they were often integrated into pilgrimages, the repositories of venerated relics, the sites of sacred places, such as "holy springs," and, of course, the center of traditional forms of liturgical religious expression. As such, the reopening of monasteries in general, and this monastery in particular, had enormous ramifications in that it allowed a plethora of additional Orthodox practices to revive by making accessible once again a variety of sacred sites. Although the fortunes of monastic life were somewhat reversed once again during Khrushchev's antireligious campaign from 1958 to 1964, ultimately, Kenworthy argues, the reopening of monasteries softened the state's antireligious rhetoric to one condemning "false holy places" and the "superstition" such sites evoked among "religious fanatics." Paradoxically, this left the Soviet state engaged in the same enterprise that had long preoccupied the Russian Orthodox Church: delineating legitimate, sanctioned religious sites and practices from popularly ordained ones. On some level, the state's efforts to promote atheism ended up echoing and reinforcing a message that the Russian Orthodox Church had long sought to advance.[23]

Pilgrimages often feature monasteries as their final destinations and incorporate broader, more flexible understandings of the sacred, which have traditionally been designated and embraced far more fervently by the laity than by clergy. Such popular forms of religious practice illustrate the dynamics of lived religion, as opposed to a narrow view of institutionally anchored religious practice. With her analysis of pilgrimages in chapter 5, Stella Rock argues that the Soviet authorities tried to capitalize on the Russian Orthodox Church's own quandaries with popular religiosity and use them for their own purposes. Pilgrimages, as quintessential forms of believer-led popular and public religiosity, posed particular challenges for the Church because they often did not constitute or include sanctified ecclesiastical ritual.

With the restraints placed on the Russian Orthodox Church and the limited possibilities for religious practice this offered, the most devout lay believers were able to lead believers in forms of religious expression that transformed them into pilgrims. Rock argues that pilgrimages in Soviet Russia grew increasingly independent of formal liturgical practices and clerical regulation, as they have in other parts of the world, and their occurrence increasingly relied on the initiative of individual believers. Even when traditional destinations of pilgrimage were desecrated or otherwise made unavailable, Rock notes how believers often substituted natural elements, such as springs and rivers, as sacred sites during pilgrimages. These adaptations allowed some pilgrimage practices to carry on, which ultimately resulted in a multiplication of the number of sites designated as sacred and worthy of veneration, and bequeathed leadership and authority to lay activists who organized and managed these mass religious events.

Another vivid example of how the state's intervention in organized religion triggered changes in formal religious practices and in established understandings of clerical authority is depicted by Nadieszda Kizenko's analysis of confessional practices in chapter 6. She shows how confession shifted from being a one-on-one event between a believer and a member of the clergy to a collective confession done publicly, which was often led by elders. This change was brought about due to the sharp reduction in the number of clergy available to hear confession. Moreover, although fewer people actually participated in confessions, the experience tended to be quite meaningful for those who did, yielding "confessional families," or groups that routinely participated together. Kizenko notes that, ironically, such shifts in confessional practices were part and parcel of a larger trend of confessional change that was operative not just in the USSR but in Orthodox communities abroad as well. Although the Russian Orthodox Church as an institution has always maintained its commitment to tradition and continuity, the ultimate success of the laity during the Soviet period to adapt basic practices to the conditions at hand to ensure their continuous enactment is notable.

Interestingly, over the course of the Soviet period not only who confessed and how they confessed changed, but also what constitutes a sin that should be confessed. Kizenko details the ways in which fundamental Soviet values were validated in the course of confessions as believers confessed to the sins of "speculation" and riding public transportation without paying, for example. In this way, Orthodox confessional practices were altered by the very state whose politics and policies confessional practices reinforced as righteous.

Although the Russian Orthodox Church was increasingly accommodated after World War II, and overall tactics to promote atheism shifted from raw coercion to propaganda, others were still targeted for repression. Religious groups, such as the Baptists and the Jehovah's Witnesses, which are analyzed here (and one could also add the Pentecostals, the Adventists, and a host of others), found postwar legislative and registration policies so restrictive that they preferred to go underground and lead a clandestine existence. This, not surprisingly, earned them the full wrath of the state—which included a roster of repressive techniques ranging from denying access to higher education to forcibly removing children from the home to prevent religious indoctrination.

In chapter 7, Olena Panych analyzes one of the coping mechanisms that the separatist, dissident Baptists in the USSR embraced as a means to maintain their group cohesion, bestow status on selected members, and uphold the integrity of their practices in the face of ever-present threats of harsh repressive measures. The dissident Baptists' confrontation with the Soviet state dramatically influenced the tenets of their faith, how they expressed and propagated their beliefs, and how the cultural practices of their communities evolved over time—all of which set these Baptists apart from their coreligionists elsewhere in the world. Key to understanding their experiences in Soviet society is a genre of biographical and autobiographical writings that they developed in response to state repressions, including exile and time spent in labor camps. These writings provided a religiously infused interpretive framework, almost a template, with which to understand the predicament of believers in a society that professes to be atheist. They offered conceptual tools to forge meaning into the suffering that believers endured and ways to cope with social isolation and depravation. Ultimately, Panych argues, the reading, writing, and study of these memoirs emerged as a form of empowering religious practice in and of itself, which distinguished dissident Baptists from other believers in the USSR and other Baptists in the world.

The Jehovah's Witnesses formed one of the few religious groups that incurred the wrath of Soviet authorities as much as the dissident Baptist believers did. However, in chapter 8 Zoe Knox takes the opposite perspective in analyzing this encounter between devout believers and hostile state authorities. Rather than analyzing how certain believers understood and experienced antireligious policies, she analyzes how the Jehovah's Witnesses were perceived by the Soviet authorities and by Soviet scholars of religion who were charged with formulating antireligious propaganda and advancing the spread of atheism.

Therefore, in one instance, we see Baptist believers depicting state officials as an evil threat; and in the other, we see state officials asserting that the threat to social stability rests with evil believers, most notably the Jehovah's Witnesses. Ironically, in both cases, the portraits of an "evil enemy" were made for those who were already converted. Both sets of accounts, the religiously infused biographies and the secular state reports, were first and foremost used to dissuade the desertion of their own readers to the other camp. That is to say, the Baptist memoirs explored by Panych were intended to strengthen the faith and allegiance of marginalized believers in the face of state repression. The official Soviet reports, as Knox argues, repeatedly confirmed to other nonbelievers the cultish, deviant, and regressive nature of "destructive totalitarian sects," which justified the righteousness of their mission. The insular nature of each discourse and the mutual alienation between believers and state officials ensured that the efforts of both the Baptists and Soviet authorities had their intended effects only among those who already sympathized with the viewpoints expressed. Overall, Panych's and Knox's chapters thus show how self-definition was achieved for a secular state and its nonbelieving citizens as well as for devout believers in religious minority communities through the detour of the other. Fierce repression and its public justification spurred the tenacity of believers and their creative recourse to coping, which was seen as evidence of their fanaticism and used to legitimate the harsh measures taken against them. This put in place a mutually reinforcing dynamic that at once repressed and vitalized these communities.

In chapter 9, Sonja Luehrmann expands on the centrality of identifying deviance and using this to formulate antireligious policies in the postwar period. She illustrates how and why the frequent response of non-Christian believers to antireligious efforts was, ironically, to encourage the very forms of religious practice that would be classified as deviant. Luehrmann analyzes how a misguided concept of religion among antireligious activists ultimately sowed the seeds for the ineffectiveness of their antireligious efforts.

Although postwar secularizing efforts targeted to Orthodox believers were heavily invested in delineating "deviant religious practices" from "traditional" and therefore tolerated ones, other faith groups were declared deviant altogether and labeled as "sects." This led to a penchant for developing standardized, Unionwide antireligious policies that were often modeled on "deviant sects" and ignored denominational and dogmatic differences among faith groups. When policies modeled on "sects" were implemented in multiconfessional, multiethnic regions—such as in the Mari Republic, with its significant indigenous and Muslim populations—the mismatch between these policies and the wide spectrum of religious practices on the ground contributed to the failures, shortcomings, and stalled implementation of these antireligious policies, especially in areas with a plethora of non-Christian religious cultures. Moreover, Luehrmann reveals the extent to which the goal of secularizing processes in the USSR, as elsewhere in the world, was part and parcel of colonizing efforts to bring distant peoples and lands under centralized state control. Secularism was a political project that was part of an effort to homogenize the Soviet Union's ethnically and religiously diverse population in order to render them more governable.[24] As such, secularizing efforts were part and parcel of cultural policies designed to foster Sovietization and assimilation to Soviet national ideals.

Therefore, it is perhaps not surprising that, as Viktor Yelensky suggests in chapter 10, when enthusiasm for, and even the legitimacy of, socialism and Soviet national ideals faded, secularizing efforts and antireligious campaigns were also proportionally resisted. Using Ukraine as an example, Yelensky argues that on social, political, and cultural levels, Soviet officials were never able to effectively decouple religion from nationality. In fact, many of their policies fused them ever more tightly. An attack on one was equated with an attack on the other. By extension, in the final decades of Soviet rule, as disillusionment grew, resistance assumed not only forms of national assertion but also expressions of religiosity, because both constituted effective forms of protest.

In sum, the implementation of secularizing policies to promote atheism, including its waves of intensification and relaxation and regional variability, shaped the forms of religious expression that emerged across confessional groups in Russia and Ukraine over the course of the twentieth century. Looking at the secularizing tactics of the Soviet state, the ten chapters that follow suggest that one should not consider religion as if it were a bounded realm of social life. In fact, religion, culture, and politics interpenetrate to such a degree that to try to understand the dynamics of either secularization or religious practice, one needs to focus on specific discourses and practices, as these authors do, rather than exclusively on state policies or confessional history.

The relevance of religion over time in the USSR might have lost much of its formal, doctrinal religious content, but this did not eradicate the popularly held reverence for the historic achievements and contributions of religious institutions nor the ability to respond to symbols and objects deemed "sacred" within particular religious traditions. Moreover, religion in the USSR came to represent culture, community, a particular sensibility, a worldview, and even a form of spirituality in the broadest sense of the term. This created a dilemma for Soviet ideologues: they expected that once they had achieved nonbelief, indifference, ignorance, or some other cognitive vacuum, religion and its sacred symbolism and pageantry would cease to hold sway over individuals. This was clearly not the case, although the social weight of nonbelief in Russian and Ukraine is undeniable. It is, however, the direct result of the compendium of secularizing and sacralizing dynamics operative in Soviet society, which created selective affinities that culminated in what is often referred to as "nominal" allegiance. The push to secularize in the Soviet Union, which often resorted to mobilizing sacred means, resulted in large sectors of the population becoming ignorant or indifferent to doctrine and wary of religious institutions at the same time that it sensitized them to sacred experiences. This yielded individuals who still maintained some reverence for religion, which found easy expression politically in the final years of Soviet rule. By considering the intersection of religious practice and Soviet secularizing policies, we see how specific communities and their members adapted to the conditions set by socialist modernity and used them to self-define and forge meaning in their everyday lives as believers living in a state that claimed to be atheistic.

## Notes

1. For some of the most recent and impressive studies of religious practice in the Soviet period, see G. L. Freeze, "Recent Scholarship on Russian Orthodoxy: A Critique," *Kritika* 2, no. 2 (2001): 269–78; Zvi Gitelman, *A Century of Ambivalence: The Jews in Russia and the Soviet Union, 1881 to the Present* (Bloomington: Indiana University Press, 2001); Edward E. Roslof, *Red Priests: Renovationism, Russian Orthodoxy and Revolution, 1905–1946* (Bloomington: Indiana University Press, 2002); Bohdan Bociurkiw, "The Russian Orthodox Church in Ukraine: The Exarchate and the Renovationists, and the 'Conciliar-Episcopal' Church, 1920–39," *Harvard Ukrainian Studies* 26, nos. 1–4 (2002–3): 63–91; Jennifer Wynot, "Monasteries without Walls: Secret Monasticism in the Soviet Union, 1928–39," *Church History* 71, no. 1 (2002): 63–79; T. A. Chumachenko, *Church and State in Soviet Russia: Russian Orthodoxy from World War II to the Khrushchev Years* (Armonk, N.Y.: M. E. Sharpe, 2002); Nathaniel Davis, *A Long Walk to Church: A Contemporary History of Russian Orthodoxy* (Boulder, Colo.: Westview Press, 2003); Judith Deutsch Kornblatt, *Doubly Chosen: Jewish Identity, Soviet Intelligentsia and the Russian Orthodox Church* (Madison: University of Wisconsin Press, 2004); Richard L. Hernandez, "Sacred Sound and Sacred Substance: Church Bells and the Auditory Culture of Russian Villages during the Bolshevik *Velikii Perelom*," *American Historical Review* 109, no. 5 (December 2004): 1475–1504; Heather J. Coleman, *Russian Baptists and Spiritual Revolution, 1905–1929* (Bloomington: Indiana University Press, 2005); John Garrard and Carol Garrard, *Russian Orthodoxy Resurgent* (Princeton, N.J.: Princeton University Press, 2008); Robert Weinberg, "Demonizing Judaism in the Soviet Union during the 1920s," *Slavic Review* 67, no. 1 (Spring 2008): 120–53; Alexsei Beglov, *V Poiskakh "bezgreshnykh katakomb": Tserkovnoe podpol'e v SSSR* (Moscow: Arefa, 2008); Robert H. Greene, *Bodies Like Bright Stars: Saints and*

*Relics in Orthodox Russia* (DeKalb: Northern Illinois University Press, 2010); Scott M. Kenworthy, *The Heart of Russia: Trinity-Sergius, Monasticism and Society after 1825* (Washington, D.C., and New York: Woodrow Wilson Center Press and Oxford University Press, 2010); and Natalia Shlikhta, *Tserkva Tykh, Khto Vyzhyv: Radians'ka Ukraina, Seredyna 1940kh–Pochatok 1970kh rr.* (Kharkiv: Akta, 2011).

2. David E. Powell, *Antireligious Propaganda in the Soviet Union: A Study in Mass Persuasion.* (Cambridge, Mass.: MIT Press, 1975); William van den Bercken, *Ideology and Atheism in the Soviet Union* (New York: Mounton de Gruyter, 1975); Daniel Peris, *Storming the Heavens: The Soviet League of the Militant Godless* (Ithaca, N.Y.: Cornell University Press, 1998); William B. Husband, *Godless Communists: Atheism and Society in Soviet Russia, 1917–1932* (DeKalb: Northern Illinois Press, 2000); Victoria Smolkin-Rothrock, "A Sacred Space Is Never Empty: Soviet Atheism, 1954–1971," Ph.D. diss., University of California-Berkeley, 2010; and Sonja Luehrmann, *Secularism Soviet Style: Teaching Atheism and Religion in a Volga Republic* (Bloomington: Indiana University Press, 2011).

3. For an overview of scholarship on religion in China, see Mayfair Mei-Hui Yang, ed., *Chinese Religiosities: Afflictions of Modernity and State Formation* (Berkeley: University of California Press, 2008), and especially her assessment as to why consideration of popular religion after 1949 has been bypassed by Western and Chinese scholars alike, on 1–2.

4. See Dimitry Pospielovsky's trilogy: *A History of Marxist-Leninist Atheism and Soviet Antireligious Policies* (New York: St. Martin's Press, 1987), *Soviet Antireligious Campaigns and Persecutions* (New York: St. Martin's Press, 1987), and *Soviet Studies on the Church and the Believer's Response to Atheism* (New York: St. Martin's Press, 1988). Only the final volume considers religion somewhat in conjunction with secularization. See also Dimitry Pospielovsky, *The Orthodox Church in the History of Russia* (Crestwood, N.Y.: St. Vladimir's Seminary Press, 1998).

5. William B. Husband, "Soviet Atheism and Russian Orthodox Strategies of Resistance, 1917–32," *Journal of Modern History* 70, no. 1 (March 1998): 74–107; and Husband, *Godless Communists*.

6. Glennys Young, *Power and the Sacred in Revolutionary Russia: Religious Activists in the Village* (University Park: Pennsylvania State University Press, 1997), 3.

7. Several studies capture the variability of religious policies and how this affected lived religiosity in periods other than the Soviet one. See Valerie Kivelson and Robert H. Greene, eds., *Orthodox Russia: Belief and Practice under the Tsars* (University Park: Pennsylvania State University Press, 2003); John-Paul Himka and Andriy Zayarnyuk, eds., *Letters from Heaven: Popular Religion in Russia and Ukraine* (Toronto: University of Toronto Press, 2006); Mark D. Steinberg and Heather Coleman, eds., *Sacred Stories: Religion and Spirituality in Modern Russia* (Bloomington: Indiana University Press, 2007); and Mark D. Steinberg and Catherine Wanner, eds., *Religion, Morality and Community in Post-Soviet Societies* (Washington, D.C., and Bloomington: Woodrow Wilson Center Press and Indiana University Press, 2008).

8. Some studies of religious practice that include the Soviet period and illustrate this variability over time include Husband, "Soviet Atheism"; Roslof, *Red Priests*; Roy C. Robson, *Solovki: The Story of Russia Told Through Its Most Remarkable Islands* (New Haven, Conn.: Yale University Press, 2004); Zoe Knox, *Russian Society and the Orthodox Church: Religion in Russia after Communism* (London: RoutledgeCurzon,

2005); Catherine Wanner, *Communities of the Converted: Ukrainians and Global Evangelism* (Ithaca, N.Y.: Cornell University Press, 2007); and Douglas Rogers, *The Old Faith and the Russian Land: A Historical Ethnography of Ethics in the Urals* (Ithaca, N.Y.: Cornell University Press, 2009).

9. Such a view of religion is clearly stated in his "Economic and Philosophic Manuscripts of 1844," where Marx writes, "*Atheism*, as the denial of this inessentiality, has no longer any meaning, for atheism is a *negation of God*, and postulates the *existence of man* through this negation; but socialism as socialism no longer stands in any need of such a mediation. It proceeds from the *practically and theoretically sensuous consciousness* of man and of nature as the *essence*. Socialism is man's *positive self consciousness* no longer mediated through the annulment of religion, just as *real life* is man's positive reality, no longer mediated through the annulment of private property, through *communism*" (emphasis in the original). Karl Marx, *Economic and Philosophic Manuscripts of 1844* (New York: International Publishers, 1969), 145–46.

10. V. I. Lenin, "Socialism and Religion," in *Lenin Collected Works*, vol. 10 (Moscow: Progress Publishers, 1965), 86. Also available at the Marxist Internet Archive, www.marxists.org/archive/Lenin/works/1905/dec/03.htm.

11. Steve Bruce argues this view most forcefully; see Steve Bruce, *God Is Dead: Secularization in the West* (Oxford: Blackwell, 2002). A modified view of Weber's projection is given by Mark Chaves, "Secularization as Declining Religious Authority," *Social Forces* 72, no. 3 (March 1994): 749–74.

12. An exception is volume 5 (2011) of the journal *Aspasia*, which was dedicated to "Gendering the History of Spiritualities and Secularisms in Southeast Europe" and was edited by Pamela Ballinger and Kristen Ghodsee.

13. Several scholars have proposed generalized theories as to what the nature of religious change might be when brought about as a result of secularization. Rodney Stark and W. Bainbridge argue that such religious change consists of a redistribution of nonrational social functions, rather than a rationalizing of society and decline of religion. Rodney Stark and W. Bainbridge, "Secularization R.I.P.," *Sociology of Religion* 60, no. 3 (Autumn 1999): 249–73. Another view is offered by Mark Chaves, who makes the case that the essence of change that secularization triggers is a loss of authority that religious belief and religiously affiliated organizations formerly claimed. See Chaves, "Secularization."

14. Alternatively, David Martin has written that secularization should rather be thought of as "successive Christianizations followed or accompanied by recoils." David Martin, *On Secularization: Towards a Revised General Theory* (Aldershot, U.K.: Ashgate, 2005), 3–4.

15. Talal Asad, *Formations of the Secular: Christianity, Islam, Modernity* (Stanford, Calif.: Stanford University Press, 2003).

16. Talal Asad, "Reading a Modern Classic: W. C. Smith's *The Meaning and the End of Religion*," *History of Religions* 40, no. 3 (February 2001): 221.

17. The blending of supernatural and state powers culminates in what Michael Taussig has called the "magic of the state." See Michael Taussig, *The Magic of the State* (New York: Routledge, 1997).

18. The full text is given by Pospielovsky, *History of Marxist-Leninist Atheism*, 133.

19. This was originally published in *Novaya Zhizn* in 1905, and it was reprinted as "Socialism and Religion," in *Lenin's Collected Works* (Moscow: Progress Publishers, 1965) and is now available at the Marxist Internet Archive.

20. Daniel Peris, "'God Is Now on Our Side': The Religious Revival on Unoccupied Soviet Territory during World War II," *Kritika: Explorations in Russian and Eurasian History* 1, no. 1 (2008): 97–118, at 103.

21. Serhii Plokhy makes a compelling argument about why Soviet foreign policy concerns of Vatican encroachment in the Soviet Bloc drove the harsh repressive measures against the Ukrainian Greek Catholic Church in the postwar period. See S. M. Plokhy, *Yalta: The Price of Peace* (New York: Viking, 2010). See also Bohdan R. Bociurkiw, *The Ukrainian Greek Catholic Church and the Soviet State (1939–1950)* (Edmonton: Canadian Institute of Ukrainian Studies Press, 1996); and Bohdan Bociurkiw and John W. Strong, eds., *Religion and Atheism in the USSR and Eastern Europe* (Toronto: University of Toronto Press, 1975).

22. Zvi Gitelman, *A Century of Ambivalence* (Bloomington: Indiana University Press, 2001), esp. chaps. 5 and 6.

23. Andrew Stone characterizes this common undertaking between Soviet authorities and the Russian Orthodox Church as "cooperation" and "collaboration." See Andrew B. Stone, "'Overcoming Peasant Backwardness': The Khrushchev Antireligious Campaign and the Rural Soviet Union," *Russian Review* 67 (April 2008): 296–320, at 297, 304.

24. On the intersection of secularization and colonization, see Douglas Northrop, *Veiled Empire: Gender and Power in Stalinist Central Asia* (Ithaca, N.Y.: Cornell University Press, 2004); and Alexia Bloch, *Red Ties and Residential Schools: Indigenous Siberians in a Post-Soviet State* (Philadelphia: University of Pennsylvania Press, 2003).

## Chapter 1

## Subversive Atheism:
## Soviet Antireligious Campaigns and the Religious Revival in Ukraine in the 1920s

*Gregory L. Freeze*

This study reexamines Bolshevik antireligious policy in the 1920s and its role in precipitating the "great turn" (*velikii perelom*). Recent scholarship in the post-Soviet states—especially in Russia,[1] and also in Ukraine[2]—and in the West has produced a substantial corpus of works on Bolshevik religious policies in the first decade of "Soviet power."[3] In contrast to most scholarship, the focus here is not the center but the periphery (specifically, Ukraine) and the impact, not the intent, of antireligious campaigns. The task is to consider *not* what the "center" wanted to see (and wanted others to believe) but to determine how Bolshevik policies affected religious life and believers. After retreating from brute repression, in 1923 the regime embraced a new religious policy (a cultural counterpart to the New Economic Policy, NEP); the goal was to avoid antagonizing rural believers and to rely on enlightenment to eradicate "superstition" in the village. But this new strategy, like the NEP, did not produce the expected outcome: it led not to de-Christianization but to religious revival, with ubiquitous and alarming signs of religious fervor and observance. By the years 1927–28, the

Bolsheviks realized that accommodating the peasantry (*litso k derevene*) had only empowered lay activists (*tserkovniki*) and, ironically, realized decades-old aspirations of rank-and-file parishioners. The regime adopted a radical new policy, one that no longer focused just on the Church and clergy, but the church and believers.[4] The "great turn" in religious policy sought not to regulate but to demolish the local church, to repress not just bishops and priests, but also the lay *tserkovniki*.[5]

## From Repression to Retreat

In its first years, Bolshevik antireligious policy had two primary objectives: the suppression of "counterrevolutionary" clergy, and the disestablishment of the Orthodox Church. Although its objectives were clear, these policies not only failed to destroy Orthodoxy but also were fraught with unintended consequences: (1) social revolution among the clergy, and (2) the empowerment of parishioners.

### *Social Revolution in the Clergy*

Throughout the Civil War, the Bolsheviks subjected clergy to persecution, incarceration, and execution, and they continued to engage in selective repression in the 1920s. As part of the process for parishioners to register and retain control of their local church, the clergy had to file a sworn statement about their past (disclosing any earlier ties to the Whites, social origins, including the status of their parents, and their own "social position" before the Revolution), and their attitude toward Soviet power and the 1918 decree on the separation of church and state.[6] The government relegated clergy to the pariah status of *lishentsy* (the disenfranchised), set high tax rates, and applied a variety of other discriminatory measures to make life so intolerable that the clergy would renounce the Church and voluntarily defrock.[7] Subjected to material deprivation, loss of position, and anticlerical abuse,[8] some priests did abandon the clergy and published antireligious diatribes in the Soviet press (as a precondition for employment in government service).[9] Moreover, the higher tax rate made it difficult for parishes to afford a full staff—most could support only a priest and had to forgo a deacon and sacristan.[10]

Anticlerical policies precipitated a veritable social revolution in the clergy, bringing radical change. First, Soviet policies reduced and restructured the parish clergy: given the costs (exacerbated by Soviet tax policies), parishes could only support a priest (needed to perform sacraments) and had to forgo the appointment of salaried deacons and sacristans (and have unpaid laymen perform their functions). Ironically, this contraction not only enhanced the authority of the priest (as the sole representative of the Church) but helped realize long-standing proposals to prune the lower ranks, which were universally characterized as uneducated (few of whom, in contrast to priests, had a seminary degree) and of ill repute for their personal behavior. Indeed, the change expanded lay participation in church services.

Second, the massive turnover in the priesthood brought democratization—and thus an end to the hereditary clerical estate—and enabled the recruitment of priests from other social groups. Although holdovers exhibited the traditional profile (clerical origin and full seminary education), new ordinands came overwhelmingly from nonclerical backgrounds. Thus, of the 208 priests in the Tikhonite churches in Ekaterinoslav Diocese, by February 1924 only 43 percent came from the clerical estate (89 priests); 57 percent came from other social backgrounds—chiefly the peasantry (99), but also merchants and townspeople (18), and even the nobility (2). Soviet anticlerical policies achieved what prerevolutionary reform could not and, inadvertently, helped to cement new social connections between the priest and his flock.

Third, the Bolsheviks demolished the seminary system that had trained candidates for the priesthood and forced parishes to choose ordinands with a modest educational background, typically in nonecclesiastical schools, and often in mere elementary schools. Thus among the priests in Ekaterinoslav, only 80 priests (mostly holdovers) had a seminary diploma; the majority had less schooling (28 had studied in an elementary church school, 43 in secular schools, and 22 at home), and 33 even admitted to illiteracy (and presumably performed services based on rote memory). In other words, in comparison with 1914 (when virtually all priests held a seminary degree), only 38 percent in 1924 had an equivalent education. In short, the parish clergy was far smaller, had more diverse class origins, and was less educated.[11]

Fourth, the regime made the priest even more dependent on the parish for material support and appointment. On the one hand, the Bolsheviks nationalized parish church land (previously at the priest's disposal, which he either cultivated himself or leased to villagers). Although much derided by prerevolutionary clergy as demeaning and distracting, this parish plot provided a modicum of security in the absence of salaries and the vagaries of voluntary gratuities. On the other hand, disestablishment of the institutional Church gave parishioners the authority to appoint and remove priests. Though the bishops officially appointed and defended priests, they no longer had the apparatus and authority to do so; consequently the priest was loathe to disagree with parishioners' demands. Thus the Bolsheviks eliminated the principal causes of popular anticlericalism: parishioners' lack of control over appointments, the burden of providing material support for a bloated staff, and the infamous hereditary "caste" that—in social and cultural terms—profoundly set the priests apart from their flock in the prerevolutionary Church.

*Disestablishment of the Orthodox Church*

A second main thrust of Bolshevik policy was disestablishment of the Orthodox Church as an institution. The first step was to extend to Ukraine the Soviet decree of January 23, 1918, on the separation of church and state, which nationalized the Church's assets (capital, land, printing presses, churches, and schools) and denied the Church the status of a juridical entity (i.e., the *right* to own property and claim recognition from the Soviet administration and courts).[12] Apart from the well-known repression of leading bishops (including the detention and prosecution of Patriarch Tikhon), no less important was the campaign to demolish diocesan administration. Symbolically, in March 1921 the NKVD confiscated the archbishop's seal, the purpose being to disabuse the prelate, and laity, of any illusions that he had the power to issue legally binding documents.[13] The regime also impeded the efforts of bishops to maintain a chancellery and consistory (even if renamed Soviet). Hence, in a typical order of November 22, 1922, a provincial executive committee issued orders to "liquidate the diocesan council," ostensibly for deviating from its legal obligations.[14] The state also forbade the Church to impose any obligatory levies, its goal being to deprive the Church and its institutions (such as diocesan administration and seminaries) of funding and to exploit long-standing popular resentment against such assessments.[15] Because of such pressure and the dearth of funds, the Church effectively lost the capacity to regulate parish life, with power inevitably devolving from prelate to parishioner.[16] Characteristically, the diocesan chancellery in Kharkiv complained in February 1922 that many clergy were serving in local churches without any authorization by diocesan authorities.[17] Nor did authorities relent in later years. In 1924, Patriarch Tikhon appealed personally to Mikhail Kalinin (chair of the

Central Executive Committee) complaining that authorities still prevented the formation of ecclesiastical administration.[18] Hence in Ukraine, as elsewhere, power rested with the church, not the Church.[19]

Ironically, as the Bolsheviks endeavored to demolish Orthodoxy, they inadvertently empowered the Orthodox, especially zealous activists who, for decades under the ancien regime, had been demanding more authority for the parish community.[20] The parishes had already begun to take power in 1917—before the October Revolution—to the consternation of the clergy;[21] the Bolshevik separation of church and state only legalized the new status quo. Henceforth, parishioners, especially the church elder (*tserkovnyi starosta*) and parish soviet (an elected committee of core parish activists) held real power;[22] the clergy could quite legitimately deny responsibility on grounds that the parish—not the prelate or priest—held real power.[23]

Empowerment of the parish was clearly evident in the 1922 campaign to confiscate church valuables. The ostensible purpose was to provide assistance to the starving masses in the Volga region, but the Communist Party—argued Lenin and Trotsky—should exploit this opportunity to expose the antipopular, "counterrevolutionary" essence of the clergy, whom they fully expected to oppose the seizure of church wealth for such a noble and necessary cause.[24] In the event, however, it was the lay believers—the real masters (*khoziaeva*) of the parish—who mounted a fierce defense of church valuables. Although some clergy did resist,[25] the most violent opposition came from parishioners seeking to protect *their* sacred property. Communist Party functionaries had assumed that the chief barrier to implementation would come from counterrevolutionary priests, but quickly realized that parishioners, not priests, posed the main obstacle to implementation. The instinctive response was an attempt at intimidation. As authorities in one case told local agents:

> You must explain to the believers that, if we encounter any kind of hostility, as at Shuia and Voznesensk (where, under the influence of a black-hundredist outburst there were bloody confrontations), if here the black-hundredist clergy agitate against us, we will be obliged to use armed force. The clergy must take every measure to avoid such violence.[26]

As the Zhytomyr Ukom (*uezd*—i.e., county—party committee) reported in May 1923, confiscation provoked such intense opposition from the laity that even threats of brutal retribution had no effect.[27] The same report recounted how a "crowd" demonstrated against confiscation and shouted that confiscation was nothing other than "robbery."[28] The Zhytomyr confiscation committee recounted how, despite tact and circumspection, they met with a firestorm of protest by parishioners:

> We had not succeeded in passing through the church fence, when from all sides a public raced up to us. They began to scream and curse, declaring that we are plundering not for the sake of the starving, but for the communists (who are sending it all abroad).

Despite the threats, the commission completed its work but departed amid a chorus of curses—"plunderers, thieves, scoundrels, miscreants."[29]

Such resistance by parishioners forced some local authorities to stop short of full confiscation.[30] Such failures infuriated republic authorities in Kharkiv, and in a coded telegram on April 30, 1922, they complained that, "despite specific instructions, the seizure of church valuables is being conducted with inadmissible slowness." They warned that "those provincial executive committees (*gubispolkomy*) that do not complete the seizure by [mid-May] will be held accountable."[31] Such threats had little effect; a month later the party reported that commissions in six provinces (Kharkiv, Chernihiv, Nikolaev, Volynsk, Poltava, and Ekaterinoslav) "manifested inactivity and insufficient attention to the matter of the struggle against famine."[32] The local authorities were thus in an untenable situation: They were to extract all valuables, but somehow to do so without offending religious sensibilities;[33] and they were to rely on voluntary cooperation, not coercion, in performing their duties.[34] To avoid clashes based on ethnic tensions, the party—heedful of non-Ukrainian members (particularly Jews)—ordered provincial committees "to ensure that the national composition of these official commissions not give grounds for chauvinistic agitation."[35] In the event, however, neither tactfulness nor the right ethnic composition diminished parish resistance, and the campaign only served to energize the laity, especially lay zealots, in defense of their church.

Parish power also played the decisive role in the defeat of the "Living Church." The Bolsheviks, hoping to neutralize counterrevolutionary clergy by engineering a schism in the Church, deliberately sought to engineer a power struggle between "renovationists" (reform-minded, pro-Soviet clergy in the Living Church) and "Tikhonites" (those devoted to Patriarch Tikhon, traditional Orthodoxy, and—the party suspected—the ancien regime).[36] Heeding directives from Moscow,[37] party leaders in Kharkiv actively supported a "loyalist" renovationist movement[38] that supported the socialist revolution and Soviet power.[39] The renovationists eagerly demonstrated their "loyalty," as in this resolution by a renovationist assembly in Kharkiv in 1922: "With a recognition of the justness and necessity of a socialist revolution, it is necessary to separate oneself from counterrevolution, and for this it is essential to expel the reactionary-minded elements from the church, and in the future not to permit such [people] in the church."[40] The party predictably took steps to ensure that "reliable" clergy led the "Living Church"[41] and made the Tikhonite clergy the prime target of repression.[42] Thus, a report by the Gosudarstvennoye politicheskoye upravlenie (GPU, the state political directorate) in 1923 emphasized the need "to intensify the repression of the reactionary clergy, not as anti-renovationists, but as anti-Soviet activists."[43] The GPU reiterated this policy a year later, claiming that "the best companion in the anti-Soviet agitation of the counterrevolutionary and kulak [prosperous peasants] element is the clergy. The mood created among the peasantry is exploited by the clergy, on the one hand, to strengthen their influence and thereby not lose their material support, and on the other hand, to assist the kulaks."[44]

Although the Bolsheviks did sow dissension among the clergy,[45] they unwittingly provoked lay parishioners to come to the defense of traditional Orthodoxy and the Tikhonite clergy. The main battlefield, after all, was the parish, which now had control over the appointment and removal of parish clergy. When the renovationists ignored parish will and appointed a new priest, the latter met with unrelenting opposition.[46] In a typical case in Kharkiv Diocese in September 1922, when the renovationist authorities sought to replace a "reactionary" priest, Vasilii Polikarpov, they encountered resistance that initially threatened to turn violent ("some intended to perpetrate violence over the priest"). In the end, the parish soviet was able to avoid bloodshed by persuading the crowd to exercise their right as a registered parish community and to file a legal protest about the "coercion against the pastor that we have elected." The parishioners argued that the Kyiv church council of 1917 had recognized the parish as a "juridical entity" and contended that the Bolshevik regime itself had implicitly confirmed the rights of parishioners: "The decree of Soviet authorities, while not recognizing church parishes as a juridical entity, nevertheless empowered authorities to conclude an agreement with the church council. In addition, the parish councils are recognized as the full masters of their church; the pastor of the church is under their charge and responsibility."[47]

Although most parishioners paid scant attention to the renovationist-Tikhonite ecclesiastical disputes (e.g., the selection of married parish clergy as bishops),[48] they *were* vitally interested in anything that concerned parish religious practice—especially adoption of the Gregorian calendar and replacement of Church Slavonic with the vernacular.[49] The language issue, indeed, was particularly sensitive in Ukraine: here the question was *which* vernacular—Russian or Ukrainian? The majority of believers preferred Church Slavonic; the vernacularists were numerous but divided—some favored Russian, others Ukrainian. The calls for liturgical "Ukrainization" preceded the schism and fueled the autocephalous church movement, which at once repudiated the supremacy of the Russian Orthodox Church and insisted on services in Ukrainian.[50] But, to the renovationists' dismay, the majority of parishioners remained faithful to the traditional liturgy in Church Slavonic. Thus, at a district (superintendency) meeting of clergy in Kharkiv in May 1923, the clergy openly acknowledged the intensity of popular opposition and agreed to use Ukrainian "only in those parishes where a majority favor Ukrainization" and even then to do so "with caution."[51]

The schism, like disestablishment, had a "dialectical" impact; it weakened the Church but strengthened the church. Although the regime hoped that the schism would divide both the clergy and the parish, the conflict energized lay activists and intensified their commitment to traditional Orthodoxy.[52] In June 1922, for example, the anxious authorities reported that Volhynia exhibited "a noticeable increase in every imaginable kind of religious movement," chiefly in the form of unauthorized "icon processions under the pretext of imaginary miracles, icon renewals, and holy visions." The party claimed that there has been "agitation and organizational work among the population on the part of reactionary elements," and accused the clergy of "exploiting the darkness and religious feelings of the backward masses" and "thereby preparing the ground for a benighted reaction that serves the interests of those who oppose Soviet power." It therefore ordered that "all religious processions (icon processions) held without the permission of the district office of administration be stopped immediately" and added that "all initiators of organized, unauthorized religious processions are to be arrested forthwith and prosecuted for violating the orders of Soviet power, and the products and money that they collect be given to the commission for assistance to the starving."[53]

Nor did the party's call for propaganda and enlightenment bolster its control and undermine "superstition." At most, the early antireligious campaigns amounted to little more than disseminating antireligious literature (special brochures, the newspaper *Bezbozhnik*, and other materials in the village "reading room" or *chital'nia-izba*), and dispatching atheist propagandists to make speeches at factories and villages. Despite pompous claims and spectacular attempts to stage a "Komsomol Christmas" and "Komsomol Easter,"[54] the party gradually realized that it had achieved little.[55] Even zealous agitators ventured to make modest claims:

> As a positive achievement of the campaign, one should regard the greater animation of thinking among workers in the antireligious domain, which took various forms: from inoffensive debates at the workplace to conflicts in the family between the traditional old people and youth rebelling against God.[56]

That was hardly tantamount to mass "renunciations of superstition" or popular demands to close the local church. Predictably, this failure was greatest where the party was weakest: the village. An agitator from the Berdichev *okrkom* (*okrug*—i.e., district—party committee) in April and May 1923 organized fourteen rural meetings, including two "disputations" with religious leaders that attracted 3,200 villagers. But the most that he could claim was that, "as a first attempt of antireligious propaganda in the village, the campaign went very well—smoothly, without any excesses [i.e., no violent disorders in defense of Orthodoxy], with the evident sympathy of the peasant youth."[57] Rarely did propagandists report a favorable response in the village; their reticence tells all. Indeed, some propagandists admitted outright that it was simply impossible to win over the peasant masses. One enthusiastic de-Christianizer conceded that, though "such lectures are unquestionably useful and necessary," he discovered that antireligious propaganda "requires an extremely careful approach, based mainly on scientific facts"—an implicit admission of just how hard it was to vanquish superstition in the village.[58]

## The New Religious Policy

Dismayed by the failure of repression, disestablishment, schism, and reeducation, in 1923 the Communist Party abruptly changed course, with the initiative coming from Kharkiv, not Moscow. The first hint came in a decision by the Ukrainian Politburo on March 3, 1923: Although it approved the adoption of a new calendar (shifting the day of rest from Sunday to Monday) and claimed to have the support of workers, the Politburo candidly admitted that the village was inalterably opposed and therefore directed functionaries *not* to impose the new calendar on rural areas.[59] The following month, the Seventh Party Congress of the Ukrainian

Communist Party adopted a resolution on the need to build ties with the rural masses.[60] Significantly, it was only later that month that the central party, at the Twelfth Party Congress in Moscow, adopted a similar resolution.[61] Party resolutions later assigned overriding priority to strengthening the "alliance" between the worker and peasant and downplayed the goal of combating "superstition."[62]

The Ukrainian Central Committee was thus at the forefront when it adopted its "theses on antireligious propaganda" at a plenum on June 22, 1923. Although the resolution included the customary claims about "an enormous improvement in the psychology of the broad masses with respect to questions of faith and religion," the party now conceded defeat on the antireligious front:

> At the same time, one must also take into account a number of negative phenomena. Thus a significant part of hitherto passive believers have shown an extraordinary increase of interest in religion, expanding thereby the number of active defenders of religion and the church. In this sense, one must ascribe a particularly negative role to the fact that a whole number of local organizations have exaggerated their forces, and that in turn has led to an attack on religion and the church that was not sufficiently careful and that was not adequately prepared.

It was not for lack of zeal, but concerns of counterproductive results that drove the party to adopt a "soft line." The Ukrainian party leadership complained that party activists in a number of provinces (referring specifically to Donbas, Ekaterinoslav, Poltava, Odessa, and Chernihiv) were *too* aggressive and had only antagonized the village: "The closing of churches, removal of church bells, taxes on churches and church lands that were not foreseen by law, and a whole number of crude administrative measures to exert pressure taken in certain areas amid the antireligious propaganda—all this provoked some excesses [i.e., disorders], which were aimed against Soviet power and individual comrades, and generated discontent among part of the workers and peasants." The party reaffirmed the need for atheist propaganda, but admonished members to "refrain from measures that might offend the religious feelings of the popular masses," particularly the "backward" folk in the village. Such forbearance did not, to be sure, prevent the repression of clergy and disorganization of the Church; the party still encouraged voluntary defrockings (through promises of material support) and support for the Living Church ("which brings an element of support for Soviet power in this struggle"). Nevertheless, the party insisted that local authorities avoid provoking believers and, given the Ukrainian nationalist issue, "exhibit a certain caution when a battle is occurring between the Living Russian Church and the autocephalous church of Petliura supporters so that the latter cannot accuse Soviet authorities of supporting the Russian church against the Ukrainian."[63]

For the next four years, the party limited its antireligious campaign to propaganda and agitation and avoided coercion ("administrative measures" in party jargon), at least with respect to lay believers. The party conceded that de-Christianization must be incremental, even requiring "years" (as Zinov'ev had predicted), and therefore extended its timeline and set a target of more modest immediate objectives. That was evident, for example, in a directive from the Kyiv Gubkom (provincial party committee) to campaign against Church holidays ("the struggle against [religious] holidays is a battle against religion"), but to avoid "administrative excesses":

> Therefore, party organizations should use every holiday to conduct antireligious propaganda. In particular, it is essential to make thorough preparations for an antireligious campaign in connection with the coming Easter. It is essential to transform this holiday into cultural recreation and entertainment. This is all the easier to do because the holiday of Easter is traditionally linked to the agricultural life of the peasantry, as a holiday of spring, the rebirth of nature, and transition to summer time. Therefore in the village one should link Easter with the sowing campaign, with the onset of fieldwork.[64]

The party abandoned its earlier call for Komsomol Easters and categorically insisted that local authorities observe the law.[65] And, even when the parishioners acted illegally, the party admonished subordinates to avoid confrontation. In 1924, for example, the party ordered officials to combat "miracles, icon processions, and placing of crosses," but only by denying permits to hold processions (as required by law). If believers nonetheless flouted the law, local authorities were not to use force.[66]

The party likewise instructed local authorities to avoid such arbitrary "administrative" actions as the unwarranted closing of churches.[67] A party circular of June 1923, for example, castigated local zealots for illegally "closing churches in villages and the unduly hasty closing of churches in towns." Nor should local officials organize sham "resolutions from the proletariat" to justify such actions—in particular, the practice of soliciting a resolution from one community to close the church in *another* parish. Henceforth, warned the party, members must recognize that "the struggle on the antireligious front is a prolonged struggle, lasting many years, and that it is impossible to chase after quick results. One must remember that the complete extirpation of religious prejudices, which are deeply rooted in our economy, will occur only in a communist society."[68] To be sure, parishioners did sometimes abandon their churches for fiscal reasons, as, for example, in Poltava in 1925 (where the "high cost of repairs" was cited).[69] But the Ukrainian leadership demanded that such closings represent popular will; in the contrary case, authorities intervened on behalf of believers, *not* overzealous officials. For example, in November 1923 the NKVD countermanded plans to close a monastery (the bête noire of communists), because the Podolia Gubispolkom (Provincial Executive Committee) had acted "without sufficient preparation, without an initiative from the local nonparty population, without the observance of the directives of the Central Committee."[70] In general, the regime jettisoned earlier efforts to "induce" parishes to self-liquidate so that their church could be used for "cultural" uses, such as schools, clubs, and village libraries. Indeed, the GPU itself came to the defense of believers' rights. The Anti-Religious Commission in Moscow continued to battle illegal "excesses" by local authorities and issued repeated warnings to adhere strictly to the party line and state laws.[71] But the "excesses" persisted. In February 1925, for example, the GPU ridiculed officials in Radomysl'skii and Korostyshevskii districts (*raiony*) for conducting "antireligious propaganda in a rather unique way: when those seeking to celebrate the religious holiday did not wish to disperse for Christmas, they were beaten with rifles."[72]

At the same time, antireligious propaganda faded: despite ritualistic incantations about the need for antireligious propaganda, the party in fact made only a nominal attempt to reeducate "superstitious" villagers, and even these modest efforts proved inept and ineffective. A report on antireligious propaganda in 1924, for example, conceded that the party's antireligious agents "are quite poorly prepared: they have launched a broad campaign of disputations, but have had little success in propaganda." Not that they had much assistance:

> There are no methodological guides for conducting antireligious propaganda, programs for [agitation] circles, etc. The journal *Bezbozhnik* is also poorly distributed. The local press gives inadequate attention to the religious movement because of the lack of antireligious personnel on the staff.[73]

Even when antireligious propagandists did appear, they felt obliged to show extraordinary caution and avoid indiscretions that would trigger popular complaints. Hence the appearance of atheist agitators took on a conspiratorial air that bordered on the comical. The deputy head of the agitprop section in the Zhytomyr Gubkom, for example, directed that lecturers sent to the village must not under any circumstances "reveal that they have come for a special purpose," and that they should "only incidentally pursue antireligious propaganda."[74]

Beyond the fear of antagonizing believers, the weak antireligious campaign was also due to the fact that party organizations were simply overtasked: a plethora of other urgent tasks forced them to marginalize antireligious activities. Characteristically, in February 1923 the Zhytomyr Ukom listed its top priorities in agitation and propaganda (agriculture, women, and the Red Army, among others) and relegated antireligious propaganda to the very end of its agenda (along with the need to combat alcoholism, as if it were related to religiosity).[75] Such benign neglect did not escape the attention of party leaders: that same year the central Agitprop Bureau in the Ukrainian Communist Party complained that propaganda has "the character of agitation and has been conducted in the form of campaigns," concluded that local reports indicated little activity, and criticized the press for ignoring the religious issue.[76] A flurry of new directives had little effect. In April 1925, for example, one agitator—after visiting scores of settlements—reported that "antireligious literature is almost completely absent (if one does not count the flaccid brochures)."[77] That same month, at the first all-union congress of correspondents for the newspaper *Bezbozhnik,* one delegate acidly criticized the ill-timed delivery of antireligious propaganda: "We receive Easter literature around New Year's Day, Christmas literature at Easter."[78] Nor were the propagandists well prepared. In 1926, for example, the "White-guardist" emigré press reportedly gloated that a priest in Kharkiv had routed an ill-prepared propagandist, igniting queries from the central Moscow office of the League of Atheists.[79] Party reports in 1926 listed some antireligious measures (e.g., the organization of atheist circles and distribution of books), but still relegated this to the bottom of their priorities; instead, the over-tasked agitprop section chose to focus on more urgent tasks, such as providing "political literacy" for the massive influx of new members; it plainly lacked the resources to conduct antireligious propaganda.[80] As one Komsomol activist recalled: "We wanted to exclude religion, superstition, and drunkenness from popular customs, but we had neither the time nor the opportunity to do this."[81] By the end of 1927, the Ukrainian party conceded that "in recent years antireligious propaganda along all lines has been weakened or has taken a one-sided, essentially distorted character, and most often it has ceased altogether."[82]

Nor did the press do much to combat religion. According to a party report from December 1927, "the mass periodical publications refuse to use antireligious materials under the pretext that this will alienate subscribers and readers. Publishers, wrongly citing the unprofitability of antireligious publications, have sharply reduced the number of these publications and, more often, altogether exclude these from their plans." By contrast, religious groups were freely publishing books (thirty-five titles in 1926–27) and periodicals (eleven different titles, with more than 1 million printed sheets each year). In addition, various religious groups (not just Orthodox) regularly received printed material from abroad; in the first ten months of 1927, for example, they obtained ten thousand titles from abroad (not counting journals and newspapers): "All this transpires amid the complete inactivity of our publishing houses in the antireligious area (in 1925–27, only three small booklets [*knizhni*] were published), and this is happening at the very time that Narkompros [the People's Commissariat of Enlightenment] has decided to condense the size of the only antireligious organ in Ukraine (*Bezvirnik*)." The party also complained that local officials displayed an intolerable "liberalism" on religious matters. Recently, for example, officials had permitted the renovationist cleric, Aleksandr Vvedenskii, to deliver public lectures in Kharkiv. Although the All-Ukrainian Council of the League of Atheists had established cells and conducted antireligious propaganda, they did so without the support of party funds and personnel.[83]

## Religious Revival

Bolshevik antireligious policy, as the Communist Party came to recognize, led not to religious decline but to religious revival. That was evident even in public spaces: although the regime sought to restrict Orthodoxy to religious buildings, displays of piety spilled over into the public arena—most dramatically, in an epidemic of "miracles" and "icon renewals" that occurred outside parish churches and triggered spontaneous mass pilgrimages. As described in a 1923 report to the Ukrainian Central Committee,

> Enormous crowds of people are streaming to the site of the "miracles"; the dominant element in the crowd is elderly women, mostly from the prosperous strata (the poor, probably, are busy at work). . . . Crowds of many thousands (among whom are many coming from other provinces) assembled at the site of one such miracle (a weeping cross) in Kalinovka.[84]

Because attempts to suppress such phenomena met with ferocious resistance from believers,[85] the party could do little more than denounce clerical machinations.[86] These reports led the main committee for the "liquidation" of religion to conclude that some local committees had lost control over religious life: "Whole crowds, seized by religious fanaticism and without any permission of local authorities, have erected crosses [and claimed icon] renewals and all kinds of miracles. To put this condition of religious life in the *okrug* into still greater anarchy is criminal and inadmissible."[87] Party officials recorded a total of 586 incidents of "miracles" in 1924—a powerful measure of the potency and vitality of traditional popular Orthodoxy, and the failure of antireligious propaganda and agitation.[88] The religious surge in Ukraine attracted the attention of the Anti-Religious Commission in Moscow; by late 1923 it had even dispatched a special commission to investigate.[89]

Nor were sensational miracles and popular interest the only alarming indicators of support for the Church. As the Zhytomyr Okruzhkom (*okrug* committee) reported in April 1924: "The wave of religious fanaticism that spread through the broad peasant masses has, at the present moment, not only failed to cease and die out, but has provoked a corresponding reaction: it has reinforced the authority of the Church and religion."[90] Party officials in Berdichev reported a similar experience: "One has recently seen an increase in religiosity, especially among the peasantry," and they specifically cited "a wave of 'miracles' and 'icon renewals,' pilgrimages to these 'miracles,' icon processions, 'memorial services' of various religious and 'miraculous' legends, etc."[91] In 1925, the GPU reported that "Poltava is also witnessing a general upsurge in religious sentiments. In many places, where previously all the peasants had evicted the priests from their apartments, they now demand that they be returned. In one place they assaulted the chairman of the local *raiispolkom* [*raion* executive committee] because he summoned a priest from the church during religious services."[92] The local party committee in another district reported "an intensification of the religious movement in the *okrug*. There has been a significant increase in the number of requests for permission to conduct icon processions, the blessing of springs, and so on."[93]

To determine the magnitude of this revival, in 1925 the party assembled statistical data on religious observance. It found that the Orthodox Church still had a substantial number of parishes and members: 1,497 parishes and 921,880 members in the renovationist Church, 6,453 parishes and 4,819,627 members in the Tikhonite Church, and 989 parishes and 680,298 members in the autocephalous church, for a total of 8,939 parishes with 6,421,805 members.[94] The report calculated that, together with the other Christian groups and sectarians, approximately 40.8 percent of those over age eighteen were still active, registered members of a religious group.[95] Because "members" did not include the casually faithful (those who merely attended and observed, without legally becoming members of the parish commune), but only those who voluntarily registered (with attendant liabilities and responsibilities), this figure of 40.8 percent provided astonishing evidence for the continuing appeal of Orthodoxy. If one adds the timid and timorous, the number of believers clearly constituted a large majority. Indeed, party specialists on religious matters concluded that 85 percent of village residents were either registered church members or easily mobilized for this purpose; although the proportion in cities was lower (from 14 to 22 percent), even there the party found cause for growing concern.

Religious revival, to be sure, was hardly universal: the regime could also marshal some evidence of a decline in religiosity, chiefly among the young and the working class. A report from Volhynia Province in March 1923 also claimed that the youth were irreligious: "Among the youth, recently, going to church has come to be regarded as shameful, and whenever someone wants to insult another, he says 'you ought to go to church.'"[96] In January 1925, a GPU report on Cherniakhovsk *raion* reported that one village recorded "a decrease in religiosity on the part of the youth (who ridicule the priest)," and that another *raion* reported "a decrease in religiosity," with "only" 35 percent attending church.[97] Another GPU report observed that "church attendance is now declining; those who attend are mainly old women and men. In a private conversation, the priest Polikarpov himself said that neither sermons nor other religious measures now entice people to worship."[98]

But such reassuring reports were few and far between: most authorities—whether Soviet, party, or police—admitted high levels of sacrament observance, church attendance, and financial support. Thus, in the years 1924–25, contributions to religious associations in Ukraine amounted to nearly 13.9 million rubles—which authorities deemed an immense sum—reflecting not only the peasants' improved economic status but also their willingness to finance the local church.[99] Religious fervor was especially marked among the elderly, rural dwellers, and women. The predominance of women and girls was particularly salient in urban areas; according to data compiled in 1927, women comprised 62 percent of religious groups in cities.[100] Their presence was still more salient in rural areas; after visiting some twenty-nine villages in 1925, a party propagandist concluded that "the main bastion of religion is women."[101] But men were also part of the revival; data on some rural areas showed that men had a high level of religious observance and usually represented the majority of formal church members.

Most alarming for party activists, however, was the fact that religious revival was also making inroads in the bastions of Bolshevism—workers, the young, and poor or landless peasants. A report from the Secret Police (Obyedinyonnoye gosudarstvennoye politicheskoye upravlenie, OGPU) in September 1924 warned that, "under the influence of the kulaks and clergy, the youth of the poor peasants (*bedniaki*) are abandoning the village reading rooms and joining religious communities and beginning to drink."[102] The registration files of church councils and parish membership also showed that the Orthodox revival drew upon a broad social base. An analysis of lay believers in the Tikhonite churches of Poltava Diocese for 1925 (involving 515 parishes) shows that, of the 5,574 church Soviet members, 33.6 percent were kulaks, 44.1 percent were *seredniaki* (middle peasants), 21.5 percent were *bedniaki* (poor peasants), and 0.8 percent were *batraki* (landless agricultural workers). Although the suspect kulaks were disproportionately represented, the great majority of church Soviet members nonetheless came from the lower income groups. The "democratic" profile of rank-and-file members was still lower class; of the general population of believers, kulaks made up 15.5 percent, *seredniaki* made up 42.1 percent, *bedniaki* made up 37.7 percent, and *batraki* made up 4.7 percent. The renovationists had a more "proletarian" profile, with higher proportions of poor and landless peasants.[103] Still more disconcerting was evidence of a surge of piety among the "proletariat" itself. Although the dynamics were predictable (renewed industrialization drew mainly on pious villagers for labor), that was no consolation to party officials.

In short, the party found itself confronted with an upsurge "of religious sentiment among the masses." Although that observance was relatively modest in some areas (e.g., 38.1 percent in the rural areas of Artemovsk Okrug); elsewhere it was much higher and even reached prerevolutionary levels (e.g., 85.2 percent in the villages of Kharkiv Okrug). Worse still, the data showed that religiosity was rising, rather than falling. For example, the data for 1925–27 revealed an increase in Lenten observance ("fasting") in fifty-two parishes in Lubenskii Okrug (from 72,543 to 78,537) and for thirty parishes in Kharkiv (from 37,560 to 39,379). Data for confession in twenty parishes within Kharkiv district likewise showed an increase from 16,612 in 1925 to 27,803 in 1927. Even urban parishes showed growing religious observance; two parishes in Kharkiv, for example, more than tripled the confession rate (from 10,676 to 34,597) between 1925 and 1927. No less alarming was the increase in church revenues, even in urban areas. Saint Sophia's Cathedral in Kyiv, for example, reported a 48.8 percent increase in revenues in this period.[104] Thus, if measured in terms of formal membership, religious observance, or financial contributions, the data confirmed what propagandists and functionaries saw with their own eyes: a resurgence of popular Orthodoxy, especially in the village, but even in urban areas.[105] The picture could hardly have been more disquieting, especially when party functionaries read reports like this one from April 1925:

> All these villages, in terms of religiosity, represent a single picture: they believe blindly, without thinking, without reflecting; they are prepared to bear the crown of martyrdom for the holy faith, and for this of course to go over to counterrevolution, insofar as the authorities are atheistic.[106]

By 1927, the Bolsheviks could take little solace from developments in the religious sphere over the previous four years. Notwithstanding some face-saving bluster about success ("our country has a process involving the incessant destruction of religious ideology of the masses"), the data demonstrated precisely the contrary. Even in terms of institutional power, the party had reason for concern; the number of bishops (thanks to the schism) actually *increased* (from twenty-six in 1914 to ninety-five in 1927). And, despite the havoc wrought by civil war and repression, the Church actually increased the number of priests (from 10,565 in 1914 to 10,657 in 1927)—to be sure, with a 50 percent reduction in uneducated and disreputable deacons and psalmists, but a decrease lamented by few priests. Thus, though the institutional structures of the Church were in disarray, the parish infrastructure—the network of parishes and priests to minister to them—not only remained intact but had even been reinforced and reenergized by the years of revolution, civil war, and the "frontal assault" of 1921–23.

## The Politics of Piety

From the Communist Party's perspective, the Orthodox revival was tantamount to counterrevolution, which, in reductionist party rhetoric, represented nothing more than the exploitation of peasant superstition and backwardness. In a typical display of Bolshevik rhetoric, the GPU concurred that religious groups "widely exploit the low political level of the peasantry" and propagate anti-Soviet ideas.[107] It cited reports that the Orthodox clergy were blaming the country's hardships on the Bolsheviks and preaching that "the harvest failure is God's punishment of the communists."[108] In August 1924, the OGPU reported that, in Cherniakhovsk *raion*, "agitation that the [bad] harvest is God's punishment of the communists is continuing."[109]

From the party's perspective, an Orthodox revival carried two main threats. First, the party portrayed "counterrevolutionary" clergy once again as the dominant influence and principal adversary. This fear pervaded, for example, a GPU report of October 1924 about the "political-economic condition of Zhytomyr Okrug":

> The clergy continues to strengthen its position in the village and to strive, with all possible means, to win the sympathy of the broad peasant masses. And it is often successful in this. Despite the acute shortfall of grain, peasants frequently collect levies to support priests. The latter make every effort to intensify the religious feelings of the populace. In Pulinskii *raion*, a recent church holiday attracted over 3,000 people from nearby villages: Novyi Zavod, Derman, and Chekhovtsy.[110]

The GPU tirelessly emphasized the obvious: clerical influence was strongest in rural areas. For example, "in the village of Liubomirka (Miropol *raion*), the peasants—who had complained about the yoke of state taxes—collected from each household fifteen sheaves for the priest and 350 pud [6.3 tons]."[111] In another village the parishioners demanded that the clergy's former houses—confiscated earlier to create "reading huts"—be returned to the clergy.[112]

The authorities also accused the clergy of undermining the regime's secular schools and reading rooms. According to the police, some priests encouraged parents to keep their children home from state schools and to defy the authority of the local schoolteachers. Thus, the GPU reported that "under the influence of the priest, peasants in the village of Cherniaka of the same *raion* do not support the school because it does not teach religion."[113] In 1925 the GPU in Zhytomyr reported about "the activism of priests" that has given special attention to "agitation against sending children to school and visiting the village reading rooms."[114] The latter—which disseminated antireligious literature—were a particular target of clerical criticism. According to a GPU report in 1924, "in the village of Shvaikovka of Troianov *raion*, the clergy have conducted propaganda against the reading rooms, suggesting that those who sign up for the reading room are registering for a commune."[115] The police also alleged that the clergy agitated against communist youth organizations and urged parents not to permit their children to join.[116]

The GPU also accused the Orthodox clergy of overtly engaging in "anti-Soviet political agitation." A police report in March 1925, for example, stated that the sermons by clergy in Shepatovskii district "bore an anti-Soviet character."[117] In one village, the police claimed, four priests were preaching that "Soviet power is the 'power of the anti-Christ,'" and that because of this, 'God is punishing us.' Their agitation is having partial success: many are joining the church commune."[118] To intimidate parishioners, according to the GPU, some priests were predicting that an earthquake, like the one that had recently devastated Japan, would inflict divine retribution on Russia for betraying the Church.[119] The police accused one priest of preaching that "Soviet power will last only until spring, when the Poles or Petliura come and free us from the yoke of the communists."[120] Interestingly, clergy were allegedly saying that the regime's "soft line" on religion signaled defeat and capitulation, and that only encouraged expectations of still more far-reaching concessions to the Church and clergy. Some clerics even made bold to express their views on the official registration documents; one wrote, for example, that he wanted "the church to be separated from the state in the full sense of the word and that full freedom of conscience be given to each citizen."[121] In March 1925, the GPU reported rumors, actively disseminated by the clergy, that they would soon be restored to full rights of citizenship.[122]

The regime's anxiety was, in no small measure, heightened by the fact that not the "loyal" renovationists but inveterate enemies—the Tikhonites and autocephalous nationalists—prevailed in most parishes.[123] Although the regime's relations with the Tikhonites remained conflictual and tense, communists in Ukraine had a special and (in their view) more serious danger posed by the autocephalous nationalists.[124] The latter had been initially small (with some three hundred parishes in early 1922) and enjoyed little popularity among believers who opposed the replacement of Church Slavonic with Ukrainian in the liturgy.[125] However, the autocephalous movement steadily gained support and increased the number of parishes to 1,600 in 1925—roughly the same size as the Living Church itself.[126] The GPU reported that, although the autocephalous movement still had little support among women and the elderly ("the old people favor Slavonic"), it appealed to the young, men, and the intelligentsia.[127] The attractiveness to the youth—the party's prime constituency—was particularly disturbing.

Above all, the party learned that, precisely as the issue of Ukrainian nationalism intensified in the mid-1920s, the autocephalous movement in the Church had become dangerously nationalistic and openly Russophobic.[128] A party report of October 1925 stressed that the autocephalous church "appears to be more of a political group than a religious one," and emphasized that its leadership included many political reactionaries intent on reestablishing an independent Ukraine. "The attitude of the Ukrainian Autocephalous Orthodox Church," it complained, "is superficially loyal toward Soviet power, but at the same time, behind the scenes, it conducts an openly hostile policy." The OGPU calculated that 70 percent of its leadership consisted of anti-Soviet activists. The police quoted the bishop of Poltava as admitting that "the autocephalous movement is not only a church, but also a social-political movement." The OGPU accused a ranking figure, Bishop Aleksandra (Ereshchenko), of ridiculing official holidays ("The demonstration of communists is a fiction: no one would go to these things if they were not threatened with undesirable consequences") and denouncing Bolshevik persecution ("the communists oppress religious activists").[129] It also quoted provocative comments by an autocephalous priest: "The Church should raise the national spirit of the Ukrainian people, free the Church and its people. The autocephalous Church should be not a religious, but political place, which should free the Ukrainian people from every authority that does not wish to give self-determination to the Ukrainian people."[130] According to the police, one autocephalous bishop was preaching "that the Ukrainian church embodies independence, and that it is necessary to expel all other nationalities now residing in Ukraine. Up to five hundred people attended. The sermons met with a sympathetic response." The GPU noted that his anti-Soviet comments evoked strong support from the "Petliura-minded intelligentsia"; one of those present declared that "we shall achieve the independence of Ukraine through the Ukrainian Church."[131] As a meeting of the Anti-Religious Commission warned in 1925: "The main strata of the population that supports Lipkovshchina [the Ukrainian Autocephalous Church] are the exceptionally chauvinistically minded townspeople and the Ukrainian intelligentsia, who see in the Ukrainian Autocephalous Orthodox Church a base for the unification of all the independent forces for the creation, through the assistance of the church, of an independent Ukraine."[132] Although the regime once toyed with idea of recognizing the autocephalous church (to facilitate control), it ultimately rejected that idea and made the autocephalites a principal target of repression.[133]

To the regime's dismay, the fratricidal conflict within Orthodoxy had only served to spur a sharp growth of sectarianism. Already in 1923, the GPU warned that "the struggle against sectarianism requires greater determination and skill than the fight against Tikhonism and the autocephalites,"[134] and a year later authorities reported a 30-percent increase in sectarians.[135] Such warnings impelled authorities to collect more detailed information on the sectarians, and by 1925 they reported that sectarianism now had 1,578 groups with 148,627 adherents. That marked a phenomenal increase since 1917, when official tallies showed a mere 24,544 sectarians.[136]

In short, religion had not only survived but thrived. And worse still, it had taken on forms—especially the Tikhonite, autocephalite, and sectarian movements—that were especially opprobrious to the regime.

## The Great Turn in Religious Policy

By the late 1920s, the Bolsheviks—duly alarmed by the religious renaissance and the anti-Soviet political engagement of churchmen (lay and clerical)—concluded that far more radical measures were needed. In late 1927, amid the mounting crisis of the New Economic Policy, the Communist Party's leaders showed growing anxiety about the religious renaissance and began to reconsider its religious policy—just as it was doing with respect to other dimensions of the NEP.

Most important, the party now recognized that the Church had the support not only of clergy, kulaks, and nationalists, but also rank-and-file believers. Indeed, authorities came to employ a new supraclass aggregate, *tserkovnik*, to label lay activists. Although the clergy remained a favorite target, the regime realized that parish activists, not just clergy, aggressively opposed reading rooms, schools, and teachers. Hints of this awareness had come earlier. In August 1925, for example, the GPU reported that the main culprit in an organized attack on the local teacher was not the priest, but the local religious community, which denounced the teacher and demanded his removal.[137] Even while still emphasizing the leading role of kulaks and priests, the police conceded that the Church enjoyed the support of the pious masses: "In almost all of the *raions* we observe growth in the activity of church community members [*tserkovnye obshchinniki*], who, following the example of the kulaks and very often together with them, have attempted to plant their representatives in the village soviet [*sel'sovet*]. It is entirely natural that, in these cases, they have widely used the word of God and, under this smokescreen, the kulaks and the lay churchpeople could prepare well and draw over a significant number of voters to their side."[138]

Hence the "religious great turn" expanded the focus from the Church to the church, from clergy to lay *tserkovniki*. The decisive turning point was the decree of April 8, 1929:[139] This statute, which systematized and tightened the legislation on the registration and rights of religious groups, signaled a new desire to combat not merely church and clergy, but the mass of *tserkovniki* who formed the real backbone and power of the postrevolutionary parish. A further decree of October 1, 1929, by the NKVD-mandated registration of all communities by May 1, 1930.[140] The laws aside, the following months marked a massive assault on the parish infrastructure—the coercive closing of churches, seizing of churches, and repression of clergy and parish activists. Dismayed by the abortive attempt to de-Christianize and alarmed by the specter of an anti-Soviet religious revival, by the late 1920s the party concluded that it must wage full-scale war not just on the Church and clergy, but also on the lay *tserkovniki*. It was a policy consistent with the war on the village, as the "intensification of the class struggle" came to embrace not only the social and economic but also the cultural sphere. The result in the 1930s was the massive campaign to close most churches and to repress not just bishops and priests, but lay activists in the parish.[141]

## Notes

1. After some first initial, general studies—e.g., M. I. Odintsov, *Gosudarstvo i tserkov' (istoriia vzaimootnoshenii 1917–1938 gg.)* (Moscow: Izd-vo "Znanie," 1991)—Russian scholars have since produced basic works on central policy. See, e.g., N. A. Krivova, *Vlast' i tserkov' v 1922–1925 gg.* (Moscow: AIRO-XX, 1997); S. G. Petrov, *Dokumenty deloproizvodstva Politburo TsK RKP(B) kak istochnik po istorii Russkoi tserkvi (1921–25 gg.)* (Moscow: Rosspen, 2004); and Iu. N. Makarov, "Sovetskaia gosudarstvennaia religioznaia politika i organzy VChK-GPU-OGPU-NKVD SSSR (okt. 1917-go—konets 1930-kh godov)", doktorskaia dissertatsiia, Sankt-Peterburgskii gosudarstvennyi universitet, 2007. More recently, Russian scholars have added valuable provincial studies, including M. A. Drozdova, "Sovetskoe gosudarstvo i tserkov' v 1917–1927 gg. (po materialam Severo-Zapada Rossii)," kandidatskaia dissertatsiia, Pskovskii gosudarstvennyi pedagogicheskii universitet, 2009; M. Iu. Khrustalev, "Russkaia Pravoslavnaia Tserkov' v tsentre i na periferii v 1919–1930-kh godakh (na materialakh Novgorodskoi eparkhii)," kandidatskaia dissertatsiia, Pomorskii gosudarstvennyi universitet, 2004; A. G. Poliakov, "Tserkovno-gosudarstvennye otnosheniia v 1917–serердina 1920-kh gg. (na materialakh Viatskoi gubernii)," kandidatskaia dissertatsiia, Viatskii gosudarstvennyi gumanitarnyi universitet, 2007. Still,

research continues to focus on the state and party, emphasizing intentionality and the impact on the Church and clergy.

2. Scholarship on Ukraine is less substantial, but includes some major works: Andrii Kukurudza, *Demokratyzatsiia pravoslav'ia 20-kh gg. XX st.* (Rivne: Vydavets' Oleh Zen', 2008); V. O. Pashchenko, *Bil'shovyts'ka derzhava i pravoslavna tserkva v Ukraïni 1917–1930-ti roky* (Poltava: ASMI, 2004); and V. I. Silant'ev, *Bol'sheviki i Pravoslavnaia tserkov' na Ukraine v 20-e gody* (Khar'kov: Khar'kovskii gosudarstvennyi politekhnicheskii universitet, 1998).

3. Western scholarship has also tended to focus on high politics and rely on central repositories; see Arto Luukkanen, *The Party of Unbelief: The Religious Policy of the Bolshevik Party, 1917–1929* (Helsinki: Suomen Historiallinen Seura, 1994); Daniel Peris, *Storming the Heavens: The Soviet League of the Militant Godless* (Ithaca, N.Y.: Cornell University Press, 1998); Ludwig Steindorff et al., eds., *Partei und Kirchen im frühen Sowjetstaat: Die Protokolle der Antireligiösen Kommission beim Zentralkomitee der Russischen Kommunistischen Partii (Bol'ševiki) 1922–1929* (Münster: LIT, 2007); Glennys Young, *Power and the Sacred in Revolutionary Russia* (University Park: Pennsylvania State University Press, 1997); R. H. Greene, *Bodies Like Bright Stars: Saints and Relics in Orthodox Russia* (DeKalb: Northern Illinois University Press, 2010); and R. Hernandes, "Sacred Sound and Sacred Substance: Church Bells and the Auditory Culture of the Russian Village during the Bolshevik *Velikii Perelom*," *American Historical Review* 109 (2004): 1475–1504. Although limited to central archival materials, William Husband gives more attention to the popular response to antireligious campaigns; see William Husband, *"Godless Communists": Atheism and Society in Soviet Russia, 1917–32* (DeKalb: Northern Illinois University Press, 2000); and William Husband, "Soviet Atheism and Russian Orthodox Strategies of Resistance, 1917–1932," *Journal of Modern History* 70 (1998): 74–107.

4. In this chapter, as in the rest of this volume, "Church" refers to the institutional Church, and "church" refers to local parish churches, etc.

5. *Tserkovnik* in prerevolutionary parlance referred to the unordained parish clergy (as shorthand for *tserkovnosluzhiteli*); by the late 1920s and 1930s, the term denoted lay parish activists who defended their church and clergy.

6. Predictably, most gave politically correct, even fawning responses. E.g., in the registration cards for 1923, typical clerical responses to the question about their view of Soviet power: "I found it to be the most correct power," "sympathetic," and "good." Derzhavnyi arkhiv Zhytomyrskoi oblasti (State Archive of Zhytomyr Oblast; hereafter DAZhO), f. r-692 (Gorodnitskii raiispolkom), op. 1, d. 54, ll. 62–92 (Registratsionnye kartochki). In Volhynia Province in January 1923, not one of the 1,317 Orthodox clergy (Tikhonite, renovationist, autocephalite) was negative toward Soviet power or to the separation of church and state—a fact that surely attests more to circumspection than to conviction. DAZhO, f. r-1657 (Otdel upravleniia Gubispolkom), op. 1, d. 444, ll. 11–19 (Uchet dukhovenstva na territorii Volynskoi gub. na 1.1.1923).

7. See Golfo Alexopoulos, *Stalin's Outcasts: Aliens, Citizens, and the Soviet State, 1926–1936* (Ithaca, N.Y.: Cornell University Press, 2003).

8. Anticlericalism impelled priests to propose that they wear secular dress rather than the traditional cassock; as one retired priest explained, this proposal was legitimate in times "when clergymen are subjected in public places to ridicule, arrests, and executions." See the 1919 file in the Derzhavnyi arkhiv Kharkivskoi oblasti (State Archive of Kharkiv Oblast; hereafter DAKhO), f. r-230, op. 1, d. 299. In 1922, another priest

sent a letter to the bishop, which, he admitted, might seem "very liberal or reek of Bolshevism," yet requested that clergy dress and wear short hair like secular citizens. Fr. Semen Petrovskii to the archbishop of Kharkiv, October 16, 1922, DAKhO, f. r-230, op. 1, d. 1583. ll. 1–2.

9. Reflecting pride in the number of voluntarily defrocked priests, the authorities in Odessa reported that eighteen had done so in the last year. Tsentral'nyi derzhavnyi arkhiv gromads'kikh ob'edinan Ukraini (formerly the Central Party Archive of the Ukrainian SSR; hereafter TsDAGOU), f. 1, op. 20, d. 1846, l. 25.

10. See, e.g., the protocol of a church council in March 1922, which eliminated a deacon's position "because of the harvest failure, difficult material shortcomings, and contraction of the parish economy to a minimum." DAKhO, f. r-230, op. 1, d. 1768, l. 12 ob.

11. TsDAGOU, f. 1, op. 20, d. 1846. The profile of renovationist priests was not significantly different. Of 53 priests, 27 came from the clerical estate (the rest consisting of 24 peasants and 2 townsmen), and only 24 had received a seminary diploma (with 15 having studied in elementary church schools, 10 in secular schools, and 4 at home). Data compiled by the Volhynia Gubispolkom for 1923 showed 1,347 (all ranks) with this profile: 15 percent Russian, 85 percent Ukrainian; 58.1 percent from the clerical estate, 40.1 percent from nonclerical backgrounds, 46.8 percent with a seminary degree, 53.2 percent with a lower ecclesiastical, secular, home, or no formal education. DAZhO, f. r-1657, op. 1, d. 444, ll. 11–19.

12. For the resolution of the Volhynia Gubispolkom of November 10, 1920, see DAZhO, f. r-1657, op. 1, d. 430, ll. 12–13.

13. DAKhO, f. r-230, op. 1, d. 1570.

14. Ibid., f. r-1657, op. 1, d. 233, l. 2 (extract from protocol of Gubispolkom, November 20, 1922).

15. Ibid., f. r-230, op. 1, d. 1774/a, ll. 71–72 ob. (Zhurnal, January 3 / February 16, 1922).

16. Significantly, the deanships—the foundation of diocesan supervision—doubled in size. In Kharkiv Diocese, e.g., each superintendent had to serve twenty-five to thirty churches, which is roughly twice the number from prerevolutionary times. DAKhO, f. 5-230, op. 1, d. 1773.

17. Ibid., f. r-230, op. 1, d. 1774/a, l. 34 (circular to superintendents, February 8/21, 1922).

18. Gosudarstvennyi arkhiv Rossiiskoi Federatsii (State Archive of the Russian Federation; hereafter GARF), f. 5263, op. 1, d. 57 ll. 35–39; published as well in M.N. Pokrovskii and S.G. Perov, *Arkhivy kremlia: Politbiuro i tserkov' 1922–1925 gg.*, vol. 2 (Moscow: Rosspen, 1997–98), 427–29.

19. That weakness of authority was hardly unique to Ukraine, but typical of the era. Characteristically, neither the regime nor the Church could impose the new secular calendar upon the laity. See G. L. Freeze, "Counter-Reformation in Russian Orthodoxy: Popular Response to Religious Innovation, 1922–1925," *Slavic Review* 54 (1995): 305–39.

20. See G. L. Freeze, "All Power to the Parish? The Problem and Politics of Church Reform in Late Imperial Russia," in *Social Identities in Revolutionary Russia*, edited by Madhavan K. Palat (London: Macmillan, 2001), 174–208.

21. Shortly after the February Revolution, the parishioners made their long-standing grievances felt. According to one contemporary report, "hundreds of priests, deacons, and psalmists were expelled from their posts and had to wander from place to place.

Everywhere, laymen began to intervene in ecclesiastical affairs, [they] seized church keys from pastors, as well as money and property, and even took upon themselves to appoint pastors." Bohdan Bociurkiw, "The Church and the Ukrainian Revolution," in *The Ukraine, 1917–1921: A Study in Revolution*, edited by Taras Hunczak (Cambridge: HURI, 1977), 221, citing *Trybuna*, January 2, 1919.

22. E.g, in September 1921, one dean in the Kup'iansk District complained that the lay church elders, reflecting the self-importance of the parish, had assumed unwarranted powers and pretensions; one elder, he complained, is "extremely proud, arrogant, regards himself as a great orator, tolerates no kind of contradiction, even if it is just," and also opposes any levies to support diocesan administration. Report of district blagochinny (priestly superintendent) to diocesan council, DAKhO, f. r-230, op. 1, d. 1773, ll. 16–ob. 17.

23. In testimony before a revolutionary tribunal, a priest from Zhytomyr who was accused of failing to aid in the confiscation of valuables in 1922 placed responsibility squarely in the hands of the laity: "We could not tell the parish that they should give up these valuables because we are not the owners. We are social parasites, hirelings of the parish. Our master is the parish commune." The priest himself was circumspect: "Moreover, as for church property, I think the parish will be agreeable and can give up certain articles, but only those that are not needed. Here are representatives of all three confessions; each will tell you that some items are very dear to us. As a Christian, I will say that to give up these items would be a sacrilege, but some items can be given up without offending religious sensibilities." Protokol zasedaniia komissii po iz'iatiiu tsennostei, April 26, 1922, DAZhO, f. r-1820 (Revtribunal), op. 2, d. 5870, ll. 26–29 ob.

24. For this reason, the regime deliberately required clergy members to take a position on the confiscations. E.g., in Novohrad-Volynia a meeting of representatives from different confessions—convened by the authorities—resolved: "Taking into account the enormous scale of the famine, the assembly finds it necessary for clerical representatives to provide every assistance for the confiscation of valuables in accordance with the resolution of the VUTsKK of March 8, 1922." The resolution urged parish soviets to cooperate and enjoined other clergy to explain the rationale and need for the confiscations. The resolution was signed by three Orthodox priests, one Catholic priest, and one rabbi. See Protocol, May 3, 1922, DAZhO, f. p-10, op. 1, d. 151, l. 1.

25. For the case of a priest in Chernihiv, who was tried by a revolutionary tribunal "for concealing church valuables" from the confiscation commission, see the weekly report for May 1–6, 1922, TsDAGOU, f. 1, op. 20, d. 1450, l. 119. Other clergy, while admitting the need to surrender some sacred artifacts, insisted that parishioners have the option to redeem them (i.e., provide an equivalent value for the right to preserve it)—as, e.g., did the diocesan soviet in Kharkiv. See its order regarding the believers' "right to transfer things and objects without religious significance." Diocesan decree to the superintendent in the second district, February 28/March 13, 1922, DAKhO, f. r-230, op. 1, d. 1774/a, l. 1. When a bishop was put on trial in Zhytomyr before a revolutionary tribunal, he gave this testimony: "Here is my view on the seizure of valuables: the magnitude of hardship in the recent famine is unprecedented. I think that under these conditions the government should do all it can to save people—including the seizure of church valuables. However, in the case of sacred objects, in my opinion it should give believers the option to redeem them in one form or another." See DAZhO, f. r-1820 (revoliutsionnyi tribunal), op. 2, d. 3598, l. 24 (interrogation). Likewise, the minutes of an interrogation of the archbishop of Odessa, Feodosii, shows that he too

recognized the need for the Church to surrender the valuables, but warned of popular opposition. See "Stenogramma zapisi besedy pred. Odesskogo Oblispolkoma tov. Avreina s Arkhiepiskopom Feodosiem," TsDAGOU, f. 1, op. 20, d. 995, ll. 32–42. But the regime regarded passive noncooperation as counterrevolutionary resistance, and routinely ordered arrests and prosecution for such noncompliance. Thus a priest in Zhytomyr, Arkadii Iosifovich Ostal'skii, pronounced guilty of resistance, was sentenced to execution by a firing squad; the punishment, however, was ultimately reduced to five years imprisonment). His interrogation revealed that he was young (thirty-three) and a graduate of the Volhynia seminary. Although apolitical ("I am [politically] indifferent; I live exclusively for the interests of the spirit; I recognize authorities, whoever they might be"), he candidly confessed his opposition to the seizure of church valuables. Like many, Fr. Ostal'skii was skeptical that the vessels would be used for the declared purpose and was especially critical of the wanton desecration that occurred during their confiscation: (1) "The valuables are seized, in most cases, by nonbelievers and without asking the permission of the believers of a given commune; (2) in the seizure of valuables with a sacred content, they do not always act with proper respect. Thus, e.g., there are cases where holy vessels with the depiction of the face of Jesus Christ are thrown to the floor; they are taken into the hands of people with cigarettes in their mouth and caps on their head, and that offends our religious feelings." DAZhO, f. r-1820, op. 2, d. 833, ll. 15–16.

26. DAZhO, f. r-1820 (Revtribunal), op. 2, d. 5870, l. 128.

27. Report to Zhytomyr Uezdpodotkom on the Seizure of Valuables in Cherniakovskii Volost', May 25, 1922, DAZhO, f. p-6 (Zhitomirskii uezdnyi komitet), op. 1, d. 72, l. 41–41 ob.

28. Report, May 6–11, 1922, TsDAGOU, f. 1, op. 20, d. 1450, l. 120.

29. Protocol of judicial session, November 20, 1922, DAZhO, f. r-1820 (Revtribunal), op. 2, d. 5870, ll. l. 67.

30. For the case of the chairman of one confiscation commission, put on trial "for nonfeasance in the seizure of valuables" (in Donetsk Province), see the weekly report for May 1–6, 1922, in TsDAGOU, f. 1, op. 20, d. 1450, l. 119. Central authorities also complained about such nonfeasance. On April 4, 1922, party leaders distributed a circular from the Russian Communist Party: "In many areas, the commissions (for purposes of a 'peaceful seizure of church valuables') take only an insignificant part, leaving the main valuables behind." Elsewhere, Moscow complained, the commissions allowed parishioners to redeem the valuables rather than risk open confrontation. It warned that "an incomplete seizure of church valuables will be regarded as nonfeasance by local organs," with the threat of judicial prosecution. See Kosior to Gubkoms, April 4, 1922, TsDAGOU, f. 1, op. 20, d. 1450, l. 118.

31. Decoded telegram from Kharkiv, May 15, 1922, DAZhO, f. p-2, otd. 1, d. 28, l. 32.

32. Protocol of Central Commission for the Seizure of Valuables, May 31, 1922, TsDAGOU, f. 1, op. 20, d. 995, l. 9.

33. Kosior to Gubkoms, April 6, 1922, TsDAGOU, f. 1, op. 20, d. 1450, ll. 106–7.

34. A March 3, 1922, telegram from party authorities in Kharkiv complained that the commissions to seize valuables are "acting too weakly and lethargically" and admonished them to "involve the worker and peasant masses" to ensure that the clergy not "emerge as the political victor." Hence, it insisted on a public display of support "so that there is not a single factory, a single plant that has not adopted a positive resolution

on this question"—which should then be published in the main newspapers. DAZhO, f. p-2, otd. 1, d. 28, l. 13. The party also disseminated statements of peasants who purportedly supported confiscation, such one averring that "we do not need the valuables of the church when we are dying of starvation." TsDAGOU, f. 1, op. 20, d. 1450, l. 51 ("derevnia o tsennostiakh").

35. TsDAGOU, f. 1, op. 20, d. 995, l. 1 (S. Kosior to all Gubkoms, April 4, 1922). At the same time, Ukraine demanded its share of the proceeds; while complying with demands to send gold, silver, and precious stones to Moscow, the Politburo in Kharkiv insisted that "15 percent of the valuables collected" throughout the entire country remain in Ukraine, where 15 percent of all the starving were located. See the importunate note to the central relief agency in Moscow in Protocol of the Politburo of the KP(b)U, May 29, 1922, TsDAGOU, f. 1, op. 6, d. 29, l. 88 ob..

36. See Edward Roslof, *Red Priests: Renovationism, Russian Orthodoxy, and Revolution, 1905–1946* (Bloomington: Indiana University Press, 2003).

37. Rossiiskii gosudarstvennyi arkhiv noveishei istorii (RGANI), f. 89 (kollektsiia rassekrechennykh dokumentov), perechen' 49, d. 17, ll. 4–5.

38. A short précis compiled for the Ukrainian Central Committee claimed that "our work undertaken to cause a schism in the Church has been crowned with complete success." This work was necessary because "the church organization, which was formed and strengthened in the course of centuries with all its iron discipline and unity, remained almost untouched after five years of the proletarian revolution, which destroyed the very foundations of the old order." It was therefore essential to rely on more than agitation and propaganda, because "insufficient attention has been given to antireligious propaganda in the villages "to remove the peasants (who have a low level of consciousness) from the influence of the clergy." Party leaders boasted that "we organized and developed the renovationist movement." A. Sokolovskii, "Kratkii obzor o dukhovenstve," TsDAGOU, f. 1, op. 20, d. 1450, ll. 1–2.

39. See, e.g., the charter and declaration of "progressive clergy" in Poltava, in TsDAGOU, f. 1, op. 20, d. 1450, l. 96.

40. DAKhO, f. r-230, op. 2, d. 500. In return for professions of political loyalty, the renovationists expected official support, personal security, and restitution of nationalized property. The 1922 clerical assembly in Kharkiv, e.g., asked that church buildings be returned for use by the parish clergy (ibid., l. 6). For principled renovationists, the primary objective was to democratize ecclesiastical administration (eliminating "bureaucratism and chancellery arbitrariness") and to conduct religious and liturgical reforms, including vernacularization of the liturgy. See Khar'kovskii uezdnyi s"ezd, December 10, 1922, ibid., l. 3; and Protocol of Belopol'skaia iacheka belogo dukhovenstva i mirian Zhivoi Tserkvi, October 1, 1923, ibid., ll. 21–23.

41. In a sensational document assessing the members of the recently elected All-Ukrainian Synod (October 27, 1923), the GPU boasted that it had successfully induced all but one of the leading renovationists in Kharkiv to collaborate and obey its directives. The ranking Synod member, Metropolitan Pimen, "was linked with the GPU in Podolia," and the GPU was confident that "through him one can successfully channel the Synod's work in the requisite direction." Another reliable renovationist was Archbishop Andrei of Donets'k Diocese, arrested earlier during the confiscation of valuables and "recruited for the GPU at that time. He has already governed Donets'k Diocese for several months, while maintaining contact with the GPU." The GPU deemed the only other cleric "an unreliable person"—Bishop Feodosii (Sergeev) of Priluki, who

had originally conducted renovationist work, but met with failure and was now wavering in his devotion to the cause. But the GPU's key link was Archpriest B. T. Dikarev, secretary of the Synod: "From the very outset of the renovationist movement, he has taken an active role and worked under the guidance of the GPU. He organized the renovationist movement in the Crimea, was chief administrator and member of the All-Ukrainian Supreme Church Administration, and is now a member of the Moscow Synod. He is a completely reliable person, and we will conduct all our secret work through him." "Kharakteristika chlenov Ukrainskogo sinoda, izbrannogo 27 oktiabria 1923 g.," TsDAGOU, f. 1, op. 20, d. 1772, l. 121.

42. A protocol of the Ukrainian Politburo on November 23, 1923, e.g., resolved to "take measures to prevent a strengthening of the Tikhonite movement," and ordered that "the organs of the GPU intensify its work in this sphere." Protocol, November 23, 1923, TsDAGOU, f. 1, op. 6, d. 1, l. 12.

43. Doklad o polozhenii tserkvi na Ukraine, [1923], TsDAGOU, f. 1, op. 20, d. 1772, l. 30.

44. V okrispolkom i Okrparkom, Sov. sekretno, Informatsionnyi doklad o politiko-ekonomicheskom sostoianii zhitomirskogo okruga po sostoianiiu na 14 avgusta 1924 g., DAZhO, f. p-85, op. 1, d. 99, ll. 28–29.

45. Tikhonite clergy were accused of telling believers that "renovationist priests are deprived of divine blessing and are heretics who desecrate churches"; the authorities complained that "this silly propaganda has some success among the dark masses." DAKhO, f. r-230, op. 1, d. 1776. The fierce dissension within the clergy was evident, e.g., at a diocesan assembly that the renovationists, with official permission, convened in Kharkiv in 1923. As a priest from one deanery (*blagochinie*) reported, a recent assembly there elected a chairman who was an inveterate foe of renovationism. He and his supporters purportedly declared that "the Living Church has already abolished sacred relics, portrays hell and paradise as [mere] moral conceptions, and if given its way, will destroy religion." The renovationists responded with equal acrimony, proposing that the antirenovationists either acquiesce or suffer dismissal, and that authorities begin "the immediate implementation of [appropriate] measures against the band of antirenovationists." DAKhO, f. r-230, op. 1, d. 1776, ll. 1, 3, 60–60 ob. Many provincial clergy looked askance at such conflict, claiming "ignorance" in a vain attempt to straddle the fence. But the renovationists, who formally controlled whatever remained of diocesan administration, insisted that parish priests must either be "with us" or "against us." Protokol sobraniia dukhovenstva i tserkovnykh starost, 1okr. Starobel'sk. u., October 16, 1922, DAKhO, f. r-230, op. 2, d. 78, ll. 19–19a ob. Frightened with that threat, and with the possibility of denunciation for counterrevolution and arrest by the GPU, the clergy hastily added their signatures to the list of renovationists.

46. For a typical case, see DAKhO, f. r-230, op. 2, d. 671.

47. Ibid., d. 519.

48. Given the breakdown of ecclesiastical administration and regular communications, most parishioners—and even many rural clergy—had little understanding of renovationism and its battle with the old guard. As one community wrote: "Those of us who live in remote corners of Starobel'sk district, who rarely read newspapers (because it is impossible to obtain them) are not familiar with the political situation in the country and still less with such new phenomena as the renovationist movement in the Orthodox Church." Protocol of a meeting of clergy and laity, October 16, 1922, DAZhO, f. r-230, op. 2, d. 78k, ll. 19–19a ob..

49. Popular opposition to the new calendar was intense; even the Living Church, which had initially been firmly in favor of its adoption (at the behest of the state authorities), soon realized the intensity of lay resistance and retreated. Thus, at a renovationist assembly in Kharkov in January 1923, the delegates affirmed that believers adamantly opposed the new calendar ("since the celebration of church holidays under the old calendar is intimately tied to the everyday life of believers") and warned against imposing the new order. Resolution of January 13, 1923, DAKhO, f. r-230, op. 1, d. 1776, l. 2.

50. The demand for an autocephalous Ukrainian Church was already evident in 1917, and even won majority support in some dioceses (Volhynia, Odessa, Ekaterinoslav, Poltava, and Kyiv). For references and discussion, see Bohdan Bociurkiw, "The Church and the Ukrainian Revolution," in *The Ukraine, 1917–1921: A Study in Revolution*, edited by Taras Hunczak (Cambridge, Mass.: Harvard Ukrainian Research Institute, 1977), 223–24. Such sentiments informed a church council convened in 1921; attended by a broad range of clergy and laity (with a total of 421 representatives), the assembly asserted the autonomy of the Ukrainian Church (banning references to the patriarch), denied the immutability of canons, upheld the need to democratize the Church (replacing episcopal tyranny by the electoral principle), and demanded that the liturgy be conducted in Ukrainian.

51. DAKhO, f. r-230, op. 1, d. 1776, ll. 75–75 ob.

52. As a Narkomiust (People's Commissariat of Justice) directive of February 13, 1922 made clear, the regime sought to disorganize and divide the parish: "For purposes of intensifying the struggle emerging among them, reject the principle of the majority, giving the possibility for the minority to have their own church and not permitting a poll of opinion among parishioners." Protokol, February 13, 1922, TsDAGOU, f. 1, op. 6, d. 29, l. 32.

53. Volhynia Gubispolkom circular of June 15, 1922; and circular titled "On the Intensification of the Manifestations of Religious Movements in Volhynia," June 17, 1922, DAZhO, f. r-1657 (Otdel upravleniia Volgubispolkoma), op. 1, d. 430, l. 54.

54. A letter from the Berdichev party organization, e.g., made the self-congratulatory claim that "antireligious propaganda assumes the significance of a colossal factor in the cause of bringing spiritual emancipation to the working class and achieving clarity in its class consciousness." Letter to all Ukom and Raikom from Sapozhnikov (sekr. Gubkom) and Vitkovskii (sekr. Gub. KK), Kyiv, June 3, 1923, DAZhO, f. p-88, op. 1, d. 1436, l. 21.

55. Komsomol was the Communist Party's youth organization. These rowdy parodies did more to offend than to persuade. See typescript by M. Gorev, later a prominent figure in the League of Militant Atheists, "Komsomol'skoe 'rozhdestvo,'" DAZhO, f. p-6, op. 1, d. 90, l. 38. More staid were the attempts by the Agitprop (Agitation and Propaganda) section of the party to dispatch agitators to groups of workers and peasants to "expose" what religious holidays really involved. Protokol kollegii Agitpropa, March 25, 1923, DAZhO, f. p-5, op. 1, d. 166, ll. 1–1 ob.

56. Otchet o rabote agitprop otdela Berdichevskogo ukoma za fevral', mart 1923 g., DAZhO, f. p-5, op. 1, d. 166, ll. 6–9.

57. Doklad o rabote agitpropa Berdichevskogo okrkoma za aprel'-mai 1923 goda, DAZhO, f. p-5, op. 1, d. 165, ll. 7–13.

58. Report to the Zhytomyr authorities, April 4, 1923, DAZhO, f. p-88, op. 1, d. 1462, l. 20–20 ob.

59. The Politburo formally approved the resolution drafted by its Orgburo: "(a) Agitation for the shift to a Monday day of rest should bear a mass character and be limited to the city and working districts (*raion*); refrain from agitation in the village. (b) The

transfer of enterprises to a Monday day of rest should be done only when there is a real desire among the workers of an enterprise, and not through an artificially created mood. (c) Propose that all members of the Central Committee, when making trips to local areas, become familiar with the attitude of workers and peasants toward anti-religious propaganda." Protocol, Politburo, part 9, March 3, 1923, TsDAGOU, f. 1, op. 6, d. 40, l. 30 ob.. Moscow was fully cognizant of the explosive situation in Ukraine. Later that month the Politburo also exempted Ukraine from any attempt to hold a Komsomol Easter: "Have the Orgburo create a commission for a detailed study of questions of anti-religious propaganda. In view of the special conditions in the Ukraine, propose to the provincial party committees not to organize Komsomol Easters." Protocol, Politburo, March 26, 1923, part 20, TsDAGOU, f. 1, op. 6, d. 40, l. 30 ob.

60. Bohdan Krawchenko, *Social Change and National Consciousness in Twentieth-Century Ukraine* (Oxford: Macmillan, 1985), 101.

61. In a celebrated speech Grigorii Zinov'ev openly conceded that "we have just begun to penetrate the countryside" and that "we do not need 'antireligious propaganda'" on such a broad scale. Referring to the abrasive calendar reform, he declared that "I do not quite understand why we should agitate in Ukraine for the 'sabbath' to be celebrated on Monday rather than on Sunday." He warned that "in this area it is necessary [to show] great caution, because we should understand the peasant on whom much depends. We shall educate him, but this will take years." *Dvenadtsatyi s'ezd RKP(b)* (Moscow: Gos. izd-vo politicheskoi literatury, 1968), 44.

62. For a summary and references, see Philip Walters, "A Survey of Soviet Religious Policy," *Religious Policy in the Soviet Union*, ed. Sabrina P. Ramet (Cambridge: Cambridge University Press, 1993), 3–30. This policy informed the decisions of the Thirteenth Party Congress, which adopted the following resolution on June 3, 1924: "It is absolutely essential to eliminate any kind of attempts to combat religious prejudice by means of administrative measures (such as closing churches, mosques, synagogues, chapels, churches, etc.). Antireligious propaganda in the village should bear only the character of an exclusively materialistic explanation of the phenomena of nature and public life that the peasant encounters; an explanation of the origins of hail, rain, drought, appearance of pests, special properties of soil, actions of fertilizer, etc. are the best form of anti-religious propaganda. . . . It is especially necessary to give special attention to ensuring that one does not offend the religious feelings of the believer. The triumph over this can only be achieved through a prolonged work of enlightenment, which must be counted in years and decades." N. Orleanskii, *Zakon o religioznykh ob'edineniiakh RSFSR* (Moscow: Bezbozhnik, 1930), 49.

63. Tezisy po anti-rel. propagande priniatye Plenum TsK KP(b)U ot 22.06 i okonchatel'no utverzhdennye Politburo ot, July 13, 1923, TsDAGOU, f. 1, op. 6, d. 44, ll. 206–13. See the circular of June 18, 1923, in ibid., f. 1, op. 20, d. 1450, ll. 3–4.

64. Kyiv Gubkom to Okruzhkoms and Raikoms, February 29, 1924, DAZhO, f. p-88 (Berdichevskii okruzhkom), op. 1, d. 1503, ll. 20–20 ob.

65. E.g., in February 1924 the authorities reversed a local ban on meetings if fewer than fifty members appeared (DAZhO, f. r-692, op. 1, d. 34, l. 37).

66. TsDAGOU, f. 1, op. 20, d. 1843, l. 20. Surprisingly, the NKVD was even flexible on the question of the religious education of children. Though not allowing formal instruction in Sunday schools, it specifically allowed children to attend prayer meetings and, hence, to learn religious basics that way. NKVD to Gubotdel, January 7, 1924, DAZhO, f. r-692, op. 1, d. 54, l. 94.

67. The Antireligious Commission in Moscow was acutely aware of the problem; upon receiving reports of illegal closings in Murom and Vladimir, it dispatched the key OGPU functionary for the antireligious campaign, Evgenii Tuchkov, to investigate. Rossiiski gosudarstvenyi arkhiv sotsial'no-politicheskoi istorii (Russian State Archive of Socio-Political History; hereafter RGASPI), f. 17, op. 112, d. 565a, ll. 5–7.

68. Circular, June 1923, TsDAGOU, f. 1, op. 20, d. 1772, ll. 7–9. Local authorities, nonetheless, remained vigilant. Before approving the registration of a church in June 1923, local authorities first inquired at the OGPU for "clarification of the political physiognomy and former criminal record" of the charter members of a religious community. DAZhO, f. r-846, op. 2, d. 117, l. 1.

69. Information Bulletin 19, TsK KpbU, July 27–August 3, 1925, DAZhO, f. p-86, op. 1, d. 319, ll. 83–84. See similar materials in Protocol no. 22 of the Anti-Religious Commission, May 22, 1923, RGASPI, f. 17, op. 112, d. 565a, ll. 5–7.

70. Protocol ARK pri TsK, November 6, 1923, TsDAGOU, f. 1, op. 20, d. 1772, l. 5. The Communists continued to be vigilant; when a religious group in Zhytomyr proposed to register, the local Soviet authorities asked "for a clarification of the political physiognomy and former criminal record [of founders of the community]." Malinskii okrlikvidkom to GPU, June 30, 1923, DAZhO, f. r-846 (Malinskii orgispolkom), op. 2, d. 117, l. 1. Still, even if the party did not gainsay *any* use of coercion, it clearly emphasized that the principal method was to be agitation and propaganda. Circular, June 1923. Sov. sekretno, TsDAGOU, f. 1, op. 20, d. 1772, ll. 7–9.

71. Protocol, Anti-Religious Commission, July 2, 1924, RGASPI, f. 17, op. 112, d. 775, ll. 3–4.

72. Doklad GPU, February 3, 1925, DAZhO, f. p-85, op. 1, d. 320, l. 23. The following year authorities interceded in Volhynia to protect the rights of religious groups, denouncing attempts to prevent the registration of groups with fewer than fifty members as contrary to the constitution and the decree on the separation of church and state. NKVD to Gubotdel, February 8, 1924, DAZhO, f. r-692 (Gorodnitskii raiispolkom), op. 1, d. 54, l. 37. Even in the sensitive issue of the youth (with the socialization of the next generation at stake), the regime made concessions. While upholding the ban on formal religious instruction for youths (who were forbidden to attend biblical, missionary, or special youth meetings), the NKVD recognized their right to attend prayer meetings. NKVD USSR to all Gubotdels, January 7, 1924, DAZhO, f. r-692 (Gorodnitskii raiispolkom), op. 1, d. 54, l. 94. Likewise, authorities in Ukraine overruled attempts to ban the display of religious objects (such as icons) in private businesses. Protocol PB, July 13, 1923, TsDAGOU, f. 1, op. 6, d. 40, l. 77.

73. Donetskii Gubkom, "Otchet o sostoianii antireligioznoi propagandy," 1924, TsDAGOU, f. 1, op. 20, d. 1845, ll. 11–14.

74. Zavagitprop Gubkoma Segalovich, "Tsirkuliar'," sov. sekretno osen' 1923, DAZhO, f. p-85, op. 1, d. 77, l. 10.

75. The instructions on antireligious activities were terse and abstract: "In the domain of antireligious propaganda, apart from posting natural science lectures, it is necessary to conduct a struggle against the growing influence of the autocephalous, living, and other churches in the village." Monthly report of Agitprop of Zhytomyr Ukom for February 1923, DAZhO, f. p-6, op. 1, d. 90, ll. 4–4 ob. The next report on agitprop from the Zhytomyr Ukom contained the usual laundry list of urgent tasks (party education, work among women and minorities, purging the Committees of the Poor [*komnezaly*], and so forth), but did not even mention an antireligious campaign. Agenda for activities, November 15, 1922 to March 10, 1923, DAZhO, f. p-6, op. 1, d. 90, ll. 8–8 ob.

76. Doklad Otdela Propagandy, August 4, 1923, TsDAGOU, f. 1, op. 20, d. 1450, l. 22.
77. Report of N. Gurich, April 30, 1925, TsDAGOU, f. 1, op. 20, d. 2007, ll. 13–14.
78. Stenogram, Congress of Correspondents, April 19–24, 1925, GARF, f. r-5407, op. 1, d. 5, l. 3.
79. For the correspondence between E. Iaroslavskii and N. N. Popov in January 1927, see TsDAGOU, f. 1, op. 20, d. 2494.
80. See the work plan for the Korostenskii Okrkom in April 1926 in DAZhO, f. p-86, op. 1, d. 621, ll. 8–10.
81. Memoir of N. V. Fedorenko, DAZhO, f. p-2668, op. 4, d. 252, l. 23.
82. Materialy dlia obsuzhdeniia na agitprossoveshchanii po voprosu o religioznykh dvizheniiakh i ob antireligioznoi propaganda na Ukraine, December 29, 1927, TsDAGOU, f. 1, op. 20, d. 2494, ll. 12–27.
83. Material dlia obsuzhdeniia na agitprossoveshchanii po voprosu o religioznykh dvizheniiakh i ob antireligioznoi propagande na Ukraine, December 29, 1927, TsDAGOU, f. 1, op. 20, d. 2494, ll. 12–27.
84. Obzor religioznogo dvizheniia, August–October 1923, TsDAGOU, f. 1, op. 20, d. 1772, ll. 37–39. A year later the GPU in Zhytomyr reported that a letter from the Berdichev party organization, e.g., made the self-congratulatory claim that "antireligious propaganda assumes the significance of a colossal factor in the cause of bringing spiritual emancipation to the working class and achieving clarity in its class consciousness." Letter to all Ukom and Raikom from Sapozhnikov (sekr. Gubkom) and Vitkovskii (sekr. Gub. KK), Kyiv, June 3, 1923, DAZhO, f. p-88, op as a result of clerical agitation (asserting that "the drought is a consequence of the lack of faith in God"), a new pilgrimage movement to Kalinovka had commenced, comprised mostly of women. V okrispokom i Okrparkom, Sov. sekretno, Informatsionnyi doklad o politiko-ekonomicheskom sostoianii zhitomirskogo okruga po sostoianiu na 9 avgusta 1924 g., DAZhO, f. p-85, op. 1, d. 99, ll. 18.
85. E.g., the chairman of a village soviet attempted to disperse a group of people who had come to celebrate a "renewed icon," but his actions only "made the population indignant," and ultimately authorities had to send the militia to restore order. Malinsk. Raiispolkom to Otdel Upravleniia Okrispolkom, September 21, 1923, DAZhO, f. r-846 (Malinskii orgispolkom), op. 2, d. 117, l. 6.
86. As the local *raion* executive committee reported: "The above behavior bears a mass character in Andrushevskii *raion*; in addition, it should be noted that in this movement one sees the underground work of the clergy together with the heads of the commune and the kulaks." Andrushevka raiispolkom—Zhitomirskii okrispolkom, sekretno, lichno, October 25, 1923, DAZhO, f. p-85, op. 1, d. 77, ll. 3–3 ob.
87. TsDAGOU, f. 1, op. 20, d. 1772, ll. 40–48. l. 47 ob.
88. Doklad, Religioznye gruppirovki na Ukraine: sostoianie na ianvar' 1926 g., TsDAGOU, f. 1, op. 6, d. 6, ll. 79–114.
89. See, e.g., the resolutions of the commission on October 26, 1923, in RGASPI, f. 17, op. 112, d. 565a, ll. 43, 44–45.
90. Zhytomyr okruzhkom to Raiispolkom, April 23, 1924, DAZhO, f. r-692 (Gorodnitskii raiispolkom), op. 1, d. 54, l. 61.
91. Zhitomirskii Gubkom Agitprop to Vsem OKR i Raipartkomam, DAZhO, f. p-88 (Berdichevskii okruzhkom), op. 1, d. 1503, ll. 6–7.
92. TsDAGOU, f. 1, op. 20, d. 2006, l. 87 ob.
93. Information bulletins of TsK KPbU, July 2–18, 1925, DAZhO, f. p-86, op. 1, d. 319, l. 65.

94. For somewhat different, but broadly similar, data for July 1, 1925, see TsDAGOU, f. 1, op. 20, d. 2007, l. 63.

95. Ibid., d. 2006, ll. 83–86.

96. Informatsionnyi obzor Volynskoi gubernii, March 10, 1925, DAZhO, f. p-85, op. 1, d. 320, l. 196.

97. Doklad GPU, January 10, 1925, DAZhO, f. p-85, op. 1, d. 320, ll. 5, 10.

98. Informatsionnyi obzor Volynskoi gubernii na March 10, 1925, DAZhO, f. p-85, op. 1, d. 320, l. 196.

99. The sums varied, but were substantial in all provinces. For the fiscal year 1924–25, the authorities reported that church contributions totaled 2.8 million rubles in Kyiv's provinces, 1.5 in Ekaterinoslav, 1.4 in Volhynia, 1.6 in Odessa, 2.5 in Podol'ia, 1.5 in Poltava, 0.9 in Kharkiv, and 1.1 in Chernigov. TsDAGOU, f. 1, op. 20, d. 2006, l. 117.

100. Material dlia obsuzhdeniia na agitprossoveshchanii po voprosu o religioznykh dvizheniiakh i ob antireligioznoi propagande na Ukraine, December 29, 1927, TsDAGOU, f. 1, op. 20, d. 2494, ll. 12–27.

101. Report by N. Gurich, April 30, 1925, TsDAGOU, f. 1, op. 20, d. 2007, ll. 13–14.

102. V okrispokom i Okrparkom, Sov. sekretno, Informatsionnyi doklad o politiko-ekonomicheskom sostoianii zhitomirskogo okruga po sostoianiu na 15 sent. 1924 g., DAZhO, f. p-85, op. 1, d. 99, l. 53.

103. The complete data set is located in TsDAGOU, f. 1, op. 20, d. 2006, ll. 90–99 ob.

104. Material dlia obsuzhdeniia na agitprossoveshchanii po voprosu o religioznykh dvizheniiakh i ob antireligioznoi propagande na Ukraine, December 29, 1927, TsDAGOU, f. 1, op. 20, d. 2494, ll. 12–27.

105. Nor was all the new piety inside the Orthodox Church: party authorities grew increasingly concerned about various sectarian groups. Although these had once enjoyed special protection (chiefly because of their purported "revolutionary" proclivities in Tsarist times), the rapid growth of sectarianism generated acute concern all across the Soviet Union, but especially in Ukraine. According to data compiled in 1925, the sectarians (from Baptists to "self-castrators" (*skoptsy*) comprised some 1,578 registered religious associations with 148,627 members (approximately 2.2 percent the size of the Orthodox population). TsDAGOU, f. 1, op. 20, d. 2007, l. 17.

106. TsDAGOU, f. 1, op. 20, d. 2007, ll. 13–14.

107. V okrispokom i Okrparkom, Sov. sekretno, Informatsionnyi doklad o politiko-ekonomicheskom sostoianii zhitomirskogo okruga po sostoianiu na 1 avgusta 1924 g. From Pomnachvolgubotdel GPU Groznyi to the nachal'nik of UChOSO Kozakov, DAZhO, f. p-85, op. 1, d. 99.

108. V okrispolkom i Okrparkom, Sov. sekretno, Informatsionnyi doklad o politiko-ekonomicheskom sostoianii zhitomirskogo okruga po sostoianiu na 9 avgusta 1924 g. From Pomnachvolgubotdel GPU Groznyi to the nachal'nik of UChOSO Kozakov, DAZhO, f. p-85, op. 1, d. 99, l. 19.

109. Informatsionnyi doklad o politichesko-ekonomicheskom sostoianii zhitomirskogo okruga, August 9, 1924, DAZhO, f. r-85, op. 1, d. 99, l. 19.

110. V okrispokom i Okrparkom, Sov. sekretno, Informatsionnyi doklad o politiko-ekonomicheskom sostoianii zhitomirskogo okruga po sostoianiu na 1 oktiabria 1924 g., DAZhO, f. p-85, op. 1, d. 99, l. 67.

111. V okrispokom i Okrparkom, Sov. sekretno, Informatsionnyi doklad o politiko-ekonomicheskom sostoianii zhitomirskogo okruga po sostoianiu na 22 sent. 1924 g., DAZhO, f. p-85, op. 1, d. 99, l. 59.

112. Informatsionnyi biulleten', July 27–August 3, 1925, DAZhO, f. r-86, op. 1, d. 319, ll. 83–84.

113. V okrispokom i Okrparkom, Sov. sekretno, Informatsionnyi doklad o politiko-ekonomicheskom sostoianii zhitomirskogo okruga po sostoianiu na 1 oktiabria 1924 g., DAZhO, f. p-85, op. 1, d. 99, l. 67.

114. Doklad GPU, March 2, 1925, DAZhO, f. p-85, op. 1, d. 320, l. 23. In another report from August 1925, the GPU reported that local priests were attacking teachers and castigating them as "agents of Soviet power." Vypiski iz svodok GPU, DAZhO, f. p-85, op. 1, d. 201, l. 8. Agents of the GPU also denounced the priest in another village for "conducting agitation against the school" and for "trying to persuade [the villagers] that the school does not teach what each person needs: to serve God." Doklad GPU, February 3, 1925, prilozhenie no. 7, DAZhO, f. p-85, op. 1, d. 320, l. 41.

115. V okrispokom i Okrparkom, Sov. sekretno, Informatsionnyi doklad o politiko-ekonomicheskom sostoianii zhitomirskogo okruga po sostoianiu na 9 avgusta 1924 g. From Pomnachvolgubotdel GPU Groznyi to nachal'nik UChOSO Kozakov, DAZhO, f. p-85, op. 1, d. 99, l. 18.

116. Informatsionnyi obzor Volynskoi gubernii na, March 10, 1925, DAZhO, f. p-85, op. 1, d. 320, l. 196. In March 1925, one priest purportedly sought to intimidate compromisers by playing on fears of a resumption of Polish/Soviet military hostilities. Retribution, he warned, would be exacted from parents who allowed their children to join the Young Pioneers, a communist youth organization: "With the arrival of the Poles, they will inflict severe repressions on all those who signed up as pioneers." Informatsionnyi obzor Volynskoi gubernii na March 10, 1925, DAZhO, f. p-85, op. 1, d. 320, l. 196.

117. Ezhenedel'nyi informatsionnyi obzor politicheskogo i ekonomicheskogo sostoianiia zhitomirskogo okruga volynskoi gubernii, 1 marta 1925 g. Sov. sekretno, DAZhO, f. p-85, op. 1, d. 320, ll. 130–62.

118. Dvukhnedel'nyi informatsionnyi obzor Zhitomirskoi oblasti na March 21, 1925, prilozhenie no. 7, DAZhO, f. p-85, op. 1, d. 320, l. 223.

119. TsDAGOU, f. 1, op. 20, d. 2006, l. 88.

120. Informatsionnyi obzor Volynskoi gubernii na March 10, 1925, DAZhO, f. p-85, op. 1, d. 320, l. 126.

121. Registration form for psalmist, 1924, DAZhO, f. r-846, op. 2, d. 157, l. 200.

122. Informatsionnyi obzor Volynskoi gubernii na March 10, 1925, DAZhO, f. p-85, op. 1, d. 320, l. 196.

123. For the pitiable plight of the Living Church despite regime support, see the report in TsDAGOU, f. 1, op. 20, d. 2007, l. 63.

124. In reality, of course, the regime continued to harass and repress the Tikhonite clergy, especially the episcopate. E.g., in a protocol of March 1, 1925, the Anti-Religious Commission proposed to use all legal means to repress the Tikhonite movement, including impeding the registration of churches, preventing the distribution of literature, and the like. TsDAGOU, f. 1, op. 20, d. 2006, ll. 56–57.

125. E.g., see the report from a parish that resisted attempts by a "small circle" of autocephalous supporters to seize control, in DAKhO, f. r-230, op. 1, d. 1510/a.

126. Dokladnaia zapiska UAPTs na Ukraine po sostoianiiu, October 15, 1925, TsDAGOU, f. 1, op. 20, d. 2007, ll. 1–9.

127. Doklad GPU, January 10, 1925, DAZhO, f. p-85, op. 1, d. 320, l. 12.

128. Bolshevik distrust was intense from the very emergence of the autocephalous movement. As the head of the Liquidation Department in the People's Commissariat

of Justice wrote in September 1921, "The Ukrainian autocephalous church, as a consequence of its remasking under democratism, is unquestionably more dangerous for the social revolution than a church which celebrates Patriarchate of Tikhon and service in the Slavonic language and nourishes the unrealizable dream of a restoration of the monarchy." Head of Likvidatsionnyi otdel NKIu to Kollegiia NKIu, September 20, 1921, TsDAGOU, f. 1, op. 6, d. 32, l. 117. Even earlier, the Ukrainian Politburo expressed concern about "the autocephalous movement and its ties with Petliura elements," and instructed the Cheka to "maintain the strictest surveillance over counterrevolution, which is concealed behind a veil of religious questions." Protocol of PB TsK KpbU, May 28, 1921, TsDAGOU, f. 1, op. 6, d. 13, l. 7. Hence, even before the formal schism of the "Living Church," the Ukrainian Politburo had begun to gather information about the "autocephalous church" and its relationship to the patriarchal ("exarchate") church. Protocol, February 25, 1922, TsDAGOU, f. 1, op. 6, d. 29, l. 40.

129. Dokladnaia zapiska UAPTs na Ukraine po sostoianiiu, October 15, 1925, TsDAGOU, f. 1, op. 20, d. 2007, ll. 1–9.

130. Doklad: Religioznye gruppirovki na Ukraine, Sostoianie na ianvar' 1926 g., TsDAGOU, f. 1, op. 6, d. 6, ll. 79–114.

131. Information bulletins of TsK KpbU, no. 19, July 27–August 3, 1925, DAZhO, f. p-86, op. 1, d. 319, ll. 83–84.

132. Zasedanie Antireligioznoi Komissii, 1925, DAZhO, f. p-86, op. 1, d. 619, unpaginated.

133. Thus, in 1925 the Ukrainian Politburo considered a proposal to legalize the autocephalous church—primarily in response to a promise to purge its ranks of counterrevolutionaries and to reaffirm loyalty to Soviet power. A resolution of the Ukrainian Politburo, October 10, 1925, declared: "Consider it possible to register the charter of the autocephalous church on condition that it express its loyalty toward Soviet power through the publication of a declaration of complete separation from the émigrés." Osobaia papka k protokolu no. 94, October 30, 1925, TsDAGOU, f. 1, op. 6, d. 1, l. 277. Such negotiations, however, came to naught, not least because of the GPU's insistent and alarming reports about the true intention of the autocephalites. By February 1926, the party adopted proposals to give special consideration to the autocephalous threat and gave orders for "further work to cause the disintegration of the autocephalites." Politburo Protocol, February 25, 1926, TsDAGOU, f. 1, op. 6, d. 6, ll. 76–133.

134. 1923 doklad, TsDAGOU, f. 1, op. 20, d. 1772, l. 30.

135. Ibid., d. 2007, ll. 26–26 ob.

136. DAZhO, f. r-86, op. 1, d. 619.

137. Vypiski iz svodok GPU, DAZhO, f. p-85, op. 1, d. 201, l. 8.

138. Spetssvodka na 1926 god, DAZhO, f. p-85, op. 1, d. 321, ll. 22–30.

139. N. Orleanskii, *Zakon o religioznykh ob'edineniiakh RSFSR* (Moscow: Bezbozhnik, 1930), 6–25.

140. Ibid., 25–26.

141. See G. L. Freeze, "The Stalinist Assault on the Parish, 1929–1941," in *Stalinismus vor dem Zweiten Weltkrieg: Neue Wege der Forschung*, edited by Manfred Hildermeier (Munich: Oldenburg Verlag, 1998), 211–34.

## Chapter 2

## From the Red Cradle: Memories of Jewish Family Life in the Soviet Union

*Anna Shternshis*

For centuries, among Jews in Eastern Europe the institution of the family has been central to retaining their identity and furthering social bonding.[1] Historically, the process of forming a family was defined for Jews by a complex web of centuries-old practices, which included the appointment of a matchmaker (*shadkhan*), who verified the religious pedigree and financial worth of the bride and the groom and negotiated with both families over an elaborate engagement and prenuptial agreements that discussed the obligations of both sides. Sophisticated celebrations accompanied each stage of the engagement and the wedding itself. After the wedding, religious law and social custom informed Jewish family life, and regulated the structure of the relationships between spouses and patterns of childrearing, including who the children would be allowed to marry.

The Jewish family was charged with ensuring Jewish survival in the Diaspora, thus preventing assimilation and intermarriage. The successful functioning of this system meant that even in the nineteenth century, throughout the Imperial Period—when Jewish enlightenment and rapid social and economic changes challenged assumptions about matchmaking, divorce, and other traditions—most Jews still created their families in accordance with Jewish religious law.[2] Thus the transformation of Jewish family structure that took place in Soviet Russia between 1917 and 1939 was nothing short of remarkable: The perception of intermarriage changed from extremely negative to largely neutral and at times positive, the process of creating a family began to exclude matchmakers, and weddings became rare—just to name a few of the numerous dramatic shifts. In fact, change in creating a Jewish family was quicker and more complete, especially when compared with shifts in practices of kosher food consumption, Jewish religious education, and general observance of Jewish traditions.[3]

Although one could explain the declining significance of religious practices by pointing to the combination of state legislation and internal processes of secularization and modernization in the Jewish community, especially its youth, one cannot fully explain why certain rituals were given up without a fight but others lingered throughout the Soviet period, often despite significant danger to those who practiced them. In this chapter, I analyze how the religious aspects of Jewish family life disappeared in early Soviet Russia, and discuss the process of transforming Jewish family life as seen through the eyes of the first generation of Soviet Jews. This analysis seeks to reveal the mechanisms of how Soviet antireligious policies and, more specifically, anti-Judaism policies worked.

Jews born between 1906 and 1930 in the Russian Empire or, after the Revolution, in the Soviet Union belonged to the first generation of Soviet Jews who began to embrace these new values and criteria for Jewish identity. In the 1930s, they went through a process of radical cultural transformation, which was catalyzed by the establishment of a system of secular education, antireligious propaganda, and, above all, the political, economic, and social reforms introduced by the Soviet regime. Because most of this group's members spoke or knew Yiddish, understood and sometimes practiced Jewish rituals, and embraced Soviet secularism, this group formed the only community of Soviet-educated citizens who experienced both Jewish religious and cultural identity and Soviet secularization to a degree that all subsequent Soviet generations did not.

In addition to being the most "Jewish" of all Soviet Jews in a religious sense, this group's members can also be seen as the most "Soviet." They grew up during the formative period of the Soviet state's ideology and political system. Many were members of the communist youth political organizations, such as the Young Communist League (Komsomol) and the

Young Pioneers. And some actively participated in creating and maintaining Soviet ideology at the grassroots level. Arguably, this was the only Soviet generation that largely internalized the values of the Soviet system and kept an overall positive attitude toward it, even after the Soviet Union collapsed.

This chapter analyzes how these Jews understood the role of their ethnicity in constructing their family lives. It is based on 474 in-depth interviews with Jews who were born between 1899 and 1930 in the Russian Empire or the Soviet Union. The interviews were conducted in the United States, Germany, Canada, and Russia.[4]

Although this is not a quantitative study, I have attempted to ensure equal representation of gender, as well as countries of origin, experiences, backgrounds, and formal education (see table 2.1). No significant variation in my respondents' backgrounds was noted by country. The respondents were highly educated (50 percent had the equivalent of a college degree, and nearly all had completed high school).

For this group of Jews, in the pages that follow I analyze differences in gender socialization and these variations' significance for future choices of spouses, as well as for patterns of courtship and choosing a partner for marriage. These findings are based on the answers that the respondents provided to these questions: "What was it like to grow up as a Jew in the USSR?" "How did you meet your spouse(s)?" and "What role did your [future] spouse's nationality play in your decision to marry him or her?" Only seven respondents (all women) never married.

## Raising Soviet Brides and Grooms: Boys and Girls in Jewish Families

Interviews of Soviet refugees in 1951 (for the Harvard Project on the Soviet Social System) revealed that during the interwar period, Soviet family values emphasized mainly secular principles, such as kindness, justice, and personal happiness.[5] Most traditional prerevolutionary values, such as a belief in God and observance of religious rituals, were gradually losing their importance. Similar trends could be observed in Jewish families. The most visible shift was in the patterns of Jewish children's upbringing, especially in differences between how parents treated boys and girls.

One way to identify these differences is to analyze the answers given by respondents as to why they were punished as children. Both female and male respondents noted that when they were punished, most often it was

Table 2.1. Data on Number of Respondents: Gender, Place of Birth, Education, and Language of the Interview

| Place of Residence | Respondents | Gender | | Place of Birth | | | | Higher Education | Yiddish Speakers |
| --- | --- | --- | --- | --- | --- | --- | --- | --- | --- |
| | | Men | Women | Ukraine | Belorussia | Russia | Poland, Lithuania, or Romania | | |
| New York | 157 | 81 | 76 | 76 | 52 | 11 | 18 | 72 | 87 |
| Toronto | 99 | 41 | 58 | 48 | 23 | 19 | 9 | 56 | 36 |
| Philadelphia | 64 | 31 | 33 | 31 | 9 | 11 | 13 | 28 | 41 |
| Berlin (including Potsdam) | 102 | 61 | 41 | 55 | 27 | 12 | 8 | 60 | 25 |
| Moscow | 52 | 19 | 33 | 39 | 3 | 10 | 0 | 43 | 18 |
| Total | 474 | 233 | 241 | 249 | 114 | 63 | 48 | 259 | 207 |

for poor grades in high school, damaging property, and mistreating younger siblings. Some of the "specifically Jewish punishments" that I recorded resulted from eating nonkosher food,[6] or, more often, from bringing nonkosher food home and socializing with non-Jews.[7] Respondents vividly remembered that girls and boys were punished for different faults in the 1920s. Girls were often penalized for not helping enough with household chores, whereas their brothers were not required to "help around the house."

A small number of women respondents said that their parents were reluctant to send them to school for fear of losing their help in the household. For example, Lilya Sh. (b. 1909) said that because her parents needed her to work at home, she did not go to school, but she did manage to learn to read and write without any formal instruction, whereas her brothers studied in schools.[8] Similarly, Esfir A. (b. 1908) recalled that her parents did not want to send her to school, and only the intervention of local teachers helped her to obtain a primary education.[9] Testimonies of these respondents are in line with how both Jewish and non-Jewish girls were treated in many families in early postrevolutionary Russia. For instance, Anne Gorsuch observed that in the 1920s, girls who lived in Moscow were less involved in political activities because of their responsibilities at home, and because many parents felt that a woman's primary work was to learn how to raise children and to take care of the household.[10]

Still, nearly 90 percent of female respondents, especially those born in the 1920s, reported that they were encouraged to go to school by their parents. Some liked to stress that one of the main differences between how Jews and non-Jews treated their children was that Jews encouraged their daughters to go to school. Efim G. (b. 1918) recalls:

> When I was six, I went to school, and I was very excited about this. But we had a neighbor who was not Jewish. He had a daughter my age. He did not want her to go to school, because he wanted her to look after their babies. My father tried to convince him to send the girl to school, but to no avail. He used to come back home, and say, "A goyishe kop iz er" (He has a Gentile head). I did not know what it meant, and when I saw this man in the street, I would tell him, "a goyishe kop." But seriously, Belorussians did not allow girls to study—they wanted them to clean the house. Jewish families were not like this![11]

Perceptions similar to Efim's of how Jews and non-Jews treated their daughters, though historically inaccurate, were widespread among respondents. Even women who did not study in school because their parents did not permit it stressed that their parents wanted them to be educated, because this was the "Jewish way." Perhaps this assertion comes from associations with later periods of Soviet history. Yet it is noteworthy that the respondents, despite knowing that Jewish girls had more limited access to education than did Jewish boys, tended to present Jews as "more advanced" than their neighbors. This attitude, which was common in many areas of daily life that were described, is one of the early expressions of Soviet-inspired Jewish identity, which equated being Jewish with being a "better person."

Jews' attitudes toward the type of education they wanted for their children also broke down along gender lines. In prerevolutionary Russia, most Jewish boys who resided in the Pale of Settlement attended *khadorim* (Jewish primary schools), which taught the basics of reading Hebrew and Bible literacy. Wealthier families sent their children to Russian or Polish gymnasia, where they received a secular education. In some cases, a secular education was supplemented by an afternoon Jewish school or a private tutor. Girls from both poorer and wealthier families were more likely than boys to receive a secular education, because they were only expected to be familiar with Jewish religious ritual, rather than have a deep understanding of it.[12] A basic secular education was regarded as important for a girl because it would enable her to trade at the marketplace and otherwise contribute to the family budget.

In the years 1922–23, shortly after the Revolution, committees for the "liquidation of the *khadorim*" were organized in towns and hamlets where Jews resided. By the end of the 1920s, the Soviet press proudly reported that all *khadorim* had been shut down; but, in fact, many were simply driven underground. David Fishman believes that "*kheyder* [i.e., a single-class school] and *yeshiva* [a school the emphasizes teaching the Talmud] actually underwent a process of consolidation and growth during the mid and late 1920s."[13] As I have shown in an earlier study, the *khadorim* continued to function well into the 1930s, albeit underground. Parents sent their children to a *kheyder* or to a private teacher for reasons that ranged from continuity with tradition to extended hours of day care.[14] Boys were much more likely to attend an underground *kheyder* than were girls. In fact, among my respondents, 140 men (out of 233 interviewed) spoke about going to a *kheyder*, only 15 women (out of 241) attended a *kheyder* or had a private teacher, and 160 women mentioned that their brothers went to a *kheyder*.

Given that my respondents arguably represent the most "Jewish"-oriented segment of their generation (due to the self-selected sample of Yiddish speakers), the percentage of those who received a Jewish religious education in the 1920s and 1930s is probably significantly higher in comparison with the general population of Soviet Jews. Nevertheless, there is a gender gap, even within this sample. Its significance lies in the fact that, when it came to educating their children, Jews did not fundamentally alter their religious practices in light of the changing Soviet policies toward religion. In other words, the religious education of boys continued despite the fact that its virtue began to disappear quite quickly after the Revolution. Girls were taught Jewish religious values at home, rather than through formal or informal schooling.

In fact, what remained consistent throughout the testimonies of the entire interwar period was that girls had far less freedom to socialize with their friends. Those born in the early twentieth century and those born in the 1920s were punished equally for spending extra hours outside the house, especially if they spent time with men and boys. Rozaliya U. (b. 1907) recalls that she was mostly punished for staying out late with her boyfriend: "We had a platonic relationship, we did not even kiss. Yet, when my mother found out I was out with him, she punished me."[15]

Olga K. (b. 1907) tells a similar story: "I was a very obedient child. I never did anything against the wishes of my parents. But I remember my mother hit me only once. I was out late because I helped in a workshop. The owner of the workshop walked me home. My mother saw us together, and she hit me so hard. . . . He had to explain that I was just helping to do some woodwork, and nothing else. But she did not believe him, or me. After that, I was not allowed to leave the house in the evening."[16]

Another respondent, Klara G. (b. 1914), specifically emphasized that she was treated differently than her brothers:

> My brothers often came home late, but I was not allowed to. Whenever I was five minutes late, my mother would beat me up. I asked my mother: "Why can [my brother] Yasha stay out late, and I can't? Why can [my brother] Petya stay out, and I can't?" She said [in Yiddish]: "Dear daughter, a man is like a glass. It can get dirty, and then you clean it, and you do not know if it was dirty. A woman is like a cloth. If it gets dirty, it will be stained forever." I did not understand her then, and yelled at her: "What glass? What are you talking about?!" I was so angry.[17]

Aside from the actual message about modesty and methods of parenting, it is noteworthy that the respondent reproduced her mother's words about the difference between men and women in Yiddish as opposed to Russian (the language of the rest of the interview). Later during the conversation, the respondent emphasized that "modesty was a Jewish virtue," and that is why, whenever she thinks about it, she does so in Yiddish. It was a rather common trend among my respondents to use folk wisdom as an explanation of their relations toward members of the opposite sex. Respondents rarely quoted Russian folk proverbs on this issue, even though most of them were quite well versed in Russian literature and folklore. They preferred to use Yiddish expressions, which they had heard from their parents (often without fully being able to understand them). Frequently, these were the only Yiddish expressions respondents knew. Yet they found that Yiddish was more suitable than Russian to best describe the issues in their families related to the differences in the upbringing of boys and girls.

Another specifically "Jewish-related" consequence of the restriction of girls' freedom was that it sometimes resulted in developing closer ties within the family and a greater familiarity with Jewish religious traditions, including the methods of kosher food preparation, ways to celebrate the Jewish holidays, and even an occasional prayer. For example, Sonya G. (b. 1923) recalls that during Passover, her brothers left the house to participate in various Soviet events, but she was required to stay at home and take part in the Seder (a festive dinner accompanied by storytelling and prayers).[18] Another respondent, Yosef S. (b. 1925), noted that his sisters were more familiar with Jewish customs than he was because "they stayed at home all the time, and I spent time in school and with other boys."[19] Indeed, because the system of formal Jewish education had been practically destroyed by the early 1930s, the only sources of knowledge of Jewish customs and rituals for children were the practices of their own families. Therefore, girls, who had less freedom to go out and did not receive a formal Jewish education, learned more about Jewish traditions than their brothers did in the home environment.

Restrictions on girls' freedom, especially for *shtetl* (small town) residents, resulted in less socializing with non-Jews compared with boys of the same age. Esfir A. (b. 1908), for example, asserted that she did not know any non-Jews until she was sixteen years of age (although it did not stop her from marrying a non-Jew just a few years later).[20] Other female respondents of her generation told similar stories, whereas women born in the late 1920s did not speak about these differences. Quite to the contrary, they liked to emphasize that their circle of friends was not limited to Jews. Anna G. (b. 1926) asserted: "We did not make a difference between non-Jews and Jews. My parents allowed us to be friends with everyone we liked, as long as they were good people."[21]

Mariya D. (b. 1928) confirmed this assertion: "We never made a difference between Jews and non-Jews when I was a child. In fact, I had more Russian friends than Jews. . . . My mother never limited us in doing anything. We could play with who we wanted to, and as much as we wanted to."[22] When I asked female respondents of this generation whether there was any difference between how Jewish and non-Jewish girls behaved, the majority said that Jewish families gave girls more freedom, did not burden them with excessive amounts of household chores, and allowed them to go out more compared with non-Jewish neighbors. Indeed, numerous respondents remembered their participation in extracurricular activities at school, such as drama and singing workshops. Many women remembered spending their free time dancing. Etya G. (b. 1918) said: "Our favorite activity [after school] was dancing. We would get together at someone's house, have a record on, and dance. We especially liked the Ria Rita, the Argentinean tango, and the foxtrot. We would dance all evening. Once a week I also went dancing in a club."[23] Leon Dennen, an American journalist who visited Jewish collective farms in Russia in 1932, also observed that dancing was extremely popular among young Jewish women.[24]

Interestingly, men of the same generation presented quite a different picture of Jewish girls' leisure time during the prewar period. A typical testimony is by Ilya F. (b. 1910), a teenager in the mid-1920s: "When we were young, we liked going to out dancing. But there were no Jewish girls there. We danced with *shikses* [non-Jewish women, with a pejorative connotation]. Jewish girls were not allowed. . . . We met Jewish girls at home parties, but most Jewish girls were not allowed to go there as well. We boys went to the movies sometimes, but girls never went with us. It was not proper for a Jewish girl."[25]

Ilya's wife of fifty-eight years, Sima F. (b. 1911), was present during this conversation. When Ilya finished a sentence, she winked at me, and quietly said: "This is what they all thought, but I knew how to dance and in fact, we went out to dance as well."

When Ilya, who has trouble hearing, asked his wife to repeat what she told me, she replied: "Nothing important. Continue with your story!"[26]

This exchange illustrates an interesting phenomenon in how the respondents constructed their ethnic and gender identities. Although there is no evidence that the behavior of Jewish young women and girls was different from that of non-Jews, many respondents agreed with Ilya's sentiments. It is noteworthy that during the interview, Ilya repeatedly emphasized that he was brought up as an "internationalist" and thus did not think about nationality at all. However, when it came to evaluating his choice for a marriage partner, as well as other aspects of gender relations, his judgment was specifically ethnic.

Analysis of numerous testimonies confirms that there were indeed differences in how Jewish boys and girls were treated during the pre–World War II period. Girls tended to spend more time at home with their parents, whereas boys took part in various activities outside their family circles. Girls were also generally punished more than boys were for being friends with non-Jews. In my analysis of the marital choices made by men and women, it is evident that women paid more attention to the ethnicity of potential spouses. This does not mean that they were more likely to choose a Jew (which is not true, according to this sample), but rather that they gave this matter more thought. Perhaps this attitude is a consequence of the greater influence that parents (and therefore traditional Jewish values) had on them during their adolescent years.[27] Thus, even during the Soviet era, women continued to be the carriers of religious traditions, or remnants of traditions that gave meaning to a Jewish identity.

It is important to note that differences between how boys and girls were treated at home were not as pronounced when respondents spoke about their own experiences, but rather when they spoke about their friends, family members, acquaintances, and, especially often, "generally" about Jews and non-Jews. Actual experience frequently did not coincide with respondents' ideas of what they thought the Jewish experience was supposed to be. For example, women respondents spoke about dancing with non-Jews as often as men did, yet respondents of both genders asserted that dancing "was not a Jewish activity." The meaning of the word "Jewish" here has little to do with what Jews indeed practiced. Rather, most frequently it meant something that the respondents considered positive. Perhaps this is one of the justifications that people used when selecting a Jewish spouse, and it is arguably the most important lesson in the determination of their ethnic identity that both boys and girls learned in their childhood.

## Courtship and Choosing Marriage Partners

The first decree of Soviet family law—the Code on Marriage, the Family, and Guardianship—which was issued by the Bolshevik government in October 1918, eliminated the validity of religious marriage and gave legal status only to civil marriage. It set up local bureaus of statistics known as ZAGS (Otdel Zapisi aktov grazhdanskogo sostoyaniia, Civil Registry Office) for the registration of marriages, divorces, births, and deaths.[28] The code reduced the significance of legal marriage, because it abolished the concept of illegitimate children and provided women with full control of their earnings after marriage.[29] The abolition of religious marriage also meant that previous religious restrictions on legal marriage, such as the need for both partners to be of the same faith, were no longer legally valid. In 1926, a new law was introduced that gave equal status to registered and unregistered marriages. It eliminated discrimination against children born out of wedlock and in some ways released men from taking responsibility for their offspring. Divorce also became easier; it was enough for only one partner to announce the end of the marriage in a newspaper. A person's divorce was not even indicated in his or her passport until 1936.[30] In general, the legal status of the family was close to nonexistent—until the legislation changed again in 1944.[31]

In addition to this relaxed legislation pertaining to marriage, the processes of industrialization, collectivization, and the Great Terror had an equal, if not greater significance, for men's and women's decisions regarding the type of family they wanted to create. For example, the massive migration from villages to larger cities broadened the choice of potential mates among urban residents. At the same time, numerous arrests and deportations narrowed the possibilities of villagers. The arrest of relatives, a fate faced by many during the late 1930s, physically destroyed many families.[32]

The changing value of marriage in society also affected the choice of partners. In the 1920s, works of fiction and popular culture posited the notion that romantic love should replace economic and social incentives to enter into a legal marriage. The ability to reject material incentives, one's lineage, and parents' wishes for the sake of romantic love, which began in nineteenth-century Russia, was essentially legislated in early Soviet Russia. The "noble" family lineage was presented as no longer desirable because of the implications for limiting social mobility. Instead, a proletarian background, or at least an alleged proletarian background, promised a more stable future. The Soviet media actively propagated the attractiveness of belonging to the Communist Party for both men and women. Although these incentives were only slowly translated into actual practices, at least in the 1920s, some of the notions that Soviet propaganda advocated found a popular response: an attack on matchmaking.

Imperial-era Jewish intellectuals and enlighteners (*maskilim*) had already developed a rich and complex culture of attacking the practices of Jewish traditional matchmaking before 1917. In fact, the criticism of matchmaking and Jewish family life in general constituted the most important topic of Yiddish literature in the nineteenth century. Alexander Abramowitch (Mendele Moykher Sforim), Sholem Rabinowitch (Sholem Aleichm), Israel Aksenfeld, and many others devoted long novels to exposing what they believed to be the greatest maladies of Jewish society—the practices of early arranged marriages and the exploitation of women by forcing them to provide family income while the men were students, and especially the practice of living together with in-laws. By 1917, the urban Jewish intelligentsia—which constituted a small, yet influential part of the Jewish society—had internalized many aspects of this criticism, and was ready to embrace the ideal of romantic love as an important part of Jewish family life. The majority of the Jewish population, however, still relied on matchmaking and other traditional practices to create and maintain their families.

Therefore, Soviet antireligious propaganda in the Yiddish language targeted matchmaking as the embodiment of bourgeois culture and values. Although it did not directly promote interethnic marriages, the inclination to marry a person of the same ethnic group or religion was presented as "backward" compared with the new policy of internationalism in personal relations. Even in the 1930s, when the superiority of Russian national culture was trumpeted in the Soviet press, the propaganda of ethnically diverse marriages did not cease. Although the majority of people still married within their ethnic group, intermarriage was no longer rare. Perhaps the most famous portrayal of Jewish interethnic courtship, weddings, and marriages is the film *Seekers of Happiness* (made in Moscow in 1936), in which Roza, a Jewish settler in Birobidzhan, marries the ethnically Russian Korney, and their union is celebrated at an elaborate wedding, complete with Jewish food, Western-style dancing, and Russian folk music. It seems equally important that most respondents who saw the movie did not remember that it ended in intermarriage, but rather quite fondly remembered the representation of Jewish daily life.[33] Yet intermarriage did not repulse, did not shock, and did not seem unacceptable any longer.

As part of its effort to promote internationalism, the Soviet government launched a campaign in 1919 against anti-Semitism, which continued well into early 1930s. The main theme—which was taken up in numerous newspaper articles, cartoons, agitation-inducing and propagandistic theater performances (agitprop), and movies—was that hostility between different nationalities, including between Jews and Christians, was encouraged by the Tsarist government in order to divert attention from "real" problems such as class struggle. An additional objective of the campaign was to convince the audience that all the Jewish religious rituals and traditions were just as meaningless as those of any other religion and thus were not especially harmful to the surrounding population. In other words, the propaganda aimed to destroy the image of Jews as both economic exploiters and as a mysterious religious sect. Rapid integration into the new Soviet regime also raised the status of Jews in society. Myths like "Jews make good husbands" pervaded popular culture. Mikhail Beyzer suggests that the increased role of Jewish men in the new Soviet economy made them more attractive in the eyes of non-Jews from the mid-1920s through the 1930s.[34] In other words, Jews who wanted to "marry out" of their faith usually had a good chance of finding a non-Jewish spouse in the 1930s.

It seems that it would have been natural for Jews to marry non-Jews in quite significant numbers in the 1920s and 1930s. Even within Jewish society, as Mordechai Altshuler has pointed out, "a union between a Jew and non-Jew no longer entailed publicly rejecting their past and changing their religion, or demonstratively integrating themselves into the life of a different nation that abhorred their origins."[35] Altshuler's data reveal that, in Moscow, nearly 50 percent of all Jews intermarried, and so did more than 15 to 18 percent of Jews in Ukraine and Belorussia.[36]

Of the 129 men and women in my sample who married before the war, only 18 married non-Jews, 8 of whom came from larger cities, such as Moscow and Leningrad. Fewer than 10 percent of the respondents from smaller towns married non-Jews. Thus, the majority of respondents probably had a more pronounced Jewish identity compared with other Jews of their generation. However, as becomes evident from the testimonies recounted below, even these people did not have clear reasons and motivations for marrying a Jew. They insisted that choosing a Jewish partner was a matter of instinct rather than principle, and very few were able to present any intellectual justification for this choice.

Most respondents suggested that they did not see marriage and the creation of a family as the most significant, or even an important, event in their lives. Quite to the contrary, people described the process of meeting their future spouse, their decision to get married, and their wedding (or marriage registration) quite casually in between telling other stories about their education, career, and migration, which they considered more worthy of attention.

For example, all respondents in the generation born before 1914, and whose marriages occurred in the 1930s, stated that they had decided to get married without any consultation with their parents. It was not rare for parents to be notified only after their children were officially married. For instance, Yosef V. (b. 1907) met his future wife, Serafima, through a friend in Odessa in 1932, when he came for a visit. After a short stay, Yosef went back to Moscow and later invited Serafima to join him. Upon her arrival, the young couple got married at ZAGS and settled down. Both parents were notified several months after the event.[37] Similarly, Ilya Sh. (b. 1913) met his future wife while both were attending a university, and they decided to get married upon graduation in 1938. He did not even tell his parents about the event; as he explained, "They lived far away, and I did not see how it was their business."[38]

Women were more likely than men to ask for permission to marry, but even in these cases, parents' opinions were supplementary, not obligatory, and respondents expected approval, not permission. Olga K. (b. 1905) recalls that even when she asked her father whether she should marry her boyfriend in 1931, her father replied: "You are the one to live with him. So you should decide. Do whatever you feel is right."[39]

Grigorii B. (b. 1910) asserted that he prepared his bride-to-be for the first meeting with his parents: "I taught her how to make good impression, how to speak. . . . My mother really liked her. She said, 'This girl is a real human being [*eto chelovek*].'"[40] It was important for Grigorii to emphasize that the "universal" appeal of the young woman was significant for his mother, more than the fact of her Jewish lineage. In the context of his entire testimony, this story of his mother's approval of his bride is an illustration of his appreciation of his mother's accommodating or even progressive nature, as opposed to the story of him valuing her opinion in the matter of choosing a spouse.

Of course, even in my respondents' stories, not all parents agreed with their children's choices. Some respondents in this group remembered parents' negative reactions. Parents protested against the age or background of the prospective bride or groom. For example, Lilya Sh. (b. 1909) told a story of a girlfriend who decided to marry a man twelve years her senior: "Her mother was trying to convince my friend not to do this, but to no avail. My friend had to run away from home, but she fulfilled her dream."[41]

Some respondents also remember conflicts related to the background of the betrothed. Olga K. (b. 1905) stated that her parents did not want her to marry a Lithuanian Jew, but a Ukrainian one, because "Ukrainian Jews are kinder and nicer people." When asked whether she followed their advice, Olga replied: "Actually, I did not. I married a non-Jew, an Austrian man, who was a Communist and escaped from Austria to live in the Soviet Union, and my parents loved him![42]

The respondent's discussion of the role of nationality in her choice of spouse demonstrates a deep ambivalence. On one hand, she was aware of the role of nationality, which was why she provided a story about Lithuanian and Ukrainian Jews. On the other hand, she downplayed the fact that she actually married a non-Jew. This could mean two things. Perhaps the respondent was saying that marrying the "right kind" of Jew was harder than marrying a non-Jew, and thus she chose a non-Jew to avoid dealing with it. Or she could have meant that she had rebelled against her parents' "small" worldview and thus married someone completely outside the faith. In either case, she emphasized that the value of being Jewish had lost its significance for her—and also for her parents, because they approved of her choice.

Olga's children were less aware of their Jewish background than of their Austrian background because of suspicious attitudes to foreigners, especially from Austria, during World War II. This respondent's Jewish identity, whether religious or cultural, did not seem to have much significance for choosing a spouse and for other areas of her life.

Olga, like many other respondents born between 1906 and 1914, met her future husband at work. Others mentioned places such as schools, universities, and social gatherings. No one described the participation of a matchmaker or even a relative who introduced them and helped them to avoid marrying a person with close genetic ties. The independent choices of marital partners in the 1920s led to the destruction of one of the most important rules of traditional Jewish community life: marrying within the ethnic group. Many respondents confirmed that, indeed, the ethnicity of their future spouse did not play an important role in their decision to marry that person.

Thus, Grigorii B. explained: "I wanted a good wife, a good person. I did not think about nationalities."[43] Veniamin Sh. (b. 1907) agreed: "I thought very little about it [the ethnicity of my wife]. This was not a factor."[44] And Ilya Sh. confirmed: "I wanted a smart, interesting wife; her nationality did not interest me. These were times when it did not matter."[45] But what made it not matter?

Such testimonies were especially common among men born between 1906 and 1914 in urban centers. Female respondents, however, spoke more of their difficulties and the complexities related to the background of future spouses. Lilya Sh. (b. 1909) reveals:

It was in 1926. I was seventeen, and I fell in love. It was in Odessa, I was on the beach. There was beautiful weather. . . . Many young men tried to court me there. . . . I was with my sister. One man asked me, right there on the beach: "Marry me. I fell in love with you at first sight!" I hated such advances. Then suddenly, another young man approached us. He had a big book, and he did not pay any attention to me. He asked my sister: "Can I leave my bag with you? I would like to go swimming." Then he went to swim. Suddenly, I started worrying about him. It had been forty-five minutes. I said [to my sister]: "Sonya, something happened to him." She said, "Don't worry, he will come back, his things are all here." Indeed, he soon came back, thanked my sister, took his things and left. He did not even look at me. . . . I had not seen the young man for several days. My sister left, but I stayed to enjoy the sea a little more. . . . One day I went to the communal shower. I stood in the line, and suddenly, I saw him behind me. . . . There was a long line, and we stood together for a while. . . . Then we went together to wait for the tram. Then he said: "Let's take a walk." We walked together. I had a wonderful feeling. . . . Eventually, we took the tram, he wanted to pay for me, but I paid for myself. Then he walked me home, and asked me out to the theater. I agreed. Until now I do not know how I agreed so easily to go with an unknown man. Then he came to pick me up at home. My mother met him, and she liked him. We went to the theater. In the theater, he only looked at me. This is how our romance started. But then I found out he was Russian. . . . And I did not want to upset my family. So we broke up. I thought about him all the time. I thought about him during the war, when I was already married. But I was not brought up this way. I could not be with him. It still hurts when I think about him.

A.S.: Thus, the only reason you did not remain with him was that he was not a Jew. Is this correct?

L.S.: I could not upset my mother.

A.S.: How did your mother argue that you had to marry a Jew?

L.S.: My mother did not say that. She explained that all nationalities are equal. We did not think that Jews were special. However, I remembered . . . that my grandfather called every gentile a "goy." I did not want him to call my husband that. I later married a Jew. He was a wonderful man. We have great children. And I always thought that I did the right thing. Yet, I missed Shura [the Russian man].[46]

This respondent remembered the details of her first courtship with a Russian man unusually clearly, and she was very articulate (which I hope justifies the length of the quotation). Her testimony illuminates some of the doubts and contradictions that could surround choosing a spouse for young Jewish women in the late 1920s. Although the respondent demonstrated that the final decision was hers and that her mother did not interfere with it, it was clear that family background and values, asserted by her grandfather, played a more important role in this young woman's life than those she learned from Soviet propaganda messages. It is also quite possible that the respondent told only the "partial truth," and that her parents protested more than she remembers or chose to tell. It is, however, noteworthy that Lilya, like many other respondents of her generation but unlike respondents of later generations, decided to present her decision to marry a Jew as a conscious one and not as coincidental.

Some respondents remember sharper arguments in their families pertaining to intermarriage. The story of Esfir A. (b. 1908), a Jewish woman who married a Russian man, is illustrative:

> I met my future husband by chance. After I finished university and came back home, I met an old grade school friend, Vasily. We studied together until fifth grade. He introduced me to a friend of his, whose name was also Vasily. They were close friends, and they both fell in love with me. I liked the first Vasily, but then he was drafted into the military in 1937 and was killed. The second Vasily came to tell me the news, and brought me my picture that was found in Vasily the soldier's pocket. Then we started dating, and I eventually married him.
>
> A.S.: He was not Jewish, was he?
>
> E.A.: He was Russian. I am the only one of my four sisters who married a Russian man. All three others married Jews. But my brothers married non-Jews—they both have Russian wives.
>
> A.S.: What was your parents' attitude to the fact that you married a non-Jew?
>
> E.A.: My mother died young, when I was sixteen. My father married again, and his wife was a bitch, even though she was Jewish. So he could not really argue with me. When I married a Russian man, my father did not tell me anything. He just said: "I am so happy your grandfather did not live to see this." You know why I married a Russian man? When I graduated, I could not find work. When I would come to the human resources department, they would look at my passport and would say that the position had already been filled. . . . But after I got married, I had a Russian last name, . . . even though my first name and patronymic [remained Jewish].[47]

Esfir suggested that her father could not protest effectively against her decision to marry a non-Jew because his second marriage to a Jewish woman was not successful. In her mind, these were important arguments, which could not be countered by relevant Jewish tradition that insisted on people marrying within the ethnic group. Also, Esfir's belief that marrying a Russian would help her social mobility outweighed her father's wish for her to have a Jewish family.

Esfir's father was obviously unhappy with her choice, but he lacked the persuasive arguments to prevent her from marrying a non-Jew. Reasons such as having Jewish children, creating a Jewish family, and observing the laws of Judaism were not relevant in the rapidly modernizing Soviet Union. A remarkable feature of this testimony is that though the respondent's father was strongly against her marriage, the respondent presented it as almost a situation without conflict. When asked whether her father protested, her first reaction was to say "no." Perhaps other respondents also exaggerated their parents' acceptance of their choices. After all, these people were being interviewed almost seventy years after the events had taken place, when the family contradictions and conflicts of the 1930s could have seemed less sharp or painful. Esfir, like most participants in the study, stayed married to her first spouse for a long time, and it is possible that in describing her parents' attitudes toward her choice of spouse, she was projecting the later relationship, not initial reactions. The lack of acknowledgment of conflict in interfaith marriages might also be explained by the fact that respondents' choices did not radically contradict their parents' wishes, because parents largely saw interfaith marriage as unfortunate but not shameful. Indeed, many interviewees who married later in the 1930s asserted that their parents did not oppose intermarriage at all. Quite to the contrary, they often thought that Soviet policies of national equality were quite beneficial to the Jewish community.

However, some respondents who married before the war emphasized that marrying a non-Jew was not an option for them. Thus Iona K. (b. 1906) explained:

> I was a Komsomol member, and an internationalist. But it did not even occur to me that I could marry a non-Jew.
>
> A.S.: Was it because you thought it would upset your parents?
>
> I.K.: It would upset my parents, but this was not the reason I wanted a Jewish woman. I just was brought up this way. When my first wife died, I went to Riga, because I heard there were many single Jewish women there. But even when I married for the first time, I only wanted a Jew.[48]

Efim G. (b. 1918) agreed with this statement. He recalled: "I wanted to marry a beautiful, smart, funny, and domestically oriented woman. . . . But all these qualities mattered only if she was a Jew. Otherwise, I would not even look at her."[49]

Both Iona and Efim came from the same Belorussian small town, Parichi. But their views were certainly not confined to this one location. A Leningrader, Vladimir Ya. (b. 1917), stated that he remained single later than his brothers and sisters and did not get married before the war because there were no available Jewish women: "I believed in love and all high ideals, but I could not get married just to get married. I also liked beautiful women, but they all happened to be gentiles [*shikses*]. I was a very handsome man, and I could get any woman I wanted, and what can I tell you, I was not a monk. . . . But to marry, to create a family, I only needed a Jew. . . . That is why I got married quite late, in 1955, and she was Jewish."[50] When asked why it was so important for him to marry a Jew, the respondent said, "This was how I was brought up," but he was not able to provide any specific explanations.

Despite the fact that a similar number of the men and women in this survey chose to marry non-Jews, a willingness to emphasize their Jewish identity and the role it played in their personal choices seemed to be more pronounced among women of this generation than among the men. This could be explained by the closer ties that women maintained with their families, and also by the different patterns of upbringing for boys and girls discussed above. Some respondents suggested that it would be easier to build a family with someone of a similar background and thus chose a Jewish mate. Some women stated that they did not think about the possibility of marrying a non-Jew because their circle of friends consisted almost entirely of Jews. But an absolute majority asserted that they had "accidentally" chosen a Jew, and that they did not think about the identity of their partner. This was the first and the last generation of Soviet Jews to hold such attitudes. Those who got married after World War II dealt not only with their own upbringing but also with state-sponsored anti-Semitism and an increased awareness of their Jewishness caused by knowledge of the Holocaust and postwar events in the Soviet Union. These factors led to a more conscious choice of a Jewish partner in the 1940s, despite the increased level of secularization and assimilation among Soviet Jews.

## Wedding Ceremonies

The wedding ceremony was one of the most elaborate rituals among Eastern European Jews. The full ceremony could last for a few days, but the preparation for it could take years. First, matchmakers would identify the couple, and the parents would agree to the match. At a special ceremony, the fathers would sign a written document, signifying their agreement to marry off their children. Then they would exchange small gifts. The engagement party would follow. Closer to the wedding day, more substantial gifts would be exchanged between the two families. During the prenuptial weeks, the groom would be given a special place at a Sabbath synagogue service, when he would bless the Torah. The bride would host a Saturday night gathering for her female guests, complete with food and dance. Sometimes, meals for the poor would also be organized. At the end of the week, the bride would go to the ritual bath (*mikvah*), where she would go through the traditional ritual of purifying herself physically and spiritually for her wedding day. After the ritual, there would be another party for her female friends.

The wedding day would include the ceremony of "seating the bride," during which her hair would be unbraided and cut. The groom would deliver a short sermon in the synagogue. Both the bride and the groom would fast. At the wedding itself, the couple would stand under the wedding canopy, and the groom would recite specific words and put a ring on his bride's finger in front of two witnesses, and then the marriage would become legally binding. The bride would receive the marriage contract (*ktubah*), which stated her husband's obligations toward her. Then seven blessings would be pronounced, including the benediction over the wine. Afterward, guests would join the wedding party for the feast and dancing.

Each part of this wedding celebration has deep social, cultural, and, of course, spiritual and religious meanings—all of which have changed somewhat over time. Ever since the early nineteenth century, ethnographers have studied the meanings of dances performed at Jewish weddings throughout Eastern Europe. Yiddish folksongs richly describe the nuances of the bride's feelings during the wedding, relationships between the new in-laws, the challenges of being a young wife, and many other aspects of the wedding, which show it to be a life-altering event.

The historian ChaeRan Freeze suggests, on the basis of an analysis of nineteenth-century ethnographers, that the Jewish wedding "firmly grounded the marriage in religious symbol; the fasting, benedictions and religious allusions served not only to consecrate the union but also make participants cognizant of its deep spiritual significance. Although lacking the theological sacramentalism and attendant 'indelibility' doctrine of the Catholic and Orthodox churches, the betrothal and wedding wrapped the new union in religious meaning."[51]

Astonishingly, despite decreasing levels of religious observance among upper- and middle-class Jews in the Russian Empire,[52] along with numerous variations among Jewish religious subgroups (Hassidic and Misnagic to name the two major ones), the wedding ceremony continued throughout the nineteenth century.[53] Even more astonishing, however, was the rapid disappearance of the ceremony from the daily lives of Soviet Jews. Among my respondents, not a single one went through the Jewish wedding ceremony if they were married before 1946 (after 1946, the story is quite different). Mordechai Altshuler confirms that, in combination with a range of socioeconomic changes in the Soviet Union, religious weddings among Jews declined dramatically in the 1920s and almost disappeared in the 1930s.[54]

Moreover, even though Soviet antireligious propaganda attacked virtually every aspect of Jewish daily life, it barely focused on the wedding ritual itself, despite its popularity and strong religious significance, to say nothing of the considerable expense associated with doing it "properly."[55] Altshuler also notes that even Jewish religious authorities did not insist on religious weddings for young couples, because if these couples would not be able to obtain a religious divorce (*get*), any children from a future marriage would be considered *mamzerim* (illegitimate), the lowest possible status in Jewish society. Jewish law prohibited *mamzerim* from marrying anyone except other *mamzerim* or slaves, and there is no simple or legal way to erase the stigma. Many rabbis preferred the "lesser evil" of people living as unmarried under Jewish law, so that their children would still be legitimately Jewish.

My respondents were not aware of any of these matters of Jewish religious law (Halachah) when they married. Many had never even met a rabbi. Most respondents who were married in the 1930s did not have a wedding celebration, whether secular or religious. Especially for young, urban Jews, weddings consisted of the act of signing registration documents in ZAGS. Fira G. (b. 1921) describes her wedding as follows:

> Vitya and I studied together at the university. In 1941, we were both supposed to graduate. Right before final exams, he suggested that we go to the ZAGS and register. I replied, "All right, let's go." That is it. We went there, and signed the papers. The office was located right in front of the Odessa Opera Theater. Then I took my final exams, and moved into his empty apartment with him.[56]

Fira did not even recall telling her parents about the event, let alone a celebratory dinner.

Similarly, Ilya Sh. (b. 1908) recalls his wedding to his first wife as something that he did in between other errands on the same day in 1935:

> I was friends with this woman for a long time. We studied together at the university, we both majored in medicine. We spent all our time together; we studied for tests, and we saw each other every day. But then we decided that we were not destined to get married, even though we loved each other. For a year we stopped dating. Then I was at some party, and realized that she was the one for me. I walked into her apartment, and told her, "I think we should get married." She said: "I am going to take a vacation in Koktebel [Crimea] tomorrow, with my girlfriend. I will come back in a month, and then we can talk about it." I said, "No, I need an answer now." She said, "No answer." I said: "Then it is no." So we said good-bye to each other. I walked home. It was midnight. I came home. My parents were awake (at that time I still lived with my parents). My mother said, "A woman came and brought you this letter." I opened the letter, and it said, "I agree." I ran to the post office to call her (we did not have a phone at home). I told her that I got her letter. She said, "That is good. But tomorrow I am still going to Crimea. If you can, join me." Immediately I went to the railway station and bought a ticket. Then I called her again, and said, "I am all set to go to Crimea." She replied, "This is wonderful, but first we have to get married." Then we met the next day, at 10 a.m., went to the ZAGS, took our passports, and got married. Then I went home to pack my things. My train was leaving at 2 p.m., and hers at 6 p.m. We met in Crimea, and spent our honeymoon there.[57]

The process of registering a marriage is described as a technicality, not as a major event recording a rite of passage. Although Ilya's bride preferred to register their relationship officially, she did not insist on a wedding or even a celebration. In fact, when people did have a special dinner for close friends, it was described as something extraordinary for the time. Olga K., who got married in 1937 in Moscow, reports:

> I got married to an Austrian man. We registered at ZAGS. But in Austria, you see, they had weddings. Even though he was a Communist, he wanted a wedding. So we had a little evening [party], mostly with his Austrian friends, ten or fifteen people. We were very poor, so there was not much to eat there. But it was a dinner, and most of my friends who got married at the time had no celebration at all.[58]

Most respondents did not feel that they needed to justify the absence of a wedding ceremony; but if they did, poverty was named as the main reason. Veniamin Sh. (b. 1908) explained that when he got married in 1929, his family hosted a little dinner for him, his new wife, and only a couple of relatives, because "that was not an easy year, there was absolutely no food."[59]

Esfir A. (b. 1908), who got married in 1932, had a similar experience: "We did not have a wedding. Neither I, nor my husband had money. My father bought a big bottle of beer, my mother fried a goose, and that was our wedding."[60]

Rozaliya U. (b. 1907) elaborated on additional reasons for the absence of her own wedding ceremony, and also specified that it was because of poverty:

> A.S.: Did you have a wedding?
> R.U.: People gathered; a cake was baked. During this time, there were no big weddings. Only rich people like policemen or noblemen had them. If simple people had big celebrations, one would look funny at them. Ordinary people did not do that.[61]

It is hard to say whether the respondent explained past events from her current perspective or how she understood them at the time. It is remarkable, however, that even though Rozaliya grew up in Bobruisk, a Belorussian town densely populated by Jews, she did not think that a wedding could serve as an expression of religious or ethnic identity. Rather, she saw it as a social event that reflected the wealth of the family, as it did in pre-revolutionary Russia. Many respondents attributed the lack of observance of religious holidays and customs to poverty, and not to the fact that Soviet ideology did not support religious rituals.

The decline of wedding celebrations was a general trend not only in urban centers but also in smaller villages and *shtetlekh* (the plural of *shtetl*). David Ransel, in his study of Russian village women, noted that in the 1930s church weddings became rarer, but two-day dinner celebrations were still the rule for anyone getting married.[62] Similarly, the only Jewish respondents who reported having attended or even having had a Jewish wedding came from or got married in *shtetlekh*.

Although the original goal of the project was to record traces of traditional Jewish life that survived in *shtetlekh* until the Holocaust, I made special efforts to find informants who had Jewish weddings, or attended one, before the war. About half my respondents reported that they attended a wedding before the war, and half had some sort of a wedding ceremony that included a celebratory dinner. In fact, some respondents chose to speak about weddings as the most memorable aspect of *shtetl* life before the war. Grigorii B. (b. 1918) left his native *shtetl* Arynin at the age of nine. The only clear memory he had was, "There were weddings, *khupes* (wedding canopies), and lots of music at those weddings. When there was a wedding, I ate everything I wanted. . . . Everyone was invited."[63]

Several respondents were able to recall some specific customs associated with the Jewish weddings in the *shtetl*. For example, Mariya K. (b. 1920), a former actress of the Moscow State Yiddish Theater, was most impressed with the klezmer music performed at Jewish weddings that she attended:

> When I was a child, I attended Jewish weddings. I remember klezmer bands. Musicians who lived in our town sometimes teamed up to play at weddings. Usually, klezmer bands consisted of four people. For weddings, there was always a fiddler, a drummer, a flutist, and cello. My two cousins got married, and I danced at their weddings. I was eight. The guests used to pay the musicians, . . . but I did not pay. I just danced, and I danced really well, and guests asked me to dance more.[64]

The details of the account of the wedding, such as methods of payment for the musicians and her own dancing, suggest that the respondent is probably quite accurate in her description. Indeed, Jewish wedding music made the biggest impression on those who attended such events in the 1930s. Viktor Kh. (b. 1919) recalls that a last peaceful event he attended in his home *shtetl* in Piliava, Ukraine, was "a merry Jewish wedding [of my cousin], with musicians, klezmers who played Jewish dances, like *freylekhs*."[65] Some respondents vaguely remembered other customs associated with traditional weddings practiced before the war. Here is a fragment of my conversation with Faina Ya. (b. 1921):

> A.S.: Have you ever seen a Jewish wedding?
> F.Y.: Of course.
> A.S.: How were they celebrated?
> F.Y.: There were *khupes*. Musicians walked around. They would come to pick up the bride, and then pick up the groom. A *khupa* [ceremonial canopy] usually stood near the synagogue.
> A.S.: Did you have a *khupa* when you got married?
> F.Y.: We had nothing. We went to register in ZAGS, came home, ate boiled lamb and soup. About ten of our friends came over, we sat down, drank a bit, they congratulated us. We did not see anything fancy. We were poor. But our children had weddings. My daughter had 350 guests.[66]

Once again, the respondent attributes the lack of an elaborate wedding ceremony to the poverty of the family.

Typically, when former *shtetl* residents describe traditional weddings, they tend to speak of events organized by their neighbors or extended family but not their own ceremonies. In fact, among all the respondents who got married before the war, only Fira F. (b. 1919) asserted that she had a *khupa* at her own wedding (in 1939):

> We had a very modest wedding. There was a *khupa*, and everything else necessary. We were very poor, we did not have money to pay for everything, so we had a very modest wedding, but all of the customs were observed.
> A.S.: How did your wedding go?
> F.F.: I only remember the *khupa*, but it was according to all the rules. . . .
> A.S.: Were there musicians at your wedding?
> F.F.: Oh yes, we had *klezmorim*, they played *freylekhs* and all other necessary music. . . . I have been at other real Jewish weddings. There were rich Jews, they had hand-made things. . . . But our wedding was simple.[67]

Some respondents called their wedding Jewish simply because there were no non-Jews invited. Iona K. (b. 1907) described the ceremony of his wedding as modest, but "proper":

> A.S.: Did you have a wedding with your first wife [in 1928]?
> I.K.: Yes, we had a wedding in Bobruisk, in my wife's parents' house.
> A.S.: Was it a Jewish wedding?
> I.K.: Well, there were no Russians invited, only Jews.
> A.S.: Did you have a *khupa*?
> I.K.: No, we did not.
> A.S.: Who officiated at the ceremony?
> I.K.: We went to ZAGS.
> A.S.: Were there musicians at the wedding?
> I.K.: There were no musicians, one person played the accordion, but especially for us. It was a small ceremony, just for the family. I did not want to organize anything in a club.[68]

The only Jewish element of this wedding was the fact that all the guests were Jewish. However, this respondent, unlike many others who came from smaller *shtetlekh*, was not apologetic about the lack of an elaborate ceremony. For him, the fact that the wedding took place among Jewish friends and family was sufficient to feel that he had a "proper" Jewish celebration. It is interesting that he did not mention the possibility of getting married in a synagogue, but rather suggested a club as a possible alternative. This testimony demonstrates that even though the respondent was proud of retaining "Jewish values" in the organization of his marriage ceremony, he did not see religion as a necessary or integral part of a Jewish wedding.

Other *shtetl*-born respondents directly asserted that they did not want to have a Jewish religious wedding ceremony for political reasons. Grigorii B. (b. 1906) explained:

> I got married in 1930. . . . When I got married, I did not have a wedding. We went to the ZAGS, and registered. What kind of wedding could I have? I had an important Soviet job. My father was a good man, he understood that, and did not insist on a wedding.
>
> A.S.: There was no celebration at all?
>
> G.B.: Of course there was a celebration. It lasted several days, and people came over, wished us happiness. There was food, drink. . . . Everything was normal.[69]

It is noteworthy that even though the respondent had a three-day celebration to mark the beginning of his married life, he answered "no" to my question about a wedding. He did not consider his three-day celebration a "real" ceremony, because for him the word "wedding" meant a Jewish wedding with the *khupa*, not just a dinner with family and friends. The majority of *shtetl* respondents, just like their urban counterparts, said that they did not have weddings. Urban respondents usually meant that they had no celebration at all, whereas *shtetlers* meant that they did not have a religious ceremony.

To summarize, all the respondents who got married in the interwar period did not see their marriages as the most important event of their lives, and did not typically have a wedding ceremony, whether religious or secular. Those who honored the event with some sort of celebration usually opted for a small dinner for family and friends, rather than an elaborate party. Even *shtetl* residents, who were more familiar with Jewish traditions, usually did not have a religiously influenced ceremony, though they were more likely to organize a celebratory party or dinner. They were also more inclined to add specifically "Jewish" meaning to their ceremony—such as inviting only Jewish guests, playing Jewish music, or serving Jewish food—even though they did not have elements of a traditional religious wedding. In other words, this study of interwar *shtetl* weddings illustrates the transformation of what was considered "Jewish" among Soviet Jews. In the case of weddings, this notion changed from a Judaism-based religious ceremony to a gathering of Jewish people. This transformation played an important role in shaping Jewish identity in the Soviet Union in subsequent years. The rise of ethnic awareness among Soviet Jews in the late 1940s strengthened some of the interwar values, such as "to be a Jew is to be with other Jews."

## Conclusion

This analysis of the transformation of the Jewish family in early Soviet society reveals the nuances of how Jewish identity began to combine new Soviet values with prerevolutionary Jewish ones. The transformation started with changing how boys and girls were brought up. Although both genders were encouraged to get a secular education and eventually take advantage of the opportunities for social mobility provided by the Soviet regime, girls more than boys were expected to maintain closer connections with their families, behave "more modestly," and eventually choose a Jewish partner for marriage. When it came to marriage, girls were more likely than boys to choose a Jewish spouse, possibly because of closer connection with their parents, although this study suggests that most Jews still overwhelmingly chose other Jews as marriage partners.

Respondents of both genders spoke of their perceptions of Jewish women as "more modest" compared with others, yet the in-depth interviews revealed that these perceptions were not factually based. However, perceptions can be as important as the facts, and this is analogous to another trend, prevalent in the 1940s, of equating being Jewish with "being a good and smart person"—an important mark of Soviet Jewish identity during the late Soviet period.

One of the surprising findings of this study is the fact that the transitional generation of Soviet Jews very quickly abandoned the rituals and customs associated with family traditions. Not a single respondent mentioned observing any Jewish religious virtues, such as the celebration of Jewish holidays, let alone the laws of family purity associated with marrying a Jew. Given that my sample included "the most Jewish" of all the Soviet Jews, among whom the rate of intermarriage was very low, this finding signifies quite quick success for the Soviet antireligious policies and propaganda regarding the importance of religious-based ideals in building families. Although some institutions—such as *khadorim*, matzo bakeries, and even small kosher slaughterhouses—continued to operate despite quite significant repression throughout the 1930s, matchmaking, which could have been done in a low-key way, disappeared almost overnight. So did elaborate Jewish weddings, complete with klezmer musicians. The reason for this quick transformation was the decreased significance of the marital union in general, among Jews and non-Jews alike, both due to Soviet legislation, the weakening of religious institutions, and a lack of people who could supervise the observance of Jewish laws that regulated the creation of Jewish families. In addition, many folk practices associated with weddings also disappeared quickly, partially because they seemed extravagant after the civil war, and due to the poverty and deprivation brought on by the Holodomor (the Ukrainian Famine of 1932–33) and collectivization.

However, even more astonishingly, matchmakers and Jewish weddings made a widespread comeback in the late 1940s, even in the cities, when the rate of intermarriage declined due to an increase in anti-Semitism in Soviet society.[70] Yet in the 1920s and 1930s, youngsters abandoned Jewish practices without too much resistance from their parents, who were mostly from a generation of Jews who had traditional marriage ceremonies before the Revolution.

In fact, the Jewish rituals associated with marriage, divorce, and choosing a spouse were among the first to disappear among young Soviet Jews, even before many fully stopped celebrating the Jewish holidays, maintaining a sense of the Jewish community, and observing the laws of *kashrut* (i.e., kosher laws, which insisted on the consumption of meat from animals slaughtered according to Jewish law, and not mixing dairy and meat products). And, surprisingly again, the Jewish wedding ceremony was the only ritual that resurrected itself, albeit in a different form, when all other expressions of Judaism and secular Jewish culture went deep underground in the 1940s to 1980.

I believe that this phenomenon can be partially explained by the fact that, in the 1920s and 1930s, most Jews did not believe that they would need to create and maintain endogamous families in order to protect themselves from a generally hostile society. Similar to their embrace of the advantages of social mobility provided in the Soviet policies of the 1920s, they welcomed the possibility of creating families that were "Soviet" in spirit, that is, families that did not reject Jewish traditional values explicitly but also did not foster them. As with many other types of behavior, however, this one characterized only the lives of a single generation of Jews, who contributed to the Soviet experiment of creating a new society. This experiment failed, but millions of Soviet and post-Soviet Jews continue to maintain some of the ideas and ideals of the only true "Soviet and kosher" generation of Jews.

## Notes

1. Research for this chapter was conducted with the help of two grants from the Rabbi Israel Miller Fund for Shoah Education, Research, and Documentation of the Material Claims Conference against Germany (grants 1413 and S028); both grants were received jointly with Zvi Gitelman. Additional funding came from the Social Sciences and Humanities Research Council of Canada and the Connaught New Staff Matching

Grant at the University of Toronto. Selected earlier parts of this chapter appeared in "Choosing a Spouse in the USSR: Gender Differences and the Jewish Ethnic Factor," *Jews in Russia and Eastern Europe* 2, no. 51 (Winter 2003): 5–30.

2. For a definitive study on this topic, see ChaeRan Freeze, *Jewish Marriage and Divorce in Imperial Russia* (Boston: Brandeis University Press, 2002).

3. For more on the content of this identity, see Anna Shternshis, *Soviet and Kosher: Jewish Popular Culture in the Soviet Union, 1923–1939* (Bloomington: Indiana University Press, 2006), xiii–xxi.

4. The interviews were conducted in the United States (New York and Philadelphia), Germany, Russia, and Canada. The respondents were interviewed about Jewish daily life in Ukraine, Belorussia, and Russia before World War II. The interviews consisted of open-ended questions about respondents' experiences during their lives. I used a combination of an open call for volunteers in the form of a letter to the editors of Russian-language newspapers and, at a later stage, the snowball method for collecting interviews. The questionnaire drew on suggestions by Paul Thompson. See his *The Voice of the Past: Oral History*, 2nd ed. (New York: Oxford University Press, 1988).

5. Alex Inkeles and Raymond Bauer, *The Soviet Citizen: Daily Life in a Totalitarian Society* (Cambridge, Mass.: Harvard University Press, 1959), 228.

6. Yurii P., interview by the author, Berlin, June 2002.

7. Samuil G., interview by the author, New York, March 1999.

8. Lilya Sh., interview by the author, Berlin, June 2002.

9. Esfir A., interview by the author, Potsdam, June 2002.

10. Anne Gorsuch, *Youth in Revolutionary Russia: Enthusiasts, Bohemians, Delinquents* (Bloomington: Indiana University Press, 2000), 32.

11. Efim G., interview by the author, Brooklyn, February 1999.

12. On the education of Jewish girls in the Russian Empire, see Eliyana R. Adler, *In Her Hands: The Education of Jewish Girls in Tsarist Russia* (Detroit: Wayne State University Press, 2011).

13. David Fishman, "Fate of Religious Education," in *Jews and Jewish Life in Russia and the Soviet Union*, edited by Yaacov Ro'i (Ilford, England: Frank Cass, 1995), 252.

14. Shternshis, *Soviet and Kosher*, 4–5.

15. Rozaliya U., interview by the author, Moscow, June 2001.

16. Olga K., interview by the author, Moscow, June 2001.

17. Klara G., interview by the author, Philadelphia, February 2001.

18. Sonya G., interview by the author, New York, February 1999.

19. Yosef S., interview by the author, Brooklyn, March 1999.

20. Esfir A., interview.

21. Anna G., interview by the author, Brooklyn, March 1999.

22. Mariya D., interview by the author, Berlin, June 2002.

23. Etya G., interview by the author, Brooklyn, January 1999.

24. Leon Dennen, *Where the Ghetto Ends* (New York: King Alfred, 1934).

25. Ilya F., interview by the author, Berlin, June 2002.

26. Ilya and Sima F., interview by the author, Berlin, June 2002.

27. Or this could be in the sense that the maternal line conferred a Jewish identity and also gave that Jewish identity meaning. Women, here as in other instances, are carriers of traditions that give meaning to certain identities.

28. Wendy Goldman, *Women, the State and Revolution* (Cambridge: Cambridge University Press, 1993), 51.

29. Ibid., 52.

30. Robert Thurston, "The Soviet Family during the Great Terror," *Soviet Studies* 43, no. 3 (1991): 557.
31. Lewis Coser, "Some Aspects of Soviet Family Policy," *The American Journal of Sociology* 56, no. 5 (March 1951): 429.
32. Thurston, "The Soviet Family during the Great Terror," 553–74.
33. Shternshis, *Soviet and Kosher,* 166–70.
34. Mikhail Bezyzer, *Evrei Leningrada* (Moscow: Gesharim, 1999), 84.
35. Mordechai Altshuler, *Soviet Jewry on the Eve of the Holocaust* (Jerusalem: Yad Vashem, 1998), 73.
36. Ibid., 76.
37. Yosef V., interview by the author, Berlin, June 2002.
38. Ilya Sh., interview.
39. Olga K., interview.
40. Grigorii B., interview by the author, Berlin, June 2002.
41. Lilya Sh., interview by the author, Berlin, June 2002.
42. Olga K., interview.
43. Grigorii B., interview.
44. Veniamin Sh., interview by the author, Moscow, June 2001.
45. Ilya Sh., interview by the the author, Moscow, June 2001.
46. Lilya Sh., Berlin, June 2002.
47. Esfir A., interview.
48. Iona K., interview by the author, Berlin, June 2002.
49. Efim G., interview.
50. Vladimir Ya., interview by the author, Berlin, June 2001.
51. Freeze, *Jewish Marriage and Divorce,* 49.
52. Natan Meir, *Kiev, Jewish Metropolis: A History, 1859–1914* (Bloomington: Indiana University Press, 2010), 150–89; and Benjamin Nathans, *Beyond the Pale: The Jewish Encounter with Late Imperial Russia* (Berkeley: University of California Press, 2004).
53. Freeze, *Jewish Marriage and Divorce,* 44.
54. Altshuler, *Soviet Jewry on the Eve of the Holocaust,* 64.
55. Shternshis, *Soviet and Kosher,* chap. 1.
56. Fira G., interview by the author, New York, March 1999.
57. Ilya Sh., interview by author, Moscow, June 2001.
58. Olga K., interview.
59. David Sh. (Venianmin is the name in the text), interview by the author, Moscow, June 2001.
60. Esfir A., interview by the author, Moscow, June 2001.
61. Rozaliya U., interview by the author, Moscow, June 2001.
62. David Ransel, *Village Mothers: Three Generations of Change in Russia and Tataria* (Bloomington: Indiana University Press, 2001), 88.
63. Grigorii B., interview.
64. Mariya K., interview by the author, Moscow, June 2001.
65. Viktor Kh., interview by the author, New York, August 1999.
66. Faina Ya., interview by the author, Berlin, June 2002.
67. Fira F., interview by the author, Berlin, June 2002.
68. Iona K., interview by the author, Potsdam, June 2002.
69. Grigorii B., interview.
70. Shternshis, "Choosing a Spouse in the USSR."

# Chapter 3

# Christianity and Radical Nationalism: Metropolitan Andrei Sheptytsky and the Bandera Movement

*John-Paul Himka*

This chapter is a study of the confrontation between a Christian clergyman and a violent nationalist movement in Western Ukraine during World War II, and between Christian principles and a largely secular ideology that subordinated everything, including traditional Christian ethics, to the victory of the national cause.[1] Unlike the Church's conflict with communism, the conflict with nationalism was complicated by the strong sympathy of many within the Church, including the hierarchy, to the aspirations of the national movement. The latter had now become embodied in an organization that routinely murdered in the name of the nation and yet enjoyed widespread popularity among co-nationals, particularly among the youth and even young clergy. In practice, the response of Christian leaders to such situations has ranged from total endorsement to total opposition; or they have tried as much as possible to avoid engaging with the problem. In the case studied here, that of the leader of the Ukrainian Greek Catholic Church, Metropolitan Andrei Sheptytsky, we are dealing with oppositional engagement and the difficulties it posed.

The city of L'viv, of which Sheptytsky was archbishop, is situated geographically and culturally between Kraków and Kyiv. Sheptytsky was only one of three Catholic archbishops in L'viv, along with his Roman Catholic and Armenian Catholic confreres. He was the Greek Catholic archbishop of L'viv, as well as the metropolitan of Halych. L'viv had been founded in the mid–thirteenth century by a prince of the Rus' principality of Halych and so was originally Orthodox. In subsequent centuries, it attracted many Catholic inhabitants, mainly Poles and Germans. The annexation of L'viv by Poland in the late fourteenth century weakened its Orthodox character. The patronage and protection of Orthodox princes, which allowed Orthodox culture to flourish in the northern Rus' principalities and in neighboring Moldavia, were absent in L'viv and the rest of the Halych territories, subsequently known as Galicia. By 1700, the Orthodox here had accepted the Church Union of Brest, that is, they joined the Catholic Church as so-called Uniates.

In 1772, Galicia was annexed by the Habsburg monarchy, and then ruled by the enlightened absolutists Maria Theresa and her son Joseph II. These reformers thoroughly renovated the Uniate Church of what they called the Ruthenian population. They renamed the church the Greek Catholic Church, to indicate parity with the Roman Catholic Church. Of the many reforms, the most important for this chapter's theme is the establishment of higher education for Ruthenian candidates for the priesthood. Within two generations, the system of general seminaries produced an educated clergy, which served as the basis for a Ruthenian intelligentsia. The clergy represented the Ruthenian population in the Revolution of 1848, and their children filled the ranks of the new Ruthenian secular intelligentsia, which assumed leadership of the national movement by the 1860s. But priests remained the indispensable foot soldiers of the movement among the peasantry. Throughout the villages they founded reading clubs and cooperatives, championed schools and condemned taverns, and agitated for Ruthenian candidates in elections. These clerical nation builders absorbed so much national work into their pastoral work that the distinction between such labors receded in their minds. Of course there were tensions, but in essence the Greek Catholic Church and the national movement progressed hand in hand. This was the church that Andrei Sheptytsky was to lead in the first half of the twentieth century.[2]

He was born Roman Szeptycki in 1865, the child of Polish aristocrats. On his father's side his ancestry could be traced back to a Rus' boyar family. The Szeptycki family had produced several bishops of the Uniate/Greek

Catholic Church in the past, but Roman's father had transferred to the Latin rite. The family had long been linguistically and culturally Polonized. Young Roman, on fire with a vision of service to the Catholic Church and the Ruthenian people, returned to the Greek rite of his ancestors. In 1888 he entered a Greek Catholic monastery, taking the name Andrei. He rose rapidly in clerical ranks thereafter. He was only thirty-five when he was appointed, in 1900, as metropolitan of Halych and archbishop of L'viv. His conversion to Greek Catholicism and Ruthenian nationalism was sincere and complete. His noble birth and innate talents gave him an influence in the public sphere that was unprecedented for the Ruthenians of Galicia, who had once been mocked as a nation of "priests and peasants." Sheptytsky spoke in the Austrian House of Lords in favor of establishing a Ukrainian university, and he met personally with the emperor to promote the same cause. He had access to tremendous personal wealth, and he used it generously for his people. He founded a national museum and a Ruthenian hospital in the Austrian period. Later, under the rule of restored Poland, when the Ukrainian population, as it then preferred to be called, was severely restricted in its access to higher education, he built a theological academy that functioned much like a university. Sheptytsky supported the Ruthenian/Ukrainian national movement with dedication and effectiveness, but only insofar as it did not come into conflict with Christian principles.

Sheptytsky's devotion to the Ukrainian movement was put to the test in 1908, when a Ukrainian student assassinated the governor of Galicia, a Polish count. Although it cost him in popularity, Sheptytsky roundly condemned the murder as a terrible sin, as "politics without God."[3] Although such a violent incident did not recur in the Austrian period, Sheptytsky was to confront more nationalist violence later, especially in the 1930s, when Ukrainian nationalists organized a series of spectacular political assassinations, and during World War II, when they engaged in mass political murder. The latter is our subject. We will follow Sheptytsky's judgment and responses in a difficult situation. It was a moment, as the Ukrainian historian Inna Poizdnyk delicately put it, "when an idea, to which one had devoted one's life, acquired a completely different coloration."[4]

The Ukrainian movement underwent a metamorphosis over the decades during which Sheptytsky presided over the metropolis of Halych. When he assumed office in 1900, the main activities of the movement consisted of fielding candidates in elections and building an organizational infrastructure. The mass of rural organizations, ranging from choirs to gymnastic and paramilitary organizations, created a network that functioned much like a state within a state. World War I gave the Ukrainians of Galicia military experience—they had their own unit in the Austrian service, the Sich Sharpshooters. When Austria collapsed, the Ukrainians fought to establish their own state, but they were defeated by the Poles, who outnumbered them by several times and who received training and equipment from the Western Allies. The Ukrainians of Galicia ended up as a minority in a restored Polish state that discriminated against them in many ways. The frustrated veterans in particular, but many other Ukrainians in Galicia as well, moved to a more uncompromising and ruthless form of nationalism. Before World War I, the Ukrainian movement had been left of center; now it was positioning itself on the right. In 1929 various groups merged into the Organization of Ukrainian Nationalists (OUN), which increasingly adopted the trappings of a radical right movement. It fell under the influence of fascism and national socialism, with the latter being the main influence on the eve of World War II. In September 1939, after the German attack on Poland, the Soviet Union occupied Galicia and incorporated it into the Ukrainian Soviet Socialist Republic. Many members of OUN fled to the German zone, particularly to Kraków. OUN split in 1940, resulting in the formation of a more radical, younger wing led by Stepan Bandera. This wing became dominant in Galicia and had thousands of adherents and many more thousands of sympathizers. Highly disciplined, it even managed to organize and maintain a nationalist underground under Soviet rule.[5]

On the eve of Germany's attack on the Soviet Union in June 1941, the Bandera movement coordinated its activities with Germany. The Banderites hoped that the Germans would allow them to establish a Ukrainian state, which was a total misreading of the goals of national socialism. The situation, in a nutshell, was that the Bandera movement considered Germany to be its ally, whereas Germany considered the movement to be its instrument. In 1943, Bandera broke definitively with the German occupiers; the Ukrainian police in German service, which it had infiltrated, deserted en masse to form the Ukrainian Insurgent Army (Ukrayins'ka Povstans'ka Armiya, UPA). The UPA embarked on the ethnic cleansing of Western Ukraine, killing and terrorizing Poles systematically as well as killing Jewish survivors in the forest.[6] The nationalists' murderous activities provoked conflict with the head of the Greek Catholic Church.

In some matters, the worldviews of Sheptytsky and the nationalists overlapped. Both opposed materialism and communism, championed an independent Ukrainian state, and hoped for the union of Orthodox and Greek Catholics into a single Ukrainian Church. In the 1920s, when nationalism was more a set of ideas than practices, Sheptytsky was not strongly opposed to the nationalists and identified some common ground. But after the founding of OUN, differences rose to the fore.[7]

In 1932, Sheptytsky issued his "Sermon to Ukrainian Youth." This text dealt with the generational conflict between the more moderate elders and the nationalist youth. From the nationalist side too, the conflict was understood as a fathers-and-sons issue, because the nationalists blamed their fathers' generation for having failed to achieve Ukrainian statehood. In the "Sermon to Ukrainian Youth," Sheptytsky addressed the issue of generational conflict and warned the young nationalists against the dangers of radicalism, violence, and intolerance:[8]

> And you have also this defect, that you all too often want to force your ideas and outlook on others, sometimes even using force and blind terror. You have little of what earlier generations called tolerance. . . . This is not, Ukrainian Youth, exclusively your failing. This is a worldwide tendency, which produced on the one hand fascism and the clear inclination in many states toward dictatorship and on the other hand Bolshevism.[9]

Sheptytsky was to clash with the nationalists several times over the ensuing years because of his objections to their violent methods, especially political assassinations. He had already been insisting for decades that political murder is still murder and therefore a grave sin.

One of the most intense moments of conflict between Sheptytsky and the young nationalists came in 1934 when they killed Ivan Babii, the director of the Ukrainian Academic Gymnasium. Sheptytsky condemned them harshly: "If you want to treacherously kill all those who oppose your work, you will have to kill all teachers and professors who work for the Ukrainian youth, all fathers and mothers of Ukrainian children." He reminded them that "a crime is always a crime," and "one cannot serve a holy cause with blood-stained hands."[10] The intervention of the metropolitan was perceived in Ukrainian society as an extraordinarily strong condemnation of the nationalists' activities.[11] OUN responded by attempting, with the connivance of another bishop, to have Sheptytsky removed from the metropolitan throne.[12]

In spite of these ideological and moral differences, Sheptytsky was still able to maintain relations with nationalist leaders, operating perhaps on the distinction between the sin and the sinner. Andrii Melnyk, a prominent member of OUN, and later the leader of one of its factions, was a friend of the metropolitan and managed his estates for a time in the 1930s. After the

Soviets occupied Galicia in 1939, Sheptytsky protected a nationalist leader who was in danger of being arrested and passed money to him.[13]

Although on the eve of Nazi Germany's attack on its former Soviet ally the Bandera faction of OUN had been working closely with the Germans, the Germans had given them no firm assurances about the establishment of a Ukrainian state. The Banderites decided therefore to present them with a fait accompli. They proclaimed the formation of a Ukrainian government on the very day that the Germans took L'viv, June 30, 1941.

Before the official proclamation of the state, representatives of the Bandera movement called upon Sheptytsky, to get his endorsement. The men who came to see the metropolitan were Yaroslav Stetsko, who was designated to head the Ukrainian government, and Father Ivan Hryniokh, chaplain of the nationalist battalion Nachtigall. The two convinced the metropolitan to give his blessing to their initiative but considered it prudent to withhold certain information from him. They did not tell him, for one thing, that they were acting without German approval. They understood that the leader of the church was a cautious man whose policy, like that of Catholic bishops as a whole, was to work within parameters set by state authorities rather than to foment rebellion. Metropolitan Sheptytsky had previously cooperated with the Soviet government that had preceded the Nazi occupation, refraining from preaching resistance to this atheistic and murderous regime. Moreover, Sheptytsky was genuinely pleased when the Germans marched in, liberating his archeparchy (i.e., an archdiocese of an Eastern church) from the Bolsheviks. Hence he would not have been party to any action that could be considered rebellious. The Banderites also hid from the metropolitan that they constituted only a faction of the Organization of Ukrainian Nationalists and were not representative of broader circles in Ukrainian politics. The split between the Melnyk and Bandera factions of OUN had taken place in Kraków in 1940—that is, in the German zone of occupation—whereas Sheptytsky was in the Soviet zone. Although the OUN underground in L'viv seems to have been aware of the differences between the factions, Sheptytsky learned of the split for the first time only after he had already endorsed the Banderite state. Finally, the Banderite representatives kept from the metropolitan that they planned to unleash a campaign of furious violence against national minorities and communists. Sheptytsky did not expect this. In his pastoral letter of July 1, Sheptytsky wrote that he expected from the new government "wise, just leadership and measures that would take into consideration the needs and welfare of all citizens who inhabit our land, without regard to what faith, nationality, and social stratum they belong."[14] Instead, on the very day that the pastoral letter was issued, the militia of the new government carried out a horrific pogrom against the Jewish population of L'viv, which alienated the metropolitan.[15] The violence was not limited to the capital city: the militias and other OUN units killed Jews in particular, but also communists and Poles, in towns and villages throughout Western Ukraine.

Sheptytsky was deeply upset by the deceptions and violence that accompanied his first close acquaintance with the Bandera movement. He took a number of steps to restrict and oppose their influence. One line that Sheptytsky pursued at first was to work for the reunification of OUN so that the more moderate elements within the organization, which he identified with the Melnyk faction, could control the radicalism of the nationalist youth, which he identified with the Bandera faction. Although Sheptytsky had opposed OUN ideology and practice long before the split, in the concrete situation of summer 1941, he preferred the return to influence of the OUN faction headed by Melnyk, who had Catholic associations and was a personal friend. An appeal to the clergy of July 5, 1941, called for all patriots to abandon party feuds and to work together in unity and harmony. Two days later Sheptytsky wrote a letter to Melnyk urging him to come to an agreement with Bandera and to eliminate the split that was so harmful to Ukrainians.[16] In August he organized and hosted a meeting between leaders of the two factions.[17] Nothing came of his efforts to reunite OUN, however; the Bandera movement consolidated its hold on political life in the territory of Sheptytsky's metropolis. After violence between the factions intensified, and especially after the assassination of two leading members of the Melnyk faction on August 30, 1941, Sheptytsky issued a text on October 5, 1941, condemning murder. This was clearly aimed against political murder within the Ukrainian political community, motivated by "blind hatred toward brother Ukrainians born into the same nationality."[18] He again called for unity in a pastoral letter of December 1941.[19] In a document of December 10, 1942, he wrote: "I am struck by the tale told by a priest who returned from western Germany, where he worked in a camp for laborers. The rural youth there were so entangled in quarrels and so divided that heated disputes, full of mutual hatred, between 'Melnykites' and 'Banderites' did not cease. They hated each other more than representatives of two enemy nations. And what can one say about those numerous murders, which no one has been able to stop?"[20]

A letter to the clergy of July 10, 1941, a version of which was published in the L'viv daily newspaper *Ukrains'ki shchodenni visti*, was a decisive statement of opposition to Banderite politics. It again expressed grave concerns over the split within the nationalist movement.[21] It also, however, called on pastors and elders in communities to form municipal governments. "Where there is not yet an administration and local militia it is necessary to organize the election of a community council, mayor, and chief of the militia." The pastor was to pick, on his own or in consultation with prominent villagers, three farmers as justices of the peace to settle disputes. This was a direct challenge to the Banderites, who themselves wanted to control local government under the Nazi occupation. A Banderite order from the time also called for control of parishes: "Take over in the village the teachers and priests and harness them to community work under our direction. Take over the church brotherhoods. Each church must have, besides a religious character, also a national character."[22]

There was at least one case in which Sheptytsky's program for municipal government was implemented, in Peremyshliany, where Father Emyliian Kovch was elected to head the district committee.[23] The radical nationalists were not pleased. His daughter wrote in her biography of Father Kovch:

> Those who are still alive today [1994] and were at that meeting reported their disappointment that instead of enthusiasm at the declaration of Ukrainian independence, Father Kowcz was much more cautious. He asked the youth not to join the German police, warned them not to participate in any anti-Jewish or any unlawful activity against any citizens of Peremyshliany.[24]

There were surely other such cases, but they have not come to light. The Banderites, however, were in a position to impose their will, because they had armed militias or related units in many localities.

In addition, the Banderites benefited from widespread popularity. The same processes that had produced OUN had also produced nationalist sentiments throughout Galicia, even among the clergy. A group of "Christian nationalist" priests had been working out their ideology during the interwar era.[25] Before Sheptytsky's letter, on June 25, 1941, Father Lev Sohor, who was administrator in Kobylnica Ruska (today in Poland) and a sympathizer of OUN, was present at a meeting during which the nationalists organized a local militia "to remove the Jews and protect the population."[26] Afterward, on August 25, an unidentified village priest sent a strongly worded protest to the L'viv Archeparchy with regard to Sheptytsky's letter of July 10. In his opinion the Banderites had earned "the confidence, enthusiasm, and unquestioning obedience of all strata of our rural and urban population" and so deserved to put their people in charge of municipal government. "Where is our [i.e., the clergy's] authority and competence, and is our meddling or our dictation with regard to the civil administration in the village welcome?"[27]

Thus the metropolitan, in spite of the great respect he had earned from his flock, was unable, neither for the first nor for the last time, to translate his moral authority into political clout. The replacement of Banderite local administration with an alternative administration led by Christian and moderate elements was a program that Sheptytsky would advocate again later, also without much effect.

The metropolitan warned against radicalism in his letter of July 10. The Bolshevik occupation had awakened "a revolutionary spirit" in many people, but now was the time for order and duty. The population should do all that is "necessary and good for our nation and for the future of our state." He welcomed the youth who had fled the Soviets and were now returning to Galicia—a reference to the young Banderite nationalists—but he felt the need to remind them that "no human considerations and no vows taken justify a sin against God's commandment."[28]

The Bandera movement understood very well that the metropolitan's letter was directed against its policies. An OUN report on the organization of Ukrainian authority on Western Ukrainian lands, dated July 22, 1941, commented: "Obviously, this letter cannot [avoid contributing] . . . to the growth of chaos and confusion in the Western oblasts."[29]

Sheptytsky's rejection of the Bandera movement also found expression in a condemnation of the movement's greeting. Like many radical-right movements of the time, the OUN Bandera had developed a greeting and raised-arm salute. One person would say "Glory to Ukraine!" The other would answer "Glory to the heroes!" In an instruction of September 6, 1941, Sheptytsky noted that "Glory to Ukraine!" was used to replace the traditional greeting of Western Ukraine, "Glory to Jesus Christ!" Sheptytsky wrote, "Of course, no Ukrainian can have anything against the slogan 'Glory to Ukraine!' but to use this phrase to replace the act of religious glorification of Christ is a clear tendency to displace Christ and put the fatherland in his place, which is a sign of a clear godless tendency that fools naive Ukrainian patriots."[30] Here he was reiterating on the symbolic level a point he had been making since the early twentieth century: the nation is good, but it cannot displace God and his laws.

Sheptytsky considered the Bandera faction to be a rebellious movement of insufficiently responsible, hot-headed youth. It was perhaps in the second half of 1941 that he allegedly called them "unserious people" and "snot-nosed kids" (*smarkachi*).[31] On July 22, 1941, he specifically condemned "the spontaneous behaviour of one faction of the Organization of Ukrainian Nationalists."[32]

In his many writings from the spring of 1942 and later that condemned Ukrainian participation, mainly as policemen, in the extermination of the Jews,[33] Sheptytsky occasionally referred specifically to the Banderites. He did so by framing his remarks in generational terms, speaking of the Banderites as "children" or "youth." In his pastoral letter of April 14–15, 1942, Sheptytsky wrote: "Among our children there have been found people who are so foolish and conscienceless that they summon upon the whole nation even heavier divine punishments." Only the Most Holy Mother of God can help stay God's anger and intercede on behalf of "those whose hands are stained with blood" that they be granted "mercy and the grace of repentance."[34] In his pastoral letter of June 1942, "On Mercy," Sheptytsky spoke about the pain of parents whose children have gone wrong. These children had been the pride and joy of their parents, but now they have become "a heavy cross and a painful source of shame. . . . What a pain for a father to see his son, stained with shedding innocent blood, a son from whom all the neighbors and acquaintances turn away in disgust."[35]

As I have argued elsewhere, one reason that the metropolitan decided to support the formation of a Ukrainian Waffen-SS division was that he feared what the nationalist youth would do in the period between the German withdrawal and the Soviet reoccupation.[36] He preferred that young Ukrainians be in a regular army unit, with discipline and with chaplains that he appointed. He considered this the lesser evil even though by this time, spring 1943, he rejected Nazi Germany entirely. His concern, in part, was to support an alternative to the anarchic violence that he associated with the Banderites, having in mind the bloody events of early July 1941. This view is confirmed by something that Sheptytsky told an KGB informer within weeks of the Soviet reconquest of L'viv on July 27, 1943. He said that he could justify the Melnyk faction and the men who joined the division it sponsored—their intentions were good, but they were deceived by the Germans. As to the Bandera faction and the UPA—these he condemned.[37] Such sentiments are reminiscent of Sheptytsky's thinking in summer 1941, when he decided that the Melnyk faction was a preferable alternative to Bandera's.

In the second half of 1943, Sheptytsky had to respond to the mass murder of Poles perpetrated by the Bandera movement, specifically by the UPA and by OUN security units. The UPA had first been active outside Sheptytsky's jurisdiction, in neighboring Volhynia, but appeared in Galicia in summer 1943. The Nazis had proclaimed Galicia *judenrein* in June of that year. There were still Jews surviving in hiding or because they held "Aryan" papers afterward, but the vast majority had been murdered. Although surviving Jews were still being killed in Galicia and Volhynia, the primary victims in Volhynia from spring 1943 and in Galicia from summer 1943 were Poles. Therefore Sheptytsky's writings against murder from summer 1943 on were concerned primarily with the murder of Poles, and not, as earlier, of Jews. A French collaborator with the Nazis, René Martel (who used the pseudonym "Dr. Frédéric"), visited the metropolitan in late summer 1943 and found him unsettled by "the Polish-Ukrainian civil war, murders, acts of sabotage against trains, the plunder of isolated villages by bands."[38]

The Germans were happy when the nationalists could be used to murder Jews, but they did not approve of their mass killings of Poles, which destabilized territories under their occupation. They therefore gave Sheptytsky a relatively free hand to denounce this set of murders forthrightly; he had not had this opportunity, of course, in relation to the murder of the Jewish population. His first pronouncement on the subject was a pastoral letter of August 15, 1943, which the Germans allowed to be circulated.[39] Sheptytsky again explicitly framed the situation in generational terms: "Appealing to the entire nation, I have in mind above all the older and more respected people of every community. It is with them, in the first place, that I want to reach an understanding." He said that for all the virtues of the youth, they were usurping leadership in the community and silencing the voice of the older generation. They were also very dangerous: "We have even been witnesses of terrible murders committed by our young people, perhaps even with good intentions, but with perditious consequences for the nation." The metropolitan said that he had many times warned against anger, national hatred, partisan quarrels, and revenge against enemies. Now he would like the elders in the community to take up these warnings as well. "You are their fathers. . . . Warn your sons against crime." He appealed to the elders to take steps to rescue those in danger of death (meaning Polish inhabitants of villages). Sheptytsky also addressed himself directly to the nationalist youth:

> Do not let yourselves be provoked to commit any iniquitous acts. It is only, after all, in the interests of our enemies to urge our people to take unwise steps that could in the future bring, and even must bring, great damage to our people. Do not let yourselves be deceived by people who present as a necessity acts which are against God's law. Remember that you will achieve nothing good through actions that are opposed to God's law.[40]

Once again, Sheptytsky's admonitions against national political violence fell on deaf ears. Among the Ukrainian clergy, there was a minority who helped and hid Poles in danger of death; but there was also a minority that encouraged the murders. Inna Poizdnyk, who studied the behavior of the Greek Catholic clergy during the UPA's massacre of Poles, concluded that the influence of the hierarchy's letters and appeals on priests was minimal.[41]

In November 1943, Sheptytsky authored a joint pastoral letter signed by the entire Ukrainian episcopate. It is a text that is not often cited, and here I will quote it extensively:

> Christian righteousness has been lost to such a degree among people that one simply does not want to believe that these were once Christians, and maybe once good Christians, who today are worse than pagans...
>
> Bad example, the use of liquor, disobedience to parents, the neglect of religious obligations and of catechism teaching, the sin of impurity, and above all the cruelty of war, which is conducted not only on the battlefields, but extends far [beyond] . . . and destroys before our eyes the lives of the most innocent people—all this accustoms one to robbery, bloodshed, and even murders. Some, thinking that by joining bands they will by their own will avoid the burdens of war, such as labor, requisitions, and the like, bring not only on themselves, but also on the entire nation still more terrible repressions and the death penalty. All this together also brings about the misfortune that a child of God, the child of Christian parents, forgets to such an extent about his honor, about the honor of his parents and nation, about his Christian upbringing, about God's law, about his own happiness and salvation, that he leaves his house and, giving himself into the service of bandits, steals with them, robs, or, what is not very removed from that, he stains (God forbid!) his hands with the blood of innocent murdered people. . . .
>
> All of us [bishops] at every opportunity remind you [the faithful] of this obligation of Christian love. As always, so now we warn you against every hatred, because not only in private life, but in civic and political life the Christian cannot hate even his most determined enemy. One can defend oneself, one's children, and the entire nation against him, but one cannot allow hatred into one's heart or exclude him from prayers and the love of neighbor. One must have vis-à-vis one's enemies a wide, all-embracing Christian love. . . .
>
> A curse of our time is that in wartime murder has proliferated among the people, as a result of which thousands who have done nothing wrong leave this world. Murder is such a clear, terrible crime, it calls so clearly to heaven

for revenge, that a person who has even a drop of Christian blood left must turn with disgust from murder and from those who have their hands stained with the blood of innocent people. . . . Of course, we condemn all murder, no matter who commits it; we condemn all crimes, those of which we are the victims and those crimes which our own people might commit.[42]

The themes raised in this powerful, even desperate letter are the same ones that Sheptytsky had raised earlier in relation to the murder of the Jews—the condemnation of murder, the instruction to love one's neighbor, and the need to make murderers social outcasts in the community.[43]

Noteworthy in the November letter is that Sheptytsky spoke not only of individuals who committed murder, as he had heretofore, but of entire bands who robbed and killed. He also referred to bands in a letter to the Latin-rite archbishop of L'viv, Bolesław Twardowski, of November 15, 1943, written therefore roughly at the same time as the pastoral letter quoted directly above. Archbishop Twardowski had previously written to the Greek Catholic metropolitan to intervene to stop the murder of Latin-rite priests and their faithful, that is, the Poles of Galicia. In response, Sheptytstky wrote:

> In the complete chaos of the present moment all the worst elements rise to the surface and run wild. In the statistics of murders, I think that murders connected with robbery occupy a very important place—and Latin-rite priests have in general a reputation of being rich people; the attack on the parish rectory is more profitable and easier for the bandits than the attack on other buildings. Bolshevik partisans, Jewish bands, agitators of revolutionary Polish organizations of Warsaw, who in their publications even brag about murders committed by Poles, act with impunity in the country. Probably in many cases personal grudges are at work, especially in forest regions. For many years it is not national, but social hatred among those who punish people for stealing wood but do not even want to sell it. In the country are bands of various deserters and everywhere a multitude of perverted, sadistic individuals who have a need for human blood.[44]

In this response, Sheptytsky lists every possibility except that Ukrainian nationalists were involved in the killing. Is it possible he did not know that there were Ukrainian nationalist bands? No, because we have a report he wrote to the Vatican about the murder on the previous day of the Orthodox metropolitan Aleksii (Hromadsky) by unidentified partisans. (Now it is clear that Metropolitan Aleksii was killed by the UPA, either unintentionally or intentionally.[45]) In Sheptytsky's report, dated May 8, 1943, that is, not long after the murder of Poles began in Volhynia, Sheptytsky characterized the kinds of partisans who roamed the region: "All of Volhynia and part of Galicia are full of bands that have a certain political character. There are some bands composed of Poles, others of Ukrainians, others indeed of communists. And besides this there are the true bandits, among whom are people of all nationalities—Germans, Jews, and Ukrainians."[46] Andrei Sheptytsky's brother Klymentii told a German collaborator in late summer of 1943 that there were seven kinds of bands active in Galicia, one of which was "bands of Ukrainian nationalists, who are equally hostile to Germany as to Poland and Russia."[47] Thus Sheptytsky was well aware, from early on, that there were politically Ukrainian bands—that is, nationalist units—but refrained from even acknowledging their existence, let alone their complicity in the murder of Poles, in his letter to Archbishop Twardowski.[48]

Indeed, there is much in the correspondence with L'viv's Latin-rite archbishop that does not seem consistent with Sheptytsky's usual positions. It is true that relations between Sheptytsky and Twardowski were far from cordial, but their mutual dislike cannot account for the substance of Sheptytsky's letter, although it may have influenced the tone.[49] A more weighty factor would have been the historic rivalry between the Latin and Greek Catholic archbishops of L'viv. Already in the nineteenth century and earlier, relations between the Polish Roman Catholic and Ukrainian Greek Catholic hierarchs had undergone much strain. By the time Sheptytsky became metropolitan in 1900, the two churches' leaders regularly confronted each other over national issues. During censuses, the Latin Catholic hierarchs would urge all their flock to report Polish as their language of communication, even if it was in fact Ukrainian; they also founded Polish-language schools and new Roman Catholic churches to strengthen the Polish element in the population of largely Ukrainian-inhabited Eastern Galicia. The Ukrainian hierarchs, of course, repaid them in the same coin. The Polish hierarchs opposed and the Ukrainian hierarchs championed the reform of the suffrage in the Austrian crown land of Galicia and the establishment of a Ukrainian-language university in L'viv. After the collapse of the Habsburg monarchy and the reestablishment of a large Poland, the metropolitan was thrust into the role of representative and leader of the stateless Ukrainians. In sum, the correspondence between the two archbishops in 1943 took place in the difficult context of a long-standing, institutionalized conflict.

The correspondence began with Twardowski's letter of July 30, 1943. Twardowski informed Sheptytsky that some Ukrainians were openly calling for the destruction of the Polish population, that "bloody murders with a clear political character" were being committed, and that the "frightening incidents" that had been going on for some time in Volhynia might spread to Galicia. As we know, on August 15, 1943, Sheptytsky issued the pastoral letter calling upon the elders of the community to restrain the youth and to protect the endangered population. But three days later he answered Twardowski with a letter that presented a list of Ukrainian grievances against the Poles: the pacification of 1930, robberies of Ukrainian villages by Polish officers a few months before the outbreak of the war, the robbery and murder of Ukrainians by Polish troops after the outbreak of the war, the murder by the Polish underground of Ukrainian activists in the Podlachia and Chełm regions during the war, the anti-Ukrainian activities of Poles who registered as Volksdeutsche, and attacks on Ukrainians and even Ukrainian priests at the present moment. He also called upon the Latin-rite archbishop to write pastoral letters to restrain the faithful under *his* jurisdiction.[50] Sheptytsky sent a follow-up letter on September 13, 1943, in which he wrote that "in the Chełm region and Podlachia such political murders [of Ukrainians by Poles] now number over five hundred."[51] This information definitely came to him from Ukrainian political circles,[52] and he later used it to blame the Poles for starting the massacres.[53] In the first "concept" of his letter to Twardowski of November 15, 1943, but not in the actual letter, Sheptytsky wrote: "The Ukrainian parties of Bandera and Melnyk deny responsibility for the murders; they steadfastly maintain that they have forbidden their members to kill Poles."[54] From this statement we can conclude that Sheptytsky was in contact directly or indirectly with the leaders of the nationalist factions and discussing the murder of the Poles with them. Whether he believed them or not is uncertain, but he did omit their denial from the letter he actually sent to Twardowski.

Clearly, the metropolitan had difficulty in breaking solidarity with the Ukrainian national movement, even in such a virulent form. He had stood with the national movement before World War I, championing causes that struck him as matters of elementary justice, such as expanding the suffrage and the representation of Ukrainians in legislative bodies or founding a Ukrainian-language university. He hoped that in the struggle between Poles and Ukrainians after the collapse of the Habsburg empire that at least Western Ukraine would acquire statehood. He also hoped that the interwar Polish state would treat its large Ukrainian minority decently. But many policies of the Polish authorities deeply disappointed him—the radical reduction of Ukrainian-language education at all levels, the brutal pacification campaign of 1930, the destruction of Orthodox churches in the years preceding World War II, to name just the most important matters. All the chauvinistic policies of interwar Poland, and the much more tragic and horrific situation of Ukrainians under Soviet rule, wounded him deeply. The same historical situation that produced the white-hot anger of the nationalists produced the profound pain of the metropolitan. This was the context that made him reluctant to give Bishop Twardowski much satisfaction, while at the same time doing everything he could think of to correct his own stiff-necked faithful.

In Sheptytsky's texts directed outward, he made a point of dissociating the Ukrainian movement from the murders. In two letters to the Vatican about the Holocaust, he emphasized that the Germans were the ones behind the murders, even though they had initially tried to blame Ukrainian militias and the Ukrainian population.[55] In his letters to Archbishop Twardowski, he went further: not only did he deny the responsibility of Ukrainian political organizations for the slaughter of Poles, but he even cast doubt on the extent to which Ukrainians were involved at all. Moreover, he took the opportunity of the correspondence to raise Ukrainian grievances against the Poles and to demand that the Polish bishop restrain *his* people. These texts are in sharp contrast to the inward-directed texts, particularly the pastoral letters, which paint a picture of a large number of Ukrainians who have committed robberies and murders that were at least in part motivated by politics and national hatred.

This contrast indicates a certain loyalty to the national movement and to the national group vis-à-vis those outside the group. I cannot exclude the possibility that it may also be indicative of some wishful thinking on Sheptytsky's part or of his giving the national movement the benefit of any doubt. Moreover, were Sheptytsky to have conceded much to Archbishop Twardowski, he would have been perceived as an outright traitor by the people entrusted to his spiritual care. Referring to a different, but related context, Shimon Redlich clearly identified Sheptytsky's problem:

> Sheptyts'kyi, as a leader of the Uniate Church and as a symbolic focus of Ukrainian national aspirations was forced into an impossible situation. He tried to preach Christian morality while not dissociating himself from the nationalistic elements. He was torn between his moral and humanist values and his compassion for frustrated Ukrainian nationalism. . . . The Church leaders were striving to preserve their influence in circumstances of rapid erosion. Sheptyts'kyi should be viewed in precisely this context. His situation was even more difficult than that of his ecclesiastic contemporaries.[56]

If he hoped to retain any authority among his flock, Sheptytsky could not risk being considered a traitor.

In the inward-directed texts, there can be little doubt that Sheptytsky was signaling that he was talking about, and sometimes to, the adherents of OUN Bandera. Not only do the references to political and national motivations hint in this direction, but a much clearer indication is Sheptytsky's repeated formulation of the perpetration of murder in generational terms. Contemporaries could not misunderstand this reference. Certainly the Polish underground understood that there was a struggle between Sheptytsky and the Banderites for moral authority in Ukrainian society. They identified the "youth" of Sheptytsky's letters with OUN and saw Sheptytsky and OUN at odds over the issue of murder.[57]

One more document from this set of problems remains to be mentioned, an undated pastoral letter titled "Peace in the Lord! (On the Murder of Priests)."[58] This document was written after the middle of October 1943 and perhaps as late as the spring of 1944, probably in response to Archbishop Twardowski's complaints about the murder of Latin-rite priests.[59] It condemns religious hatred, "the pagan principle of vengeance," and the extension of hatred also to the kin of the perceived offender. It makes the point that even the pagans did not kill the defenseless, as was the case at the time Sheptytsky was writing. It is interesting that this text not only condemns the murder of Latin-rite priests, but also the murder of Orthodox priests. There is no overt identification of who the metropolitan believed the murderers to be, but we know that the UPA at that time killed both Latin-rite priests[60] and Orthodox clergymen.[61]

After the Soviets reconquered Galicia, Sheptytsky once again condemned the activities of the UPA, this time by name at a clergy synod held on September 7, 1944, less than two months before his death:

> The situation of the peasants has today become unbearable because of the UPA and various partisan units. All these organizations also accept people who are fleeing from any kind of warfare and would not want to serve in any army. But among them are also people who do not listen to God's law, nor to the voice of the Church, and consider themselves called to punish people with death for alleged crimes that perhaps were not even committed.
>
> For three years I have not stopped reminding [everyone] that a man is not allowed to deal death to another. . . .
>
> And meanwhile there are young men . . . who carry on the function of executioners in convictions in which they have been the prosecutors, judges, and defense attorneys. And there are so many of them that we have to speak of an entire army.[62]

A nationalist historian has interpreted these statements as part of Sheptytsky's tactics to save the Church under renewed Bolshevik rule—that is, condemnation of the UPA was directed at Soviet informers at the synod.[63] However, it is consistent with all that we know of Sheptytsky's attitude to the Bandera movement in previous years. Although Sheptytsky remained opposed to the nationalists, many of his clergy had moved even closer to the nationalist underground as the Bolsheviks approached Galicia.[64] Andrei Sheptytsky passed away on November 1, 1944.

The Bandera movement was not preoccupied with the truth. It countered the metropolitan's many condemnations of its activities by distributing leaflets that said that Sheptytsky had given his special blessing to OUN.[65] Nationalists after the war, and to the present, continued to intimate that Sheptytsky and OUN were thinking and acting in tandem. They made a hero of Sheptytsky, using his prestige to add luster to their own reputation. Of great importance to them was that Sheptytsky had been an active rescuer of Jews. They used Sheptytsky to deflect charges that Ukrainian nationalists participated in the Holocaust. In the postwar era, the Soviets were also interested in portraying Sheptytsky as having been in league with the Banderites. This made it easier to justify their destruction of the Greek Catholic Church in 1946, as it was presumably linked with fascist atrocities and treason. But as we have seen, these mythologized versions of the Sheptytsky–Bandera movement relationship bear no resemblance to the truth.

If Metropolitan Sheptytsky had not expressed adamant opposition, it is likely that OUN, and the Bandera faction in particular, would have developed a much cozier relationship with the Church, as did equivalent movements in Eastern Europe (the Ustasha in Croatia, the Legion of the Archangel in Romania, and the Hlinka Guard in Slovakia). Much of the Banderite leadership came from clerical families, including both Bandera and Stetsko. There were certainly many in the clergy who sympathized with them. The Banderites made some use of religious forms. Stepan Lenkavsky, a Banderite ideologue, had earlier, in 1929, written "The Ten Commandments of a Ukrainian Nationalist"; there was no mention here of God, and the morality invoked was violent and nation-centered rather than Christian.[66] During the war, the Banderites produced "A Prayer to Ukraine," which had no reference to God or the Mother of God. Its opening invocation was: "O Ukraine, Holy Mother of Heroes, come down into my heart." The prayer was for the faith, will, courage, and strength to die for and dissolve into a strong and united Ukraine.[67] To distinguish itself from the Melnyk faction of OUN, the Bandera faction began to use its own emblem in July 1941 that bore a cross made out of a sword (*khrestomech*).[68] At the various meetings called to celebrate Stetsko's proclamation of a Ukrainian state in summer 1941, Greek Catholic clergymen held prayer services as well as memorial services for "Ukrainian heroes killed by the Bolsheviks."[69] During the war, the Banderites certainly had a religious policy. In addition to their often deadly hostility to the Autonomous Orthodox and Roman Catholic clergy, already mentioned, they took a decidedly negative view of Baptists.[70] They also killed Jews, although religious motives were less important than national ones. The Banderites used religion as an instrument, but they were not at all guided by it. Characteristically, they did not bother to institute a regular chaplaincy in the UPA, a fact that Sheptytsky noted with bitterness in his speech of September 7, 1944:

> And if somehow units of some kind of army were formed, then it was the obligation of priests to serve the nation as chaplains; and these chaplains are not by any law responsible for the actions of the army in which they serve. And the Ukrainian Insurgent Army forced our boys to enter its ranks, and this could be a justification for the youth that in the UPA there also served priests who were their chaplains. But of such I know nothing; rather, I know that there were no [chaplains].[71]

This chapter has focused on how one man oriented himself in a difficult conflict of principles at a grave time in European history. On the one hand, he was a Christian bishop. On the other hand, he was a champion of Ukrainian national aspirations, yet he found it necessary to condemn the activities of those who came to embody those aspirations. It was a choice between Christian universalism and nationalism, between "thou shalt not kill" and "the nation above all." Perhaps put so starkly it seems that the correct choice was clear, but Sheptytsky was working in an atmosphere in which murder had become a commonplace—committed by Soviets, Nazis, and nationalists. The forces of peace and mercy were barely visible. The effectiveness of his actions and protests was weak, although perhaps further research in chancery records and the proceedings of disciplinary courts may reveal more effective intervention in concrete instances. From the published record it seems that Metropolitan Sheptytsky's voice was audible, but his people had hardened their hearts and stopped their ears. He wanted to condemn the crimes committed by the people with whom he identified, but he did not want to condemn the people as a whole nor even the cause in the name of which the nationalists committed their violent acts. He tried to retain solidarity with the Ukrainian cause, particularly when responding to the Latin-rite archbishop. He kept communications open with Ukrainian politicians of the nationalist camp. Sometimes it seems that he might have believed them too readily. To influence their murderous politics, he had to retain a certain degree of credibility among Ukrainian leaders. One has the feeling that he went as far as he could in opposing the Bandera movement without alienating the Banderites to the extent that they would have condemned him and his church root and branch. Analysis of his responses shows that he was clearheaded about the need to condemn ethnic cleansing and political murder as it was happening. But it was not easy for him to grasp all the complexities of the situation, and it proved impossible for him to offer effective resistance.

## Notes

1. This chapter is based on research supported by the Social Sciences and Humanity Research Council of Canada as well as the Pinchas and Mark Wisen Fellowship at the Center for Advanced Holocaust Studies at the U.S. Holocaust Memorial Museum. I benefited tremendously from the comments of many readers of my earlier drafts.

2. See John-Paul Himka, *Religion and Nationality in Western Ukraine: The Greek Catholic Church and the Ruthenian National Movement in Galicia, 1867–1900* (Montreal: McGill–Queen's University Press, 1999).

3. John-Paul Himka, "Sheptyts'kyi and the Ukrainian National Movement before 1914," in *Morality and Reality: The Life and Times of Andrei Sheptyts'kyi*, edited by Paul Robert Magocsi (Edmonton: Canadian Institute of Ukrainian Studies, 1989), 29–46.

4. I. Poizdnyk, "Ounivs'ki ianychary' chy 'kandydaty na prestolu," in *Storinky voiennoi istorii*, no. 11 (Kyiv: Instytut istorii NAN Ukrainy, 2007), 295.

5. The classic, but not unproblematic, study of OUN and its armed forces is John A. Armstrong, *Ukrainian Nationalism*, 2nd ed. (Littleton, Colo.: Ukrainian Academic Press, 1980).

6. On the murder of the Poles, see Timothy Snyder, "To Resolve the Ukrainian Question Once and for All: The Ethnic Cleansing of Ukrainians in Poland, 1943–1947," *Journal of Cold War Studies* 1, no. 2 (Spring 1999), 86–120; and Timothy Snyder, *The Reconstruction of Nations: Poland, Ukraine, Lithuania, Belarus, 1569–1999* (New Haven, Conn.: Yale University Press, 2003), 166–201. Snyder summarized the results of his research in *Bloodlands* (New York: Basic Books, 2010), 326–27.

7. Anton Shekhovtsov, "By Cross and Sword: 'Clerical Fascism' in Interwar Western Ukraine," *Totalitarian Movements and Political Religions* 8, no. 2 (2007): 275–76. This article mistakenly identifies Sheptytsky as himself a nationalist by sympathy, a view that may derive from precedents in Soviet historiography. Sheptytsky's political allegiance, however, was to the moderate Ukrainian National Democratic Union (known by the Ukrainian acronym UNDO) and not to OUN. See O. Ie. Lysenko, "Relihiine pytannia u teorii ta praktytsi ukrains'koho natsionalizmu v pershii polovyni XX st.," *Ukrains'kyi istorychnyi zhurnal*, no. 6 (2000): 38; and Bohdan Budurowycz,

"Sheptyts'kyi and the Ukrainian National Movement after 1914," in *Morality and Reality*, ed. Magocsi, 54–57.

8. Anatol' Mariia Bazylevych, "Vvedennia u tvory mytropyta Andreia Sheptyts'koho," in *Tvory Sluhy Bozhoho mytropolyta Andreia Sheptyts'koho: Pastyrs'ki lysty, Andrei Sheptyts'kyi* (Toronto, 1965), vol. 1, B213–15.

9. Ibid., B214. This excerpt from the text is also found in Kost' Pan'kivs'kyi, *Roky nimets'koi okupatsii* (New York and Toronto: Zhyttia i mysli, 1965), 143.

10. Cited by Lysenko, "Relihiine pytannia," 38–39.

11. Pan'kivs'kyi, *Roky nimets'koi okupatsii*, 140.

12. Liliana Hentosh, the author of a number of important works on Sheptytsky, in a discussion with the author, June 2010. Hentosh saw documents to this effect in the Vatican archives.

13. K. E. Dmitruk, *S krestom i trezubtsem* (Moscow: Izdatel'stvo politicheskoi literatury, 1979), 20; Ihor Zahrebel'nyi, "Vladyka Andrei—Kniaz' tserkvy i narodu," *Banderivets'* (February 2010): 14, http://www.banderivets.org.ua/?page=pages/zmistd0/201002/article12.

14. Orest Dziuban, ed., *Ukrains'ke derzhavotvorennia: Akt 30 chervnia 1941: Zbirnyk dokumentiv i materialiv* (L'viv: Piramida, 2001), 126.

15. "The anarchistic eruptions of hate and revenge that occurred in L'viv before and during the German entry dampened the Metropolitan's sympathy for OUN." Hansjakob Stehle, "Sheptyts'kyi and the German Regime," in *Morality and Reality*, ed. Magocsi, 127. On the pogrom, see John-Paul Himka, "The L'viv Pogrom of 1941: The Germans, Ukrainian Nationalists, and the Carnival Crowd," *Canadian Slavonic Papers* 53, nos. 2–4 (June–December 2011): 209–43.

16. V. Iu. Malanchuk et al., eds., *Pravda pro Uniiu: Dokumenty i materialy* (L'viv: Kameniar, 1968), 301.

17. Oksana Surmach, *Dni kryvavykh svastyk: Hreko-katolyts'ka tserkva v period nimets'koho okupatsiinoho rezhymu v Ukraini (1941–1944 rr.)* (L'viv: Spolom, 2005), 114–15; Kost' Pan'kivs'kyi, *Vid derzhavy do komitetu* (New York and Toronto: Zhyttia i mysli, 1957), 89–90.

18. Zhanna Kovba, ed., *Mytropolyt Andrei Sheptyts'kyi: Dokumenty i materialy 1941–1944* (Kyiv: Dukh i Litera, 2003), 45–47.

19. Pan'kivs'kyi, *Roky nimets'koi okupatsii*, 33.

20. *Diiannia i postanovy l'vivs'kykh arkhyieparkhiial'nykh soboriv 1940–41–42–43 pid provodom Sluhy Bozhoho Mytropolyta Andreia Sheptyts'koho* (Winnipeg: Archieparchial Jubilee Committee, 1984), 211.

21. Zahrebel'nyi, "Vladyka Andrei," 15.

22. Cited in Lysenko, "Relihiine pytannia," 40.

23. Father Kovch soon distinguished himself in assisting the Jews and was arrested by the Gestapo for these activities in 1942. He perished in a gas chamber at Majdanek in 1944. In 2001, Pope John Paul II beatified him.

24. Anna Maria Kowcz-Baran, *For God's Truth and Human Rights* (Ottawa: Emil & Olena Baran, 2006), 55.

25. Lysenko, "Relihiine pytannia," 38; Shekhovtsov, "By Cross and Sword," 280–81; John-Paul Himka, "The Place of Religion in the Ukrainian National Revival," in *Nationalisierung der Religion und Sakralisierung der Nation im östlichen Europa*, edited by Martin Schulze Wessel (Stuttgart: Franz Steiner, 2006), 97.

26. Dziuban, *Ukrains'ke derzhavotvorennia*, 77–78, 93.

27. Lysenko, "Relihiine pytannia," 42–43.

28. Kovba, *Mytropolyt Andrei Sheptyts'kyi*, 12–13. Andrii Krawchuk, *Christian Social Ethics in Ukraine: The Legacy of Andrei Sheptytsky* (Edmonton, Ottawa, and Toronto: Canadian Institute of Ukrainian Studies Press, Metropolitan Andrey Sheptytsky Institute of Eastern Christian Studies, and Basilian Press, 1997), 240, links this text with Rabbi Lewin's request to Sheptytsky for intervention in the L'viv pogrom, but the timing—more than a week after the L'viv pogrom took place—makes this seem unlikely as does the content of the letter, which warns against internal discord. Mykhailo Khomiak, who was a well-informed contemporary, wrote that the text was a warning against fratricidal war. M. Khom'iak, "Diial'nist' Mytropolyta Kyr Andreia pid nimets'koiu okupatsiieiu," *Lohos* 6, no. 3 (July–September 1955): 214–23, and no. 4 (October–December 1955): 294.

29. Volodymyr Serhiichuk, *OUN-UPA v roky viiny: Novi dokumenty i materialy* (Kyiv: Dnipro, 1996), 261.

30. Kovba, *Mytropolyt Andrei Sheptyts'kyi*, 38.

31. Mieczysław Adamczyk, Janusz Gmitruk, and Adam Koseski, eds., *Ziemie Wschodnie: Raporty Biura Wschodniego Delegatury Rządu na Kraj 1943–1944* (Warsaw and Pułtusk: Muzeum Historii Polskiego Ruchu Ludowego and Wyższa Szkoła Humanistyczna im. Aleksandra Gieysztora, 2005), 45.

32. Krawchuk, *Christian Social Ethics*, 236. I am not certain that these are Sheptytsky's words or the words of the source Krawchuk cites, which was not available to me.

33. On OUN members in the Ukrainian Auxiliary Police and the involvement of this police force in the Holocaust, see Gabriel N. Finder and Alexander V. Prusin, "Collaboration in Eastern Galicia: The Ukrainian Police and the Holocaust," *East European Jewish Affairs* 34, no. 2 (Winter 2004): 95–118.

34. Andrei Sheptyts'kyi, *Pys'ma-poslannia Mytropolyta Andreia Sheptyts'koho ChSVV. z chasiv nimets'koi okupatsii* (Yorkton, Sask.: Biblioteka Lohosu, 1969), 92–93.

35. Ibid., 167.

36. John-Paul Himka, "Metropolitan Andrei Sheptytsky and the Holocaust," forthcoming, *Polin* 26 (2013).

37. Serhii Bohunov et al., eds., *Mytropolyt Andrei Sheptyts'kyi u dokumentakh radians'kykh orhaniv derzhavnoi bezpeky (1939–1944 rr.)* (Kyiv: Kyivs'kyi natsional'nyi universytet imeni Tarasa Shevchenka, Tsentr ukrainoznavstva; Derzhavnyi arkhiv Sluzhby bezpeky Ukrainy, 2005), 264.

38. Dr. Frédéric, "Abschrift, Übersetzung," September 19, 1943, report, Mémorial de la Shoah, Musée, Centre de documentation de documentation, juive contemporaine, CXLVa-60, 1.

39. Adamczyk, *Ziemie Wschodnie*, 93 (dating), 95–98 (discussion by the Polish underground's Eastern Bureau), and 101–5 (text of the letter).

40. Ibid., 104.

41. Poizdnyk, "Ounivs'ki ianychary'," 292–301, esp. 296. Earlier, in September 1939, OUN, which was not yet divided into two factions, took advantage of the Soviet invasion and the communists' encouragement of class warfare to kill Poles in Galicia. Father Kovch at that time assisted and protected Poles and preached against the murder of civilians, including women and children. Kowcz-Baran, *God's Truth*, 95–96.

42. Sheptyts'kyi, *Pys'ma-poslannia*, 419–20, 422–23.

43. The details are given by Himka, "Metropolitan Andrei Sheptytsky."

44. Józef Wołczański, "Korespondencja arcybiskupa Bolesława Twardowskiego z arcybiskupem Andrzejem Szeptyckim w latach 1943–1944," *Przegląd Wschodni* 2, no. 2 (6) (1992–93): 482.

45. For the view that this was unintentional, see Armstrong, *Ukrainian Nationalism*, 206. For the view that this was intentional, see Friedrich Heyer, *Kirchengeschichte der Ukraine im 20: Jahrhundert—Von der Epochenwende des ersten Weltkrieges bis zu den Anfängen in einem unabhängigen ukrainishcen Staat* (Göttingen: Vandenhoeck & Ruprecht, 2003), 303–5.

46. Pierre Blet et al., eds., *Actes et documents du Saint Siège relatifs à la seconde guerre mondiale, Vol. 3: Le Saint Siège et la situation religieuse en Pologne at dans les Pays Baltes 1939–1945*, 2 parts (Vatican City: Libreria Editrice Vaticana, 1967), part 2, 790.

47. Dr. Frédéric, "Abschrift, Übersetzung," 1.

48. In the original "concept" of the letter to Twardowski of August 18, 1943, Sheptytsky had written that "various bands roam everywhere, among whom, I'm sure, there are communists and Poles and Ukrainians and Jews and German deserters." Wołczański, "Korespondencja," 479.

49. Athanasius McVay, "A Lack of Tact and of Delicacy: The Difficult Relations between Archbishops Sheptytsky and Twardowski of L'viv," *Annales Ecclesiae Ruthenae*, May 1, 2010, http://annalesecclesiaeucrainae.blogspot.com/2010/04/lack-of-tact-and-of-delicacy.html.

50. Wołczański, "Korespondencja," 471–72.

51. Ibid., 474. The same was reported by Dr. Frédéric, "Abschrift, Übersetzung," 2.

52. For background on the figure of five hundred Ukrainian activists murdered by Poles in the Chełm region and Podlachia, see Czesław Partacz and Krzysztof Łada, "Kto zaczął? Polacy i Ukraińcy na Lubelszczyźnie w latach 1941–1943," in *Antypolska akcja OUN-UPA 1943–1944: Fakty i interpretacje*, edited by Grzegorz Motyka and Dariusz Libionka (Warsaw: Instytut Pamięci Narodowej, 2002), 33–40.

53. Letter to Archbishop Twardowski of November 15, 1943, quoted by Wołczański, "Korespondencja," 481.

54. Ibid., 479.

55. Himka, "Metropolitan Andrei Sheptytsky."

56. Shimon Redlich, "Metropolitan Andrei Sheptyts'kyi, Ukrainians and Jews during and after the Holocaust," *Holocaust and Genocide Studies* 5, no. 1 (1990): 48.

57. Adamczyk, *Ziemie Wschodnie*, 45, 68, 93, 95–98.

58. Sheptyts'kyi, *Pys'ma-poslannia*, 431–32.

59. Wołczański, "Korespondencja," 477, 483.

60. From the memoirs of a Holocaust survivor in Volhynia: "The retreat of the Germans had left a clear field for the Banderas. They went about their business of massacring Poles. . . . They threw priests and other men into wells." Jacob Biber, *Survivors: A Personal Story of the Holocaust*, Studies in Judaica and the Holocaust, no. 2 (San Bernardino, Calif.: Borgo Press, 1989), 36. In the L'viv Archdiocese alone, the UPA killed forty-eight Roman Catholic priests. Alexander Statiev, *The Soviet Counterinsurgency in the Western Borderlands* (Cambridge: Cambridge University Press, 2010), 86.

61. In addition to Metropolitan Aleksii (see the text above and n. 45 above), the UPA killed other Orthodox churchmen. Heyer, *Kirchengeschichte der Ukraine*, 303–5. According to Lysenko, in "Relihiine pytannie," 45, OUN killed thirty Orthodox churchmen in Volhynia by 1944. On September 11, 1943, a UPA security service revolutionary

tribunal hanged Manuil (Tarnavsky), the bishop of Kovel-Volodymyr in the Autonomous Orthodox Church. They accused him of collaborating with the NKVD and later with the Gestapo. Sluzhba Bezpeky UPA, "Za zradu—smert'!" *Do zbroi* (vydaie politychnyi viddil UPA), no. 5 (November 1943): 12. See copy in the U.S. Holocaust Memorial Museum Archives (hereafter USHMM), RG-31.017M, reel 1, Derzhavnyi Arkhiv Rivnens'koi Oblasti, f. 30, op. 1, od. zb. 16, f. 65v.

62. Bohunov, *Mytropolyt Andrei Sheptyts'kyi*, 274.
63. Zahrebel'nyi, "Vladyka Andrei," 16.
64. Poizdnyk, "Ounivs'ki ianychary'," 298.
65. Ibid., 297.
66. Stepan Lenkavs'kyi, *Ukrains'kyi natsionalizm: Tvory*, edited by Oleksandr Sych, 2 vols. (Ivano-Frankivsk: Lileia-NV, 2002-03), 1:454–59; Alexander J. Motyl, *The Turn to the Right: The Ideological Origins and Development of Ukrainian Nationalism, 1919–1929* (Boulder, Colo.: East European Monographs, 1980), 142.
67. USHMM, RG-31.026, reel 14, Tsentral'nyi derzhavnyi arkhiv hromads'kykh ob"iednan' Ukrainy, f. 57, op. 4, od. zb. 342, f. 85.
68. "Symvolika Ukrains'kykh Natsionalistiv," *Virtual'nyi muzei ukrains'koi falerystyky*, http://ua-orden.org/simvolika-ukra%D1%97nskix-nacionalistiv.html; Orest Dziuban, "L'vivs'ki pechatky 1941 roku iak pam"iatky ukrains'koho derzhavotvorennia," *Ukrains'ka spadshchyna*, http://donklass.com/arhiv/histdisk/heritage/heritage/istorija/doslidzhennja/DzyubLvivPech/DzyubLvivPech01.htm.
69. Lysenko, "Relihiine pytannia," 41. On the meetings themselves, see Grzegorz Rossoliński-Liebe, "The 'Ukrainian National Revolution' of 1941: Discourse and Practice of a Fascist Movement," *Kritika: Explorations in Russian and Eurasian History* 12, no. 1 (Winter 2011): 83–114.
70. See the memoirs of a Ukrainian Baptist from Volhynia: Mykhailo Podvorniak, *Viter z Volyni. Spohady* (Winnipeg: Tovarystvo "Volyn'," 1981), 137, 156–59, 181, 184, 187–88, 191, 206. Kost Pankivsky mentions an incident of a Banderite speaking against Baptists in a village, calling them "of the German faith." Pan'kivs'kyi, *Roky nimets'koi okupatsii*, 332. A Jewish survivor wrote in her testimony after the war that she had been protected by Baptists (Shtundists) until the UPA attacked the community. See Archiwum Żydowskiego Instytutu Historycznego, 301/1011. The testimony is in Yiddish. I read it in an English translation in a manuscript in preparation at Florida Atlantic University titled "First Reports: An Anthology of Early Holocaust Testimonies Taken from Record Group 301 of the Jewish Historical Institute of Poland," edited by Felix Tych et al.
71. Bohunov, *Mytropolyt Andrei Sheptyts'kyi*, 275.

## Chapter 4

## The Revival of Monastic Life in the Trinity-Sergius Lavra after World War II
*Scott Kenworthy*

For the cycle of Easter services in April 1946, clergy from the Russian Orthodox Church were able to celebrate in the great Dormition Cathedral of the Holy Trinity–Saint Sergius Lavra—Russia's central shrine—for the first time since the Bolsheviks had closed the monastery a quarter of a century earlier. For the feast of the Holy Trinity forty days later, Patriarch Aleksii I conducted the services, which signaled the official reopening of the monastery. This was a major event in the life of the Russian Orthodox Church, for it meant receiving back one of its most sacred sites; it also signaled that momentous changes had taken place in the Soviet Union itself. According to one of the first new monks, "the spiritual upsurge, connected with the opening of the Trinity-Sergius Lavra, was very great."[1] Trinity-Sergius was resuming its role as a vital spiritual center of Russia.

 The Trinity-Sergius Lavra was the most important monastery and spiritual center of Muscovy since the death of its founder, Saint Sergius of Radonezh, in the late fourteenth century. Moreover, the monastery enjoyed a revival, particularly as a center of pilgrimage, in the century leading up to the Revolution of 1917. Precisely because of the monastery's prominence and influence, it became one of the first targets of the Bolshevik antireligious campaign. The monastery was closed in 1919, and in 1920 its churches were permanently closed for services. Some of the former monks resettled in apartments in Sergiev Posad (renamed Sergiev in the 1920s and Zagorsk in the 1930s) or in the Lavra's hermitages in the same town, which transformed themselves into agricultural collectives in order to survive. These remaining communities were closed by 1929, and throughout the 1920s and 1930s former monks were subject to sporadic arrest and persecution. During the Terror of 1937–38, the NKVD systematically rounded up and executed all of the former Trinity monks who remained in the region. Thus, in the first decade after the Revolution, major monasteries were closed but smaller hermitages were able to continue, while monks were subjected to sporadic harassment or arrest. From 1928 onward, all monastic communities were eliminated and the persecution of monks grew more systematic until it reached its apex a decade later. In short, after 1928 the Stalinist state viewed monasticism as completely incompatible with Soviet ideology, and being a monk made an individual a priori anti-Soviet and an enemy of the people.[2]

Although the Soviet state nearly eradicated the Church during the Great Terror of 1937–38, World War II brought a dramatic reversal in church-state relations. This manifested itself in a greater tolerance showed toward the Church for the duration of Stalin's reign. One particularly important dimension of this change came with the reopening of the Trinity-Sergius Lavra in 1946, a move that was requested by the Church leadership that Stalin agreed to fulfill. This chapter examines the fate of Trinity-Sergius from its reopening in 1946 to Khrushchev's renewed antireligious campaigns of the late 1950s and early 1960s. It will pay particular attention to the efforts to reconstitute an authentic monastic brotherhood in the first phase of the monastery's renewed existence and analyze the degree to which it was able to do this with only limited interference of the state. Second, it places the revival of monastic life in the broader context of the postwar religious revival in the Soviet Union and in particular the role that Trinity-Sergius played in that revival, both as a manifestation and a facilitator of it. Finally, it will consider the impact of Khrushchev's antireligious campaign on the monastery and the ways in which the monastery resisted and negotiated with the Soviet state in order to continue to pursue its own goals.

## Background

The Soviet antireligious campaign culminated in the Terror, of which religious clergy and activist believers were a main target. Although the massive wave of arrests and executions died down by the middle of 1938, the closure of churches continued until the outbreak of war. At the same time, the pact the Soviets made with the Nazis in 1939 resulted in the acquisition of territories—including parts of Ukraine and Belorussia as well as Moldova—that included many Orthodox churches and monasteries, many of which the Soviets began to close before the war. With the war, however, the situation fundamentally altered. The head of the Church, Metropolitan Sergii (Stragorodskii), famously called Russian believers to stand by the motherland on June 22, 1941—even before Stalin made any announcement.[3] Religion became one of the elements in the ideological struggle between the Nazis and the Soviets, as Orthodox believers were initially allowed to open churches in Nazi-occupied territories, and some clergy made declarations of loyalty to the Nazis. There was also a religious revival on Soviet territory, and the Soviet authorities were willing to turn a blind eye to this revival for the sake of the war. Moreover, the Church made massive contributions by raising donations to support the war effort.[4]

The most dramatic change came when Stalin met with the Church's leaders at the Kremlin on September 4, 1943, the first such meeting between Soviet and Church leadership. During this meeting, the hierarchs presented a series of requests, including the release of certain clergy from the gulag, the ability to hold a council to elect a patriarch, the opening of educational institutions for training clergy, and the possibility of publishing church literature. Stalin made great promises, not all of which he kept—but many of which he did. It was a dramatic reversal of policy toward religion.

Although this reversal of state policy has often been interpreted as the state recognizing its need of the Church and believers to defeat the Nazis, recent research demonstrates that the situation was more complex—not the least of all that this meeting between Stalin and Church leaders came after the victory at Stalingrad, when the course of the war had already shifted. To be sure, this meeting in a sense was recognition of the Church's active patriotic service during the first years of the war, and made official changes in policy that had unofficially already taken place (such as allowing the Church to receive donations and distribute them or allowing the reopening of churches). There had also been a shift in Stalinist ideology to a focus on more traditional Russian nationalism, which could find room for the Orthodox Church, as well as a call for unity of all Soviet citizens against the common enemy. The Soviets had to neutralize Nazi propaganda that they were defenders of Christianity in Russia, which appeared to be born out by the reopening of churches in occupied territories. Equally important were international factors: Stalin sought positive relations with Britain and the United States, which were often critical of Soviet antireligious policy. Furthermore, Stalin was planning to extend Soviet influence in the postwar period, and envisioned the Orthodox Church playing an important role in this endeavor (particularly in Eastern Europe and the Balkans).[5] In other words, Stalin hoped the Russian Orthodox Church would play a leading role among the Orthodox Churches in Eastern Europe and this would serve as one more means for him to influence those societies.[6]

Stalin also created the Council for Russian Orthodox Church Affairs to serve as an agency to implement the new policy, and appointed Georgii Karpov as its head. Stalin instructed Karpov not to interfere in the internal life of the Church. The Council for Russian Orthodox Church Affairs was under the direction of the Soviet of Ministers, thus making it an organ of executive power, and it was initially intended to serve as a link between the government and the patriarch. The Council later became the instrument for implementing state policy toward the Church and therefore for controlling the Church. The Council appointed commissioners at the local level to carry out its work; Aleksei Trushin became the commissioner for the Moscow region and would serve as the immediate interface between the Soviet government and the Trinity-Sergius Lavra for the following four decades.[7]

Changes began immediately after the historic meeting between Stalin and the Church leaders: a council of bishops was held that elected Sergii as patriarch, the first since Tikhon's death in 1925; the council also made an appeal to the Christian world against fascism. The Church continued to collect donations for the war effort, such as supplying two tank divisions; in all it donated some 300 million rubles during the war. In turn, the government made concessions to the Church. The *Journal of the Moscow Patriarchate* began publication. The Church began to organize seminaries and theological academies, and by 1947 there were two academies and ten seminaries. The infrastructure of the Church also had to be reconstituted. On May 15, 1944, Patriarch Sergii died; the following year, the Church held a council, which included participants from other Orthodox patriarchates, and Metropolitan Aleksii (Simanskii) was elected the new patriarch. The Council ratified a new charter for the Church, which had been worked out with the Council for Orthodox Church Affairs. It had committees for education, publishing, finances, and foreign relations. Moreover, the possibility of a church council served to reconcile schisms that had arisen since the 1920s, and many from the Renovationists on the "left" to those on the "right" that had rejected Sergii's 1927 declaration returned to the patriarchal church. The Church was granted juridical personhood—denied since 1917—which enabled it to have bank accounts and possess property.[8]

## Monasticism during and after World War II

The centrality of monasticism for Russian Orthodoxy meant that its revival was an inseparable feature of the revival of the Church as a whole. Although all monasteries in the Soviet Union had been closed by 1930, by the end of the war there were about 100 monasteries, which included 40 that were reopened in the occupied territories and another 60 that were in the western regions not part of the Soviet Union before 1939 (especially Ukraine and Moldova, and the famous Pskov-Caves Monastery, located in Estonia between the wars) that had never been closed. Indeed, examination of the documents concerning monasteries from 1944 to 1947 reveals just how radically Stalinist policy had changed toward the Church. In 1944, Karpov received complaints against local Soviet organs of power that they were confiscating the lands and property of monasteries and expelling the monks. In response, the Council for Russian Orthodox Church Affairs conducted an investigation. This investigation revealed that the majority of monasteries were engaged in patriotic activities, including donations for the defense fund, operating military hospitals, and caring for the wounded. Therefore, as Karpov reported to Molotov (as first deputy premier of Stalin's cabinet) in October 1944, the Council considered the liquidation of monasteries inappropriate, and proposed that existing monasteries be allowed to use their land ("on the basis of labor collectives") and their buildings.[9] In February 1945, Karpov received instructions to work together with the patriarch and the newly constituted Holy Synod to come up with rules for monasteries. Moreover, the Council for Russian Orthodox Church Affairs was to collect information about all the existing monasteries and prepare a report about their legal and economic situation. In the meantime, monasteries were to be allowed to continue to use their land, livestock, and buildings.[10]

The report, prepared by I. V. Pokrovskii, legal consultant for the council, considered 75 monasteries, which included 32 convents (with 3,125 inhabitants) and 33 men's monasteries (with 855 inhabitants). Two-thirds of the inhabitants were over 60 years of age. Two of the monasteries were in the Russian Federation, 42 in Ukraine, 23 in Moldova, 3 in Belorussia, and 4 in the Baltic Republics. Forty-six monasteries (in Moldova, the Baltic republics, and Western Ukraine) had operated continually, while 29 had been closed in the 1920s and reopened during the German occupation. Naturally, those that never ceased functioning were better off. The report described the monasteries in Moldova as having well-organized field crops and gardens, vineyards and wine making, beekeeping, shepherding, and milling operations; Pokrovskii also noted that conditions were better before 1940 (i.e., before Moldova was taken over by the Soviet Union), and had since worsened. Moreover, many of the monasteries enjoyed great authority among believers and were visited by a great number of worshippers. For example, some 12,000 to 15,000 people visited the Pochaev Lavra per day on great religious holidays, many coming from great distances and various parts of the Soviet Union. Moreover, most pilgrims were young, and they often stayed for several days.[11] Pokrovskii concluded: "The investigation has not established the presence of harmful influence of the monasteries on the surrounding population, [or] disloyal attitude toward the Soviet regime." The majority of local authorities positively characterized the monasteries in their regions, such as one official who described a local convent as the "best economy in the district, living by its own personal labor and rendering necessary assistance to the district," so that he considered the preservation of the monastery "necessary."[12]

Pokrovskii's report noted a few problems, such as the lack of a written rule (a founding document that governs the life of the community) for many of the monasteries. He also reported instances of conflict between the monastic brotherhoods that were reopened in German-occupied territories and the institutions that had been located on the monastery grounds for the previous decade. Nevertheless, the report's conclusions and recommendations were mostly favorable to the monasteries. On the negative side, he stated that monasteries should not be permitted to operate schools (as some were evidently doing). At the same time, he recommended that those with developed agriculture should be preserved, and any lands that had been confiscated should be returned. The central authorities should instruct respective republic or regional governments to allow monasteries with insufficient land to be apportioned more from locally available lands (so long as the monasteries work the land by their own labor). Finally, the authorities should satisfy the requests of monasteries to remove those institutions that occupied monastery grounds after their closure as interfering with monastery activities.[13]

The contrast between the policies—and even the very language—of the Stalinist state in the mid-1940s and those of the late 1920s and the 1930s is radical. Antireligious propaganda disappeared between 1941 and 1947.[14] Between 1928 and the war, simply being a monk or nun de facto meant that one was anti-Soviet. During the Terror (less than a decade earlier), having maintained one's association with members of a former monastic brotherhood was equivalent of forming a "secret," "illegal" monastery that in itself was a counterrevolutionary activity and punishable by death. The very fact that monastics had influence on believers and commanded their respect was in itself bad and constituted an alternative ideology that Soviet power could not tolerate.[15] In 1945, despite the acknowledgement that monasteries enjoyed "great authority" among the believers and attracted large numbers of pilgrims—the majority of whom were young, always a sensitive point for Soviet propaganda—Pokrovskii's investigation concluded that the monasteries were neither disloyal nor a harmful influence. Equally striking, monasteries were praised for their well-ordered economies, the existence of which was regarded as "necessary" by many local officials. The central authorities intervened on behalf of monasteries to ensure that they remained in full control of their land and property, and be given back land and property that had been expropriated—even to the detriment of other Soviet institutions.

In secret correspondence to Karpov in November 1946, the Soviet of Ministers stated that they heard of instances in which local organs of power had violated Soviet laws on the Church by extorting money from clergy, interfering with services (sometimes in rude and offensive ways), and disrupting the internal life of the Church—thus "forgetting that the Church in our country is a private organization"; Karpov was to take measures to ensure that such violations did not happen.[16] The very admission that there were "private organizations" (*chastnaia organizatsiia*) in the Soviet Union, and that they were to be protected by law—in secret correspondence, no less, not propaganda meant for public consumption—signaled a fundamental change in perception. In short, the contrast between the 1930s and the 1940s was not simply a change in tactics, but reflected a revolutionary shift in attitudes. To be sure, Stalin did not have a "conversion" (as is sometimes popularly believed in Russia today) and did not become sympathetic to the Church, and his intentions were clearly to use the Church for his own purposes. Nevertheless, the Church's authority was no longer a threat that had to be eliminated at all costs; rather, the Church's aura was to be co-opted to serve the legitimacy of the Stalinist state.

## The Reopening of Trinity-Sergius

Of all the institutions restored to the Church in the 1940s, certainly the most symbolically important was the Trinity-Sergius Lavra. Though the one hundred or so other monasteries had either never been closed, or were reopened by local clergy and believers under German occupation, only Trinity-Sergius was opened by order of the Soviet authorities and located in the heart of Russia. The reopening of the Lavra was a sign of the changed attitudes of the Stalinist state. Decisions to allow the monastery to reopen and to authorize the return of buildings were made at the highest level. Just as Lenin had personally edited and signed the decree that turned the Lavra into a museum in 1920, so Stalin personally directed that Trinity-Sergius be given back to the Church.[17] And not just the monastery was given back—so were the relics of Saint Sergius of Radonezh, which had been so contested in the years after the Revolution.[18] Relics continued to be important for Russian popular belief in the prerevolutionary period and became one of the early targets of Bolshevik antireligious campaigns. The Bolsheviks believed that if they could prove relics to be frauds, people would lose their faith and abandon the Church, but the campaign largely backfired.[19] Indeed, the return of these relics was exceptional, for very few relics were returned to the Church by the Soviet authorities.[20] World War II witnessed a profound religious revival in the Russian Orthodox Church in general, which found expression in the mass reopening of churches and a great outpouring of faith in those churches and in pilgrimages to monasteries and sacred sites. The renewed life at Trinity-Sergius gave expression to this revival both in its monastic life, as new recruits began to join, and as a center of pilgrimage for tens of thousands of worshippers. Moreover, the reopening of the monastery and the return of the relics of Saint Sergius gave further impetus to the religious revival after the war, especially in central Russia, which had not experienced as much freedom during the war. Certainly believers regarded the restitution of Trinity-Sergius and the return of Saint Sergius's relics as a victory for Orthodoxy over atheism.

The decision to return the Lavra to the Church was made in 1945, and the transfer to the Church's control began in the spring of 1946.[21] Patriarch Aleksii had a personal connection with the Lavra, where he had been ordained before the Revolution, and made its reopening one of his first tasks as patriarch.[22] On August 15, 1945, Aleksii wrote a bold letter to the Council for Russian Orthodox Church Affairs arguing for the reopening of Trinity-Sergius. He asserted that the reopening of the Lavra was central to the strengthening of the Orthodox Church because church life in Russia had, for so long, been intimately connected with it: "The Lavra was the spiritual center of the Russian Orthodox Church to which believers were drawn from all ends of Russia."[23] The Lavra held such a special position both because of the veneration for Saint Sergius and his relics, and also because of the role that the Lavra played at key moments in Russian history (e.g., Saint Sergius's blessing of Dmitrii Donskoi before the battle against the Tatars, withstanding a siege during the Time of Troubles), which gave the monastery not only a spiritual, but also a patriotic significance. The monastery was not only of central importance to Russian believers but was well known to foreigners, a great number of whom expressed the desire to visit it.

However, the patriarch continued, the monastery was in great disrepair and filled with a motley array of inhabitants, thus spoiling the impression of visitors to the architectural monument. Aleksii therefore requested that the Lavra be returned to the Church and that the inhabitants be removed, with the exception of the museum and its workers, with whom the Church could work to restore the monastery. Aleksii further requested that the buildings of the former Theological Academy be returned to the Church so that the academy could be reopened there; he also expressed the "daring thought" that the Council ask the central government to permit the return of the relics of Saint Sergius:

> If the Government found it possible to satisfy my request and the lamps before the reliquary of Saint Sergius could be lit, this one circumstance could witness before the whole world that is interested in the church life of our [Soviet] Union about the condition of the Orthodox Church in it. On the other hand, all believers would value this act as the clearest expression of the relationship that the Soviet government has to the Church.[24]

Clearly, Patriarch Aleksii was presenting arguments designed to appeal to the Soviet government: that the Lavra was not only centrally important to the Russian Orthodox Church for spiritual reasons, but also for patriotic ones; it was valued, moreover, not only by Russian believers but by foreigners as well, and returning the monastery to the Church would permit the restoration of its buildings for foreign visits. Finally, he boldly asserted that the Soviet government must demonstrate to the world and to Russian believers that it did support (or at least tolerate) the Russian Orthodox Church to which the return of the Lavra and the relics of Saint Sergius would be a testimony. On August 21, Georgii Karpov sent a report to the Soviet of People's Commissars with the patriarch's request, and Molotov reported back to Karpov that there were "no objections."[25]

On April 11, 1946, Patriarch Aleksii heard news from the Council for Russian Orthodox Church Affairs that the Dormition Cathedral was being transferred to the Patriarchate.[26] The first service was held in the Dormition Cathedral (Uspenskii Sobor) on Holy Friday in 1946. On Saturday evening, the reliquary with the relics of Saint Sergius was transferred to the Dormition Cathedral (the Trinity Cathedral still belonged to the museum); although the police had locked the gates after the pilgrims had left, people discovered what was taking place and found a way back in. People gathered to witness the revival of the Lavra, and the enormous cathedral and the square in front were full of worshippers for the Paschal vigil. It was the first Easter service celebrated at Trinity-Sergius in over a quarter century, and those present felt the momentous nature of the occasion.[27] At the end of April, Patriarch Aleksii wrote to Karpov to communicate his own gratitude and that of many others for Karpov's direct role in taking their request to the government, for the reopening of the Lavra has "aroused an entire wave of joyful feelings among believers." Aleksii was particularly grateful to Karpov for taking his request for the return of both the Lavra and the relics of Saint Sergius directly to Stalin, and mentioned the numerous times when Karpov intervened to hasten the process of their transfer to the Church: "Your name will always be connected with the great and joyful fact of the renewal of life in the Lavra." Aleksii also sent a letter of gratitude to Stalin through Karpov.[28]

The patriarch came and celebrated the liturgy for the feast of the Holy Trinity, and that day in 1946 was considered the official reopening of the Trinity-Sergius Lavra. The new monastery faced enormous challenges. To begin with, the monastery grounds were not only occupied by a museum and other institutions, but a great number of people were living on the grounds as well. As a result, the monks themselves had to settle initially in private apartments in the city. Buildings were returned to the monastery only gradually, and they had to build up the community essentially from nothing.[29] They also faced hostility by museum workers and local authorities. Nevertheless, the Church at this point seemed to have the support of Karpov (and therefore the Council of Russian Orthodox Church Affairs) and even the highest levels of government. In July 1946, Patriarch Aleksii I wrote a personal and confidential letter to Karpov in which he complained about hindrances from the museum and requested that even more buildings, including the chapel over the well (which would later be the center of controversy) and the Refectory Church of Saint Sergius, be turned over to the Church. He asserted that satisfaction of these requests would "confirm more eloquently than any words the fact—unquestionable for us, but disputed by our ill-wishers—of the favorable relationship of our government to the religious questions of Russian believers, and even more broadly—the fact of freedom of the Orthodox Church in our [Soviet] Union."[30] The patriarch used such language because the government itself had expressed its intentions in this way. Even though such expressions were likely not sincere, the fact that they were made meant that the patriarch could appeal to them to try to get what the Church wanted. And it worked: in this case, as in many others (at least until the death of Stalin), the Soviet of Ministers granted the patriarch's request.[31]

## Reestablishing the Brotherhood

In the initial period after its reopening, the leadership of Trinity-Sergius ensured the restoration of authentic monastic life with surprising autonomy from outside interference. The greatest challenge came, first of all, with establishing a monastic brotherhood after monasticism had been virtually eliminated and few experienced monks remained. Patriarch Aleksii chose Archimandrite Gurii (Viacheslav Egorov, 1891–1965), whom he knew in the early 1920s at the Aleksander-Nevskii Lavra in Petrograd, to take the lead in renewing monastic life at Trinity-Sergius. Gurii had become a monk in 1915 while studying at the Saint Petersburg Theological Academy. He was a well-known religious activist who went out to the working class districts of the city to minister to factory workers, and after the Bolshevik Revolution he helped establish the Aleksander-Nevskii brotherhood, which brought together clergy and laity in defense of the Church.[32] During the 1920s, he was arrested and exiled, rearrested, and sent to the dreaded White Sea Canal, where many political prisoners were sent to work (and many to die).[33] After serving his time, he settled in Uzbekistan, where he escaped the Terror by remaining under the NKVD's radar. Gurii was to serve as prior of Trinity-Sergius for less than a year before he was installed as bishop of Tashkent.[34] Nevertheless, his excellent organizational skills together with his deep monastic experience guided him in giving shape to the newly opened Lavra, and he played a key role during a crucial moment in reconstituting the monastery.

Archimandrite Gurii gathered experienced monks to form the initial brotherhood and laid a solid foundation for the flowering of monastic life, despite the hardships of rebuilding from nothing in a less-than-hospitable environment. The first brothers of the Lavra constituted a remarkable collection of experienced monks (including a few from the prerevolutionary Lavra) and clergy together with a few young men who had served in the army who joined the monastery as novices. Few, however, remained at the Lavra for very long, and many went on to become bishops.[35]

It also took time to reestablish a routine of monastic life—particularly as, for most of 1946, only the Dormition cathedral was returned to the Church and the monks did not live at the monastery. According to Ioann (Vendland), the monks lived in private apartments, "went about in civilian clothing, and only on the territory of the Lavra put on their cassocks. Each one knew his obedience for the week."[36] Those obediences, or work assigned by the monastery, included church services (e.g., prayer services at the relics of Saint Sergius, memorial services, and hearing confessions). Trushin of the Council of Russian Orthodox Church Affairs also reported how each monk fulfilled his obedience (everything from cleaning and candle sales to sacristan and steward), and that the brothers conducted four services a day, beginning at 6 a.m. All of the brothers lived on an equal basis (except for the abbot) and did not receive payment for their services, although they did obtain food and clothing from the monastery.[37] In short, Gurii succeeded in reviving prerevolutionary monastic traditions at Trinity-Sergius, which became what Nikolai Mitrokhin termed the "ideological and organizational" center of the postwar Russian Church. Mitrokhin also alleges, however, that Gurii reestablished the prerevolutionary intellectual—and political—traditions of the Lavra, including its monarchist, nationalistic, and xenophobic views, although he does not provide much in the way of concrete examples of these manifestations.[38]

In August 1946, after Gurii was consecrated bishop and left for Tashkent, a former member of the prerevolutionary Trinity-Sergius collective, Archimandrite Ioann (Dmitrii Razumov, 1898–1990) became the new prior.[39] Ioann had become a novice before the Revolution and was tonsured a monk in the 1920s; in the 1930s he served close to Metropolitan Sergii. He remained the prior of Trinity-Sergius until November 1953, when he was consecrated bishop of Kostroma. In June 1953, Karpov must have proposed Ioann as an episcopal candidate for Arkhangelsk, which Patriarch

Aleksii I resisted because Ioann was evidently resistant to leaving the Lavra. Moreover, Aleksii himself was reluctant to lose Ioann because his administration of the Lavra was very valuable to the patriarch.[40] He ended his career as metropolitan of Pskov, where he served until his retirement in 1987 and death in 1990.[41]

One of the most notable early inhabitants of the renewed Lavra was Archimandrite Veniamin (Viktor Milov, 1887–1955), whose powerful sermons suggest the uncompromising nature of the Lavra in the first years after its reopening. He had become a monk in 1920, was sent to the gulag from 1929 to 1932, and then arrested and exiled again during the Terror. He came to Trinity-Sergius directly from exile in June 1946, and he lived at first in a private apartment like the others.[42] Veniamin served the early liturgy in the church located in the crypt of the Dormition cathedral on Sundays and feast days. In his sermon for the first Christmas celebration at the reopened Lavra (January 7, 1947), for example, he began with the words from the Gospel of Luke, "Glory to God in the Highest and peace, goodwill among men" (Luke 2:14). He asked his listeners why they did not find this peace, and why reality contradicted the benediction of the angel. A more accurate description of contemporary conditions would be the "unrolling of the scroll of woes over our Fatherland," a reference to Ezekiel, chapter 2. "Is it possible to speak of peace in our present life when the sons of Russia, under the influence of pernicious teachings unknown of old, tear to pieces the maternal heart of the Motherland with internecine fratricidal war, despising every authority and trampling up everything holy, having fallen in love with the egotism of the modern superman?" Christ brought peace, Veniamin continued, but people have turned away from Him. If everyone followed Christ's teachings, then there would be peace in the world: "Then there would be no ground or basis for the appearance of ill will in political, social and economic life, which we run into now."[43] Although Veniamin did not name the "pernicious teachings" he had in mind—and perhaps it could have been a reference to Nazism as well as communism—the essential message was clear: human ideologies could not bring peace; only following Christ brought peace. It was particularly bold of Veniamin to make it clear that his message had broad, social connotations and political implications, and that he was not only speaking about "inner" peace.

A particular theme of Archimandrite Veniamin's sermons was the shame people felt about their faith before nonbelievers—something his listeners very likely struggled with. In a sermon during Great Lent, he cited Christ's words that "whoever is ashamed of me and of my words in this adulterous and sinful generation, of him will the Son of man also be ashamed" (Mark 8:38). In Veniamin's day, he stated, it was in fashion to reject everything, to reevaluate everything, to overthrow authority—and that this negation has included even Christ: "Try now anywhere in society to speak about Christ or even to cross yourself—everyone will laugh. Tell them that you pray every day and keep the fasts—and they will take you for a dimwit or a crank [*chudak*]." The true followers of Christ must follow His call, and this included casting aside the "absurd prejudices of society."[44] In another sermon, he criticized contemporary believers for hiding their faith "for the sake of a piece of bread," or even rejecting Christ for the sake of security and a more comfortable life.[45] In short, Veniamin preached powerfully to his listeners not to compromise or hide their faith, despite possible consequences of being despised in society or suffering in their career—and he was one who could speak with authority.

The brotherhood continued to grow steadily throughout 1946, reaching twenty-one by the end of the year.[46] A year later, there were thirty-five brothers, which remained roughly the size of the brotherhood until the end of the 1940s, as there was a lot of turnover in the early years. In 1947 there was a predominance of ordained clergy (twenty-five), with only three monks and seven novices.[47] There were also many who were older; seventeen of the monks were more than fifty-five years of age, while six were younger than thirty-five and twelve were between thirty-five and fifty-five. The majority were of peasant background (eighteen), and the fewest came from workers' families (four); six were from white-collar families (*sluzhashchie*), and seven were sons of clergy. Only three had a theological education, and the vast majority (twenty-four) had a "lower" education. In the years 1947–48, the brotherhood drew in more brothers who had become monks before or during the Revolution, many returning directly from exile or the gulag, as well as a few émigrés who returned to the Soviet Union after the war to serve the Church. Although many of the monks had been in prison or exile before the war, Trinity-Sergius was also attracting new recruits, many of whom had fought in the war, including some who had even been decorated. The monastery was also starting to attract younger recruits, several of whom were born in the late 1920s and early 1930s.[48] In short, despite the rapid turnover in the early years, the Trinity-Sergius brotherhood was reconstituted with a mix of both older, experienced monks and new recruits.

## The Late Stalin Period, 1946–53

A shift in church-state relations occurred in 1948, and this was palpable at Trinity-Sergius. According to Shkarovskii, by 1948 it became clear to Stalin that his grandiose dream of finally realizing Moscow as the "Third Rome," a world religious center, was going to fail. Therefore, he grew less interested in granting the Church the types of concessions it had been receiving for the previous five years, and the Soviet authorities began to tighten the reins on the Church. The number of open churches was reduced, and the Church's donations for patriotic aims—which won respect among the people—were stopped, while the government made up for the loss of income by taxing the Church. The number of seminaries was reduced, and the state renewed support for antireligious propaganda. Nevertheless, the Church was still useful to Stalin in other areas, such as advocacy for the peace movement. From 1949 until his death in 1953, Stalin showed less interest in the Church, which left a greater role for the Council for Russian Orthodox Church Affairs. The Church had less freedom than in the immediate postwar years, but there was no active repression.[49] In short, Stalin did not fundamentally change his policy toward the Church, although there were many in the Communist Party who viewed the wartime toleration of the Church as a tactical move to be reversed after the war was over and chafed against Stalin's policy.[50]

The reopening of Trinity-Sergius brought about a "spiritual uplift," in the words of Ioann (Vendland), not only for the monastic brotherhood, but also for Russian Orthodox believers more broadly in the postwar years. As soon as the monastery was open, pilgrims began coming in great numbers. According to Trushin, access to the relics of Saint Sergius was available from 6 a.m. until midnight. During the summer of 1946, an average of 100 to 200 pilgrims came to the Lavra per day on ordinary days, 1,500 to 2,000 on Sundays, and 4,000 to 6,000 people per day on great feasts. Moreover, these people came not only from the surrounding villages and from Moscow, but from many other cities and towns.[51] Trushin's report for 1947 noted that visitation to the Lavra on ordinary days had declined somewhat, although on major feast days the level of pilgrimage remained the same as before.[52] In his report for 1949, he optimistically observed that visitation to the monastery declined both on ordinary days and on the great feast days, and that "there are significantly fewer people than there were in 1946 after [the Lavra's] opening."[53] However, the number of pilgrims continued to rise thereafter, so that a decade later, in 1956, authorities estimated between 10,000 and 15,000 pilgrims visited for each of the great feast days.[54] Clearly, the upsurge in pilgrimage to Trinity-Sergius was not merely a temporary phenomenon inspired by the traumas of the war and the momentary elation of the monastery's return, as Soviet authorities evidently hoped in the late 1940s. Rather, once religious practice had once again become more openly permitted, it only continued to intensify.

As in the nineteenth century, more pilgrims resulted in increased income for the monastery.[55] In 1946, Trinity-Sergius received 300,000 to 400,000 rubles per month in the summer from candle sales, donations, and other collections, and about half that amount in winter months. The following year, the figures had declined somewhat (100,000 to 150,000 in winter months) and, according to Trushin, these figures were reduced three to four times after a monetary reform.[56] Despite this, however, the level of income continued to increase together with the level of pilgrimage, so that in 1957 the income ranged from 400,000 rubles (in January, the slowest month) to slightly more than 1 million in August (the highest). Thus in 1947, the total income for the year was 2 million rubles, whereas in 1957 it was 7 million. Also, as in the nineteenth century, the greatest single source of income came from candle sales. For the mid-1950s, the average annual income from candles and memorial services was 3 to 4 million rubles (i.e., more than half of total income), with 800,000 to 950,000 rubles from the sale of prosphora, 1 to 1.5 million from collection plates passed around during church services, 0.5 to 1 million from the sale of church goods (presumably books and icons), and 500,000 to 800,000 in pure donations. Typically, these donations were made by ordinary private persons in relatively small sums (100 to 500 rubles), although occasionally there were some anonymous donors who gave large donations (from 1,000 to 3,000 rubles).[57] This enormous rise in income, which was part of a broader phenomenon of the Church receiving a substantial flow of cash from believers, not only demonstrates the continued rise in pilgrimage and the devotion of the believers to the monastery, but clearly provided the monastery with significant economic power.[58]

Offsetting rising income, Trinity-Sergius also had major expenditures during the first decade of its renewed existence—especially for renovating buildings. As was mentioned above, the buildings of the monastery were only gradually given back to the Church. Sovnarkom decreed in 1940 that the entire complex of Trinity-Sergius was to be transformed into a "museum city" (*muzei-gorodok*), and significant sums were set aside for the renovation of the buildings; the outbreak of the war, however, prevented this plan from being fulfilled.[59] Although a museum had been established in the former Lavra in 1920, only those buildings and artifacts considered artistic or historical treasures fell into the direct control of the museum—especially the sacristy and the Trinity Cathedral.[60] Some of the churches (e.g., the Dormition Cathedral) remained unused, while some had been used for other purposes. In addition to the museum, a pedagogical institute (in the former Theological Academy), an arts and crafts school, the town theater (in the Academy's chapel), a clothing repair shop, and the town bakery were located inside the monastery grounds. In addition to these activities, there were a large number of local inhabitants living on the grounds. By 1946, most of the buildings had been neglected and were in dreadful shape.[61]

The highest levels of the Soviet government dictated which buildings of the old Lavra would be handed over to the reopened monastery, and when. Thus, the Church received only the Dormition Cathedral in April 1946. In October of that year, by decree of the Soviet of Ministers, the Moscow Patriarchate received the Refectory Church of Saint Sergius and accommodations in the basement—which finally made it possible for the monks to begin living on the grounds of the monastery—together with the bell tower, the chapel with the spring near the Dormition Cathedral, and the small church of Saint Mikhei near the Refectory. The Moscow Patriarchate began restoration work immediately, spending significant sums of money.[62] In 1947, the Patriarchate received the metropolitan's apartments and some of the buildings of the former Theological Academy. Evidently, as soon as they succeeded in renovating the buildings they had been given, the patriarch would press for more. Thus in May 1948, Aleksii wrote to Karpov requesting the return of the Trinity Cathedral and the Church of the Holy Spirit, justifying his request both on the success of the Church's restoration work and again appealing to the notion that such actions would demonstrate the state's "favorable" relationship to the Church both to believers and to foreigners. As before, the patriarch's requests were supported by Karpov and confirmed by the Soviet of Ministers.[63] The following year, the pedagogical institute, the bakery, and the clothing repair shop were moved out and the monastery was given those buildings. The return of buildings was very gradual, and there were still over a thousand civilians living on monastery grounds until the mid-1950s.[64]

Because the buildings were in such a desperate state of disrepair when returned to the Church, the Moscow Patriarchate immediately began renovation and restoration. The restoration work was extremely expensive. In

1946, the Church spent 1 million rubles on the Dormition cathedral alone, reroofing and painting, putting in new plumbing and electricity, and the like.[65] Between 1946 and 1948, by which time it had received the main churches and part of the Theological Academy, it spent 8 million rubles. By 1957, 30 million rubles were spent on restoration work, of which 13 million were provided by the Patriarchate, and the rest by the monastery itself. Great sums of money spent on renovation decreased by the mid-1950s because the majority of the buildings had been returned and because the Church and the monks were doing more of the work themselves.[66]

The restoration work did not always proceed smoothly or without problems. The work on the Dormition cathedral, for example, was evidently carried out by the head of the building sector (*stroiuchastka*), but instead of doing it through the official building sector he worked through private contracts and employed relatives and other people close to him. Moreover, he charged the Lavra exorbitant sums for shoddy work. Naturally, Archimandrite Ioann and Patriarch Aleksii were outraged, as was Trushin.[67] Nevertheless, the Church was quite successful overall in its restoration work, so much so that they had a large picture book printed showing what the buildings looked like before and after the restoration. Patriarch Aleksii requested that Karpov give a copy to Stalin, stating that their success in restoring the Lavra "justified the great trust" that Stalin showed the Patriarchate in returning to it such an invaluable treasure as the architectural ensemble of the Lavra.[68]

The monastery was not free from outside interference in restoring its buildings. In 1950, for example, the monastery wanted to restore a pool with a canopy at the chapel over the well that had been originally built in 1872, but had been demolished as lacking historical and artistic value; the administration for the preservation of architectural monuments, however, did not allow the monastery to restore this pool. Further, the administration felt it necessary to warn the monastery that the bell tower was in a dangerous state of disrepair and needed to be taken care of immediately.[69] In 1951, Stalin himself signed a document about certain structural work on the Dormition Cathedral (pertaining to the walls and foundation) directed by the central restoration workshop of the Academy of Architects of the USSR at a sum of 120,000 rubles—which was charged to the Moscow Patriarchate.[70] In summary, during the first decade of the renewed Lavra, the Church carried out an enormous amount of restoration work, mostly at its own expense, but tension between the monastery's autonomy and state dictate persisted.

Until other institutions were removed from the territory of the monastery, the coexistence of ecclesiastical and civil institutions provoked tensions. Contrary to the conflicts between these institutions one might expect, the problem, as far as the Soviet authorities were concerned, was the opposite—that they were getting along too well. This was particularly true after the Moscow Theological Academy and Seminary were reinstalled in its former location. The reestablishment of theological education had been one of Metropolitan Sergii's key demands at the historic meeting with Stalin in 1943. Soon after the war, theological courses began in Moscow, where they were temporarily located at the Novodevichii convent. Then the Soviet government returned some of the buildings of the former academy in 1947, and after they were renovated, the Academy began operation in its former home in 1948—although it was still sharing the space with the pedagogical institute, and the town theater continued to occupy the church.

In 1949, Trushin reported that the presence of state institutions on the same territory as the monastery was very undesirable—primarily because the theology students and the monks could influence the students at the pedagogical institute and the arts and crafts school. He cited examples of this negative influence, arguing that the prior, Archimandrite Ioann, and other brothers had attracted some of the arts and crafts students to become either novices in the monastery or seminarians. In order to attract them, the monks allegedly made orders for arts and crafts from these students and paid inflated prices, invited them to meals in the monastery refectory, and supported them in other ways. Trushin then cited specific examples of one person who applied to the Theological Academy and two others who requested to become novices. Moreover, the theological students at the Academy were having a similar influence among the students of the pedagogy institute, which was located in the same building. Finally, there were other tensions—in particular, the Academy was agitating to have the town bakery removed from its cafeteria, and in particular to have the theater removed from its chapel.[71] Although this language and perception of the harmful influence of the church indicated a shift in thinking that more closely resembled earlier Soviet rhetoric, it is significant that the solution to the problematic situation was to remove the government institutions and return everything (with the exception of the museum) to Church control.

The shift in state policy toward the Church became palpable in 1948 at Trinity-Sergius, as the authorities began looking at the monastery and its influence on believers with greater scrutiny. Trushin's apprehension about the monastery's influence on local students was one such case. Much more ominously, in 1948 Trushin prepared a list of five monks who had prior convictions for "anti-Soviet activities" (four in 1937–38, one in 1941), and stated that these monks should be denied the right of residence as "having passport limitations"—a tactic that the authorities commonly employed to remove undesirable clergy.[72] One of them, Hierodeacon Iosif (Evseenok; 1897?–1968), had joined the Lavra's Gethsemane Skete in the 1920s; he was arrested in 1937 and sentenced to ten years in the gulag, and he joined the Lavra directly from exile. In Trushin's report on the Lavra for 1949, he noted that there were seven monks of the Lavra who had been repressed for "anti-Soviet activity" (three of whom were also on the earlier list); it is not clear how long they remained, but it is clear that the Soviet authorities were keeping closer watch, especially on "repeat offenders"—those who had previously been arrested.[73] Moreover, Archimandrite Veniamin (Milov) was "called in" to the local police in 1949, never to return to Trinity-Sergius; he was exiled to Kazakhstan, perhaps because of his uncompromising sermons.[74] Such outspoken preaching was no longer to be tolerated. As of February 1949, roughly half of the brothers present in the monastery a year earlier were gone; although it is not entirely clear why all of them left, a number were exiled or transferred because they were perceived as "anti-Soviet," no doubt precisely because of such uncompromising preaching or religious activism.[75]

Clearly, the "golden age" for the Lavra was the brief period between 1946 and 1948, which was in general a period of religious revival, and when Soviet authorities granted the monastery a remarkable degree of freedom. Trinity-Sergius used its freedom well to reestablish a strong brotherhood of experienced monks, many of whom had suffered for the faith, and to attract promising new recruits. Moreover, Trinity-Sergius retook possession of the relics of Saint Sergius, which it again made available for veneration by pilgrims, and reestablished the monastery as Russia's sacred center and foremost pilgrimage destination. Pilgrims brought with them money, which the monastery in turn used to restore and renovate the churches after decades of neglect. By 1948, Stalin's attitude toward the Orthodox Church had cooled; the authorities thus curtailed some freedoms at Trinity-Sergius, became more watchful of monks previously repressed for "anti-Soviet activities," and ceased to tolerate outspoken preaching. Nevertheless, the shift in 1948 was by no means a complete reversal of Stalin's wartime policy toward the Church, as the monastery continued to recruit new monks and draw ever-larger numbers of pilgrims for another decade.

## Trinity-Sergius in the Middle 1950s

The period between Stalin's death in 1953 and Khrushchev's full assumption of power and the resumption of the antireligious campaign in 1958 was a particularly complex one in church-state relations. Shortly after Stalin's death in the spring of 1953, Karpov submitted a proposal to the Central Committee to strengthen the role of the Council for Russian Orthodox Church Affairs, and his suggestions were based on acceptance of the religious revival and attempted to come to terms with and cooperate with the Orthodox Church. His proposals were rejected by Communist Party functionaries who regarded the revival of religious life as a cause for concern, not cooperation; clergy were to be regarded as ideological opponents rather than reliable citizens. In June 1954, the Central Committee passed a resolution to strengthen "scientific atheist propaganda" and began to take measures against the Church. This new policy elicited protest and opposition from the Moscow Patriarchate and believers, as well as dismay from the leadership of the Council for Russian Orthodox Church Affairs, and this provoked leading figures in the Soviet government (Malenkov, Voroshilov, and Molotov) also to oppose it; by November 1954 the government reversed the policy back to relative tolerance.

The Orthodox Church continued to play a "useful" role (as far as the Soviet government was concerned) in the international arena through its involvement in the world peace and ecumenical movements. In all, the years 1955–57 were relatively stable ones in church-state relations. Indeed, in 1955 clergy who had been exiled in 1948–49, such as Veniamin (Milov), were allowed to return to church service (Veniamin was consecrated bishop of Saratov, but was to live only another six months). The situation was a precarious one, however, as there were competing forces in the Communist Party as to whether the postwar policy toward the Church should continue, or whether there should be a return to a more vigorous policy of eradicating such obsolete remnants of the past as religion. The tide began to shift in 1957, as Khrushchev sought support among the "ideologues" of the party who were opposed to the policy of cooperation with the Church, while Khrushchev himself wished to reinvigorate communist ideology and eliminate "relics" such as the Church.[76]

The story of Trinity-Sergius during the post-Stalin years of the Soviet Union exemplifies much of the Church's experience. Trinity-Sergius experienced a change in leadership at the same time as the Soviet Union itself. In November 1953, the prior, Archimandrite Ioann (Razumov), was consecrated bishop. He was replaced by Archimandrite Pimen (Izvekov, 1910–90) in January 1954. Pimen had been tonsured a monk at the Lavra's Paraclete Hermitage as a seventeen-year-old in 1927. In the 1930s he served as a parish priest in Moscow, and became prior of the Pskov-Caves Monastery beginning in 1949; he gained a reputation for his abilities of putting into good order whatever was in his charge. As prior of Trinity-Sergius, Pimen was also engaged in restoration, such as of the church of the Theological Academy and other work of renovation and repair. He evidently distinguished himself in this and as an administrator, so that in November 1957—after less than four years as prior of Trinity-Sergius—he was consecrated bishop, ending his career as patriarch of the Church from 1971 to 1990.[77]

The period when Archimandrite Pimen (Izvekov) served as prior was a relatively quiet one for the monastery. Indeed, perhaps the situation was too easy, and the monastery was growing too wealthy, for there is some evidence that there was a decline in monastic discipline under Pimen.[78] At the time of Stalin's death, the Church was still not in charge of much of the territory of the monastery and continued to share the grounds with city inhabitants, which was a source of constant consternation for the monastery not only because these people did not care for the buildings they occupied, but also because their lifestyles contrasted with the atmosphere of the monastery and its pilgrim visitors.[79] As an expression of the moderate line the government was taking at the end of 1954, Malenkov met with Patriarch Aleksii on December 11. Among only a few requests, the patriarch asked Malenkov about transferring all structures of the Lavra to the Church.[80] Malenkov promised to satisfy the requests, but the promises were met only a year later when the Council for Russian Orthodox Church Affairs took the side of the patriarch, advocating the satisfaction of such requests in response for the Church's continued international role.[81] Finally, in August 1956 the Soviet of Ministers passed a resolution "On the Transfer to the Moscow Patriarchate of Buildings Located on the Territory of the Trinity-Sergius Lavra." In order to fulfill this, it also instructed the Moscow provincial Executive Committee to build three apartment buildings over the following three years "for the resettling of the tenants, numbering 1,150 persons, who are living in the buildings situated on the territory of the Trinity-Sergius Lavra."[82] However, as it turned out, the Moscow Patriarchate itself had to pay for the construction of the new homes, and the pace of construction was painfully slow.[83] It therefore took more than a decade before the monastery finally assumed control of most of its territory and was freed from the interference of large numbers of civilian inhabitants—although it continued to share the grounds with the state museum until the 1990s. Indeed, Patriarch Aleksii's attempts to remove the museum in 1958, and the government's refusal to do so, are indicators that the times were already changing.[84]

As with the Church as a whole, the primary strategic function that Trinity-Sergius played for the Soviet government was as an international showpiece. Soviet authorities were aware that, as an architectural ensemble and museum, Trinity-Sergius had universal significance, and that it was a place to take important guests.[85] However, it had great significance even as a monastery, as a means to try to dispel Western criticism about the treatment of religion in the Soviet Union. But having esteemed visitors was also in the Lavra's interests. Thus Archimandrite Ioann had tried to restore the Dormition Cathedral quickly in part in preparation for the visit of Elliot Roosevelt, President Roosevelt's son, in 1946, who was received by Archimandrite Ioann during the visit.[86] Receiving foreign visitors at the monastery became a regular practice. In 1957, during a world youth and student festival that convened in Moscow, a group of 750 foreign Christians came to Trinity-Sergius (including some pastors and parliamentarians from Germany and Britain), and there were some 700 participants from the Soviet Union. Soviet authorities, naturally, focused on the impressions made on the foreign visitors, and reported one Catholic student from Belgium as saying that "they have lied to me for ten years that religion in the USSR has been kept down. Attending meetings in Zagorsk and conversing with clergy, I am convinced of the opposite."[87] During the relatively peaceful time of the mid-1950s, such visits might serve the interests of both church and state. During the Khrushchev persecutions, however, foreign visits would become much more contested.

By 1957, the brotherhood of the monastery had grown and diversified significantly, compared with a decade earlier. There were eighty-nine brothers as of January 1, 1957 (six more than the previous year), of whom fifty-three were ordained clergy and the remainder monks or novices. Although the largest number of brothers, forty-one, were older than fifty-five years, a significant number of the brothers (thirty-one) were younger, between nineteen and forty years. The monastery lost ten brothers in 1956: one died, one was laicized, four transferred to other monasteries, and four (presumably all novices) were expelled for "immoral behavior" such as drunkenness, playing cards, and meeting with women. There were sixteen new brothers received in 1956 (in contrast to twenty-seven in 1955). What particularly caught Council for Russian Orthodox Church Affairs commissioner Trushin's attention was that, for the first time, the majority of the new brothers were young; he named seven of these recruits, four of whom were born in the years 1937–38. Archimandrite Pimen (Izvekov) explained to Trushin, however, that the youngest ones were received in the monastery on the recommendation of the seminary—where they had applied as students but which lacked adequate vacancies to receive them—in the hopes that they would be received the following year.[88] In fact, however, the trend continued the following year. The number of new postulants joining the Lavra sharply increased in the mid-1950s, while their age and previous experience decreased. Until 1953, according to Trushin, the monastery received three to ten people per year, of whom only two to three were joining a monastery for the first time in their lives. Between 1954 and 1957, by contrast, the Lavra received twenty-three to thirty new recruits per year, of whom nineteen to twenty-five—a much higher percentage—were entering a monastery for the first time. Of the eighty-six inhabitants at the beginning of 1958, a total of twenty were monks at the time they joined the Lavra, thirty-two took vows at Trinity-Sergius, and thirty-four were novices—in short, 77 percent (sixty-six men) joined a monastery for the first time when they came to the Lavra and were younger than forty years of age.[89] The fact that monasteries were attracting increasing numbers of young recruits was particularly disturbing to the Soviet authorities for a variety of reasons, not the least of which was that it indicated the failure of Soviet indoctrination of young people—a key concern of antireligious ideologues. Although the number of recruits was not enormous, the very fact of growth in the number of youths who were willing to dedicate themselves entirely to the Church, whether by going to the monastery or to the seminary, was understood as a failure of Soviet antireligious policies.

Although the monastery had significantly increased the number of new postulants in the mid-1950s, in fact it was turning away many more than it was accepting. From 1946 to 1957, the monastery received some 500 requests to join, of which 226 were accepted. Pimen explained to Trushin that a great number of people who applied to join were old and were not taken because they would be "excess ballast" for the monastery; understandably, the monastery preferred younger men who could take on more of the tasks the monastery required. Many other people were rejected because they were psychologically inappropriate for monastic life, or they were morally corrupt and "looked upon the monastery as a more comfortable place for their residence."[90] The monastery had also lost 140 people over the years (80 monks and 60 novices), no doubt to a variety of causes (death, transfer, promotion, expulsion); nevertheless, the high rate of losses perhaps prompted the monastery to be more cautious in receiving new recruits.[91] Thus Pimen explained that they were trying to accept only those people who "sincerely wanted to devote themselves to the service of the monastery," which they did on the recommendation of the monastery's own monks.[92] This last point made Trushin particularly suspicious. Although Pimen claimed that they were not actively recruiting and that people came of their own accord, the fact was that the monks were recruiting, and this—from Trushin's perspective—was clearly a problem, a violation of what the Soviet authorities regarded as permissible. He cited specific examples of locals that the monks had tried to recruit, and other cases in which monks who were on leave to visit their families recruited among former neighbors.[93] In short, the Soviet authorities such as Trushin evidently were willing to accept monasteries so long as they primarily served as refuges for older, former monks. However, the fact that the monastery was receiving many new postulants who were younger appeared to them more threatening because it was a sign that the monastery was actively—and successfully—recruiting, that is, young Soviet men were drawn to the service of the Church, a phenomenon that paralleled the rise in seminarians in the mid-1950s.[94]

Because Trushin blamed the monastery for recruiting new postulants, his next step was to indicate the main culprits in this process. He pointed to four monks, including Archimandrite Iosif (Evseenok), who had been exiled in 1948, but had returned, most likely in 1955, when other clergy had been allowed to return from exile. The others that Trushin pointed to included Hieromonk Nikon (Preobrazhenskii, b. 1899), Hieromonk Mikhei (Alykov, b. 1899), and Hieromonk Arsenii (Romashchenko, b. 1888). Moreover, Trushin regarded these four monks in particular as not only a problem with regard to recruiting new monks, but perhaps even more because of their influence over pilgrims. Trushin, in a report to Karpov from the end of January 1957, pointed out that both Nikon (Preobrazhenskii) and Iosif (Evseenok) had prior convictions for anti-Soviet activities. Nikon, according to Trushin, was "severely anti-Soviet," demonstrated heightened interest in foreigners who visited the monastery, and constantly tried to engage them in conversation. A religious "fanatic," he also conducted "harmful ideological activity among the youth (females)," whom he tries to work up into a "religious spirit." He supposedly "prophesied" and also encouraged people to visit the Lavra and pray to God more often. Moreover, in 1947 he had spoken against participation in local and national elections, while in

1948 he had expressed anti-Soviet opinions in the presence of foreigners at the time of the celebration of the five-hundredth anniversary of the autocephaly of the Russian Church.[95] Indeed, one pilgrim who visited Trinity-Sergius in those years portrayed Nikon as well-educated and well-versed in literature, philosophy, and art, and therefore well-respected among the pilgrims and very able to lead foreign visitors—precisely the kind of monk who was dangerous from the Soviet point of view.[96]

Trushin described other troublesome monks as religious "fanatics" who expressed anti-Soviet attitudes. Archimandrite Iosif (Evseenok), according to Trushin, had broad connections with people who had been previously repressed. "On fulfilling religious rites he actively strove to cultivate a zealous attitude toward religion in visitors," and he also told pilgrims about the holy springs in Zagorsk and talked them into going. He further recruited females to join convents in Moldova. Like Nikon, he allegedly expressed anti-Soviet views openly, including among foreigners who visited the Lavra. Mikhei (Alykov) enjoyed great authority among the believers who regarded him as prescient (*prozorlivyi*) and able to cast out demons. He also actively tried to instill religious spirit in the youths with whom he interacted. Finally, Arsenii (Romashchenko), a former school teacher who was tonsured at the Pochaev Lavra and transferred to Trinity-Sergius in 1954, "concentrated" around himself youths (males) and "there are a series of signals," according to Trushin, "which speak to the fact that Romashchenko practices homosexuality."[97] Trushin first attempted to draw Karpov's attention to these four monks at the end of January 1957, asserting that their continued presence at the Lavra was "not desirable" and that they should be transferred to some other monastery—thus anticipating the change in government policy that would come later in the year. However, it appears that Karpov did not accept his proposals, for toward the end of the year Trushin repeated the same information about these monks.[98] On his own power and authority Trushin could not have monks transferred; rather, he had to get Karpov's support, who in turn pressured the patriarch to transfer them. At the same time, Trushin's attitudes appear to have reflected or anticipated those of other party and government officials who opposed the Church's continued revival more than the relatively tolerant leadership of the Council for Russian Orthodox Church Affairs, and thus anticipated Khrushchev's antireligious campaign.[99]

Clearly, there was a dramatic growth of religiosity in the postwar Soviet Union. Although Soviet officials tried to explain this away as a reaction to the horrors of the war, such an explanation could not account for the continued growth of religiosity throughout the 1950s. Indeed, what was particularly troublesome for Soviet officials was not the expressions of religious faith and increased church attendance; rather, it was the substantial number of young people—products of the Soviet system and Soviet education—who decided to dedicate themselves completely to church service, whether by studying theology and entering the priesthood or by joining monasteries. This phenomenon indicates that at least a significant minority of the population was disenchanted with communist ideals.[100]

## Khrushchev's Antireligious Campaign

Although one commonly associates the Khrushchev period with the "Thaw"—the program of de-Stalinization and liberalization in the cultural sphere—with regard to religion, "de-Stalinization" meant the end of the postwar policy of toleration for the Church and a return to the policies closer to the prewar persecution of religion. The shift began behind the scenes, evidently already in 1957 with personnel changes in the Council for Russian Orthodox Church Affairs—because the old personnel were those who fulfilled Stalinist policies on the Church. The antireligious campaign between 1958 and 1964 did not proceed consistently. There were periods when the government scaled back the campaign, particularly in light of international developments (such as improving relations with Rome in 1962–63). Nevertheless, the total effect of those years was tremendous. The number of churches in the Soviet Union was cut nearly in half (from 13,414 in 1958 to 7,523 by 1966), and the number of clergy was also drastically reduced. The number of seminaries was dramatically cut, and great pressures were applied to deter potential candidates from entering a seminary. Religious institutions and clergy were charged exorbitant taxes that they were unable to pay. Although the persecution was certainly not as brutal as it was in the period between 1928 and 1938, hundreds of clergy were removed from their posts, arrested, sent to camps, or exiled, and hundreds of believers were also exiled.[101]

Just as with the Bolshevik Revolution from 1917 to 1921, the Khrushchev antireligious campaign began with the monasteries. As in the revolutionary period, the role of monasteries as centers of pilgrimage and in the strengthening of popular piety made them particularly important targets to destroy or weaken if antireligious propaganda was to succeed. Unlike parish churches, which required a group of twenty laypeople to agree on registering the church with the authorities, monasteries had no official interface with the government and were therefore harder to control.[102] In October 1958, the Soviet of Ministers passed a resolution to take stock of monastic land with the intention of taking some of it away, to charge rent for the use of buildings (previously used free of charge), and to study the monasteries with the intent of reducing their number.[103] This was followed by actual monastery closures. The monks were expelled from the Kievan Caves Lavra in January 1959, while later that year most of the land was taken away from the Pskov-Caves Monastery and plans were made to close most monasteries. The Council for Russian Orthodox Church Affairs forbade the Moscow Patriarchate from giving subsidies to monasteries without its permission and forced it to stop receiving recruits younger than thirty years of age. Dozens of monasteries were later closed, often requiring the use of force and great numbers of police and KGB. In June 1963, the authorities arrested all of the monks at the Pochaev Lavra, although defenders of the monastery submitted a petition to the World Council of Churches and the United Nations, causing such an international scandal that the monastery was allowed to remain open. Despite this victory, the overall effect of the campaign was devastating as the sixty-three monasteries and skites in 1958 were reduced to only nineteen by 1966.[104]

The rise of Khrushchev and the reversal of policy toward religion coincided with a change of leadership at Trinity-Sergius. Pimen (Izvekov) was succeeded by Pimen (Khmelevskii), who was born in Smolensk in 1923, and thus was the first prior of the Lavra to be born after the Revolution. He had become a monk in the occupied Minsk region during the war, and after finishing seminary studied at the Moscow Theological Academy before serving the Russian mission in Palestine (1955–57).[105] He was prior from 1957 to 1965, precisely during the most difficult time of the Lavra's postwar existence. Pimen (Khmelevskii) was able to defend the monastery and hold his own, despite intense pressures. During his time as prior, he tonsured as monks the next generation of the Church's leadership, including Patriarch Aleksii II (1990–2007) and Metropolitan Filaret of Minsk. He also taught at the Theological Academy at the same time he served as prior of the Lavra. In 1965, Pimen was ordained bishop of Saratov, where he would remain as bishop (later archbishop) until his death in 1993.[106]

Only after the antireligious campaign had begun in earnest were Trushin's proposals regarding troublesome monks at Trinity-Sergius followed. He reported in 1958 that several monks were transferred—and not only the ones he mentioned the previous year—including Iosif (Evseenok), but also Archimandrite Serafim (Shinkarev), Hegumen Tarasii (Mishin), Hieromonk Savva (Ostapenko), and Schemamonk-Hierodeacon Varnava (Zaitsev). Evidently, Nikon (Preobrazhenskii) was also transferred at this time on Trushin's insistence to a monastery at Odessa.[107] Trushin considered Savva (Ostapenko) a problem because he "made prophecies," told visitors not to work on feast days and not to participate in political campaigns.[108] Savva was transferred to the Pskov-Caves Monastery, where he would remain for most of the rest of his life—and become widely respected throughout the Church as one of the most popular spiritual guides in Russia.[109] Even after these monks were removed, however, Trushin was still not satisfied, for he feared that "there can be no doubt that there are people such as Savva and Varnava among the inhabitants [of the Lavra] who, by more hidden methods, influence those around them by igniting religiosity."[110] The crackdown on activist monks whose primary crime was encouraging people to take their faith seriously was a sign of the escalating persecution of religion that encroached on the walls of Trinity-Sergius. Moreover, the very language that was employed—by which a dedicated monk was dubbed a "religious fanatic" automatically having an "anti-Soviet attitude"—is reminiscent of the language of the 1930s.

The Khrushchev-era antireligious campaign did more than target a few activist monks, however. In its effort to destroy the hold that religion had on people, one of their primary targets was pilgrimage and the holy things that drew pilgrims. In his report for 1956, Trushin stated that "the activity of the Lavra, as in previous years, was directed to spreading its influence. The presence in the Lavra of the 'relics' of its founder—Sergii Radonezh, the continually operating chapel over the well with 'holy water,' the periodic services of the Patriarch, the frequent visits of foreign church delegations, the existence of the 'holy' spring near Zagorsk, all attract a great number of pilgrims to the Lavra."[111] The following year he also noted the great number of pilgrims that came, especially for the great feasts; some 15,000 pilgrims came to each of the major feasts for several years running.[112] Thus, much to the dismay of antireligious activists, pilgrimage remained strong—or was even growing—in the mid-1950s, and the draws were the traditional ones that drew pilgrims before the Revolution: monasteries, relics, solemn liturgies, and holy springs.[113]

The Soviet authorities wished to curtail these mass pilgrimages, and the question remained as to how.[114] In many places they simply closed the monasteries, although they did not accomplish what they wanted in every case (as in Pochaev). Trinity-Sergius had already become too much a fixture for foreign visitors to be closed. Perhaps they had learned from the past that attacking relics directly was too contested and too problematic,[115] and any renewed attempt in such a direction would only bring a great outbreak of protest and negative public and international attention. Instead, the Central Committee of the Communist Party attempted a more clever method: in November 1958 they passed a resolution "On the Measures to Cease Pilgrimage to So-Called Holy Places."[116] However, rather than attacking established holy places, they claimed they were reducing pilgrimage "where the organizers turn out to be shriekers, holy fools, and other kinds of dubious persons, using these places for spreading superstition, igniting religious fanaticism and extracting from the population great monetary sums."[117] By attacking what they labeled as "illegitimate" pilgrimages and pilgrimage organizers, the Soviet authorities cast themselves into the role of defining what constituted "superstition" and what constituted legitimate religion—a paradoxical role, particularly as they had previously defined all religious belief as equivalent to superstition.

The resolution had the desired effect, for Patriarch Aleksii sent out a circular letter to the diocesan bishops, to be distributed to the clergy, who in turn were to make clear to the faithful that "there should be no place for pilgrimage to places not revered by the Church." Patriarch Aleksii himself pressured Trinity-Sergius to prohibit any monks from going to a recently closed holy spring a few kilometers from the monastery.[118] Trushin made no attempt to prohibit veneration of the relics of Saint Sergius at the Lavra. Rather, he attacked the chapel over the well that was a source of holy water—which, he argued, "is also used for the spread of superstition, igniting religious fanaticism and extorting money from the believers." This chapel, he continued, was open from early morning until late in the evening: "The water of this spring is considered just as 'holy' among the believers as in any other 'holy spring,' organized by shriekers, holy fools, and other doubtful elements." This was proven, as far as Trushin was concerned, by the long lines that formed after every service for the pilgrims to get their holy water—which sometimes took hours. Trushin therefore proposed to Karpov that he speak to the Patriarch about closing this "holy well."[119] It is not clear, however, that Trushin ever succeeded in getting what he wanted. The authorities would, however, turn to more coercive means, including arresting pilgrims and detaining them until they signed statements swearing never to return to the Lavra. Then, on March 18 and 19, 1961, the police entered the churches during service and arrested, detained, and interrogated pilgrims. Archimandrite Pimen vigorously protested to the chief of the Zagorsk police that his officers had violated the law of freedom of conscience, and he further disputed the excuses in the police chief's reply.[120]

The Trinity-Sergius Lavra became a key destination not only for Russian Orthodox believers, but also for foreign tourists and dignitaries, and this also became a point of contestation between the Soviet authorities and the monastery during the Khrushchev era. In 1957, for example, Trushin reports that 3,089 foreigners visited the Lavra from 45 countries, while in 1960 it received some 9,000 foreign visitors.[121] In 1960, the Intourist office sent a proposal to Trushin that detailed the problems. They brought foreigners to the Lavra because of its exemplary architectural ensemble and rich collection of Russian art. The Intourist organizers encountered problems, however, in that the museum workers often complained that serving as guides would interfere with their scholarly work. As a result of the museum's lack of involvement, the clergy of the Lavra had taken the initiative in guiding visitors. In short, Intourist proposed to Trushin that the scientific atheism department of the Zagorsk museum play a more active role in providing foreigners with tours, perhaps even providing them free of charge as the monks did, as well as making the monastery more "comfortable" for such visitors (by improving eating and bathroom facilities and also removing beggars from the entrances and pilgrims who sit on the lawn to eat).[122]

Despite the typical image of the Orthodox Church in the postwar Soviet period as being completely controlled and infiltrated by the Soviet authorities, a closer examination of church-state relations on the ground reveals a more complex picture. We have already seen a few instances in which Trushin did not get what he wanted. A particularly enlightening document is Trushin's report about his discussion with Archimandrite Pimen (Khmelevskii) in April 1961. Trushin posed a series of questions and demands: first, the icon shop was not to remain open throughout the day selling church goods (presumably including books), but trade in such wares should only be conducted in church and during church services—no doubt to restrict access to such items. Pimen responded that he could not give a final answer on this and would have to consult the patriarch—but that he was willing to fulfill Trushin's request if the patriarch gave his "blessing." Second, Trushin explained a second time that Pimen did not have the right to refuse the local authorities permission to check the monastery's bookkeeping records and other financial documentation. Pimen responded that, after a previous conversation, he took this up with the patriarch and resolved it affirmatively. Third, Trushin had evidently explained earlier to

Pimen that the monks were not to escort foreigners who visited the monastery. Trushin claimed it was still happening, but Pimen asserted that the monks had stopped giving tours. Fourth, Trushin demanded that Pimen turn away several novices that they had received, as having been denied the right of residence. Pimen responded that he would have to take this up with the patriarch as well. The Soviets had forced the patriarch to confirm all tonsures of new monastic recruits as a way to ensure greater control over the process, but now Pimen was using it as a way to defer meeting Trushin's demands; in short, he was using Soviet requirements against them.[123] From this exchange it is clear that the Soviet authorities sought to control the Church and its leaders, but that often Church leaders themselves were able to resist this control through a variety of means (deferring decisions, obfuscating, claiming they had already fulfilled a request, and so on) as well as to negotiate—and this at the height of Khrushchev's persecution.

Later that year, Trushin complained that the museum administration did not have a free hand in deciding what to do with the buildings of the Lavra, because the Soviet of Ministers gave the buildings to the monastery. Trushin was particularly insistent that the chapel over the well and the icon shop were violations of the law, as if he could take decisive action—although clearly he was unable to. Pimen asserted that he would only do what Trushin asked—for example, that the brothers would receive only church-related foreign delegations but not other foreign visitors—but "in reality this is not so at all," Trushin protested. "In contrast to the previous priors, this one is the most clever. He has become completely impudent and unrestrained. Evidently, we will have to take him out soon and put in place another, more tactful, who will take Soviet laws into consideration."[124] Despite Trushin's intention to replace him with someone more compliant, Pimen remained prior until 1965, at which point, instead of being sent to a remote monastery for his "uncooperativeness," he was made bishop and sent to Saratov.[125] Indeed, he even outlasted Khrushchev and his antireligious campaign. Despite that fact that his tenure as prior coincided with Khrushchev's antireligious campaign, Archimandrite Pimen pushed both the Church hierarchy and the Council for Russian Orthodox Church Affairs to allow the brotherhood to increase to one hundred monks, although the local authorities repeatedly denied the right of residence to new recruits. He was more successful in continuing the restoration of the monastery and in finally relocating the last remaining inhabitants who did not belong, even though the former involved struggle with the museum and the latter struggle in the courts. He also directed his attention to the monastery's inner life, providing it with a new monastic rule that remained in effect for forty years.[126] Clearly Archimandrite Pimen (Khmelevskii) was a strong figure who could hold his own, and while Trushin and the Soviet authorities that interfaced with the monastery did not find churchmen compliant to their demands, they were also unable to have them removed at will.

Trinity-Sergius succeeded in weathering the Khrushchev antireligious campaign and even maintaining some autonomy both because of its strong leadership and because of its prominent status as a "showpiece" for foreign visitors. For monasticism as a whole, however, Khrushchev's antireligious campaign had devastating consequences. There were between 60 and 70 monasteries and convents open in the Soviet Union during the 1950s (already a significant reduction from more than 100 in the immediate postwar period), but by the end of the Khrushchev era there were only 18.[127] Until perestroika in the late 1980s, the Soviet government maintained this status quo, but became particularly restrictive in allowing new monastic recruits. Thus the brotherhood of Trinity-Sergius, which numbered 89 brothers in 1957, had declined to 65 (62 monks and 3 novices) after Khrushchev because the local police refused to allow any new recruits to register their residence at the monastery. By 1973, that number had fallen to 57.[128] The fundamental turning point in church-state relations came with the preparation for, and then the celebration of, the millennium of the Christianization of Rus' in 1988, when Gorbachev permitted widespread freedom for the Church, including the reopening of churches and monasteries. Even before the collapse of the Soviet Union at the end of 1991, the Russian Orthodox Church was again witnessing a resurgence of monasticism, and in those few short years over 100 new monasteries were opened.[129]

## Conclusion

The picture that emerges of Trinity-Sergius in the postwar years challenges the prevailing depiction of the Russian Orthodox Church as completely compromised, infiltrated, and controlled by the Soviet government and the KGB. Although the highest levels of Church authority, especially in the late Soviet period, certainly did not have great freedom of action, the evidence is clear from both Church documents and even Soviet records that, on the ground, Trinity-Sergius had a surprising degree of autonomy especially during the late Stalin period. Contrary to what the Soviets were fond of declaring to the West, there was no "freedom of religion" in the

Soviet Union. It is also true that the most uncompromising and outspoken monks, especially after 1948, were often transferred to remote monasteries or exiled. The priors of Trinity-Sergius, however, appear to have been quite adept at learning to play the system to ensure the maximum degree of autonomy possible under the circumstances and to pursue their own interests—and not those of the state. In case after case, from vigorous preaching to the faithful to selling religious objects to pilgrims to guiding foreign visitors through the monastery and giving them their version of things, the monastery stubbornly pursued its own interests despite the challenges of Trushin and the state apparatus. Remarkably, even at the height of Khrushchev's antireligious campaign, Trushin was unable to have the uncooperative prior of Trinity-Sergius removed as he so ardently wished. Although the highest level of church authority—the Patriarchate—may have been seriously compromised under the Soviet regime, it evidently was also able to act as a shield to protect lower levels of the Church and preserve at least some autonomy. And though that autonomy was very limited, Trinity-Sergius certainly exercised it to the extent of its abilities and to a remarkably successful degree. Though not free, neither were these churchmen mere puppets of the regime—let alone KGB agents.

Peter the Great and the enlightened hierarchs of the eighteenth-century Russian Church attempted to rationalize and contain the manifestations of the sacred and expressions of piety through categorizing accepted phenomena (e.g., relics of long-revered saints and miracles associated with them) and unacceptable phenomena—particularly the appearance of new miraculous icons or holy springs—which were then labeled "superstition."[130] The Soviets attempted to "disenchant" and secularize the world completely by doing away with all manifestations of the sacred. Failing to accomplish this goal, they were reduced to half measures that were not unlike those of Peter the Great and his churchmen; unable to extinguish believers' veneration for the relics of Saint Sergius of Radonezh, and ultimately unable even to divorce the relics from the monastery he founded, the Soviets instead turned to attacking "false" holy places and "superstition" (such as Trinity-Sergius's well with holy water) in order to combat pilgrimage and "religious fanaticism." Paradoxically, this placed Soviet authorities in a position of having to define what distinguished legitimate religious practice from "superstition." Yet even here the Soviets failed, because that well with holy water is to this day immensely popular (as I have myself witnessed on many occasions)—probably second in importance only to the relics of Saint Sergius. Although the extent to which the Soviets succeeded in secularizing Russian society should not be underestimated, the irony is that it is precisely these manifestations that most strongly persist today—Russian Orthodox believers may be more likely to go to a holy spring for its healing waters than they are to stand through an entire liturgy in church.[131]

Despite decades of state-sponsored atheism and antireligious campaigns, the Soviets did not succeed in eliminating religion in Russia. On the contrary, the postwar period was one of religious revivals, which can be seen in the tremendous upsurge of churches being reopened, in the increasing number of pilgrims to Trinity-Sergius, and the growth in the number of young postulants who wished to join the monastery. Ultimately, undiluted Bolshevik ideology failed in the Soviet Union so that, beginning with World War II, Stalin and the Soviet state were falling back on old bases for national identity—and in that picture Orthodoxy could once again find a place; but this also spelled the beginning of the end for Soviet ideology and the Soviet project. The return to religion even increased in the 1960s, when one of the side effects of Khrushchev's de-Stalinization campaign was a decline in the legitimacy of Soviet ideology and an increase in the search for alternatives. As at other times in Russian history, it is precisely at such moments of social questioning and transformation that monasticism experienced revival.

## Notes

1. Ioann (Vendland), *Kniaz' Fedor (Chernyi), Mitropolit Gurii (Egorov): Istoricheskii ocherki* (Yaroslavl: Izd-vo DIA-Press, 1999), 129.

2. Scott M. Kenworthy, *The Heart of Russia: Trinity-Sergius, Monasticism and Society after 1825* (Washington, D.C., and New York: Woodrow Wilson Center Press and Oxford University Press, 2010).

3. Dimitry Pospielovsky, *Russian Church under the Soviet Regime* (Crestwood, N.Y.: St. Vladimir's Seminary Press, 1984), 1:194–95.

4. On the Russian Orthodox Church before World War II, see I. A. Kurliandskii, *Stalin, vlast', religiia* (Moscow: Kuchkovo pole, 2011); and, during World War II, see Daniel Peris, "'God Is Now on Our Side': The Religious Revival on Unoccupied Soviet Territory during World War II," *Kritika* 1, no. 1 (2000): 97–118; Steven M. Miner, *Stalin's Holy War: Religion, Nationalism, and Alliance Politics, 1941–1945* (Chapel Hill: University of North Carolina Press, 2003); M. V. Shkarovskii, *Natsistskaia Germaniia i Pravoslavnaia Tserkov'* (Moscow: Izd. Krutitskogo Podvor'ia, 2002); Shkarovskii, *Politika Tret'ego reikha po otnosheniiu k Russkoi Pravoslavnoi Tserkvi v svete arkhivnykh materialov 1935–1945 godov (Sbornik dokumentov)* (Moscow: Izd. Krutitskogo Podvor'ia, 2003); Shkarovskii, *Tserkov' zovet k zashchite Rodiny: Religioznaia zhizn' Leningrada i Severo-Zapada v gody Velikoi Otechestvennoi voiny* (Saint Petersburg:

Satis, 2005); O. Iu. Vasil'eva et al., eds., *Russkaia Pravoslavnaia tserkov' v gody Velikoi Otechestvennoi voiny 1941–1945 gg.: Sbornik dokumentov* (Moscow: Izd. Krutitskogo Podvor'ia, 2009).

5. See M. V. Shkarovskii, "Russkaia pravoslavnaia tserkov' v 1943–1957 godakh," *Voprosy istorii*, no. 8 (1995): 36–37.

6. See Tat'iana Volokitina, Galina Murashko, and Al'bina Nosokova, *Moskva i Vostochnaia Evropa: Vlast' i tserkov' v period obshchestvennykh transformatsii 40–50-kh godov XX veka* (Moscow: POSSPEN, 2008); and T.V. Volokitina et al., eds., *Vlast' i tserkov' v vostochnoi Evrope 1944–1953 gg.: Dokumenty rossiiskikh arkhivov*, 2 vols. (Moscow: Rosspen, 2009).

7. On the council, see Tatiana A. Chumachenko, *Church and State in Soviet Russia: Russian Orthodoxy from World War II to the Khrushchev Years*, translated by Edward E. Roslof (Armonk, N.Y.: M. E. Sharpe, 2002). On Trushin, see Edward E. Roslof, "'Faces of the Faceless': A. A. Trushin Communist Over-Procurator for Moscow, 1943–1984," *Modern Greek Studies Yearbook* 18/19 (2002/2003): 105–25. On the period more broadly, see M. V. Shkarovskii, *Russkaia Pravoslavnaia Tserkov' pri Staline i Khrushcheve* (Moscow: Izd. Krutitskogo Podvor'ia, 1999); and M. V. Shkarovskii, *Russkaia Pravoslavnaia Tserkov' v XX veke* (Moscow: Veche, Lepta, 2010).

8. Shkarovskii, "Russkaia pravoslavnaia tserkov' v 1943–1957 godakh," 37–40; Chumachenko, *Church and State*, 15–86; and Aleksei Beglov, *V poiskakh "bezgreshnykh katakomb": Tserkovnoe podpol'e v SSSR* (Moscow: Izdatel'skii Sovet Russkoi Pravosalvnoi terkvi, 2008).

9. Karpov's report to Molotov, October 1944, Gosudarstvennyi arkhiv Rossiiskoi Federatsii (State Archive of the Russian Federation; hereafter GARF), f. 6991, op. 2, d. 18, ll. 45–49.

10. GARF, f. 6991, op. 2, d. 18, l. 84.

11. I. V. Pokrovskii, "Doklad o rezul'tatakh obsledovaniii pravovogo i khoziaistvennogo polozheniia monastyrei," GARF, f. 6991, op. 2, d. 18, ll. 3–11. There is no date on the report, but it appears to have been prepared in late 1945. It is also unclear why Pokrovskii counts fewer monasteries than other reports.

12. Pokrovskii, "Doklad," GARF, f. 6991, op. 2, d. 18, l. 12.

13. Ibid., ll. 12–15.

14. Chumachenko, *Church and State*, 82.

15. See Kenworthy, *Heart of Russia*, chap. 9; and Jennifer Jean Wynot, *Keeping the Faith: Russian Orthodox Monasticism in the Soviet Union, 1917–1939* (College Station: Texas A&M University Press, 2004).

16. Secret Memorandum from N. Chesnokov of Sovnarkom to Karpov, November 15, 1946, GARF, f. 6991, op. 1, d. 82, l. 67.

17. Vladislav Tsypin, *Istoriia Russkoi tserkvi, 1917–1997* (Moscow: Izd. Spaso-Preobrazhenskogo Valaamskogo monastyria, 1997), 329.

18. Kenworthy, *Heart of Russia*, chap. 8.

19. Robert H. Greene, *Bodies Like Bright Stars: Saints and Relics in Orthodox Russia* (DeKalb: Northern Illinois University Press, 2010).

20. Andronik (Trubachev), *Zakrytie Troitse-Sergievoi Lavry i sud'ba moshchei prepodobnogo Sergiia Radonezhskogo v 1918–1946 gg.* (Moscow: Izdatel'skii Sovet Russkoi Pravoslavnoi tserkvi, 2008), 297–99; Chumachenko, *Church and State*, 81.

21. On the reopening, see Sergei Boskin, "Paskha 1946 goda: Otkrytie Lavry Prepodobnogo Sergiia," *Russkii arkhiv*, no. 1 (1990): 119–32; also printed, with

the same title, in *Troitskoe slovo*, no. 4 (1990): 16–30; and G. A. Pyl'neva, *V Lavre prepodobnogo Sergiia: iz dnevnika (1946–1996)* (Moscow: Podvor'e Sviato-Troitskoi Sergievoi Lavry, 2006), 8–17. (Details differ on some points.)

22. "Sviateishii Patriarkh Aleksii I i vosstanovlenie Sviato-Troitskoi Sergievoi Lavry," *Al'fa i Omega* 22, no. 4 (1999): 193–200.

23. *Pis'ma patriarkha Aleksiia I v Sovet po delam Russkoi Pravoslavnoi Tserkvi pri Sovete Narodnykh Komissarov-Sovete Ministrov SSSR 1945–1970 gg.*, 2 vols. (Moscow: Rosspen, 2009–10), 1:67.

24. Ibid., 68–69.

25. Ibid., 69.

26. Makarii (Veretennikov), "Arkhimandrit Gurii—Pervyi namestnik vozrozhdennoi Troitse-Sergievoi lavry," *Troitskii sbornik*, no. 2 (2002): 340.

27. Boskin, "Paskha 1946 goda," 124–27; Pyl'neva, *V Lavre prepodobnogo Sergiia*, 11–12; and Andronik (Trubachev), *Zakrytie Troitse-Sergievoi*, 297–99.

28. Letter of Patriarch Aleksii I to Karpov, April 29, 1946, *Pis'ma patriarkha Aleksiia*, 1:149.

29. Makarii (Veretennikov), "Arkhimandrit Gurii," 341.

30. Letter of Patriarch Aleksii I to Karpov, July 2, 1946, *Pis'ma patriarkha Aleksiia*, 1:169.

31. See ibid., n. 1.

32. See M. V. Shkarovskii, *Aleksandro-Nevskoe bratstvo 1918–1932 gg.* (Saint Petersburg: Pravoslavnyi Sankt-Peterburg, 2003).

33. Ioann (Vendland), *Kniaz' Fedor (Chernyi), Mitropolit Gurii (Egorov): Istoricheskii ocherkii*, 81–117; Makarii (Veretennikov), "Arkhimandrit Gurii," 337–38.

34. He passed away in 1965 when metropolitan of the Crimea. See "Gurii (Egorov)," *Pravoslavnaia Entsiklopediia* (Moscow: Tserkovno-nauchnyi tsentr 'Pravoslavnaia entsiklopediia,' 2000), 13:473–74.

35. On the first inhabitants, see Boskin, "Paskha 1946 goda," 127–32; Sergii Golubtsov, *Troitse-Sergieva Lavra za poslednie sto let* (Moscow: Izd. Pravoslavnogo bratstva Sporuchnitsy greshnykh, 1998), 97–100; and Archimandrite Tikhon (Agrikov), *U Troitsy okrylennye: Vospominnaniia* (Sergiev Posad: Trinity-Sergius Lavra, 2000); note that this work was published in three parts in two books—parts I and II in the first book, and part III in the second book. On the author of these memoirs, see Tikhon (Agrikov), *Zhizneopisanie, propovedi, pis'ma* (Sergiev Posad: Trinity-Sergius Lavra, 2008).

36. Ioann (Vendland), *Kniaz' Fedor (Chernyi), Mitropolit Gurii (Egorov)*, 129.

37. Tsentral'nyi gosudarstvennyi arkhiv Moskovskoi oblasti (Central State Archive of Moscow Oblast; hereafter TsGAMO), f. 7383, op. 1, d. 11, l. 9.

38. Nikolai Mitrokhin, "Arkhimandrit Naum i 'naumovtsy' kak kvintessentsiia sovremennogo starchestva," in *Religioznye praktiki v sovremennoi Rossii: Sbornik statei*, ed. K. Russele and A. Agadjanian (Moscow: Novoe izdatel'stvo, 2006), 133. Mitrokhin maintains that Gurii was sent to Tashkent as a kind of exile because of his conservative monastic views, although from Vendland's account it appears that he expected to end up in Tashkent from the beginning of his service as Trinity-Sergius prior. See Ioann (Vendland), *Kniaz' Fedor (Chernyi), Mitropolit Gurii (Egorov)*, 128. On the Lavra's prerevolutionary monarchism, nationalism, and anti-Semitism, see Kenworthy, *Heart of Russia*, chap. 7.

39. *Pis'ma patriarkha Aleksiia*, 1:184.

40. Letter from Aleksii I to G. G. Karpov, July 23, 1953, *Pis'ma patriarkha Aleksiia*, 1:711, 717.

41. See Konstantin Malyk, "Vyskokopreosviashchennyi mitropolit Ioann," *ZhMP*, no. 12 (1990): 42–44; "Ioann (Razumov)," *Pravoslavnaia entsiklopediia*, 23:439–40.

42. "Veniamin (Milov)," *Pravoslavnaia entsiklopediia*, 7:637–38; Veniamin wrote a memoir in the years 1928–33 that is a remarkable account of the years before and after the Revolution. See Episkop Veniamin (Milov), *Dnevnik Inoka* (Sergiev Posad: Sviato-Troitskaia Sergieva Lavra, 1999).

43. Episkop Veniamin (Milov), *Krupitsy slova Bozhiia* (Sergiev Posad: Sviato-Troitskaia Sergieva Lavra, 1999), 77–81. Manuscripts of Veniamin's sermons from 1928 and from 1946 to 1949 were published in this volume for the first time.

44. Veniamin (Milov), *Krupitsy*, 81–84.

45. Ibid., 85.

46. Trushin's report to Karpov on the conditions and activities of the Church in Moscow and the Moscow region, January 10, 1947, TsGAMO, f. 7383, op. 1, d. 11, l. 9. That number included 6 archimandrites, 5 hieromonks, 3 hegumens, 2 hierodeacons, 1 priest, 1 monk, and 3 novices. Hereafter, "Trushin's report" will refer to the regular reports that he submitted on the conditions of the Church in Moscow and the Moscow region to the Council for Russian Orthodox Church Affairs.

47. In Orthodox monasticism (by contrast with Roman Catholic religious orders), monks are frequently not ordained to holy orders, so this preponderance of ordained clergy is unusual.

48. See the list of brothers with brief biographical information as of January 1, 1948, Trushin's report of November 2, 1948, TsGAMO, f. 7383, op. 1, d. 14, ll. 3–7, and for February 1949, Trushin's report for March 12, 1949, ibid., d. 17, ll. 37–39. See also Pyl'neva, *V Lavre prepodobnogo Sergiia*, 30–37.

49. Shkarovskii, "Russkaia pravoslavnaia tserkov' v 1943–1957 godakh," 46–50.

50. Chumachenko, *Church and State*, 87–89.

51. Trushin's report, January 10, 1946, TsGAMO, f. 7383, op. 1, d. 11, l. 9.

52. Trushin's report, November 11, 1948, TsGAMO, f. 7383, op. 1, d. 14, l. 8.

53. Trushin's report, March 12, 1949, TsGAMO, f. 7383, op. 1, d. 17, l. 40.

54. Trushin's secret report on the activities of Trinity-Sergius for 1956, November 6, 1957, TsGAMO, f. 7383, op. 1, d. 41, l. 32.

55. On the nineteenth century, see Kenworthy, *Heart of Russia*, 183–86.

56. Trushin's report, November 11, 1948, TsGAMO, f. 7383, op. 1, d. 11, l. 9; d. 14, l. 8.

57. Trushin's report, February 3, 1958, TsGAMO, f. 7383, op. 1, d. 44, ll. 13–15; Trushin provided averages of sources of income for the 1952–57 period.

58. Roslof, "'Faces of the Faceless,'" 115.

59. Trushin's report, March 12, 1949, TsGAMO, f. 7383, op. 1, d. 17, l. 34ob.

60. On the politics and establishment of the museum, see Kenworthy, *Heart of Russia*, 306–12, 319–25.

61. Trushin's report, March 12, 1949, TsGAMO, f. 7383, op. 1, d. 17, ll. 34ob–35ob. Tikhon, *U Troitsy okrylennye*, part I, 45, also mentions the disrepair of the grounds at the time the monastery was reopened.

62. Karpov's memorandum to Trushin, October 8, 1946, TsGAMO, f. 7383, op. 1, d. 9, l. 23.

63. *Pis'ma patriarkha Aleksiia*, 1:370–72.

64. Trushin's report, March 12, 1949, TsGAMO, f. 7383, op. 1, d. 17, ll. 34ob–35. See also op. 3, d. 3, ll. 27–28; and *Pis'ma patriarkha Aleksiia*, 1:370–72, 376–77, 473.
65. Trushin's report, January 10, 1946, TsGAMO, f. 7383, op. 1, d. 11, ll. 8ob–9.
66. Trushin's report, February 3, 1958, TsGAMO, f. 7383, op. 1, d. 44, ll. 19–20.
67. Trushin's secret memorandum to Karpov, January 11, 1947, TsGAMO, f. 7383, op. 1, d. 12, l. 5.
68. *Pis'ma patriarkha Aleksiia*, 1:536.
69. Head of the administration for protection of architectural monuments Sh. Ratiia to Archimandrite Ioann, February 8, 1950, TsGAMO, f. 7383, op. 3, d. 3, l. 43.
70. Stalin's order of October 6, 1951, GARF, f. 6991, op. 2, d. 44, l. 64.
71. Trushin's report, March 12, 1949, TsGAMO, f. 7383, op. 1, d. 17, ll. 35ob–36ob.
72. Trushin's list of previously convicted monks, 1948, TsGAMO, f. 7383, op. 1, d. 15, l. 42. The names were Archimandrite Nifont (Bugaevskii), Hieromonk Iona (Nebogatov), Hieromonk Veniamin (Gorodkov), Hierodeacon Iosif (Evseenok), and Hierodeacon Serafim (Shustov). On removing clergy for passport restrictions, see Chumachenko, *Church and State*, 113.
73. Trushin's report, March 12, 1949, TsGAMO, f. 7383, op. 1, d. 17, l. 39ob. On the phenomenon of "repeat offenders," see Chumachenko, *Church and State*, 113.
74. *Za Khrista postradavshie: goneniia na Russkuiu pravoslavnuiu tserkov' v 1917–1956: biograficheskii spravochnik* (Moscow: Izd. Pravoslavnogo Sviato-Tikhonovskogo bogoslovskogo instituta, 1997), 239–40. For his letters from exile, see *Dnevnik Inoka*, 145–249.
75. Mitrokhin implies that the first generation of the Lavra's monks were exiled because restoring a conservative monastic ethos also meant reviving anti-Soviet monarchist political views, although there is no direct evidence for this in the documents.
76. Shkarovskii, "Russkaia pravoslavnaia tserkov' v 1943–1957 godakh," 50–55; Chumachenko, *Church and State*, 125–41.
77. "Na netlennuiu zhizn' prikhodu dnes'," *ZhMP*, no. 8 (1990): 9–11.
78. This is a particularly scandalous denunciation by an employee of the Lavra who accused one of the senior monks of getting him drunk and then raping him, and also alleged that many of the monks were practicing homosexuality. See TsGAMO, f. 7383, op. 3, d. 10a, l. 100.
79. Archimandrite Ioann complained of the contrast between the church bells calling pilgrims to prayer alongside drunken shouts and the blasting radio of military personnel housed in the Lavra's buildings. See the letter of Patriarch Aleksii I to Karpov, May 30, 1953, *Pis'ma patriarkha Aleksiia*, 1:697–700.
80. *Pis'ma patriarkha Aleksiia*, 2:99–100.
81. Shkarovskii, "Russkaia pravoslavnaia tserkov' v 1943–1957 godakh," 52–54; Chumachenko, *Church and State*, 128.
82. Soviet of Ministers decree on the transfer of buildings of Trinity-Sergius to the Moscow Patriarchate, August 20, 1956, GARF, f. 6991, op. 2, d. 44, l. 1g.
83. See *Pis'ma patriarkha Aleksiia*, 2:182–84, 225, 276–77.
84. Patriarch Aleksii I's letter to Karpov, not later than June 2, 1958, *Pis'ma patriarkha Aleksiia*, 2:225–26.
85. E.g., in April 1945, Winston Churchill's wife visited the monastery.
86. Tsypin, *Istoriia Russkoi tserkvi*, 340.
87. Karpov's report to Trushin about the Festival of Youth, August 21, 1957, TsGAMO, f. 7383, op. 1, d. 40, ll. 219–20.

88. Trushin's secret report on the activities of Trinity-Sergius for 1956, November 6, 1957, TsGAMO, f. 7383, op. 1, d. 41, ll. 28–30.

89. Trushin's report, February 3, 1958, TsGAMO, f. 7383, op. 1, d. 44, ll. 15–17.

90. Trushin's secret report on the activities of Trinity-Sergius for 1956, November 6, 1957, TsGAMO, f. 7383, op. 1, d. 41, l. 30.

91. Trushin's report, February 3, 1958, TsGAMO, f. 7383, op. 1, d. 44, ll. 15–16.

92. Trushin's secret report on the activities of Trinity-Sergius for 1956, November 6, 1957, TsGAMO, f. 7383, op. 1, d. 41, l. 30.

93. Trushin's report, February 3, 1958, TsGAMO, f. 7383, op. 1, d. 44, ll. 16–19. A number of districts in Moscow Province provided a few recruits each year to the monastery or the theological schools, whereas ten had come from Moscow itself.

94. Chumachenko, *Church and State*, 138. On Soviet anxieties about religion among the youth, see also chapter 8, by Zoe Knox, in the present volume.

95. Trushin's secret report to Karpov, January 31, 1957, TsGAMO, f. 7383, op. 1, d. 41, ll. 1–3; Trushin's secret report on the activities of Trinity-Sergius for 1956, November 6, 1957, ibid., l. 31.

96. Pyl'neva, *V Lavre prepodobnogo Sergiia*, 31. See also Tikhon, *U Troitsy okrylennye*, part III, 29–47.

97. Trushin's secret report to Karpov, January 31, 1957, TsGAMO, f. 7383, op. 1, d. 41, ll. 2–3.

98. Trushin's secret report on the activities of Trinity-Sergius for 1956, November 6, 1957, TsGAMO, f. 7383, op. 1, d. 41, ll. 31–32.

99. See Roslof, "'Faces of the Faceless,'" 117.

100. See Chumachenko, *Church and State*, 71.

101. See M. Shkarovskii, "Russkaia pravoslavnaia tserkov' v 1958–1964 godakh," *Voprosy istorii*, no. 2 (1999): 43–58, which recently appeared in translation as "The Russian Orthodox Church in 1958–1964," *Russian Studies in History* 50, no. 3 (Winter 2011–12): 71–95; Chumachenko, *Church and State*; and Shkarovskii, *Russkaia Pravoslavnaia Tserkov' pri Staline i Khrushcheve*, 359–93.

102. Shkarovskii, "Russkaia pravoslavnaia tserkov' v 1958–1964 godakh," 42–44.

103. Resolution of the Soviet of Ministers, October 16, 1958, GARF, f. 6991, op. 2, d. 44, l. 118.

104. Shkarovskii, "Russkaia pravoslavnaia tserkov' v 1958–1964 godakh," 44–46; see also Chumachenko, *Church and State*, 143–88; Nathaniel Davis, *A Long Walk to Church: A Contemporary History of Russian Orthodoxy*, 2nd ed. (Boulder, Colo.: Westview Press, 2003), 33–45; and Michael Bourdeaux, *Patriarch and Prophets: Persecution of the Russian Orthodox Church Today* (New York: Praeger Publishers, 1970), 85–116. For many discussions of monasteries in Patriarch Aleksii I's correspondence, see *Pis'ma patriarkha Aleksiia*, vol. 2.

105. See Pimen (Khmelevskii), *Dnevniki: Russkaia Dukhovnaia missiia v Ierusalime 1955–1957* (Saratov: Izd. Saratovskoi eparkhii, 2008).

106. L. Vladyshevskaia, "Pamiati arkhiepiskopa Saratovskogo i Vol'skogo Pimena," *ZhMP*, no. 4 (1994): 139–44. A remarkable collection of documents—including his diary, letters, reports, and remembrances about Pimen—has recently been published: Pimen (Khmelevskii), *Dnevniki: Sviato-Troitskaia Sergieva Lavra, 1957–1964* (Saratov: Izd. Saratovskoi mitropolii, 2011).

107. See Golubtsov, *Troitse-Sergieva Lavra*, 132, 203 n. 22; on several of these monks, see Tikhon, *U Troitsy okrylennye*, part III.

108. Trushin's report, February 3, 1958, TsGAMO, f. 7383, op. 1, d. 44, ll. 14–15.

109. See his obituary in *ZhMP*, no. 3 (1981): 29, which states that he was transferred to Pskov in 1955.

110. Trushin's report, February 3, 1958, TsGAMO, f. 7383, op. 1, d. 44, l. 15.

111. Trushin's report on activities of Trinity-Sergius for 1956, November 6, 1957, TsGAMO, f. 7383, op. 1, d. 41, l. 32.

112. Trushin's report, February 3, 1958, TsGAMO, f. 7383, op. 1, d. 44, l. 14. During the summer these pilgrims came not only from the environs of the monastery, but from Moscow and other cities. Most pilgrims were middle-aged to older women, and they came both individually or in groups of five to ten persons.

113. On pilgrimage before the Revolution, see Kenworthy, *Heart of Russia*, chap. 5; Chris J. Chulos, "Religious and Secular Aspects of Pilgrimage in Modern Russia," *Byzantium and the North/Act Byzantina Fennica* 9 (1999): 21–58; Chris J. Chulos, *Converging Worlds: Religion and Community in Peasant Russia, 1861–1917* (DeKalb: Northern Illinois University Press, 2003); Christine Worobec, "Miraculous Healings," in *Sacred Stories: Religion and Spirituality in Modern Russia*, edited by Mark D. Steinberg and Heather J. Coleman (Bloomington: Indiana University Press, 2007), 22–43; Roy R. Robson, "Transforming Solovki: Pilgrim Narratives, Modernization, and Late Imperial Monastic Life," in *Sacred Stories*, ed. Steinberg and Coleman, 44–60; Greene, *Bodies Like Bright Stars*.

114. See also chapter 5, by Stella Rock, in the present volume.

115. Kenworthy, *Heart of Russia*, 312–19; Greene, *Bodies Like Bright Stars*.

116. Shkarovskii, "Russkaia pravoslavnaia tserkov' v 1958–1964 godakh," 44.

117. As summarized in Trushin's secret memorandum to Kaprov, April 1, 1959, TsGAMO, f. 7383, op. 1, d. 47, l. 35.

118. Karpov's notes on a meeting with Patriarch Aleksii, GARF, f. 6991, op. 2, d. 227, l. 71. I am grateful to Stella Rock for this reference.

119. Trushin's secret memorandum to Kaprov, April 1, 1959, TsGAMO, f. 7383, op. 1, d. 47, ll. 35–36. See Chumachenko, *Church and State*, 155. On shriekers, see Christine D. Worobec, *Possessed: Women, Witches and Demons in Imperial Russia* (DeKalb: Northern Illinois University Press, 2001).

120. Pimen (Khmelevskii), *Dnevniki: Sviato-Troitskaia Sergieva Lavra*, 44–45, 95–96, 444–48, 453–57. Shkarovskii, in "Russkaia pravoslavnaia tserkov' v 1958–1964 godakh," 46, mentions a similar episode for October 1960.

121. Trushin's report, February 3, 1958, TsGAMO, f. 7383, op. 1, d. 44, l. 20; Director of the Zagorsk museum, G. Okskii, July 1961, TsGAMO, f. 7383, op. 3, d. 30, l. 216; see also Pimen (Khmelevskii), *Dnevniki: Sviato-Troitskaia Sergieva Lavra*, 9.

122. Intourist representative Ankudinov to Trushin, Information on deficiencies in showing foreign tourists the Zagorsk museum, September 12, 1960, TsGAMO, f. 7383, op. 1, d. 51, ll. 28–30.

123. Trushin, Information on the reception of Prior Archimandrite Pimen (Khmelevskii), May 19, 1961, TsGAMO, f. 7383, op. 3, d. 30, ll. 209–10.

124. This document evidently constitutes minutes of a meeting concerning the Zagorsk museum in 1961. See ibid., l. 220.

125. See Sergii Golubtsov, "Venok na mogilu: Arkhiepiskop Saratovskii i Vol'skii Pimen (Khmelevskoi) v bytnost' namestnikom Troitse-Sergievoi Lavry," in Pimen (Khmelevskii), *Dnevniki: Sviato-Troitskaia Sergieva Lavra*, 394.

126. For an overview, see Pimen (Khmelevskii), *Dnevniki: Sviato-Troitskaia Sergieva Lavra*, 3–52, and throughout the volume for relevant documents.

127. Davis, *Long Walk to Church*, 164–66.

128. Report of Pimen (Khmelevskii) to Patriarch Aleksii I, August 14, 1959, *Pis'ma patriarkha Aleksiia*, 2:278–79; Council for Religious Affairs, statistical data on churches and monasteries for 1967, GARF, f. 6991, op. 6, d. 25, l. 17; and Trushin's report on statistical data for 1972, GARF, f. 6991, op. 6, d. 480, l. 83.

129. Davis, *Long Walk to Church*, 172–74.

130. See Christine Worobec, "Lived Orthodoxy in Imperial Russia," *Kritika* 7, no. 2 (2006); 329–50; Gregory L. Freeze, "Institutionalizing Piety: The Church and Popular Religion, 1750–1850," in *Imperial Russia: New Histories for the Empire*, edited by Jane Burbank and David L. Ransel (Bloomington: Indiana University Press, 1998), 210–49.

131. For this type of religious practice, see Jeanne Kormina and Sergey Shtyrkov, "St. Xenia as a Patron of Female Social Suffering: An Essay on Anthropological Hagiology," in *Multiple Moralities and Religion in Contemporary Russia*, edited by Jarrett Zigon (New York: Berghahn, 2011), 168–90.

## Chapter 5

## "They Burned the Pine, but the Place Remains All the Same": Pilgrimage in the Changing Landscape of Soviet Russia

*Stella Rock*

In 1989, a group of believers appealed to their bishop to secure permission for the procession of the cross that their pious ancestors had promised Saint Nicholas to hold annually. This procession, from the regional center of Kirov to the village of Velikoretskoe, had been illegal for thirty years. That year, though the local authorities refused permission to process via the "traditional" circular route of about 150 kilometers, diocesan clergy were permitted to lead pilgrims about 7 kilometers to Velikoretskoe and to celebrate a liturgy at the riverside shrine. Disregarding this officially sanctioned procession, a group of several hundred walked the circular route from Kirov, following elderly pilgrims who had continued to make the same journey, in secret, for decades.[1]

Despite substantial legislative restrictions and social pressures, Orthodox Christians continued to undertake private acts of peripatetic devotion, to join religious processions and to gather at shrines, throughout the Soviet period. Although Christian pilgrimage is a flexible religious practice and therefore is able to adapt to social and political change in a way that liturgy is not, Orthodox pilgrimage is centered on physical proximity to the holy, usually in the form of icons or relics, and rituals led by the clergy.² How Russian Orthodox believers continued to seek out and experience sacred space as these traditional channels to the sacred were restricted, destroyed, or desecrated is the focus of this chapter, which is based largely on local government and church records, memoirs,³ newspaper reports, and *samizdat* documents. In the pages that follow, I seek to examine how pilgrim practice adapted to the changing landscape of Soviet Russia through the lens of the Velikoretskoe procession of the cross.⁴ Bearing in mind the variable nature of Soviet policies toward the Russian Orthodox Church, and recent research that challenges the "believer–versus–Soviet citizen" model of historiography, it begins by addressing the changing nature of the threat that pilgrimages posed to the Soviet state, from the October Revolution to the Khrushchev period, and the efforts of Soviet authorities—sometimes in collaboration with the clerical hierarchy—to control it.⁵

## Pilgrimage as Public Spectacle, Political Protest, or Petitioning of the Supernatural?

Although the government's relationship with the ecclesiastical hierarchy varied over the Soviet period, at best the authorities sought to marginalize religion and relegate it to the private sphere. The various methods and policies—some counterproductive—by which the authorities attempted to curb religious practice have been well documented, but in attempting to curtail pilgrimage, the Soviet authorities were undertaking a massive task. The late nineteenth and early twentieth centuries saw, in the words of one scholar, an "explosion of peripatetic energy" as Russian Orthodox believers embraced the travel opportunities offered and promoted by emancipation, improved transport, high-profile canonizations, and a flourishing literature on saints and shrines.⁶ In response to this rise, the clergy promoted processions of the cross as a form of priest-led pilgrimage, which facilitated the regulation of pilgrim behaviors and made the vast number of shrine visitors more manageable.⁷ These religious processions, although generally starting and ending at a church or shrine, publicly testified to the porous boundary between the secular and the sacred. By carrying icons and crosses through streets and fields, believers effectively declared civic space sacred, and they demonstrated Orthodox Christianity's privileged position in Russian society.

The Bolsheviks swiftly set about erasing Russian Orthodoxy's very public stamp on civic life with the 1918 decree on the separation of church and state. Instructions on how to implement the decree, issued on August 24, 1918, banned the conducting of religious rituals in public places, and required "the written permission of the local Soviet authorities, which must be secured by the organizers each time in advance" for any religious procession.[8] Nevertheless, some effort was made by the authorities to accommodate demands for public religious practice, and they demonstrated a pragmatic laxity in applying legislation at critical points and places.[9] Later Soviet legislation clarified that religious processions, which were "an integral part of the liturgy" (e.g., at Easter) and processed around the "cult building" could be held without prior permission so long as the procession did "not interfere with the normal traffic of the street."[10] For nonessential processions, and those which strayed away from church grounds (e.g., traveling to shrines, carrying icons from parish to parish) permission still had to be gained in advance from the local authorities.

The need to confine religion to the private sphere was not the only reason for controlling public prayer and processions. In the febrile atmosphere that followed the October Revolution, processions proliferated, some of which were organized in protest at specific government measures such as the 1918 decree,[11] or to commemorate those who had been killed by the Bolsheviks in defense of the Church.[12] Even processions that were not clearly articulating opposition to a particular government measure, were—and are—sometimes difficult to distinguish from political protest.[13] In the summer of 1918, for example, the Red Army issued an order to mobilize young men from a Siberian village, Merkushino. The villagers refused the request (declaring that the men were needed for the harvest), attacked the government representatives who had announced the mobilization, and arrested ten members of the local Soviet. The memoirs of a local communist eyewitness record that the villagers then went on a "crusade" (*krestovyi pokhod*) against the Bolsheviks in Verkhutor'e, but church sources stress that this was a straightforward pilgrimage to the relics of their local saint, Saint Simeon of Verkhotur'e. The procession, apparently composed mainly of women and led by a priest with a cross, was escorted by peasants carrying hunting rifles and pitchforks. Whether or not the peasants' primary motivation was to take their troubles to the shrine of the local wonder-worker, the procession was interpreted by the Soviet authorities as armed insurrection and savagely repressed.[14]

Processions of the cross—legal and illegal—might also create, or result in, political protest and public disorder. Young observed the use of processions of the cross to disturb electoral processes in village life in the 1920s and early 1930s,[15] and in 1943 a religious procession in the Penza region, which began as thirty women processing through the town with icons, attracted over a hundred participants and ended in anti-Soviet agitation as one of the women leaders began to declaim against collective farms, "supposedly in the throes of religious ecstasy."[16] Large masses of people were unpredictable, and as conditions in the countryside worsened, such gatherings increased.

Bemoaning an increase in religious activity in 1921, especially in areas affected by famine, Soviet officials in the Viatka district (now Kirov Oblast) complained that priests sent their peasant parishioners "for permission for some [public] prayer service, [or] procession of the cross that has been held in a given region since . . . ancient times," and that in the face of spontaneous, unauthorized processions of the cross attracting crowds of thousands, "the local authorities are powerless to do anything."[17] Although the authorities feared civil unrest, the motive of those organizing processions was often to end drought or ward off an epidemic. In addition to being a traditional form of pilgrimage, processions of the cross are also defensive or apotropaic actions, organized in response to "extraordinary circumstances," such as invasion, famine, drought, and outbreaks of disease.[18]

Public demonstrations of Orthodox piety were also prompted by manifestations of religious fervor that proliferated in the 1920s. Icons and letters from heaven miraculously appeared, wondrously renewed icons and apple trees attracted hundreds and sometimes thousands of pilgrims, and an appearance by the Mother of God prompted tens of thousands to carry crosses to a sacred site in Right Bank Ukraine.[19] The responses of the authorities to these phenomena varied across time and place. Central government was sometimes dismayed by the excessive enthusiasm with which regional atheist agitators and Komsomol youth attacked local shrines, but local authorities could also behave in ways that reflected sympathy for the locally miraculous at odds with the central drive to marginalize or eradicate religion.[20] In 1922, for example, an unfortunate local official in the Voronezh region who had permitted a procession with a miraculously renewed icon was put on trial, as well as the group of believers who were deemed to have spread rumors about the miracle.[21]

It was not uncommon for local officials to use their powers to ensure that religious processions and pilgrimages did take place, perceiving them as beneficial for the local community rather than as demonstrations of resistance to Soviet power.²² The extraordinary tale of the members of the local *ispolkom* (executive committee) in Ostashkov, in the Tver region, who in 1920 made a pilgrimage to venerate the relics of Saint Nil Stolbenskii on his feast day and gave state employees a holiday so that they too could visit his shrine, reflects the continuing importance of local saints. As Greene has so clearly demonstrated, communities that accepted Soviet authority were nevertheless often reluctant to reject the local wonder-worker with whom they had a long and reciprocal relationship, and on whom they depended for good harvests, health, and clement weather.²³

Saints of national importance also continued to draw pilgrims from across the Soviet Union. An émigré writer who made a pilgrimage to Saint Seraphim's shrines of Diveevo and Sarov in 1926 wrote that "both the young and old rose up and hastened to Sarov. I remember how a whole pilgrimage set out from our city [Kyiv] with those distinguished clergymen . . . and after them stretched the lay people. Some soulful, inexplicable, but powerful need to visit the Saint enveloped everyone. Some on returning back related what they saw and experienced, and were immediately replaced by others. And this happened everywhere."²⁴ Reflecting on the subsequent closure of Saint Seraphim's shrines, this pilgrim interpreted the nationwide peripatetic impulse as a portentous indicator of the devastation to come.²⁵

Monastic centers such as Diveevo and Sarov, repositories of the wonder-working shrines and icons sought out by Orthodox pilgrims, were subjected to forcible exposés of their "fraudulent" relics from 1919 through the early 1920s. These exposures were contentious even among the Communist Party faithful and perceived by some to be spreading religiosity rather than dispelling it, as well as unnecessarily embittering believers.²⁶ Although relics were supposed to be transferred to museums,²⁷ this often proved impractical and the bodies were simply reinterred and continued to attract pilgrims like those from Ostashkov, who venerated Saint Nil a year after his remains were exposed. Even those displayed in public museums sometimes became the locus of pilgrimages.²⁸ By the 1920s, many monastic communities had reinvented themselves as workers' cooperatives or agricultural communes, or had been turned into state farms worked at least partly by their former inhabitants, which enabled them to remain in the locus of the shrine and to continue receiving pilgrims.²⁹ When the Diveevo commune was finally closed in August 1927, this reflected a nationwide campaign against monasticism, which ensured that by 1930 no functioning Russian Orthodox monastery remained on Soviet soil.³⁰

The 1929 Law on Religious Associations ushered in further devastation, with a decade of mass closures of churches and arrests of clergy.[31] This legislation made holding religious marches, rituals, and ceremonies outside a religious organization's location even more difficult, although illegal processions, sometimes attracting hundreds of participants, continued sporadically in the 1930s.[32] As clergy numbers dwindled, laity increasingly took over the organization of processions and public prayers, and as shrines were closed and desecrated, natural features such as springs increasingly became the locus of the sacred.[33] One pilgrim, Vera Vasilevskaia, recounts how when she made a secret pilgrimage to Diveevo more than a decade after the convent's closure, it seemed that beneath the "anthill" of Soviet life, the sacred continued to flow in Diveevo, symbolized most powerfully by the holy springs that refused to remain buried:

> After the closure of the monastery they assiduously filled them in with earth, in order to obliterate people's memory of their grace-giving power. But it didn't help: now here, now there the spring water broke afresh through the earth's surface. To begin with it surprised me when I saw how someone passing by would bend down to the ground, looking and listening attentively to something. Drawing nearer I heard the rapturous whisper: "the spring is flowing!" The spring was filled in again, and again flowed free—a living symbol of God's unquenchable mercy to humankind.[34]

Although, by the late 1930s, the Orthodox essentials of sacraments and relics were almost unobtainable, pilgrims like Vera continued to search out the sacred in secret.[35]

## "Why in Our Times Do Such Wild Rites Still Exist?" Secularized Sensibilities and the Postwar Rise in Pilgrimage

Evidence for pilgrim practices in the 1930s is slim, but as has been well documented, policy changes ushered in by World War II and international politics significantly improved the fortunes of the Russian Orthodox Church from 1943 onward, and public displays of Orthodoxy increased during the war years.[36] Although further instructions forbidding processions and prayers at venerated places were issued by the Council for Russian Orthodox Church Affairs in February 1944, the late 1940s saw a notable rise in the number of believers participating in processions and mass acts of pilgrimage.[37] A 1949 report on "religious survivals manifested in the fulfillment of rites and mass prayer at illegal (unregistered) churches" identified a number of sites that were attracting large numbers of pilgrims. Some sites, like Lake Svetloyar, at which ten thousand pilgrims gathered in 1948, or the holy apple tree in Voronezh region, which—despite being felled—drew "a crowd of pilgrims," were natural features apparently unconnected with former church shrines. Others were the wells, springs, or ruins of former monasteries and churches, such as the "thunder well" on the site of a former chapel in Orlov Oblast, at which "prayers take place without the participation of the clergy, as in this region there are no churches," or the ruined church in Chuvashia, where "amid heaps of rubble and bricks," an icon of Saint Nicholas the Wonderworker was placed, at which believers left money, food, and candles.[38]

The massive postwar increase in pilgrimages about thirty years after a revolution that was supposed to make religion irrelevant was an embarrassing anomaly. Public processions were still occasionally perceived as dangerous, because by their very nature they were uncontained, difficult to control, and comprised an arena in which unregistered clergy and anti-Soviet agitators could spread sedition,[39] but increasingly they were viewed as public manifestations of a mindset (unscientific, superstitious, reactionary) that was incompatible with socialist progress.[40] "Why in our times," lamented a journalist observing pilgrims at Lake Svetloyar in 1959, "do such wild rites still exist? Can we really call the people crawling [round the lake] our contemporaries?"[41] Pilgrimages were also portrayed as facilitating behaviors, such as drunkenness and fighting, that were damaging to Soviet society, with the disruption to agricultural work caused by summer pilgrimages in particular singled out in a secret July 1954 report from the Central Committee of the Communist Party of the Soviet Union and in newspaper stories criticizing the resurgence of pilgrimages.[42]

"Our successes do not depend on 'Saint Nicholas' or 'the Savior,' nor on 'gods' or 'saints,' but on the selfless, creative work of workers, collective farm workers and intelligentsia," *Kirovskaia Pravda* protested in 1955, faced with the annual pilgrimage to Velikoretskoe.[43] Greene has demonstrated the fervent efforts that believers made to keep their wonder-workers physically accessible so that they might be directly appealed to in times of need, but thirty years after the campaign against relics Soviet bureaucrats were bemused to discover that believers, like the pilgrim who walked from Urdmurtia to Velikoretskoe in 1949 after his legs were healed, were still vowing to visit a shrine in return for some benefit.[44] Despite decades of propaganda campaigns and scientific atheist education, it was clear that many Soviet citizens continued to rely on supernatural agents of change.

In response to this increasing demonstration of religious belief in the postwar period, Soviet authorities renewed legislative restrictions and increased efforts to restrict access to the sacred. Khrushchev's antireligious campaign ushered in a significant period of repression, and whereas earlier legislation had already made religious processions, rituals, and ceremonies outside of a religious organization's location illegal without prior permission, the instructions issued in early 1961 for applying the 1929 law explicitly forbade clergy or religious associations to organize pilgrimage to "so-called holy places."[45]

The tactic of co-opting the Church hierarchy into efforts to curtail extra-church religious practice should also be noted. Already in 1948, the Holy Synod had been prompted to adopt a resolution that reminded the clergy with regard to "the performance of these liturgical services [intercessory prayers, e.g., for rain or clement weather] in public places, and also the conducting of processions of the cross from one locality to another, as a clear violation of the principle of the separation of church and state, this cannot be permitted by diocesan authorities."[46] When, on November 28, 1958, the Presidium of the Central Committee of the Communist Party of the Soviet Union adopted the resolution "On Measures for Stopping Pilgrimages to So-Called Holy Sites," it was backed up by a letter from the Patriarchate in 1959 to all dioceses. The patriarch declared it necessary for parish clergy to receive "appropriate instruction so that false, supposedly holy, memorials should not replace our genuine shrines and church rituals," and for local believers to be told that "pilgrimage to so-called 'holy sites' not venerated by the Church" was not permissible. Finally, diocesan clergy were requested to report back on measures taken to eliminate such "illegal and unauthorized phenomena."[47]

Across the Soviet Union, local authorities launched a campaign to shut down the holy places in their regions. The annual summer procession to the springs at the Kursk-Korennaia hermitage attracted up to 15,000 pilgrims annually in the postwar period, but on March 31, 1959, the Council for Russian Orthodox Church Affairs reported the successful closure of this pilgrimage.[48] At the same meeting, the failure of the Kirov regional authorities to eradicate the Velikoretskoe procession of the cross was raised.[49]

## A Case Study: The Velikoretskoe Procession of the Cross

The Velikoretskoe procession of the cross commemorates the miraculous appearance of an icon of Saint Nicholas on the banks of the Velikaia River, apparently in the fourteenth century, and its relocation to the medieval regional center of Khlynov (currently still called Kirov, but local residents are currently debating a return to the prerevolutionary name of Viatka). Clergy escort the icon from the diocesan cathedral in Kirov to the riverbank shrine at Velikoretskoe, in time to celebrate the anniversary of its appearance on June 6 (new style), before returning it to the cathedral. Pilgrims might accompany the icon the entire way or ceremonially escort it out of the city and/or into the shrine. In the prerevolutionary period, venerating the icon in the place of its miraculous appearance rather than walking the circuit was the pilgrims' primary goal; post-Soviet pilgrims are more focused on the procession itself, which now annually covers the circular route between June 3 and 8.

*Late Imperial Pilgrimage Practice*

The structure of this pilgrimage has varied significantly in the period of its documentable history, and its fourteenth-century origins are contested by some.[50] The date, route, and duration of the procession have changed, and until the ecclesiastical authorities ruled that the procession should travel overland in the late eighteenth century, the icon and accompanying clergy traveled to Velikoretskoe by boat.[51] The process of movement and mode of travel were of less importance for pilgrims than the goal of venerating the icon at the riverbank shrine, and a participant in the 1892 procession observed that whereas peasant pilgrims accompanied the icon on foot, better-off townsfolk caught the ferry and then continued their journey by horse.[52] The wonder-working icon itself, and the clergy who helped believers fulfill their obligations to God, Saint Nicholas, and their deceased relatives, were central to the pilgrimage experience.

Upon arrival into the village, the icon was carried first to the Transfiguration Church (one of several), where an evening vigil service took place. On the following day prayers were said before the visiting wonder-working icon, and before the resident local icon of Saint Nicholas in Saint Nicholas's Church. After a liturgy, the former was carried in festive procession down to the riverbank chapel where a water blessing service was conducted.[53] In the late nineteenth century, according to the then-priest of Velikoretskoe, "every one of the pilgrims visiting Velikoretskoe . . . considered it a holy obligation to celebrate a *moleben* [supplicatory prayer service] before this image [of Saint Nicholas]."[54] In addition to making offerings in return for a *moleben* celebrated by local clergy, pilgrims also requested memorial services for their dead, which took place in the local cemetery church.[55]

In addition to these clerically administered rituals, pilgrims collected water from a fountain in a chapel between the churches in the village, considering it holy because the fountain was cross-shaped, and "almost every pilgrim considered it a duty to take home water from the spring where the miraculous icon appeared."[56] Pilgrims might also make offerings by throwing money and jewelry into the water, and these and other behaviors, have been perceived as less than orthodox by some observers.[57] In 1869, an unfavorable article about the procession in the secular newspaper *Golos* provoked the diocesan newspaper to dismiss the offering of sheep to Saint Nicholas (misunderstood as some sort of "sacrifice"), ordering of prayers for healthy livestock, washing babies in spring water, searching for "curative herbs for [protection from] illness, and porous stone," and the driving of wooden stakes into graves as phenomena that belong "not to the Velikoretskoe procession of the cross but to a minority of the dark Russian simple people."[58] Clerically unregulated pilgrim practices, which became an important lever in Soviet efforts to shut down the pilgrimage, have been perceived or misread as "superstitious" by Tsarist and Soviet observers alike.[59]

*Conflicts and Continuity: Early Soviet Practice*

The icon seems to have been carried in procession annually throughout the 1920s, although the Renovationist schism affected the riverside shrine as it did the diocese as a whole.[60] According to Father Andrei Dudin, a local historian and deputy leader of the Velikoretskoe procession, in 1921 the diocese witnessed an increase in processions attended by significant numbers of people.[61] Nevertheless, by 1925 only 2,000 to 2,500 peasants accompanied the icon from Viatka Cathedral to Velikoretskoe,[62] compared with the 50,000 pilgrims who made it to the banks of the river a decade earlier.[63]

The icon itself became a point of friction in the middle to late 1920s. Renovationist cathedral clergy heading the procession that carried the icon into Velikoretskoe in 1925 were met by local "Tikhonite" clergy who contested their right to officiate at the *moleben* to Saint Nicholas in the village churches. "Tikhonite pilgrims, led by the church council, prevented the Renovationists from entering the church service and they began to conduct the ritual on the place of the icon's 'appearance' in the open air." They were not allowed to perform even this ritual, however, because the cathedral's icons were snatched away from them and carried into the local church. One Renovationist priest narrowly escaped being thrown into the river during the fracas.[64] Though some pilgrims joined in the fray, others visiting the shrine were scandalized by these conflicts and complained that they had been unable to fulfill their promise to celebrate a *moleben* because the priests were busy squabbling.

*Improvising the Sacred: Pilgrimage without the Icon*

Viatka Diocese, like the rest of the country, suffered large-scale repression and church closures after 1929,[65] and in the chaos surrounding the 1930 closure and subsequent demolition of Viatka Cathedral, the icon disappeared.[66] Although the icon could no longer be ceremonially escorted to Velikoretskoe by cathedral clergy, and the procession's ceremonial departure point was no longer accessible, in the early 1930s significant numbers of believers continued to mark the traditional feast by traveling to the riverside shrine. The parish priest in Velikoretskoe was rewarded with a gold cross for having managed a "huge convergence of pilgrims" and having ensured that the celebrations were orderly and "marked by a festive procession of the cross to the place where the image of Saint Nicholas appeared" in 1932, presumably using the local icon of Saint Nicholas in the absence of the wonder-working original.[67]

Velikoretskoe's last remaining church—which had been temporarily closed several times in the mid-1930s, ostensibly as a measure against epidemics—was vandalized by hooligans from the local children's home and closed in 1938. The priest was arrested, and despite continual petitioning of the authorities by local believers, the church remained closed for almost a decade.[68] With no cathedral, no functioning church at the shrine, and no icon, one might expect the pilgrimage to have disappeared, but a request to reopen Velikoretskoe's Church of the Transfiguration in 1946 was accompanied by the explanation that "annually believer-pilgrims came here from 100 and 1000 km [away] to bow down before the holy place and honor Saint Nicholas the Wonderworker and bathe in the Velikaia River. . . . And nowadays pilgrim-believers come from May 21 to 30."[69] Velikoretskoe's believers had, of course, a vested interest in proving a need for their church, but a 1956 report by the regional commissioner for the Council for Russian Orthodox Church Affairs also claimed that pilgrimages continued "even during the years of the Great Patriotic War [i.e., World War II, 1941–45]."[70]

Pilgrimages during the 1940s were no doubt facilitated by the reopening in 1942 of Kirov's Saint Seraphim's Church as a diocesan cathedral, and the greater wartime leniency toward demonstrations of Orthodox piety.[71]

In 1948, a year after Velikoretskoe's Church of the Transfiguration had been reopened, the procession attracted an estimated 1,500 pilgrims from Kirov and neighboring regions and republics—a relatively small number in contrast to other pilgrimages such as the Kursk Korennaia procession, but significant enough to concern the authorities.[72] By the mid-1950s, both the Kirov clergy and the local Council for Russian Orthodox Church Affairs had noticed a significant rise in religiosity.[73] Although, in May 1955, an article in *Kirovskaia Pravda* noted that "isolated individuals" continued to abandon important agricultural work for pilgrimage to the river,[74] 3,500 to 4,000 people made the pilgrimage to Velikoretskoe that year, and this number almost doubled the following year.[75]

Despite the absence of a wonder-working icon, pilgrims in the 1950s appear to have adhered to a strict calendar, gathering in Kirov on June 3, and walking 75 kilometers to arrive in Velikoretskoe at about 2 p.m. on June 5 in an organized fashion.[76] Not all pilgrims traveled together, however; 100 to 150 True Orthodox Church members walked behind the column, and they continued to keep to themselves at the riverside shrine.[77] Although, in 1948 and 1949, the bishop refused to give pilgrims icons to carry in the procession, by the early 1950s believers had secured a large copy (measuring 80 by 60 centimeters) of the miracle-working original from an elderly local man to carry in the procession, in addition to their own icons.[78] In 1954 and 1955, the parish priest apparently held this icon at the church in Velikoretskoe, sending the pilgrims back to Kirov without it.[79]

Once Velikoretskoe Church reopened, the pilgrims and clergy were able to organize an appropriately festive entrance into the village. In the early 1950s, the Velikoretskoe bell-ringer, specially decorated with ribbons, would meet the pilgrims at a pine tree, 4 kilometers from the shrine, where they gathered to pray before entering the village. There he would collect offerings of money, bread, and eggs from the pilgrims, and lead them from the pine tree to Velikoretskoe Church, singing prayers to Saint Nicholas on the way.[80] According to the local commissioner for Russian Orthodox Church affairs, after the liturgy pilgrims fulfilled "a series of religious rituals" until evening, when most returned to Kirov—leaving about 1,500, who returned to Kirov on June 8 and 9.[81]

This "series of religious rituals," developed in the absence of the wonder-working icon and with the reduced input of clergy during the 1930s and 1940s, included traditional forms of icon veneration. In addition to kissing and passing under the large icon carried in procession, pilgrims purchased photocopied icons of Saint Nicholas from a church in Kirov to wear on their chests.[82] Collecting water from the spring was equally essential, and pilgrims took this home with them, just as their prerevolutionary counterparts had done. Pilgrims also collected sand and pine tree roots as well as the little stones apparently sought by some late Imperial-era pilgrims. Soviet pilgrims appear to have sought stones with the image of Saint Nicholas or the Mother of God on them (called "little icons" by contemporary pilgrims),[83] and some pilgrims interpreted the shape and size of stones they found on the riverbank to discern the future.[84] One woman was observed rejoicing over a stone that she experienced as "a find that God himself had sent her, in exchange for her husband and only son, killed in the war."[85] The collecting of natural souvenirs was not confined to the laity; a priest visiting the closed shrines in Diveevo and Sarov in 1971, for example, took water and "little stones" from a spring home with him.[86] The distribution of stone fragments painted with small images of Saint Seraphim—popular pilgrim souvenirs in contemporary Diveevo—was also recorded in 1926.[87] Taking home souvenirs, often a piece of the fabric of a shrine, is a widespread practice, and given the restricted possibilities it is not surprising that naturally available materials became increasingly significant to Soviet pilgrims.[88]

These rituals also reflect the continuing desire for contact with Saint Nicholas in his own locality, and the entire site could be considered holy by virtue of its connection with him. Elements from a holy place also convey the sanctity of their location; pilgrims to Diveevo collected, and continue to collect, flowers and soil from the holy moat (*kanavka*), which "sometimes protected them from attacks of the enemy."[89] And a pilgrim there in 1926 expressed his belief that the entire area was sanctified by its connection with Saint Seraphim and the Mother of God: "How grace-filled every small rock and blade of grass is here, blessed by the Mother of God and ever blessing all those who visit these places."[90] The small stones collected by Velikoretskoe pilgrims were a direct and tangible connection with the saint, and some pilgrims even spotted his image in the crown of a large pine on the banks of the river.[91] Despite the absence of their wonder-working icon, pilgrims could still experience Saint Nicholas's proximity and power via the natural features of the shrine.

The nature of these rituals, however, became an important issue in the subsequent closure of the shrine. One of the most frowned-upon rituals, condemned by contemporary clerics and Soviet officials alike, was the throwing of clothes into the river by those with bodily ailments. According to elderly local Communist Party members, in Velikoretskoe in the first decade of the Soviet period (i.e., before the icon disappeared), "there was no veneration of pines, no bathing and they didn't throw clothes in the water."[92] Though the testimony of party members to party officials may be unreliable, contemporary pilgrims born in the first two decades after the Revolution also testified that "earlier" people did not throw linen into the water in order to gain miraculous healing.[93] The clothes cast on the water would correspond with the body part in need of healing—in cases of infertility, for example, pilgrims might cast their undergarments (*pantalony*) into the water, whereas the lame might throw in socks.[94] This in some ways mimics the practice of laying clothing on a shrine or icon, and then wearing them or using them to dress invalids who were unable to make the pilgrimage themselves.[95] In the absence of wonder-working relics or icons, pilgrims may have assumed that the river—made holy by the feast day—would transfer the same healing grace. However, some reports imply that the clothes were left floating in the water, and diocesan clergy recall this being the case in the early 1990s,[96] so they may also have been leaving the clothes as offerings, as recorded at one northwestern spring in 1931.[97]

A similar flexibility in relating to the sacred may be observed in the changing rituals associated with pine trees. Nineteenth-century pilgrims would hang the wonder-working icon on an impressively large pine near the village of Mediany, as they rested on the way to Velikoretskoe, and make prostrations before the icon.[98] As noted above, Soviet pilgrims also rested at a particular pine tree 4 kilometers outside Velikoretskoe, but in 1956 this tree "somehow or other burned down." That year, the pilgrims stopped there anyway. "You could often hear that 'they burned the pine, but the place remains all the same,'" the local commissioner for Russian Orthodox Church affairs observed in his report, noting that pilgrims took "cinders and even earth from under the former pine."[99] By 1958, only a few pilgrims stopped at the site of the pine tree, while most prayed 2 kilometers away in a field, but nevertheless in 1959 the commissioner recommended that the spot be sown with rye, because crops function "better than any fence" in keeping pilgrims away.[100] Pilgrims also venerated a pine on the riverbank, a phenomenon that post-Soviet clergy have continued to oppose as a Soviet accretion.[101] According to Father Dudin, Soviet pilgrims unable to reach the fenced-off spring on the riverbank took to standing outside the fence on the top of the hill overlooking the bank, and hanging the icons they'd brought with them on a pine tree, while they recited the *akathist* (hymn dedicated to a saint or holy event) to Saint Nicholas:

In time the belief was created that that this pine is also the place of the icon's appearance, people forgot that a spring gushed at the place of the icon's appearance and a chapel was built [there]. Unfortunately this superstition, and several more, are still followed by unenlightened pilgrims. Many of them attribute magical strength to this pine and, instead of prayerfully joining the Lord's liturgy, they spend time at it, naively hoping to receive healing.[102]

Because pilgrims apparently venerated pine trees before the barriers were erected, it seems likely that the transference happened earlier, when pilgrims continued to stop at traditional resting places marked by large trees upon which the icon had once hung. In the absence of the icon, the saint's presence was still acknowledged at the pines on which his wonder-working image had once rested.

*Pilgrimage without the Holy: Cutting Off the Channels of the Sacred*

According to Beglov, local registered clergy participated in the procession until 1949, but because it is unlikely that there were clergy to participate in any pilgrimage to Velikoretskoe for the period in which the diocesan cathedral was closed, they may have participated for about six years in two decades.[103] From 1948 onward, the diocese refused to give out icons for the procession, but "despite continual warnings from the local bishop that the procession of the cross is prohibited and won't happen, believers spontaneously gather, bringing icons from [their] flats, and go out to the river, and on the way believers from other hamlets and villages join in."[104] That year the Velikoretskoe priest and priests from neighboring villages were already celebrating at the shrine as the pilgrims arrived. Once the icon was installed in the church, five clerics celebrated a *panikhida* for the dead, while in the riverbank chapel three local men read the Psalter.[105] Local laity, as elsewhere, took a leading role in the pilgrimage while the clergy were unable to and acted as guides for visiting groups from all over the Soviet Union—and, according to one report, as healers[106]—but though they might read the Psalter or the *akathist* to Saint Nicholas, they could not celebrate the intercessory prayers for the living and dead that pilgrims required, conduct the water-blessing ceremony, or dispense the sacraments.

Although in 1949 the pilgrims were still able to avail themselves of clerical intercession at the shrine, the small group of pilgrims who also walked back from Velikoretskoe to Kirov that year was refused a *moleben* by clergy in the diocesan cathedral.[107] A decade later, Velikoretskoe Church was forbidden to hold a service as the pilgrims entered the village, or to collect money from pilgrims, "since a service on that day in the church [June 5, Thursday] is not connected with any calendrical church feast."[108] The local bishop was also called upon to write annually to every parish reminding them of the ban and asking them to dissuade their parishioners from joining the pilgrimage. Father Balyberdin, a local historian and former diocesan secretary, observed that because the first day of the pilgrimage fell on the Feast of Pentecost in 1963, Bishop Ioann was prevailed upon to send a further letter to priests in Kirov, Slobodskoi, and the village of Chudinovo, forbidding festival liturgies in these churches. Only exceptional conditions, he surmises, could have persuaded the clerical hierarchy to take such steps.[109]

The grounds for co-opting the local clergy into the struggle to curtail the pilgrimage were set out by the local commissioner for Russian Orthodox Church affairs in June 1958. "Year after year," he declared, "this local festival changes more from Orthodoxy into some sort of pagan ritual, idol worship."[110] However, when the local authorities first tried to win Bishop Polikarp's support by pointing out the superstitious nature of the local traditions that accompanied the pilgrimage, the bishop replied that "he also considered intolerable the distortion of Christian rituals during this pilgrimage (the veneration of a pine tree, hill, stones, mixed sex bathing, throwing undergarments into the water, etc.)," but believed that the distorted rituals rather than the pilgrimage itself should be eliminated.[111] The bishop seems to have adopted the tactic of procrastination, promising to inform the Velikoretskoe priest of the need to combat such rituals, and to observe the pilgrimage himself "incognito."[112] However, following the November 1958 resolution, "On Measures for Stopping Pilgrimages to So-Called Holy Sites," and the subsequent patriarchal letter,[113] the following year the bishop was forced to instruct all clergy that the pilgrimage was now banned (although, as he pointed out privately, the patriarch's letter only concerned places not recognized as holy by the Church).[114]

In co-opting the clerical hierarchy to stamp out manifestations of spontaneous religiosity, the Soviet bureaucracy played on a dynamic that has been much discussed with regard to Russian Orthodoxy but is perceptible in any Christian community with an ecclesiastical hierarchy. What constitutes superstitious rather than Orthodox behavior has preoccupied the clergy since the first centuries of conciliar Christianity, and a significant element of this concern relates to authority and the role of sanctifying ecclesiastical ritual: Who has the authority to discern, and dispense, the holy?[115] The Soviet masterstroke was to substantially reduce clerical participation and then use the clerical hierarchy to find nothing holy at the pilgrimage site.

In May 1959, Bishop Polikarp was compelled to inform believers at Saint Seraphim's Cathedral that neither he nor any other priest would be blessing participation in the pilgrimage.[116] Yet despite the bishop's instructions, leafleting by the authorities, and a local propaganda campaign, pilgrims still set off from the cathedral on June 3. According to the 1959 report by the regional commissioner for Russian Orthodox Church affairs, the pilgrims traveled in small groups to the villages of Monastyrskoe and Gorokhovo, where they then formed two columns and processed into Velikoretskoe, accompanied by atheist agitators.[117] A crowd gathered around the church—which had been forbidden to hold a service—and was informed via megaphone that all the holy sites were closed. Many pilgrims, the report continues, returned home without the usual canisters of holy water—because the spring had not been blessed, "that sort of water we get at home too."[118]

The argument that without ecclesiastical ritual the place could not be considered holy was more clearly articulated by Polikarp's successor, Bishop Ioann, who in 1964 explained how a shrine becomes holy in a missive to parishes. The pilgrimage to Velikoretskoe had once upon a time had "its own religious meaning (a church functioned there, a procession of the cross was conducted)," he declared, but without these features it had no religious basis, and to continue making the journey was to willfully go against the Church. Not only were the clerically led rituals central to the pilgrimage; without them, nothing at the site could be considered sacred:

> That which is sanctified by the Church through sacraments and prayers really becomes—for the believing person—a holy object. Therefore I, your archbishop, beg all to guard against spiritual delusion. Do not ascribe holiness to those elements—water, the springs at the Velikaia River, and other items that pilgrims venerate there—because nowadays the Church does not sanctify anything there. The Church even sanctifies the water of such a holy river as the Jordan, in which Christ the Savior himself was baptized, and only after sanctification is [the river] considered holy. Exactly thus it deals with all other holy objects that believers venerate. But it strictly forbids the deification of these items.[119]

Eradicating all clerical contributions was not enough to stamp out pilgrimage, however, because in the absence of registered clergy, believers (often former monastics and elderly laity) arranged their own processions and prayers. To curtail the Velikoretskoe pilgrimage, the local authorities also applied the earlier method of simply removing the material fabric of the sacred. Preempting a massive campaign of church closure,[120] the local commissioner recommended that the Velikoretskoe hospital grounds be widened to include the pine grove on the banks of the river, the spring, and the derelict riverbank chapel, and that pilgrims be prevented from accessing the hospital grounds: "Thus the place where traditionally pilgrims gather on the banks of the Velikaia river, where they look for holy stones and collect sand and water, and also venerate the second pine, will be isolated."[121]

Harsher measures followed; the Velikoretskoe priest was moved, and the lay organizers of the pilgrimage were arrested.[122] In 1960, according to Boris Talantov, a local believer and samizdat writer, "the beautiful [riverside] chapel was blown up, the spring surrounded by a high fence, and the Transfiguration Church was illegally closed. On May 11, 1961, at 4 a.m., the interior of this architectural monument was barbarically destroyed."[123] Pilgrims reaching the shrine that year found that not only were they unable to celebrate a liturgy or *moleben*; their church had been desecrated, and the chapel and spring were inaccessible.

*Responding to Desecration*

One elderly resident of Kirov recalled the shock of desecration as follows:

> And then we came to the Velikaia River, . . . that church they'd shut. They already didn't allow services [to be held there]. So Saint Nicholas the Wonderworker was on the church there, right up high, a portrait, just as if [he were] alive. But now they'd whitewashed him. I stand and cry and think, we came to Nicholas the Wonderworker, well such tears ran down, really that was how it was for me, he really was not visible, all whitewashed, but it was clear that this was an icon. But anyway, all this, you know, we grieved over a bit, [and then] went to bathe. Went, that is, to . . . the river, went into it and you come out of the river as if you were coming straight out of the bathhouse. Some kind of warmth . . . it feels so very good, and so. . . . But they'd built a high fence all the way up, as high as a ceiling, probably, and you couldn't get to the holy water. They fenced off the water, everything . . . shut away. What are we to do? . . . You know, we're [just] walking and wailing. Why did we come here, and we have nothing, we read the *akathist* to Nicholas the Wonderworker somewhere, just to ourselves.[124]

The impact of the church's desecration was devastating for most of the believers, and gave rise to popular tales about the subsequent misfortune and miserable deaths of those who had carried out the destruction.[125] Although one local woman felt bereaved at the loss of those elements that, for her, were an essential aspect of the pilgrimage—the image of the local wonder-worker, the opportunity to bathe—desecration could also give rise to a deeper spiritual experience. Likewise, another pilgrim, Vera, who was from Moscow, set off to Saint Seraphim's shrines despite the puzzlement of fellow Christians who wondered why she would go there—"now, when everything there is ruined and nothing remains"—discovered a profoundly Christian experience in the ruins of the pilgrimage site:

> Those who were here earlier, and who remember the monastery in its former flourishing appearance, and consider that here in Sarov there is nothing, might experience, perhaps, before the appearance of this broken cross, only sorrow or indignation and not share my feelings! The abandoned and broken cross in this blessed forest created, it seemed to me, a closer and more palpable suffering of the Savior than the most artistically depicted and preserved Crucifixion in rich and splendid churches.[126]

Despite—or perhaps because of—its ruinous condition, Sarov monastery rose before her "silently and majestically." She recalled, "I felt that although there was no longer luxury and magnificence here, neither monks nor holy icons, the grace of God had not left these walls."

Jeanne Kormina has observed the search for "authenticity" and the correlation of age and value among contemporary pilgrims, discussing the notion of holy places or objects as *namolennye*—a term that implies the special power accrued as a result of veneration. The more prayers said over an object or in a place, the more grace or "holy energy" it accumulates.[127] As sites trod by a saint retain an invisible footprint of grace, so do sites formerly occupied by built or natural sacred objects. Nineteenth-century peasants continued (to the consternation of the clerical hierarchy) to collect soil from the site of a church that had not existed for two centuries, reflecting—like continued rituals at Soviet-closed shrines—a popular understanding of the sacred that was broader, more flexible, and more durable than that of the clerical hierarchy.[128]

Although Khrushchev's antireligious campaign did not dampen the desire of some pilgrims, as one observer of the time noted, making a pilgrimage subsequently became an almost monastic feat, with those undertaking it often being people strongly drawn to the monastic life.[129] The subsequent drop in pilgrims to Velikoretskoe indicates that—for many—a desecrated shrine was not worth the risk entailed in traveling to it. In 1960, an estimated 500 pilgrims reached Velikoretskoe by June 6; but after the 1959 ban, pilgrims also began to travel to the riverbank in small groups all year round—one of the reasons given for closing the church. The church's income records revealed that pilgrims were donating money throughout June, July, August, "and even September."[130] In 1961, however—though at least 130 pilgrims attempted to undertake the journey (up to 10 of them by catching a train from Kirov)—not a single pilgrim made it into Velikoretskoe on June 5 or 6.[131]

Pilgrimage to Velikoretskoe also became the territory of elderly people. A major concern for Soviet bureaucrats was the number of young and working-age pilgrims, because this indicated not only potential damage to work quotas but also the strength of a religion that was supposed to be dying out as new scientifically educated Soviet citizens replaced generations educated in prerevolutionary Russia. No less than 15 to 20 percent of Velikoretskoe pilgrims in 1955 were young or middle-aged, and those singled out in the local commissioner's report included a family whose members had walked 170 kilometers from their *kolkhoz* (collective farm) to the river ("first the husband and wife bathed, then they helped the old folk and little children to bathe"), and a local pioneer seen bathing and hunting for stones with her mother.[132] By 1961, it was the old who continued to battle the secular authorities and to defy the clerical hierarchy, as each year the police and volunteer constabulary were drafted to "courageously hunt down old men and women, catch and fine them for simply quietly and peaceably walking the road to Velikoretskoe village."[133] This geriatricization in part reflected the fact that local collective farms were forbidden to give workers time off during the period of the feast, but this phenomenon can be interpreted more broadly as continued religious action for the benefit of the community by the older generation while the younger generation worked and raised children—a practice reminiscent of Davie's "vicarious religion" in secularized Western Europe.[134] Pilgrim tradition holds that Saint Nicholas punishes the community if the vow made centuries ago is not upheld.[135]

It is difficult to draw a clear picture of the numbers of pilgrims attempting the journey in the years after the ban, but the fact that the district management committee of a local soviet of workers' deputies found it necessary to issue a ruling about the pilgrimage ban again in 1975, claiming that pilgrimage to Velikoretskoe was causing "great material damage" by distracting workers from their agricultural labors, suggests that working-age people were still trying to absent themselves for the feast in the early 1970s.[136] Under sustained harassment, however, the pilgrimage became a memory maintained predominantly by local women. One pilgrim, Iulia, who undertook the journey in the mid-1970s when she was in her early forties, recalled how her sister prepared for their pilgrimage:

> [My sister] is such a brave one, she wrote down everything, every point, how to [get] there, that's there and back, indicated all the little villages, she wrote everything in that (*laughs*). She drew up her own plan and everything, well, something [was known], of course, some people already walked [the route] earlier, so, of course, they asked around, but she basically did that.[137]

Iulia could not remember whether they had sought a blessing from a priest to undertake the pilgrimage (a requirement stressed by contemporary clergy),[138] and she also thought they probably had not carried an *akathist* with them—the pilgrimage had by then become completely laicized. Samizdat sources from the early 1980s record small and larger groups of 200 to 250 believers attempting to reach the river on June 6,[139] and in 1984 the authorities managed to stop a group of 30 pilgrims several kilometers outside the shrine. The composition of this group concerned local bureaucrats, although they celebrated the fact that the number of participants had dropped dramatically. Although "there were no fanatically emotional organizers from the town of Kirov among [the pilgrims]" and only twenty elderly local women attempted to participate, young people under age thirty-five from outside the local area had appeared among the pilgrims, and several pilgrims holding responsible jobs (factory directors, trade union inspectors) attempted to reach the village by car.[140] A range of measures to quash this unusual interest was implemented, and by 1986 a mere eight pilgrims were recorded as attempting to reach the riverbank at Velikoretskoe—all women residents of Kirov town (although more may have attempted the journey unnoticed).[141]

The local authorities continued to battle the practice with all the resources available to them until 1989. At the request of local believers, the bishop appealed for the pilgrimage to be permitted in 1988, but that year six police blockades were set up along the pilgrimage route. In contrast, a local priest in a parish near Rostov Velikii managed to organize a procession around the entire village, culminating in an open-air address to a crowd of over a thousand.[142] When the first full-length procession from Kirov to Velikoretskoe was finally permitted in 1992, the elderly women who had maintained a memory of the "traditional" route became local celebrities upon whom neophyte pilgrims, academics, and urban intellectuals relied for insight into how the pilgrimage should "properly" be conducted—some even credited them with the ability to summon clement weather for the procession.[143]

## Conclusion

Pilgrim practices in Velikoretskoe, as elsewhere in the Soviet Union, adapted during the decades in which pilgrimages became increasingly detached from liturgical practices and clerical regulation. Manifestations of spontaneous religiosity during the Soviet period reflect the findings of recent research in European societies where institutional Christianity has been marginalized, which suggest that instead of religiosity dying out in "secularized" societies, more individualized ways of experiencing the sacred develop.[144] As a structure, pilgrimage is well suited to resist periods of secularization and political change, and it has shown a marked and continual rise in Europe as individuals move from an institution-based faith to a more flexible manner of accessing the sacred.[145]

The innate flexibility of pilgrimages made it hard for Soviet authorities to eradicate them in the same way that it was, and is, difficult for clerical hierarchies to regulate them. However, during the Soviet period the authorities manipulated the ever-present dynamic between institutional and lived religiosity to impose on would-be pilgrims, in tandem with the ecclesiastical hierarchy, a narrow vision of clerically dispensed sacredness. They also cut off access to Orthodox channels of grace—removing relics and icons, closing churches, blocking holy springs, and forbidding clerics to bless or celebrate with pilgrims. In their absence pilgrims developed new rituals, and relied on guidance from respected laity (often older women) who subsequently became the repositories of religious memory that did not necessarily reflect institutional norms.

Pilgrims' experience of desecrated space was diverse—for some it had become profane by virtue of the absence of clerically sanctified elements, whereas for others it represented a more emotively Christian experience. Still others found that in the absence of a human-made religious environment and clerical channels of grace, natural elements both testified to, and transferred, spiritual power. What remained in place once a shrine was destroyed was its history, human and divine. As Vera Vasilevskaia mused, in the midst of devastation, a shrine accumulates holiness that is not only retained by the walls, but by the natural world around it: "The traces of prayers and spiritual feats are imprinted and remain in the surrounding countryside so clearly [that] they seem almost accessible to the perception of external senses."[146]

## Notes

1. Fr. Andrei Dudin, interview by the author, Kirov, June 1, 2009. See also "Ne boites krestnogo puti!" *Voskresenie* 12 (2000); A. Logvinov, "Reka Velikaia, 5 Iiunia . . . ," *Komsomol'skoe plemia*, 27 (June 8, 1989), 7; and Gosudarstvennyi arkhiv Kirovskoi oblasti (State Archive of Kirov Oblast; hereafter GAKO), R-2169, op. 45, d. 11, l. 138.

2. Victor Turner and Edith L. B. Turner, *Image and Pilgrimage in Christian Culture: Anthropological Perspectives* (New York: Columbia University Press, 1978), 231.

3. Although these memoirs necessarily reflect the retrospective perceptions of the educated pilgrim, they offer invaluable observations of practices, which, to a great extent, crossed social and educational divides.

4. I am grateful to the Keston Institute for a grant that allowed me to access the archive of the Keston Center for Religion, Politics, and Society, at the J. M. Dawson Institute of Church-State Studies of Baylor University in Waco, Tex., and to the British Academy for a grant to participant-observe the revived Velikoretskoe procession in 2009. I am also indebted to Alexander Agadjanian, Miriam Dobson, Andrei Dudin, Katja Tolstaja, Catherine Wanner, and Christine Worobec for helpful suggestions and constructive criticism during this chapter's final draft.

5. Historians who have challenged this believer–versus–Soviet citizen dichotomy include Andrew B. Stone, "'Overcoming Peasant Backwardness': The Khrushchev Antireligious Campaign and the Rural Soviet Union," *Russian Review* 67 (April 2008): 296–320; Glennys Young, *The Power and the Sacred in Revolutionary Russia: Religious Activists in the Village* (University Park: Pennsylvania State University Press, 1997); and Douglas Rogers, *The Old Faith and the Russian Land: A Historical Ethnography of Ethics in the Urals* (Ithaca, N.Y.: Cornell University Press, 2009).

6. Chris Chulos, *Converging Worlds: Religion and Community in Peasant Russia, 1861–1917* (DeKalb: Northern Illinois University Press, 2003), 5; Christine Worobec, "The Unintended Consequences of a Surge in Orthodox Pilgrimages in Late Imperial Russia," *Russian History* 36 (2009), 62–76.

7. Worobec, "Unintended Consequences," 67.

8. "O poriadke provedeniia v zhizn' dekreta 'Ob otdelenii tserkvi ot gosudarstva i shkoly ot tserkvi' (Instruktsiia)," in *Otdelenie tserkvi ot gosudarstva: Sistematizirovannyi sbornik deistviushchego v SSSR zakonodatel'stva*, 3rd ed., edited by P. V. Gidulianov (Moscow: Iuridicheskoe izd., 1926), 628–29 (first published in *Izvestiia*, August 30, 1918).

9. An NKVD circular issued in 1925 acknowledged that believers wishing to organize "marches, processions of the cross, prayer services and so on" in streets and public squares were finding it "extremely difficult" to secure permission from the local *uezd* (county) authorities, even when the procession was to be held only within a village's boundaries. This instruction, and one issued in the Ukrainian Soviet Socialist Republic

in 1924, clarified which organs were responsible for granting permission, depending on whether the processions covered one or several villages, or larger regional towns, or crossed gubernatorial boundaries. "Tsirkuliar NKVD ot 12 fevralia 1925 g. no. 73" and "Tsirkuliar NKVD USSR ot 25 avgusta 1924 g. no. 46," quoted in *Otedelenie tserkvi ot gosudarstva*, ed. Gidulianov, 53–54.

10. "O religioznykh obedineniiakh," April 8, 1929, in *Zakonodatel'stvo o religioznykh kul'takh: Sbornik materialov i dokumentov* (Moscow: Iurodicheskaia literatura, 1971), 83–99, esp. 96. See also Aleksei Beglov, *V poiskakh "bezgreshnykh katakomb": Tserkovnoe podpol'e v SSSR* (Moscow: Arefa, 2008), 177. That they were permitted by law did not preclude harassment; e.g., see the Very Rev. D. Konstantinov, *Stations of the Cross: The Russian Orthodox Church 1970–1980* (London, Ont.: Zaria Publishing, 1984), 86–87.

11. Vladimir Stepanov, *Svidetel'stvo obvineniia: tserkov' i gosudarstvo v Sovetskom Soiuze* (Jordanville, N.Y.: Holy Trinity Monastery, 1987), 208.

12. "O meropriiatiiakh, vyzyvaemykh proiskhodiashchim goneniem pravoslavnuiu tserkov," April 1918, http://www. orthedu. ru/ch_hist/20-vek/opredelenie1918.htm.

13. Contemporary Russian nationalists have appropriated the form and used it to significant effect on National Unity Day.

14. *Sviashchennomuchenik Konstantin Merkushinskii* (Ekaterinburg: Novo-Tikhvinskii zhenskii monastyr, 2008), 22–24. The periodical *Tserkovnye vedomosti* [Church News] recorded that in February 1918 alone, religious processions in Voronezh, Shatsk (Tambov region), Tula, and Kharkov were fired upon. See Lev Regelson, *Tragediia Russkoi Tserkvi 1917–1945* (Paris: YMCA Press, 1977), 229–30.

15. Young, *Power and the Sacred*, 248–51.

16. Steven Merritt Miner, *Stalin's Holy War: Religion, Nationalism, and Alliance Politics, 1941–1945* (Chapel Hill: University of North Carolina Press, 2003), 145. This report is reproduced by Beglov, *V poiskakh "bezgreshnykh katakomb,"* 269–72.

17. This is quoted from a July 1921 report transcribed in Gosudarstvennyi arkhiv sotsial'no-politicheskoi istorii Kirovskoi oblasti (State Archive of Socio-Political History of Kirov Oblast; hereafter GASPIKO), f. 6774, op. 1, ed. khr. 141 (*Teksty dlia publikatsii v "Eparkhial'nom vestnik"' k 2000-letiiu Rozhdestva Khristova*), ll. 1–2, from f. 1, op. 2, ed. khr. 215. See also Beglov, *V poiskakh "bezgreshnykh katakomb,"* 177, who notes that in 1924 the GPU recommended that local believers in areas affected by crop failure should not be prevented from conducting religious rituals.

18. See, e.g., *O sviatykh ikonakh i krestnykh khodakh v voprosakh i otvetakh* (Moscow: Kazak, 1999).

19. Kate Brown, "Danger! Local Culture at the Crossroads," *East-West Review*, Spring 2010, 10–11. See also "Moskovskie pisma: dokumenty 20-x godov," *Russkaia mysl'*, December 16, 1976; William B. Husband, "*Godless Communists*": *Atheism and Society in Soviet Russia, 1917–1932* (DeKalb: Northern Illinois University Press, 2000), 143, on an "epidemic of miracles"' in the 1920s; Lynne Viola, *Peasant Rebels under Stalin: Collectivization and the Culture of Peasant Resistance* (New York: Oxford University Press, 1996), 53–54; Steven Smith, "Nebesnye pis'ma i rasskazy o lese: 'sueveriia' protiv bol'shevizma," *Antropologicheskii forum* 3 (2005), 280–306.

20. See, e.g., Husband, "*Godless Communists*," 48; Sheila Fitzpatrick, *Stalin's Peasants: Resistance and Survival in the Russian Village after Collectivization* (New York: Oxford University Press, 1994), 34.

21. *Revoliutsiia i Tserkov'* 1–3 (1922), cited by Regelson, *Tragediia*, 275.

22. Young, *Power and the Sacred*, 199–200, 240–42.

23. Robert H. Greene, *Bodies Like Bright Stars: Saints and Relics in Orthodox Russia* (DeKalb: Northern Illinois Press, 2009), 194.

24. A. P. Timofievich, "A Pilgrimage to Diveyevo," in *St. Seraphim Wonderworker of Sarov and His Spiritual Inheritance*, edited by Helen Kontzevitch (Wildwood, Calif.: Saint Xenia Skete, 2004), 270. Timofievich was a medical doctor who emigrated from the Soviet Union to Germany at the end of World War II, and then on to the United States. His pilgrimage recollections were first serialized in 1951 in *Pravoslavnaia zhizn'*.

25. Other memoirists confirm this nationwide impulse. See, e.g., *K batiushke Serafimu: Vospominaniia palomnikov v Sarov i Diveevo (1823–1927)* (Moscow: Otchii Dom izd., 2006).

26. S. A. Smith, "Bones of Contention: Bolsheviks and the Struggle against Relics 1918–1930," *Past and Present* 204 (2009): 155–93; Chulos, *Converging Worlds*, 109. Patriarch Tikhon observed in 1920 that the "insulting of St Sergius [of Radonezh]' relics evoked a great outburst of religiosity, manifested in the intensified pilgrimage to His health-giving shrine," as quoted by Regelson, *Tragediia*, 267–68.

27. As a Narodnyi Komissariat Iustitsii (People's Commissariat of Justice) circular of August 25, 1920, observed, "Housing 'relics' in museums is the most rational method of eliminating future exploitation of prejudice and superstition. Similar relics relating to other religions (e.g., Egyptian mummies) were placed in museums a long time ago, along with other remains of old cults, which is no offense against religious conscience, no persecution of one or another faith."' Reproduced in Gidulianov, *Otdelenie tserkvi ot gosudarstva,* 69.

28. Smith, "Bones of Contention," 175, 186.

29. See Jennifer Jean Wynot, *Keeping the Faith: Russian Orthodox Monasticism in the Soviet Union, 1917–1939* (College Station: Texas A&M University Press, 2004); O. Iu. Vasil'eva, "Sudby Russkikh monastyrei v XX veke," in, *Monashestvo i monastyri v Rossii XI-XX veka: Istoricheskie ocherki*, edited by N. V. Sinitsyna (Moscow: Nauka, 2002); and Charles Timberlake, "The Fate of Russian Orthodox Monasteries and Convents since 1917," *Donald W. Treadgold Papers* 103 (1995). William G. Wagner offers an illuminating case study in "Paradoxes of Piety: The Nizhegorod Convent of the Exaltation of the Cross, 1807–1935," in *Orthodox Russia: Belief and Practice under the Tsars*, edited by Valerie A. Kivelson and Robert H. Greene (University Park: Pennsylvania State University Press, 2003), 211–38.

30. See chapter 4, by Scott Kenworthy, in the present volume; Wynot, *Keeping the Faith*, 119, 162; and Vasil'eva, "Sudby Russkikh monastyrei," 336–38.

31. Dimitry V. Pospielovsky, *Soviet Anti-Religious Campaigns and Persecutions* (Basingstoke and London: Macmillan, 1988); Anna Dickinson, "Quantifying Religious Oppression: Russian Orthodox Church Closures and Repression of Priests, 1917–41," *Religion, State and Society* 28, no. 4 (2000): 327–35.

32. "O religioznykh obedineniiakh," 96.

33. Iu. V. Geras'kin, "Bor'ba Sovetskoi vlasti s palomnichestvom k sviatym mestam (40–60-e gg. XX v.)," *Vestnik Moskovskogo gosudarstvennogo oblastnogo universiteta: Seriia "Istoriia i politicheskie nauki,"* no. 2 (2008); Beglov, *V poiskakh "bezgreshnykh katakomb,"* 177–79. Beglov (ibid., 72, 184–85) also argues that most places of underground pilgrimage in the 1920s, 1940s, and early 1950s were springs at the sites of former churches and monasteries, which in the absence of functioning churches became

gathering places for prayer and liturgical services. A. A. Panchenko notes that given the dearth of village churches in the postwar years, locally venerated shrines incorporating holy springs, stones, trees, and crosses "practically replaced churches"' for many rural dwellers. See A. A. Panchenko, *Issledovaniia v oblasti narodnogo pravoslaviia: Derevenskie sviatyni Severo-Zapada Rossii* (Saint Petersburg: Izd. Aleteiia, 1998), 77.

34. Vera Vasilevskaia, *Pravedniki nashego vremeni: Katakomby XX veka—Vospominaniia*, 85–86, Keston Archive, Baylor University, Waco, Tex. (hereafter Keston), SU/Ort S. V. Ia. Vasilevskaia's memoirs have been published as *Katakomby XX veka: Vospominaniia* (Moscow: Fond imeni Aleksandra Meniia, 2001), http://krotov.info/history/20/1930/ktkmb0.html.

35. Beglov makes a convincing case for the continuation of pilgrimage until the early 1950s in *V poiskakh "bezgreshnykh katakomb,"* although his primary focus is the dynamic between legal and illegal (unregistered) church activity.

36. See Kenworthy's exploration of the impact of this changing religious policy on the significant national shrine of Trinity–Saint Sergius Lavra, reopened in 1946 after more than two decades. See Kenworthy, chap. 4, this volume.

37. Beglov, *V poiskakh "bezgreshnykh katakomb,"* 186. See also Miner's reference to the head of the Central Committee's Directorate of Propaganda and Agitation 1944 memorandum to party activists, citing several icon processions and public prayers for rain as examples of clergy who tried to extend church influence, "rudely breaking Soviet law in the process," Miner, *Stalin's Holy War*, 151.

38. Council of Russian Orthodox Church Affairs report published in Beglov, *V poiskakh "bezgreshnykh katakomb,"* 290–96.

39. Beglov, *V poiskakh "bezgreshnykh katakomb,"* 110.

40. See, e.g., Stone, "'Overcoming Peasant Backwardness,'" 296–320.

41. V. Mal'tsev, "'Sviatoe' ozero," *Smena* 12 (1959): 15.

42. See Joan Delaney Grossman, "Khrushchev's Anti-Religious Policy and the Campaign of 1954," *Soviet Studies* 24, no. 3 (1973): 374–86; N. S. Timasheff, "The Anti-Religious Campaign in the Soviet Union," *The Review of Politics* 17, no. 3 (1955): 329–44; "Current Soviet Press Attacks on Religion," Soviet Affairs Analysis Service, Institute for the Study of the USSR, Munich, Germany, October 13, 1959.

43. "O religioznom prazdnike 'Nikoly velikoretskogo,'" *Kirovskaia Pravda* 104 (May 28, 1955): 4.

44. Council of Russian Orthodox Church Affairs report from July 5, 1949, reproduced by Beglov, *V poiskakh "bezgreshnykh katakomb,"* 286–90.

45. *Zakonodatel'stvo o religioznykh kul'takh*, 153.

46. *Zhurnal zasedaniia Sviashennogo Sinoda ot 25 avgusta 1948 no. 18*, Gosudarstvennyi arkhiv Rossiiskoi Federatsii (State Archive of the Russian Federation), f. 6991, op. 1, d. 148, l. 51. See also Tatiana A. Chumachenko, *Church and State in Soviet Russia: Russian Orthodoxy from World War II to the Khrushchev Years* (Amronk, N.Y.: M. E. Sharpe, 2002), 111; Beglov, *V poiskakh "bezgreshnykh katakomb,"* 106.

47. This citation is from an uncatalogued photocopy of the patriarch's letter held in the Viatka Diocesan Archive (with thanks to Fr. Andrei Dudin). See also Chumachenko, *Church and State*, 155, 216 nn. 43 and 44.

48. Beglov, *V poiskakh "bezgreshnykh katakomb,"* 180–82.

49. A. Balyberdin, *Bezumie: Khrushchevskie goneniia na Viatskoi zemle* (Viatka: Bukvitsa, 2006), 74–75. This detailed study of religious repression in the Kirov region in 1959–64, and the dissertation that preceded it, provided a vital starting point for this case study.

50. Daniel C. Waugh, "Religion and Regional Identities: The Case of Viatka and the Miracle-Working Icon of St. Nicholas Velikoretskii," in *Die Gerschichte Russlands im 16. und 17: Jahrhundert aus der perspective seiner Regionen*, edited by Andreas Kappeler (Wiesbaden: Harrossowitz Verlag, 2004), 259–78.

51. See "O rasporiazheniiakh i postanovleniiakh kasatel'no Velikoretskago krestnago khoda," *Viatskiia eparkhial'nyia vedomosti* 18 (September 16, 1869): 380–97. For an overview of the procession's history, see Daniel Waugh, "We Have Never Been Modern: Approaches to the Study of Russia in the Age of Peter the Great," *Jahrbücher für Geschichte Osteuropas* 49 (2001): 321–45; and Andrei Dudin, "Velikoretskii krestnyi khod," *Velikoretskaia Ikona Sviatitelia Nikolaia: Istoriia i sovremennost'* (Viatka: Bukvitsa, 2008), 61–127.

52. S. V. Kurbanovskii, "Na 'Velikoi reke': Vpechatleniia bogomol'tsa," *Kalendar' Viatskoi Gubernii na 1893g* (Viatka: Gub. tip., 1892), 256. I am most grateful to Daniel Waugh for this and other nineteenth-century sources.

53. Kurbanovskii, "Na 'Velikoi reke'; O rasporiazheniiakh," 380–97.

54. Petr Makarov, "Opisanie iavleniia Velikoretskago chudotvornago obraza Sviatitelia Nikolaiia," *Dushepoleznyi sobesednik*, no. 5 (Moscow: Izd. Afonskago Russkago Panteleimonoviia monastyria, 1889), 119.

55. Kurbanovskii, "Na 'Velikoi reke,'" 268.

56. Ibid., 267–68.

57. V. A. Korshunkov, "Obriad na Nizhnem Potoke i Velikoretskii krestnyi khod: pochitanie vodnykh istochnikov v Viatskom krae," in *VIII Gertsenovskie chteniia: Materialy nauchnoi konferentsii*, edied by V. A. Korshunkov (Kirov: OUNB im. A. I. Gertsena, 2002), 77–83.

58. "O rasporiazheniiakh," 393–94.

59. The local bishop and governor discussed concerns over the killing and trading of sheep in secret correspondence from 1839 to 1840, but they did not perceive any hint of the paganism that later secular commentators observed. See GAKO, f. 582, op. 128[6/8/b] ed. khr. 178.

60. See, e.g., GAKO, f. 300, op. 2, ed. khr. 14, l. 3 (1924); "O 'Nikole ugodnike,'" *Viatskaia Pravda*, June 3, 1926.

61. Dudin, "Velikoretskii krestnyi khod," 109.

62. GASPIKO, f. 1, op. 3, ed. khr. 51, l. 20.

63. *Viatskii eparkhial'nyi vestnik* (*VEV*) 6 (50) 1994, citing a 1915 report.

64. GASPIKO, f. 1, op. 3, ed. khr. 51, l. 20 (1925); GASPIKO, f. 1, op. 5, ed. khr. 46, l. 10, ll. 10, 40–41 (1927).

65. By 1941, there were only six churches for the entire diocese; V. M. Bad'in, "Viatskaia eparkhiia v 1917–1941," in *Ocherki istorii Viatskoi eparkhii (1657–2007)*, edited by A. Dudin et al. (Bukhvitsa: Viatka, 2007), 441. In contrast, in 1914 the Viatka Diocese had 667 parish churches. See Vera Shevzov, *Russian Orthodoxy on the Eve of Revolution* (New York: Oxford University Press, 2004), 99.

66. Dudin, "Velikoretskii krestnyi khod," 108–9.

67. Tat'iana Berkhina, *Viatskie pometki* (Kirov: Dom pechati-Viatka, 2005), 14.

68. Berkhina, *Viatskie pometki*, 22–23, 26–30. A 1955 report records that the church elder and head of the village soviet believed it to have been closed in 1934 and reopened in 1946; GASPIKO, f. P-1290, op. 28, ed. khr. 43, l. 172.

69. GAKO, f. R-2169 op. 44, d. 109, l. 69 ob, l. 72 (copy sent to Moscow).

70. Dudin, "Velikoretskii krestnyi khod," 110; GAKO, f. R2169, op. 45, ed. khr. 11, l. 12, 14.

71. Balyberdin, *Bezumie*, 37. The original cathedral was demolished in the early 1930s.

72. Locals questioned about attendees at the 1949 celebrations estimated around 7,000, of whom 85 percent were locals just enjoying the spectacle. They perceived a 20 percent increase in procession participants from the year before. Beglov, *V poiskakh "bezgreshnykh katakomb,"* 289.

73. Balyberdin, *Bezumie*, 48. See also N. V. Shabalin, *Russkaia pravoslavnaia tserkov' i Sovetskoe gosudarstvo v seredine sorokovykh—piatidesiatye gody XX veka (na materialakh Kirovskoi oblasti)* (Kirov: Avtor, 2004). Kenworthy observes a similar trend during this period in the Trinity–Saint Sergius Lavra, with increasing numbers of young postulants as well as pilgrims; see chapter 4 in this volume.

74. "O religioznom prazdnike 'Nikoly velikoretskogo,'" *Kirovskaia Pravda*, May 28, 1955.

75. GAKO, f. R2169, op. 45, ed. khr. 11, ll. 5, 12.

76. Ibid., ll. 12, 14.

77. Ibid., op. 29, ed. khr. 57a.

78. A very similar description of the Kursk pilgrimage can be found in a 1958 report published by O. V. Lavinskaia and, Iu. G. Orlova, "O zakrytii pravoslavnykh monastyrei v SSSR i zapreshchenii palomnichestva k sviatym mestam (1958–1961)," *Pravoslavnyi palomnik* 4, no. 6 (2002): 54–62.

79. GAKO, f. R2169, op. 45, ed. khr. 11, l. 6.

80. GASPIKO, f. P-1290, op. 28, ed. khr. 43, ll. 164–71.

81. Dudin, "Velikoretskii krestnyi khod," 110; GAKO, f. R2169, op. 45, ed. khr. 11, ll. 12, 14.

82. GASPIKO, f. P-1290, op. 28, ed. khr. 43, 168.

83. A. A. Ivanova, "Nikola Velikoretskii v fol'klore i ritual'noe praktike: Materialy i kommetarii," *Traditsionnaia kul'tura* 1 (2005), 49–56.

84. GASPIKO, f. p-1290, op. 28, ed. khr. 43, ll. 164–71; GAKO, f. R2169, op. 29, ed. khr. 57a, l. 37.

85. GAKO, f. R2169, op. 45, ed. khr. 11, l. 14.

86. "Iz perepiski dvukh sviashchennikov," *Grani* 108 (1978), 124–51, esp. 136.

87. I. M. Andreev, "K batiushke Serafimu," in *K batiushke Serafimu*, 592–93.

88. Clerical efforts to control "often-heterogeneous" pilgrim practices, including the use of holy water and the taking of pieces of the grotto stone home with them, are explored by Suzanne K. Kaufman, *Consuming Visions: Mass Culture and the Lourdes Shrine* (Ithaca, N.Y.: Cornell University Press, 2005), 20–21. Panchenko also records that pilgrims to locally venerated rural shrines traditionally take water, bark, sand, small stones, and pieces of wax home with them; see Panchenko, *Issledovanie v oblasti narodnogo pravoslaviia*, 104.

89. Protoierei Stefan Liashevskii, "Diveev monastyr' v miatezhnye gody," in *Letopis' Serafimo-Diveevskogo monastyria* (Moscow: Palomnik, 2005), 668.

90. Timofievich, "A Pilgrimage to Diveyevo," 329. Elements (generally earth, oil, water) sanctified by physical contact with the holy were also traditional souvenirs—"'portable, palpable sanctity'"—for Byzantine pilgrims. See, e.g., Gary Vikan, *Byzantine Pilgrimage Art* (Washington, D.C.: Dumbarton Oaks, Trustees for Harvard University, 1982), 13.

91. 1949 report reproduced in Beglov, *V poisk "bezgreshnykh katakomb,"* 286–90.

92. GAKO, f. R2169, op. 29, ed. khr. 57a, l. 37.

93. Ivanova, "Nikola Velikoretskii v fol'klore."
94. GAKO, f. R2169, op. 45, ed. khr. 11, l. 13.
95. Greene, *Bodies Like Bright Stars*, 52.
96. Fr. Andrei Dudin, in a discussion with the author, Kirov, November 2010; GASPIKO, f. R-1290, op. 28, ed. khr. 43, ll. 164–71.
97. See Panchenko's discussion of cloth as a traditional offering (ribbons, head scarves, clothes, towels, etc.) at locally venerated icons and natural features associated with a holy figure, in *Issledovanie v oblasti narodnogo pravoslaviia*, 88–92.
98. Kurbanovskii, "Na 'Velikoi reke,'" 275.
99. GAKO, f. R2169, op. 45, ed. khr. 11, ll. 15–16.
100. Ibid., op. 29, ed. khr. 57a, ll. 44–46.
101. Stella Rock, "'Walking Sunday Schools' or 'Demonstrations of Marginal Mindsets'? The Procession of the Cross in Post-Soviet Russia," unpublished manuscript, 2009; *Nash Vybor: Informatsionno-publitsisticheskaia gazeta* 20 (661), Kirov, May 17, 2007, 1, 6. I am most grateful to the local historian Vladimir Korshunkov for this article, field notes, and photographs of earlier practices.
102. A. Dudin, "Velikoretskii krestnyi khod," in *Pochitanie sviatitelia Nikolaia Chudotvortsa i ego otrazhenie v fol'klore, pis'mennosti i iskusstve* (Moscow: Skanrus, 2007), 32–36.
103. Beglov, *V poiskakh "bezgreshnykh katakomb,"* 182.
104. April 1949 report, reproduced by Beglov, *V poiskakh "bezgreshnykh katakomb,"* 290–96.
105. July 1949 report, reproduced in ibid., 286–90.
106. Balyberdin, *Bezumie*, 49, 81; GAKO, f. R2169, op. 29, ed. khr. 57a, l. 36.
107. Reports published by Beglov, *V poiskakh "bezgreshnykh katakomb,"* 286–96.
108. GAKO, f. R2169, op. 29, ed. khr. 57a, l. 47.
109. Balyberdin, *Bezumie*, 154.
110. GAKO, f. R2169, op. 29, ed. khr. 57a, l. 37.
111. GASPIKO, f. P-1290, op. 34., ed. khr. 51, l. 3.
112. Balyberdin, *Bezumie*, 65–66; GASPIKO, f. P-1290, op. 31, ed. khr. 59, ll. 120–22; GAKO, f. R2169, op. 29, ed. khr. 57a, l. 46.
113. Chumachenko, *Church and State*, 216.
114. Aleksandr Gennad'evich Balyberdin, *Gosudarstvenno-tserkovnye otnosheniia v 1958–1964 gg. (po materialam Kirovskoi oblasti)*, 76–78, http://www.eparhia-vtk.ru/press/books/.
115. See, e.g., Vera Shevzov's discussion of clerical concerns around miraculously appearing icons and chapel construction in *Russian Orthodoxy on the Eve of Revolution*, 122–23, 209; and Stella Rock, *Popular Religion in Russia: "Double Belief" and the Making of an Academic Myth* (London: Routledge, 2007).
116. GAKO, f. R2169, op. 45, ed. khr. 11, ll. 58–59.
117. Ibid., l. 55.
118. Ibid., l. 56; Balyberdin, *Bezumie*, 79.
119. GAKO, f. R2169, op. 45, ed. khr. 11, ll. 83, 85.
120. "Ego sviateishestvu, sviateishemu Patriarkhu Moskovskomu i vseia Rusi, Aleksiu: Ot veruiushchikh Kirovskoi eparkhii Iiun' 1966 goda," *Vestnik Russkogo Studencheskogo Khristianskogo Dvizheniia* 82, no. 1 (1966): 3–20, esp. 10–11.
121. GAKO, f. R2169, op. 29, ed. khr. 57a, ll. 44–46.
122. Balyberdin, *Bezumie*, 81.

123. "Bedstvennoe polozhenie pravoslavnoi tserkvi v Kirovskoi oblasti i rol' Moskovskoi Patriarkhii (iz otkrytogo pis'ma Borisa Talantova ot 10 noiabria 1966 goda)," *Vestnik Russkogo Studencheskogo Khristianskogo Dvizheniia* 83, no. 1 (1967): 62–63.

124. Nadezhda Andreevna Cheremukhina (b. 1921), recorded in 2000, in *Biulleten foneticheskogo fonda russkago iazyka: Prilozhenie No. 12—Velikoretskii krestnyi khod, zvuchashchaia khrestomatiia*, edited by E. N. Moshkina, O. N. Fedianina, and V. V. Podrushniak (Kirov, 2002), 27.

125. Elena Levkievskaia, "The Silent People? Soviet Militant Atheism through the Eyes of the Russian Peasant," *Russian Studies in History* 38, no. 4 (2000): 33–52. Jeanne Kormina sees these tales functioning as "the 'myth' that sanctions the worship of a sacred locus." See Kormina, "Pilgrims, Priest and Local Religion in Contemporary Russia: Contested Religious Discourses," *Folklore* 28 (2004): 26–40.

126. Vasilevskaia, *Pravedniki*, 90.

127. Jeanne Kormina, "*Avtobusniki*: Russian Orthodox Pilgrims' Longing for Authenticity," in *Eastern Christians in Anthropological Perspective*, edited by Chris Hann and Hermann Goltz (Berkeley: University of California Press, 2010), 267–86.

128. Shevzov, *Russian Orthodoxy*, 123.

129. Tat'iana Goricheva, "Iz pisem k dukhovnomu bratu: Monastyr' Piukhtitsy," *Grani* 123 (1982): 166–89, esp. 180 (extracts from letters written on pilgrimage in 1979).

130. GASPIKO, f. P-1290, op. 35c, ed. khr. 61, ll. 8–9.

131. Balyberdin, *Gosudarstvenno-tserkovnye otnosheniia*, 125–26.

132. GAKO, f. R2169, op. 45, ed. khr. 11, l. 5.

133. Talantov, "Bedstvennoe polozhenie pravoslavnoi tserkvi." See also Balyberdin, *Bezumie*, 155.

134. For a recent articulation of this concept, see Grace Davie, "Vicarious Religion: A Response," *Journal of Contemporary Religion* 2, no. 25 (2010): 261–66. See also Douglas Rogers's exploration of the feminization and geriatricization of Old Belief in *The Old Faith and the Russian Land*.

135. See, e.g., Vladimir Krupin, "Bogom khranimaia Viatka," *Internet zhurnal Stretenskogo monastyria*, 2004, http://www.pravoslavie.ru/jurnal/158.htm.

136. GAKO, f. R2169, op. 45, ed. khr. 11, l. 97.

137. Iulia Petrovna Reshetnikova (b. 1933), interviewed in 2000, in *Biulleten foneticheskogo fonda russkago iazyka*, 28

138. See, e.g., "Palomnichestvo i turizm," *Russkii vzgliad*, http://www.poklonnik.ru/site.xp/049048054057124.html.

139. Balyberdin, *Bezumie*, 175; GAKO, R2169, op. 45, ed. khr. 11, ll. 101–2; "Soobshcheniia iz Rossii," samizdat file, Keston, SU/Ort 7/4*Posev* 11 (1981): 3–4.

140. Report reproduced by Evgenii Piatunin, "Grad Velikoretskii," *NG* (July 30, 1999): 16.

141. Galina Nagornichnykh, "Shli liudi na velikuiu," *Viatskii eparkhial'nyi vestnik* 5, no. 259 (May 2009): 13. A 1985 report lists four men and thirteen women (several of whom led groups of up to five pilgrims) known to have visited the river between June 5 and 7. The majority came from Kirov. See GAKO, R2169, op. 45, ed. khr. 11, ll. 107–8. A Council for Russian Orthodox Church Affairs report relating to the registration of Velikoretskoe parish in 1989 observed "in the [19]50s the number [of pilgrims] rose to 15,000 people, in the [19]80s it fell to 400 people." See GAKO, R2169, op. 45, ed. khr. 11, l. 116.

142. Keston News Service, no. 320, February 3, 1989, citing *Moskovskii tserkovnyi vestnik* 12 (1988).

143. "Krestnyi khod na reku velikuiu," *VEV* 6, no. 26 (1992). Vladimir Krupin has done much to raise the profile of Viatka's pilgrim pensioners; see, e.g., "Bogom khranimaia Viatka."

144. See, e.g., Robert Wuthnow, *After Heaven: Spirituality in America since the 1950s* (Berkeley: University of California Press, 1998).

145. Grace Davie, *Religion in Modern Europe: A Memory Mutates* (New York: Oxford University Press, 2002). The relevant literature on pilgrimage is too large to be summarized here, but the following work addresses a number of the issues that have shaped this chapter: Peter Jan Magry, ed., *Shrines and Pilgrimage in the Modern World: New Itineraries into the Sacred* (Amsterdam: Amsterdam University Press, 2008).

146. Vasilevskaia, *Pravedniki*, 89.

# Chapter 6

# Sacramental Confession in Modern Russia and Ukraine

*Nadieszda Kizenko*

Soviet policies toward religious communities and toward specific religious practices did not come only from an ideological commitment to atheism and secularization. In the case of Orthodox Christianity, those policies also rested on a particular suspicion of Orthodoxy as the dominant religion and "ruling faith" of the prerevolutionary Russian empire. Sacramental confession as practiced in the Russian empire before 1917 seemed emblematic of the mutual cooperation of Church and state leaders in their quest for better Christians and better Imperial subjects. In the context of rethinking religion and secularization in twentieth-century Russia and Ukraine, then, it is useful to look at how this sacrament, which had seemed so closely tied to its prerevolutionary cultural context, changed—or did not change—in very different circumstances.

## Background

Talal Asad's governmentalist approach to religion, as discussed in Catherine Wanner's introduction to this volume, has particular resonance when applied to confession. In the Russian empire, from the end of the seventeenth century to 1917, sacramental confession was a legal requirement for Orthodox Christians, required and enforced by the agents and agencies of the secular government (most notably, the Department of Police) as well as those of the Orthodox Church (most notably, the Orthodox priests who were required to maintain detailed records of the dates of parishioners' confessions and to submit those records annually to their religious consistory). The Supplement to the 1722 Spiritual Regulation of Tsar Peter the Great required priests to report anything treasonous they might hear at confession.[1] In the mid–nineteenth century, if people did not go to confession for several years, they might expect a visit from the local police, who acted as a combination of summons delivery service, investigators, and escorts.[2]

Surprisingly, such attempts to enforce participation and to undermine the confessional seal do not seem to have made confession suspect in the eyes of prerevolutionary penitents. Consistory records, liturgical texts, sermons, memoirs, paintings, church decorations, children's fiction, high literature—all testify in different ways that *govenie*, the week-long process of preparation for confession and communion, was an important marker in people's religious lives. Orthodox Christians prepared for annual confession and communion by attending daily Church services, performing works of charity, reading or listening to the prayer rule before confession, and seeking to avoid worldly distractions. After going to confession on the evening before they meant to go to communion, people were expected to abstain from all food and drink until they partook of the Eucharist at the following morning liturgy.[3] As written confessions and priests' guides indicate, most Orthodox believers followed these practices, scheduling their *govenie* for the first or last weeks of Great Lent. Thus, although confession was a private conversation between penitent and priest, the ritualized timing and performance of this action also made this sacrament a communal action that most Orthodox Christians in the Russian empire undertook at the same time. Participation in confession was both private and a sign of collective belonging to the Church and loyalty to the Russian state.

The abdication of Nicholas II ended this symbiosis. A case from the records of the religious consistory in Kazan vividly illustrates the transition. An urban worker convicted of killing another man in a drunken brawl in early 1917 joined the thick police file of criminals whose cases, upon conviction, were automatically transferred to the consistory so that they could be assigned a church penance. The Kazan police knew that it was standard procedure to halve the period of penance and temporary excommunication (*epitimiia*) if a prison sentence or lesser judicial punishment had been assigned as well. Indeed, they had standard forms for precisely this combination of jail sentences meted out by the civil courts, and terms of Church penance meted out by the consistories. When the Kazan police forwarded the worker's case to the consistory in late February 1917 so that he could be assigned his penance, they were following utterly standard prerevolutionary procedure. What set this particular case apart, though, was that by early April—days after the abdication of Nicholas II and the formation of the Provisional Government—the governor-general sent the consistory a new, terse memorandum: "Never mind this case, and never mind any other cases you may have like it. I request that you leave undone all my communications before March 17 of this year concerning the assignment of church penances to those convicted. This procedure is henceforth terminated."[4]

It was not only this procedure that was terminated. The machinery that had provided state support to sacramental penance and confession began to grind to a halt as well. The last confession-related cases in the four major consistories of the empire date from 1917. By 1918, all the consistories had closed. With no more consistories, there were no more centralized records. Individual priests in individual churches continued to keep records of baptisms, weddings, and deaths. In some cases, they maintained private records of participation in confession. But there were no more forms sent out inquiring about confession, and there was no longer any place to send them.

This is the essential problem of examining sacramental confession in the Soviet era. Although there are clear official markers mentioning confession from the first legislation of Tsar Aleksei Mihailovich calling for annual confession (1666) to the last consistory case in Kyiv in 1917, and an abundance of confession-related cases in between, there are no equivalent markers for the Soviet period. Unlike Peter the Great's Spiritual Regulation, which had signaled a new stage of church-state relations, the Soviet-era laws formally separating church and state did not explicitly mention confession.[5] The limitations placed on priests in Soviet-era churches—no formal parish-level education, no publications, no sermons—did not address confession. In fact, to scholars who normally focus on the Imperial or early modern periods or post-Soviet periods, tracking confession in the Soviet period presents a methodological challenge. When most churches have closed, does confession even exist? What traces does it leave?

## Assumptions: Confession and the Secret Police

To complicate the situation, a thicket of assumptions surrounds confession during the Soviet era. The pervasive reigning wisdom follows: In the early Soviet period, priests faced serious pressure by the Cheka and its successors to break the confessional seal.[6] In 1923, for example, the priest Dimitrii Flerin was sent to the prison camp at Solovki for refusing to do just this.[7] The direct and indirect pressures on priests created a climate compromising confessional secrecy. In reaction, priests and their spiritual children devised new forms of confession. It is not only that laypeople themselves ran the risks of being identified as believers; it is that they did not want to put their priests into an uncomfortable position vis-à-vis hostile authorities.[8] As a result of this "perfect storm," auricular confession nearly disappeared and new forms took its place. Most notably, general (public or group) confession would become the norm during, and characteristic of, the Soviet period.[9]

There is at least one problem with this widely accepted model. There is no smoking gun. That is, there is no Soviet-era equivalent of the Supplement to the Spiritual Regulation of Peter the Great, explicitly authorizing (indeed enjoining) priests to disclose anything they heard at confession. However, that in itself is not decisive. During the Imperial period, the *legislation* and the *authorization* for using confession to obtain evidence of treason existed, but the *practice* largely did not.[10] Is it possible that the pattern was reversed after 1918—no explicit legislation, but disclosure all the same? The Soviet government certainly did not recognize that priests had any legal *right* to confidentiality in their contacts with their parishioners.[11] Moreover, the Soviet Union was a country where anonymous denunciation was not only admissible, but encouraged, in prosecuting enemies of the state.[12] But even simply because people "knew" a priest was an agent of the Narodnyy Komissariat Vnutrennikh Del (NKVD; People's Commissariat for Internal Affairs) does not necessarily mean that he specifically reported confessions.[13] If he wanted to denounce people, a priest could do so without any evidence, whether obtained at confession or not. (This was another reason why the Imperial-era civil courts had refused to consider information obtained via confession—ultimately it was no more reliable than anything else.[14]) In Ukraine in 1928, clergy of every denomination, including Mennonites, Lutherans, Muslims, and Jews, worked as informants for their respective co-religionists, and were listed as such on the party's payroll.[15] But, if anything, this suggests that sacramental confession was *not* a privileged source of information, as most denominations did not practice it. One's mere presence in church, or the simple act of wearing a cross, could prompt repression, whether or not one ever went to confession. The problem remains. There is little way to know for sure whether the KGB pressured priests to reveal what they learned at confession, and thus to reach conclusions based on that assumption.

The potential source base for seeking to determine police pressure is problematic as well. Archives of the Federal Security Service of the Russian Federation (Federal'naya sluzhba bezopasnosti Rossiyskoy Federatsii, FSB), and especially records interrogating priests, might allow some idea of how consistently priests may have been asked to report on anything they might have learned via confession, whether this evidence was actually used to round up people, and so on. Alternatively, records of arrested laypeople might reveal patterns, such as denunciation by the same priest. However, FSB files are almost impossible to access unless one is a family member of those involved in the case, making it difficult to reach conclusions based on small samples. In a few cases, the NKVD did apparently seek to use information obtained through sacramental confession. The cases revolve around collectivization, especially during the First Five-Year Plan (1928–32). Then, the state sought to force peasants onto collective farms and to find class enemies. Some available NKVD interrogations of clergy at this time sought to prove that during sacramental confession, peasants sometimes asked their priests whether they should join the *kolkhoz* and that priests then tried to dissuade them. Thus, by claiming that clerics used confession for anti-Soviet agitation, the NKVD could and did repress them for anti-Soviet activity.

According to the files compiled by the NKVD on them, for example, Archimandrite Tikhon (Krechkov), Hegumen Iosif (Iatsuk), and Hieromonk Melkhizedek (Khukhrianskii) used confession to impress upon their flocks that people who joined collective farms risked the closing of their churches and losing God's grace. Father Aleksandr Mil'tonov from Voronezh said under interrogation that "if at confession a peasant would say anything about Soviet rule or blamed it, I would usually absolve him of his sins and say simply, 'Go, and sin no more.'" Priest Sakharov claimed that when peasants from different villages came to him for confession, he would ask them how things were at the collective farm. If people complained about Soviet rule, he would advise them to bear it, saying that better times were ahead.[16]

Of course, it is nearly impossible to determine how much pressure was applied to the clerics at such interrogations, or whether any of these statements were actually uttered. It does seem extremely unlikely that monks and priests, who knew something of what their flocks were going through, would go out of their way to ask provocative questions, whether at confession or otherwise. It seems similarly unlikely that peasants, who normally went to confession once a year, would choose this occasion to murmur against collectivization and Soviet rule. What is interesting here, however, is not *whether* anti-Soviet exchanges actually happened at confession, but simply that the NKVD could *claim* that they did. If the NKVD had been looking for a justification for investigating sacramental confessions, that would have been it.

Without ready access to FSB archives, the most that one can say is that some NKVD cases from both Russia and Ukraine use evidence of anti-Soviet activity supposedly obtained at confession to incriminate monks and priests, but this source does not seem to have been a central element of obtaining information or of deterring penitents. Other reasons for changes in confessional practice over the Soviet era seem more important.

## Changes over Time:
## General Confession and Spiritual Elders

For the purposes of discussing confession, stages during the Soviet era may be divided in the following way: the years 1918–28, from the decree separating Church and State to the eve of the First Five-Year Plan; 1929–39, from the First Five-Year Plan up to the German invasion, including the Terror and the famine; 1941–58, from the relative relaxation of World War II up to Khrushchev's antireligious policies; 1958–64, the years of Khrushchev's antireligious campaign; and thence to 1988.

At first glance, it might seem as if more immediate issues than confession were at stake from 1918 to 1928: Would a church or monastery stay open? Would there be a priest to serve in it? Would it be under the jurisdiction of the Living Church, or under the patriarch or his locum tenens? In the first wave of secularizing policies and the elimination of annual confession and communion records, one might expect the rates of participation in the sacraments to drop, at least among supporters of the Revolution: there was no longer any formal, governmental pressure to observe Orthodox practices, and indeed some informal and formal pressure not to do so.

If anything, strictly as regards confession, the drop in church attendance might have *removed* some of the pressure on parish priests. After all, one of the matters discussed at the Council of 1917–18 had been the phenomenon of unmanageably large numbers of people regularly seeking confession at the same time, especially on major holidays, and especially in monasteries with many visiting pilgrims. Some council delegates, like Bishop Ioann (Smirnov) of Poltava and the well-known religious writer, Evgenii Poselianin, thought that as something exceptional, a "general" confession in which the priest would read a general list of sins before the assembled penitents and then offer the option of supplementary individual confession, might be not only expedient, but even spiritually useful.[17] Such precedents for general confession in pre-Soviet practice existed: Saint John (Sergiev) had practiced general confession in Kronstadt at the turn of the twentieth century, general confession had been used during pilgrimage processions, and military chaplains in the Russian army had used a version of general confession on the eve of battle in World War I.[18] These established uses of general confession help to explain why, out of fifty-four council delegates, only five categorically opposed general confession and regarded it as harmful (at the other extreme, only four thought general confession should or might become the norm).[19] Thus, even independent of Soviet rule, though most clerics and religious thinkers continued to favor individual confessions, most also recognized that in some circumstances exceptions might be made.

The first decade of Soviet rule was such an extraordinary circumstance. General confession in Russia began to be practiced more widely, and in the capital cities of Moscow and Petrograd in particular. This did not need to stem from fears of police informants; in fact, the reasons could be simpler. As arrest without warning and even death were real possibilities, many Orthodox interpreted their situation as a return to the conditions of early Christianity, and sought the sacraments as often as possible. According to a sympathetic observer:

> The persecutions, arrests, and tortures of the faithful sharpened their religious feeling; the times called for special all-night services in which each of those present sought to confess his sins and partake of the Body and Blood of Christ, so that he might meet the coming day, in which he might await torture and death, cleansed and fortified. Given the multitude of those wishing to confess and receive communion, there could be no discussion of private confession.[20]

For at least some penitents, then, general confession in the 1920s arose out of a stronger devotional commitment and extreme circumstances, rather than laxity.

Critics such as Archpriest Valentin Sventsitskii, however, charged that general confession threatened to undermine centuries of Church discipline, and was a sign of creeping secularization (*obmirshchenie*).[21] Instead, in 1921 Sventsitskii formed discussion circles encouraging people to practice a monastic life with or without formal tonsure, including the disclosure of thoughts to a spiritual father, in secret.[22] This new model of ascetic life in the world was the second Soviet-era innovation in the sphere of confession. For devotees of Archpriest Sventsitskii, Priest Sergei Mechev in Moscow, and Hieromonk Varsonofii (Iurchenko) in Ukraine, confession to their spiritual father, often conducted outside a church or monastery, formed a hidden cornerstone of spiritual life.[23] This pattern of regular, hidden extraecclesiastical confession to a spiritual father or mother would persist and indeed expand through the Soviet period.[24] As had been the case with devotees of spiritual elders before the Revolution, sacramental absolution was less important than disclosure of thoughts and spiritual counsel.[25] Because of the closure of monasteries and convents, monasticism itself became more intimately connected to life in the world. Thus, it is possible that the conditions of persecution may have created an additional type of believer—someone who might not have considered entering a monastery before 1917. The Soviet experience, as Scott Kenworthy suggests in chapter 4 of the present volume, complicated the profile of monasticism in Russia and Ukraine, and gave both confession and monastic life an altered or added meaning they did not have before 1917.

Here it is important to distinguish between urban and rural areas, and between ordinary laypeople and those whom Max Weber described as religious "virtuosi." For urban virtuosi in the first decade of Soviet rule, general confession and secret monasticism were important developments. But ordinary rural people from Russia, Ukraine, and Belorussia, when remembering that period at a later time, had a different impression. The few interviews I was able to carry out from 1987 through 1993 with religiously observant laypeople born from 1900 through 1910 suggested that for those who continued to go to confession once a year as they had before 1917, there were few changes in how the sacrament was conducted in the early Soviet period. In particular, there seems to be little sense in this period that the average village dweller feared that the contents of his or her confession might be divulged.[26] Similarly, one of the great elders of the late Soviet period, Archimandrite Pavel (Gruzdev), upon describing the early 1920s, wrote that the nuns he knew from the Mologa convent continued to go to the Tolga monastery for confession, bringing butter, sour cream, and pea flour as gifts from their abbess to the Tolga monks. On the other hand, when those Mologa pilgrims got to Tolga, they saw that only twelve monks were left.[27] This suggests that although, for most religiously observant people, the old confessional habits remained through the 1920s—individual annual confession, giving one's name before confessing, making a donation afterward, and sometimes making a pilgrimage to a monastery specifically for confession—the external attributes to support those traditional practices—a nearby priest, and a church or monastery—were beginning to vanish.

The real turning point came in the second period, beginning with the First Five-Year Plan. The main reason for lower numbers of confessions (and, for that matter, most public religious activities) was the closure of churches. The statistics are well known: by 1939, there were only slightly more than a hundred open churches in all of the USSR, and not a single monastery. In most regions, there was only a single church; twenty-five regions were "churchless."[28] Oral histories corroborate the numbers. To take an example from Ukraine: according to Borys Petrovich Okopnyi of Melitopol' (b. 1926, grandson of two priests), church closings in Zaporizhya started in 1933. By 1935, in all of Zaporizhya, there were only three churches left: the Ascension church in Melitopol, and one dedicated to Saint Panteleimon in Belozerka and another to Saint Nicholas in the village of Tsaritsyn Kut. As Okopnyi noted, with less than a skeletal church structure and clergy members either arrested or gone underground, the number of people receiving sacraments obviously plummeted along with church attendance. Children from even the most ardently religious families had virtually no opportunity to go to confession. And this refers only to people who had not been arrested: confessional practices in prison or forced labor camps, with a larger proportion of clerics and monastics than outside "the zone," are not discussed here.[29]

The German occupation marked a turning point and a revival of Orthodox practice. With the German invasion of Zaporizhya on October 6, 1941, for example, churches reopened. Once again, at least in Zaporizhya, priests and penitents practiced confession as they had before the war: individual auricular confession in church, with prostration before and afterward.[30] Okopnyi's testimony as to the resumption of prerevolutionary practices is confirmed by other Ukrainians of the same generation. Thus, after her first confession in Kirovohrad at the age of seven, in 1942, Tamara Plyshevskaia recalls her mother sending her back to leave a donation to the priest (she had not realized she was expected to do so).[31] In Kharkiv, both before and during World War II, where the only church was divided between the Living Church group (which was nearly empty), and the patriarchal section ("packed to the gills"), parishioners intending to go to confession first gave their names to the churchwarden (*starosta*) or the sacristan (*diak*).[32] This suggests the simple point that when the opportunity to go to confession and communion again appeared in wartime Soviet Ukraine, neither priests nor parishioners had forgotten how to do it—and they did it in the way they remembered. The tradition had been derailed, but it had not been broken.

Churches in Soviet Russia were reopened as well. Although the tendentious *The Truth About Religion in Russia* was published in 1942 with the explicit goal of denying émigré accounts of religious persecution and of German toleration of Orthodox Christianity, even that book acknowledged that it was only in the last two years (i.e., with the German occupation) that "Moscow churches were crowded with worshippers, especially those who were fasting and preparing for communion. . . . All were anxious to make confession and partake of the Sacrament."[33] In 1944, what mattered to Soviet authorities were external signs of clerical loyalty: patriotic sermons, a *moleben* (supplicatory prayer service) for the Red Army, church collections for the Red Army, and so on. Confession and communion were all but irrelevant.[34]

Stalin's meeting with Orthodox hierarchs in September 1943 marked official recognition of the Church in Soviet society. From then until 1959 (with two brief interludes, in 1948–49 and 1954), the Soviet government showed little open hostility toward organized Orthodox activity, as long as it stayed within strictly prescribed limits.[35] Nevertheless, the legacy of the previous years of church closures, persecutions, and dissuasion remained in the form of too few priests and clergy for the number of believers who wished to avail themselves of their services. In Moscow Province, for example, only 215 churches functioned immediately after the war; even that small number declined by about 20 percent in the 1980s (and this for 6 to 8 million people). In the Malyi Donskoi Cathedral in Moscow, eight hundred to a thousand believers took communion on Sundays and holidays.[36] Given this numerical imbalance between priests and parishioners, it is not surprising that general confession—with the priest listing the various kinds of sin, and the flock listening to the list and repenting privately, approaching the priest for a subsequent individual confession only if they had something else to say—became the norm. Some clerics actively supported the practice, citing the holy Father Ioann of Kronstadt's introduction of it before the Revolution as prescient (and later cited the émigré Father Alexander Schmemann's Radio Free Europe broadcasts in their support).[37] A rearguard fight against general confession did persist: in 1944, for example, Archbishop Grigorii (Chukov) of Leningrad criticized the practice as being a "deviation from liturgical norms"; he was supported in 1948 by some provincial bishops.[38] But, from the postwar years onward, for the vast majority of lay believers, general confession became standard practice throughout the Soviet Union.[39]

## Postwar Confessions

This shift did not necessarily mean an inferior experience of repentance. In the hands of talented priests, postwar confession could produce remarkable spiritual fruits. Archpriests Aleksandr Voskresenskii (1875–1950), Tikhon Pelikh (1895–1983), Vasilii Serebrennikov (1907–96), Aleksandr Tolgskii (1880–1962), and Vsevolod Shpiller (1902–84) are only the best-known confessors from the Moscow region who continued the old tradition of Muscovite *dukhovniki*. Particularly telling is how Archpriest Nikolai Golubtsov (1900–1963) conducted confessions for fourteen years in the Church of the Deposition of the Robe, which was reopened in 1943. Golubstov was born in Sergiev Posad to Aleksandr P. Golubtsov, a professor at the Moscow Theological Academy, and his wife Ol'ga Sergeevna, whose spiritual father was Hieroschemamonk Aleksii (Solov'ev).[40] Father Aleksii became the young Nikolai's confessor as well. (This sharing and bequeathing of spiritual fathers within the same family, incidentally, is characteristic of devout and clerical families in the Soviet era.)[41] Remarkably, despite his undesirable (in Soviet terms) social background, Nikolai was able find employment as a scholarly bibliographer. Nikolai was ordained a priest in 1949 at the relatively advanced age of forty-nine, an indicator of difficult conditions in the late 1920s and 1930s.[42]

Father Nikolai was operating under at least two constraints. The large numbers of people in his parish meant that hearing only individual confessions was out of the question. In his parish, as in most others, confessions were heard before the liturgy, during the reading of the hours. Priests were not allowed to begin earlier, as Soviet-appointed *starosty* would open the church only twenty to thirty minutes before a service and close it almost immediately afterward.[43] Moreover, in the conditions of the 1950s and

1960s, preaching sermons was also restricted. Father Nikolai thus hit upon a novel solution that addressed both issues—a solution that other priests began to emulate. His new hybrid "homilies before confession" took the place of both sermons and formulaic general confessions.[44]

On February 28 / March 13, 1953, for example, Father Nikolai linked the liturgical occasion—the Friday of the Fourth Week of Great Lent—to what his flock ought to keep in mind during their confession and communion for the next day's liturgy. He noted that at the end of the day's service, the cross would be returned to the altar from the center of the church—and so proposed to discuss both the sufferings of the Savior and the spiritual quest for eternal life of the believers present in church. After mentioning the repentance of the good thief, he urged every person to emulate the thief (save for waiting until the last minute to confess):

> Throw out all the filth of sin from your soul, and, leaving [confession], you will feel lightness. . . . Do not undertake any action without the blessing of the priest. . . . Confess everything to God—do not be ashamed of revealing to God your sins and bad fleshly impulses, for they inescapably visit all people during their youth and sometimes in old age as well. . . . Approaching the holy chalice, you can be sure that your sins have been forgiven. At confession do not repeat sins that you have already confessed—they are forgiven. If your heart is still tormented by sins you have already confessed, that means you have not done enough good deeds, which could mute and forever banish this foulness from your immortal soul.[45]

Father Nikolai would carry through this linkage of church occasion and confession in other "lectures before confession." Soon after the above homily, for example, he used the day's patron saint, Symeon the New Theologian, to exhort his flock to repentance: "Confession is a second baptism—a baptism in the tears of repentance. You sin, but come to the Lord and plead for forgiveness."[46] According to devoted members of Father Nikolai's flock, his combination of homily, general confession, and individual confession, bore remarkable fruits, although the recognition of the general confession as inferior is worth noting:

> For the sake of [Father Nikolai's] confession, his small church was packed with people even on weekdays. With him, general confession, the mere name of which normally prompts such revulsion in the soul, always left a deep impression, and everyone thought that Father Nikolai's words were directed at him personally. [His] confession (or, more accurately, the homily before

confession) was never standard in content. It always started with a brief recounting of the saint or feast of the day, or the Epistle or the Gospel read at liturgy—and then, on that basis, went not simply a listing of sins, but a sermon understandable to everyone, penetrating into all the recesses of the soul and enlightening the conscience, calling people to a right and righteous way of life, to prayer, to repentance, and to improvement.... And when you come up to the *analoi* and say what is especially weighing down your conscience, Father Nikolai never hurried you—but did not force you to linger either; he showed no surprise at your sin, but, judging it, did not judge the repentant soul. If he found it necessary, he would then and there give a brief and decisive counsel, or utter "Forgive, O Lord!" or "Help, O Lord!" The simplicity with which he took confession eased the penitent's acknowledgment of any sin.

The Soviet-era religious writer Sergei Iosifovich Fudel' also praised Golubtsov's confessions: "I can say both for myself and many others that for many years there was not a single instance where we would return from confession to Father Nikolai with our previous dry soul."[47] It is not surprising that, at his death, Father Nikolai's disconsolate flock described him as "the last Muscovite *dukhovnik*."

Such intimacy with a priest-confessor represents something new. To be sure, some father-confessors in Imperial Russia had devotees among their flocks, particularly among educated women. In the Soviet period, however, other more public forms of religious practice, such as cross processions or pilgrimage to local or faraway shrines or even embroidering icon-covers for public display, had become harder to pursue. Because they were private and could be pursued discreetly, confession and disclosure of thoughts to a spiritual father, and a close relationship to one's spiritual father, became more central to a dedicated religious life. It is worth noting that Father Nikolai's homilies before confession and his general confessions survive only because they were transcribed by three devoted women: Nadezhda Nikitichna Frolova (b. 1927), Nina Fedorovna Zheltova (b. 1922), and Rogneda Vladimirovna Maeva (1924–2004; she was also known as Mitrodora at the end of her life, after she revealed her earlier secret tonsure, which was secret because she had become a monastic earlier in life).[48] These women and others like them formed confessional "families" reminiscent of their predecessors among the Old Believers. Soviet-era confessional "families," both among the secret monastic "virtuosi" and their lay counterparts, consisted of people linked to the same confessor who maintained contacts in other aspects of their everyday lives.[49] Such closeness among spiritual children of a father-confessor, nearly unknown in the prerevolutionary period even for such celebrated elders as those of Optina and of Father John of Kronstadt, stemmed from the sense of being the "faithful remnant" or the select and embattled few in the Soviet period.[50] This closeness to spiritual fathers persisted even amid a wide range of confessional styles. Though Father Nikolai's homily topics could be intellectually stimulating, he made a point of having his discussion of sin be accessible to the most uneducated present. Archimandrite Pavel Gruzdev, by contrast, favored a general confession that was downright colloquial and very short, saving more extended discussions about his penitents' spiritual life for private conversations outside of church.[51]

Other extraordinary Muscovite priests in the 1970s and 1980s continued the confessional focus of their predecessors. Priests Dimitry Dudko, Vsevolod Shpiller, and Alexander Men', for example, had large confessional families and used the first confession of grownups as an occasion to instruct them in Orthodox Christianity. Thus, a first confession could take the form of several conversations, inside or outside of church, where the priest learned the spiritual autobiography of the convert and taught him or her about the faith.[52] This confessional practice of the 1970s and early 1980s, like few other religious phenomena, indicates a key change in Orthodox Christianity as experienced by inhabitants of the old Russian empire. What had been a broad base of Orthodox Christians sharing a similar experience of sacramental confession, whatever their individual degrees of personal commitment—a well-prepared first experience at the age of seven, annual performance at ritual times thereafter—had moved to a far smaller subset. Sacramental confession went from something shared by even nominal Orthodox Christians to something limited to a small group—but more important for that small group. The devotional clusters of the 1970s and 1980s also indicate a shift from the discussion-confession circles around a priest or elder that arose in the 1920s. Both groups were conscious of their opposition to the existing regime. But in the 1920s, confession was both a link to the past and something that had acquired a heightened intensity for Christians facing the real risks of arrest and execution. By the 1970s and 1980s, going to confession was linked to discovery and even political dissidence, with various priests representing different political and intellectual strains as much as spiritual ones.

Not all "elders" belonged to the official clergy. Elder Sampson (Sivers), for example, had a large lay following among those who flocked to his general confessions while he was a priest—and those who distributed his spiritual talks after he was defrocked.[53] One might ask whether the *starets* (elder) phenomenon began to spread in the Soviet era further than it had in the past because the elder (man or woman) was not always linked to official church structures, which some people mistrusted after Metropolitan Sergii (Stragorodskii)'s declaration of loyalty to the Soviet regime in 1927.[54] But, even before 1917, especially in remote rural areas, it was not uncommon to have self-proclaimed elders to whom believers, especially women, would flock. Both before 1917 and after 1941, the official hierarchy enlisted the support of state agencies in seeking to clamp down on the "unofficial" elders, although the penalties obviously differed.[55]

After 1988, with more churches and more clerics, individual confession largely replaced the general one. Celebrated Muscovite confessors now explained to their numerous spiritual children that they need not feel compelled to have any contact with one another outside of church.[56] As the product of extraordinary circumstances leading to greater-than-usual closeness, the confessional family has receded into the past.

## Changing Notions about Sin and Penance

One might ask whether the notion of what constituted a sin changed at any point in the Soviet era. Maria Sil'vestrovna Plyshevskaia, for example, engaged in "speculation" in late 1938 and 1939. That is, she bought shoes and felt boots, and then tried to sell them in the Kirovohrad market. When she saw the police heading for her stand, she vanished into the crowd and managed to avoid arrest. She understood that what she was doing was a crime, and would have carried severe penalties had she been caught. Nevertheless, partly because before 1929 she had gone to fairs and supplemented her income with selling produce or handiwork, she did not regard her attempt to buy and sell as a sin *in itself*, and so did not mention it at confession, even when she began to go again.[57]

The interesting thing is whether she and others in her position were ever asked about such things at confession when the possibility of regular confession resumed. If the person does not remember, or does not choose to share the information, how can we know? If general confession is the norm, and it is left to believers' discretion whether they wish to have an individual confession at all, then there would have been no opportunity for the priest to ask. One useful source for such matters is the Soviet-era priests' tableside companions, the *Nastol'nye knigi* published in 1979, 1983, and 1988 (the very fact that no such guide had been published between 1914 and 1979 says a lot).[58] Similarly useful are notes on homilies before confession. In those, as in their prerevolutionary predecessors, priests learned how to translate the commandments into queries about their penitents' spiritual state. It is in these working guides that we can glean something of how priests in the Soviet period understood, say, the questions of "Thou shalt not steal," and how they sought to instill those attitudes in their flocks. They also offer an illustration of the impact of post-1958 repression.

The 1983 edition of the *Nastol'naia kniga*, for example, warns priests that penitents too often understand the commandment to mean burglary or theft. But the priest should explain before confession that it also covers "the resale of food and industrial products at higher prices (speculation). Riding in public transport without having paid the fare is also an act that should be regarded as a breaking of the eighth commandment."[59]

Of course, one cannot know to what extent priests actually followed these guides, whether before 1917 or afterward. One might also inquire whether the Soviet-era priests' guides should be regarded with greater skepticism than their prerevolutionary predecessors. To the first objection—a familiar one with any source that is prescriptive rather than descriptive—one might note that the prerevolutionary *Priests' Tableside Companions* frequently cite examples of their topics from the contemporary press (*Rukovodstvo dlia sel'skikh pastyrei, Tserkovnye Viedomosti*, various *Eparkhial'nye Viedomosti*, and the like). Moreover, their contents are corroborated by not only periodicals, but all other sources available—contemporary literature, art, correspondence, consistory cases, and court cases. Finally, they are the equivalent of technical manuals, clearly meant to be what they claim they are: practical tools for contemporary priests (rather than an elaborate ruse to deceive later historians or the laity).[60]

The second objection is more interesting. Should Soviet-era *Priests' Companions* be automatically more suspect? Rather than arguing from principle or deduction, I would suggest a straightforward comparison from one edition to another. What, if anything, changes over time? And what might the changes during the Soviet period tell us?

Perhaps the most striking aspect is the continuity with prerevolutionary priests' guides. As in those publications, there is a historical section and a purely technical section (which prayers are to be read in what order, what vestments the priest is to wear, where he should stand, what sequence the confession should follow, etc.).[61] There is a similar abundance of inspirational extracts from famed Imperial-era clerics and the holy fathers.[62] Priests are similarly enjoined against neglecting the confession and communion of the sick at their homes, or last rites (although there is no longer any mention of the disciplinary sanctions the priest will incur for this). Priests are still instructed to distinguish between "those superstitions that grossly contradict Orthodox teaching and piety" (e.g., using Church objects for magic rituals), and those that do not harm Orthodox and Christian morality (requests to open the Royal Doors on the iconostasis during a difficult childbirth, making the sign of the cross over one's mouth while yawning, bathing on the dawn of Holy Thursday, "and the like"). One might surmise either that the Guides were simply reproducing earlier copy—or that such practices had actually persisted into the 1980s among the kinds of people who went to church. Interestingly, although the eighteenth-century injunctions against "spreading rumors about the end of the world, false miracles and signs" had lessened by the end of the nineteenth century, they returned toward the end of the Soviet era.[63]

But there were changes from Imperial-era guides, and it is these additions and the deletions that are key to understand what, if anything, changed in the Soviet period. First, general confession was acknowledged to have become common practice, but was noted to be improper from the point of view of both liturgical theology and good church order. The proposed solution was to encourage people to stagger their confessions over different times during the four Church fasts (one might thus surmise that this goal of Imperial-era clergy had not been achieved by the end of the Soviet period).[64] Lacking that, before reading the prayer of absolution, priests were urged to give every penitent the chance to individually confess the sins that most bothered him or her.[65]

Perhaps the most significant change from the prerevolutionary guides (or, for that matter, from the statistics for the Moscow region in the immediate postwar years) is the level of familiarity (or rather, lack thereof) with the sacrament and the socioeconomic background of believers of which priest must be aware:

> Along with people who believe deeply and sincerely, . . . come people with little connection to the Church, who come to confession for the first time as adults. Most parishioners belong to the category of low- or semi-skilled laborers and peasants; if we also bear in mind that the vast majority of the faithful are middle-aged and old people who never got a real education, and completely lack systematic knowledge of Church sacraments and dogma, then the pastor, at every confession, must first, even to a minimal degree, explain the basic truths of Christianity.[66]

To be sure, prerevolutionary clerics had also bemoaned their flocks' ignorance and superstition. But by the beginning of the twentieth century, in the territories of both present-day Russia and present-day Ukraine, they could also assume that Orthodox Christians had gone to their first confession at the age of seven, and had gone to confession more or less annually. Clearly by the late 1970s, this was no longer the case.[67] Evgeniia Nikolaevna Kuzovenkova, for example, was baptized only in 1982 at the age of sixty. She had been a party member and a medical doctor. She had feared becoming baptized openly because her children might have had problems at school and work. But fearing confession in itself never entered her mind. After baptism in 1982, she continued to partake of the sacraments of confession and communion roughly once a month until her death in 2003.[68]

Also telling is the implicit acknowledgment that, because confession (along with other forms of Orthodox practice) was no longer something for all of society (particularly no longer something for young men), some sins were less relevant among those who went to confession: "Every experienced priest knows that at confession few people will admit to theft [and] robbery, not to mention premeditated murder, and one need not ask about such sins—in our day they are rare among Christians." Other comments reflect changing sexual mores: "The questions and sins provided by Church Slavonic Trebnik concern such rare perversions (incest, bestiality) that their mere utterance might provoke only discomfiture and temptation. . . . Asking about the sin of masturbation is appropriate with regard to boys, youths, and bachelors, but one should hardly pose it to girls and women."[69]

Similarly novel are detailed condemnations of theosophy, karma, and the occult. Although *bozhba*—using the name of the Lord (or His Mother) in vain or in cursing—was not new, the implacable sternness with which priests battled it at confession was, as they could deny communion if the penitent did not "decisively overcome this sin, regarding it as minor. Indeed it is precisely with this spiritual disease that should begin the fight for the spiritual health of one's flock—with this sickness, as catchy and persistent as a sniffle, and as fraught with sad consequences."[70] Neglect of church services, another perennial sin, is now explained in passing with "this is explained by a lack of Church education and an interruption of [a break in] religious traditions in the family." Clearly, what caused the break in the maintenance in religious traditions did not need to be spelled out. If a penitent says in confession that he prays "using his own words," and not those of the Orthodox prayer book, the *Guide* informs the priest that "this most often means he does not pray at all."[71] New realities about divorce may be gleaned from the comment that: "At confession priests have to hear stories about tragic family conflicts, most often arising as the result of an intemperate use of alcohol or the unfaithfulness of one of the spouses. Often in such cases the priest-confessor is asked whether such a marriage ought to be preserved or whether it would not be better to dissolve it."[72]

Finally, although prerevolutionary *Guides* mentioned abortion and infanticide as matters to ask women of childbearing age, the late Soviet-era editions discuss abortion (legal for decades) at far greater length. Particularly interesting here is the following comment:

> A woman who does not belong to the Church is warned against this action [abortion] by medical personnel. . . . However, the unbelieving woman is free to act upon herself as she wishes. Whereas for a woman who acknowledges belonging to the Orthodox Church (and clearly every baptized woman who comes to church for confession should be regarded as such), the artificial interruption of pregnancy is categorically inadmissible and forgivable only in extraordinary circumstances when carrying a pregnancy to term threatens her life.[73]

The *Guide* bemoaned that

> some priests mention this terrible sin at general confession along with other [sin]s and [then] absolve it without even having discussed it with the sinner at a personal confession, without having clarified the reasons that impelled her to this act, and without having heard from her a single word of repentance. By this they cover an unrepented sin, which is perilous for the soul of the confessing woman; they commit a crime against pastoral conscience; and they sow temptation among the other parishioners.[74]

Misogyny in the context of confession also made its first appearance in the Soviet-era priests' guides. Snide comments by clerics and hierarchs about women (and particularly educated women) at confession were not new. What is striking is that previously they had appeared not in formal, "canonical" priests' tableside companions, but only in individual essays.[75] Perhaps as a reaction to the feminization of piety in the postwar Soviet era, however, late Soviet-era priests' guides and priests' essays focus on women and their supposedly specific confession-related defects. In speaking of spiritual delusion known as *prelest'*, for example, a late Soviet-era *Tableside Companion* asserts that "the priest most often encounters such pathological phenomena in the confessions of women prone to hysteria, and this should, everything else aside, serve to test his pastoral patience."[76]

Soviet-era clerical memoirs went further than the guides. Archpriest Mikhail Ardov, for example, noted that though most of the faithful at confession need to have each word literally pried out of them, "educated women comprise a significant exception; these truly hold forth 'beyond all reason and nature.'"[77]

Thus, in several telling ways—the condemnation of "speculation" or riding in public transport for free, in the acknowledgment of little childhood exposure to religion and the relatively limited number of people who go to confession, of legal and readily available abortion and divorce—these changes in instructions for priests on how to conduct confessions seem to correspond to aspects of Soviet life in the late 1970s. In this respect, they support Maria Korogodina's contention that changes in penitentials from the fourteenth through the seventeenth century similarly reflect social and political changes in Rus'.[78] The politically engaged might wish for a more direct or trenchant commentary on Soviet-era life. However, it is precisely the relatively limited and guarded nature of priestly guidelines that gives them their verisimilitude; it is easy to imagine that these are the kinds of confessions that actually took place in the postwar era up to perestroika.

## Statistics

Such guides, homilies, and memoirs form a necessary background to assessing the few statistics on confession available for the Soviet period. Edward E. Roslof examined the reports of Aleksei Alekseevich Trushin, a regional commissioner from 1943 to 1984 for the Council for Russian Orthodox Church Affairs (later the Council for Religious Affairs).[79] In his paper, Roslof was struck by how few (fewer than ten) references there were to confession, compared with hundreds of references to baptisms, weddings, funerals, ordinations, bell-ringing, and even the blessing of livestock. The Moscow Central Municipal Archive and the State Archive of the Russian Federation kept records on income, expenses, clergy, and churches.[80] Yet on confession these archives were almost completely devoid of information.[81]

The few references to confession that Roslof did find were telling. Strikingly, as Roslof notes, in Trushin's first detailed postwar report on the activity of the Russian Orthodox Church in Moscow Oblast as of January 1, 1947, confession figured prominently. According to Trushin's calculations, in every church in Moscow region villages, up to 2,000 people had gone to confession annually (compared with up to 200 baptisms and up to 150 funerals); in Moscow itself, up to 10,000 people went to confession annually (compared with up to 800 baptisms and 1,000 funerals). Thus, nearly 1 million residents of the city and region went to confession every year (confirming the estimates of eyewitnesses from the Donskoi monastery). Given that general confession had become entrenched, and it would be impossible to determine how many people approached the priest for a follow-up individual confession, it is worth asking how Trushin reached those estimates. Because he did not provide separate statistics for communion, I would suggest that perhaps he conflated confession with communion, or rather extrapolated the number of people who had gone to confession based on how many had gone to communion (which had to be administered individually and thus could be counted).

Trushin also noted that priests told him that during exam time, students in secondary and postsecondary schools came to confession more often.[82] Although Trushin reported nothing on confession for several years after 1947, he noted in 1951 that more churches in Moscow had begun holding special services at the start of the academic year. Although one might assume that these services were simply the standard *molebens* before school, Trushin mentioned that one priest told the children "during general confession" to be conscientious in school and avoid noisy arguments on the street.[83] Similarly, in 1952, Trushin noted that a priest named Ozerov used individual confession to remind children to attend services.[84] These references, rare as they are, might suggest why, by the end of the 1950s, Council reports described confession as a tool the clergy used to agitate among the susceptible young.[85] Roslof suggests that concern over such perceived agitation may have fueled the antireligion campaign during Nikita Khrushchev's drive to revive communist ideology. In the three decades that followed, Roslof found only two other references to confession—one from 1962 recounting a priest saying to another that only women came for confession, and one from 1970 describing a priest refusing to hear the confessions of couples who had not been married in church.[86]

## Conclusion

A study of sacramental confession in Soviet-era Russia and Ukraine, then, complicates several assumptions. Certainly, for most believers, the combination of secularizing pressures, church closures, and fewer priests meant that individual confession was replaced by general confession. The routine, institutionalized aspect of confession before 1917, which had made individual auricular confession something familiar to the average Orthodox Christian believer, vanished. On the other hand, for religious "virtuosi," confession became a more central element of religious life. Indeed, in a Soviet-era innovation reminiscent of Old Belief, private confessional "families" formed around charismatic father confessors. By the late 1970s, the people who went to confession in the Soviet Union were the dedicated, those with little to lose, and, in Moscow and Leningrad, clusters of intelligentsia who had assembled around celebrated clerics. Confession had moved from being part of routine practice to becoming a sign of commitment to faith. The overall feminization of piety during the Soviet period also led to an increasing feminization of confession.

As we consider these Soviet-era changes, however, it is important to put them in a larger perspective. Given the often-perfunctory nature of annual confession before 1917, it can be argued that the general confession of the Soviet era simply took the previous *pro forma* aspect of confession a step further. If one bears in mind the infrequency with which Orthodox Christians of other nationalities went to confession, including Greeks, Bulgarians, and Serbs, and the changes in Roman Catholic approaches to the sacrament during the 1960s, one could argue that the general confession of the Soviet period, paradoxically, brought the practices of Russians and Ukrainians *more* in line with those of other traditions rather than *less*.[87] The enthusiastic revival of individual confession in both Russia and Ukraine after 1991, however, suggests that the changes during the Soviet period served as a kind of trial period for some forms of confession that were more similar to those of other traditions, only to have them rejected in favor of returning to precisely what had distinguished prerevolutionary Imperial practice (and Roman Catholic practice before Vatican II): the linkage between individual auricular confession and partaking of communion.

Finally, it is important to recall that, *in itself*, change in the practice of confession need not be automatically suspect nor automatically linked to Soviet policies. After all, the practice of penance changed substantially in the early Church, partly in response to a crisis of discipline created by persecution. In the sixth century, penance changed from being a mostly public to a mostly private act, and from being a once-in-a-lifetime opportunity to a regular, annual practice. As John McNeill and Helena Gamer noted:

The new barbarized society could not be subjected to the old discipline which had already proved too severe for the Roman Christians. After much ground had been lost and public penance had been almost extinguished, a new system was to develop, more workable in this turbulent state of society and more applicable to its needs.[88]

Why, then, should we be surprised at changes in practice in twentieth-century Russia and Ukraine? Even before the Soviet period, some Russian clerics had noted a crisis of confession. In circumstances very different from those of the Soviet Union, some émigré Russian clerics called for eliminating confession as a prerequisite for communion. Most notably, Father Alexander Schmemann of Saint Vladimir's Seminary in Crestwood, New York, devoted much of his pastoral work and writing to phasing out individual confession in favor of having Orthodox Christians partake of Holy Communion at every liturgy.[89] Indeed, between 1960 and 1990, the practice of confession changed more in the Orthodox Church of America and in the Roman Catholic Church than it did in the USSR. Perhaps the surprising thing is not how much the practice of confession changed during the Soviet period in response to secularizing pressures, but rather how little.

## Notes

1. *Polnoe sobranie zakonov* 6, no. 3984 (n.d.): 666. See "Supplement to the Spiritual Regulation of Peter the Great," in *The Spiritual Regulation of Peter the Great*, translated and edited by Alexander V. Muller (Seattle: University of Washington Press, 1972), 60–63.

2. See, e.g., the surveillance and separation of an illegally cohabiting couple who were noticed partly because they avoided confession. Sulyma and Kolomiitseva, 1856, Tsentral'nyi derzhavnyi istorychnyi arkhiv Ukrainy (Ukraine Central State Historical Archives; hereafter TsDIAK), f. 127, op. 896, d. 133.

3. For an example of guides to preparation for confession, see Protopresviter Grigorii Diachenko, *Voprosy na ispoviedi vzroslykh khristian* (Moscow: Russkii Khronograf, 1913). For laypeople's accounts of their observance, see the personal records of Ioann (Sergiev), Tsentral'nyi gosudarstvennyi istoricheskii arkhiv Sankt-Peterburga (Central State Historical Archive of Saint Petersburg), f. 2219, op. 1, d. 31 (confessions), ll. 1–220.

4. Ob otmene predanii provinivshikhsia tserkovnomu pokaianiiu, March 10, 1917, Natsional'nyi Arkhiv Respubliki Tatarstanam (National Archive of the Tatarstan Republic), f. 4 (Kazan Religious Consistory), op. 149, d. 34, l. 4.

5. Relevant legislation includes that of January 23, 1918 (separation of church and state), April 8, 1929 (on religious associations), and October 1, 1929 (the Instructions of the People's Commissariat of Internal Affairs). See Nikolai M. Orleanskii, *Zakon o religioznykh ob'edineniiakh RSFSR. . .* (Moscow: Bezbozhnik, 1930), 6–25, 170–71.

6. Bishop Leonty (Filipovich) describes such cases from Ukraine in his "Politicheskie Kontroli Nad Pravoslavnoiu Tserkoviu v Sovetskom Soiuze," manuscript in Bakhmeteff Archives, Columbia University, New York, n.d., 127, 134–36.

7. "O. Dimitrii Flerin," permanent SLON exhibit at Solovki State Historical, Architectural, and Natural Museum-Reserve, Onega Bay, Solovetsky District, Arkhangelsk Oblast.

8. Archpriest Aleksandr Golubtsov, a 1970 graduate of the Moscow Theological Academy, has compared the position of Russians and Ukrainians during the Soviet era to that of Greeks and South Slavs under Ottoman rule. If Christians think their hierarchy and clergy might be compromised, they instinctively change aspects of their spiritual life, both to avoid putting priests in an awkward position and to protect themselves. Golubov, "Lectures on the Liturgy," Jackson, N.J.; and discussion with the author, February 8, 2010. On this comparison, see also Timothy Ware, *The Orthodox Church* (New York: Penguin Books, 1986), 96–101, 111.

9. Hieromonk Iov (Gumerov), "Pokaianie: Osnova dukhovnoi zhizni," *Pravoslavnaia vera*, no. 44 (September 2010): 5, 19.

10. The only two Russian cases of denunciations over two centuries, from 1734 and 1742, ended with one denouncing priest being defrocked, having his nostrils slit, and being sent to Siberia for permanent hard labor, whereas the other was executed. Rossiiskii gosudarstvennyi istoricheskii arkhiv (Russian State Historical Archive; hereafter RGIA), f. 796, op. 15, d. 144, and op. 23, d. 366, l. 83. By the mid-nineteenth century in Ukraine, when Priest Vasilii Gritsenko from Cherkasy alerted the police to a possible crime he had learned at confession, it was the police who refused his evidence, informed the Kyiv consistory of the priest's "immodesty regarding the sacrament of confession," and asked the consistory to have him desist in the future. The priest received only a stern reprimand. TsDIAK, f. 127, op. 896 (1852), d. 92, ll. 2–5.

11. By contrast, the nineteenth-century and early-twentieth-century synods expressly upheld the confessional seal in every attempt to use material from confession in criminal cases. See RGIA, f. 796, op. 131, d. 1389, ll. 1–6.

12. Vladimir A. Kozlov, "Denunciation and Its Functions in Soviet Governance from the Archive of the Soviet Ministry of Internal Affairs," in *Stalinism: New Directions*, edited by Sheila Fitzpatrick (London: Routledge, 1999), 117–41.

13. For a discussion of a 1943 informant, Priest Nikolai Kol'chitskii, see Natalia N. Sokolova, *Pod krovom vsevyshnego* (Moscow: Izd. Prav. Bratstva sv. Ap. Ioanna bogoslova, 2002), 59.

14. See the discussion of Russian legal precedent by Senator Tagantsev in Gosudarstvennyi arkhiv Rossiiskoi Federatsii (State Archive of the Russian Federation; hereafter GARF), f. 564, op. 1, d. 641, ll. 1–3.

15. Tsentral'nyi Derzhavnyy Arkhiv Gromads'kykh Ob'ednan' Ukrainy (Central State Archive of Ukrainian Civic Organizations), f. 1, op. 16, spr. 34, avk. 94–95. I am grateful to Liudmila Grynevich for this reference.

16. Sledstvennoe delo A. Buiia, Arkhiv Voronezhskogo (Administration of the Federal Security Services of the Russian Federation), quoted by I. I. Osipova, *Skvoz' ogn' muchenii i vodu slez: Goneniia na istinno-pravoslavnuiu tserkov' po materialam sledstvennykh i lagernykh del zakliuchennykh* (Moscow: Serebriannye niti, 1998), 108, 114.

17. *Otzyvy eparkhial'nykh arkhieireev po voprosu o tserkovnoi reforme*, part II (Saint Petersburg, 1906; Moscow: Izdatel'stvo krutitskogo podvor'ia, 2004), 334–35.

Poselianin had earlier articulated his position in E. Poselianin, "Ispovied", *Tserkovnyi Golos*, no. 15 (1907): 414.

18. Protopresviter Georgii Shavel'skii, *Pravoslavnoe pastyrstvo* (Saint Petersburg: Izd. Russkogo Khristianskogo gumanitarnogo instituta, 1996), 597–602.

19. Mitred Protoierei Nikolai Balashov, *Na puti k liturgicheskomu vozrozhdeniiu: Pomestnyi sobor 1917–1918 gg. i predsobornyi period* (Moscow: Kul'turno-Prosvetitel'skii Tsentr Dukhovnaia Biblioteka, 2001), 392.

20. Shavel'skii, *Pastyrstvo*, 605.

21. Protopresviter Valentin Sventitsky, *Six Lectures on the History of the Mystery of Repentance: Against General Confession* (Jordanville, N.Y.: Holy Trinity Monastery, 1996).

22. Abbot Herman, "New Russian Confessor Achpriest Valentin Sventitsky," *The Orthodox Word*, July–August 1983, 133.

23. Jennifer Wynot, "Monasteries without Walls: Secret Monasticism in the Soviet Union, 1928–1939," *Church History* 71, no. 1 (March 2002): 63–79.

24. See, e.g., Natalia Sokolova's account of the secret nuns clustered around the elder Isaiah in the 1940s, making a living as an *artel'* of seamstresses. Sokolova, *Pod krovom*, 64–66.

25. A. Beglov, "Asketicheskaia pis'mennost' epokhi gonenii kak sistema marginalii," *Al'fa i Omega* 1 no. 54 (2009): 121–25.

26. Maria Silvestrovna Plyshevskaia (born in Belorussia), interview by the author, Jackson, N.J., March 15–18, 1993; and Marfa Samoilovna Shekhova (born in Belorussia), interview by the author, Trenton, N.J., April 1987.

27. *Rodnye moi: Rasskazy i propovedi arkhimandrita Pavla (Gruzdeva)* (Iaroslavl: Izd. Kitezh, 2004), 156.

28. See, e.g., GARF, f. 5263, op. 1, d. 891 (Kuibyshev district), ll. 2–6. See also Tatiana A. Chumachenko, *Church and State in Soviet Russia: Russian Orthodoxy from World War II to the Khrushchev Years*, edited and translated by Edward E. Roslof (Armonk, N.Y.: M. E. Sharpe, 2002), 49.

29. E.g., when in the late 1940s Gruzdev and his fellow prisoners were separated from their convoy, they tried to find a church so that they could go to confession and communion. All that held them back was not having any money to give the priest for confession. After an old man gave them 3 rubles, each had enough for confession and some candles. Gruzdev, *Rodnye moi*, 103.

30. Borys Petrovich Okopnyi, interview by the author, Jackson, N.J., February 16, 2010.

31. Tamara Ivanovna Plyshevskaia, interview by the author, Jackson, N.J., February 15, 2010.

32. Protopresviter Boris Ivanovich Kizenko, interview by the author, Jackson, N.J., February 15, 2010. This dismissal of Renovationists is confirmed in other memoirs (Sokolova, *Pod krovom*, 17), and explored by Gregory L. Freeze, "Counter-Reformation in Russian Orthodoxy: Popular Response to Religious Innovation, 1922–1925," *Slavic Review* 54, no. 2 (Summer 1995): 305–39.

33. Nicholas (Yarushevich) (metropolitan of Kyiv and Galicia) et al., eds., *The Truth about Religion in Russia, Issued by the Moscow Patriarchate* (London: Hutchinson, 1942), 89.

34. GARF, f. 6991, Sovet po delam Russkoi Pravoslavnoi Tserkvi, op. 2, d. 12, ll. 2–6.

35. See Chumachenko, *Church and State in Soviet Russi*a, x.

36. Ibid., 4–5; Nun Iulianiia (Samsonova), "Introduction," in *Besedy pered ispoved'iu*, by Protopresviter Nikolai Golubtsov (Moscow: Izd. Moskovskogo Podvor'ia Sviato-Troitskoi Sergievoi Lavry, 2009), 5; Gumerov, "Pokaianie—osnova dukhovnoi zhizni," 5.

37. Mikhail Ardov (archpriest), *Melochi arkhi . . ., proto . . ., i prosto iereiskoi zhizni (kartinki s natury)* (Moscow: Izd. imeni Sabashnikovykh, 1995), 95. Schmemann did not in fact support general confession, but he thought that individual confession need not be an inevitable requirement for communion.

38. Metropolit Grigorii Chukov, "Address, November 8, 1944," in *Selected Speeches, Talks, and Articles*, edited by Izbrannye Rechi, Slova, i Stat'i (Moscow, 1954), http://www.bogoslov.ru/text/print/1013701.html; Sovet po religii pri SM SSSR, 1948, GARF, f. 6991, op. 2, d. 34a, l. 57.

39. Conversely, "virtuosi" could have had more intimate access to confession, e.g., making one's confession after seeing a salacious theatrical performance. Sokolova, *Pod krovom*, 78.

40. The hieromonk was martyred in 1928 and canonized in Moscow in 2000. See Samsonova, "Introduction," 4.

41. See the discussion of similar phenomena given by Sokolova, *Pod krovom*, 35.

42. Golubtsov, *Besedy pered ispoved'iu*, 5.

43. Paraskeva Vasil'evna Nikitina, interview by the author, Saint Petersburg, January 1992; Gumerov, "Pokaianie—osnova dukhovnoi zhizni," 5.

44. Golubtsov, *Besedy pered ispoved'iu*, 6–7.

45. Ibid., 56–59.

46. Ibid., 72.

47. S. I. Fudel', "Vospominaniia ob otse Nikolae Aleksandroviche Golubtsove," in *Sobranie sochinenii v trekh tomakh* (Moscow: Russkii put', 2001), vol. 1, 225.

48. Their practice was to write down the confessional homilies from memory, show them to Fr. Nikolai for corrections, and then type them out. Golubtsov, *Besedy pered ispoved'iu*, 9–12.

49. Sokolova, *Pod krovom*, 89–97.

50. Indeed, many postwar priests insisted upon regular confession to a degree unprecedented in Russian practice. See Gleb Kaleda, *Domashniaia Tserkov' (ocherki dukhovno-nravstvennykh osnov sozidaniia i postroeniia sem'i v sovremennykh usloviiakh*, 3rd ed. (Moscow: Izd. Zachat'evskogo Monastyria, 2001), 58–59.

51. Gruzdev, *Rodnye moi,* 162–66.

52. O. Dimitrii Dudko, *O nashem upovanii* (Paris: YMCA Press, 1975); Dudko, interview by the author, Moscow, June 19, 1980; Yves Hamant, *Alexander Men': A Witness for Contemporary Russia (A Man for Our Times)* (Torrance, Calif.: Oakwood Publications, 1995), 120–21.

53. Hieroschemamonk Sampson Sivers, *Zhivyi i po smerti: ieroskhimonakh Sampson, graf Sivers* (Moscow: Derzhava, 2004), 25–30.

54. Mitrokhin, *Russkaia Pravoslavnaia Tserkov'*, 92–100.

55. See Irina Paert, *Spiritual Elders: Charisma and Tradition in Russian Orthodoxy* (DeKalb: Northern Illinois University Press, 2010), 179–213.

56. Protopresviter Maksim Kozlov, *Klir i mir: Kniga o zhizni sovremennogo prikhoda* (Moscow: Khram Sviatoi Muchenitsy Tatiany pri MGU, 2008), 123.

57. Maria Sil'vestrovna Plyshevskaia, interview with the author, Jackson, N.J., April 1993.

58. For confession-related issues, see, e.g., *Nastol'naia kniga sviashchennosluzhitelia*, vol. 4 (Moscow: Izd. Moskovskoi Patriarkhii, 1983), 242–87.

59. *Nastol'naia kniga*, vol. 4, 281.

60. The most widely used late Imperial *Nastol'nye knigi* include those given by S. V. Bulgakov, *Nastol'naia kniga dlia sviashchenno-tserkovno-sluzhitelei (sbornik sviedienii, kasaiushchikhsia preimushchestvenno prakticheskoi deiatel'nosti otechestvennago dukhovenstva)*, part 2 (Kharkov: Tip. Gubernskago Pravleniia, 1900) (pages pertaining to confession are indicated), 1047–112, and P. Nechaev, *Prakticheskoe rukovodstvo dlia sviashchennosluzhitelei, ili sistematicheskoe izlozhenie polnago kruga ikh obiazannosteiiii i prav* (Saint Petersburg: I. N. Skorokhodova, 1890), 176–90.

61. *Nastol'naia kniga*, vol. 4, 244–47.

62. Ibid., vol. 6, 762–74.

63. Ibid., 265. For eighteenth-century Church condemnations of "false signs and wonders," see Muller, *Spiritual Regulation*, xxix, 13–16, 62–63; and A. S. Lavrov, *Koldovstvo i religiia v Rossii, 170–1740gg.* (Moscow: Drevlekhranilishche, 2000).

64. Given that the churches in Moscow and Saint Petersburg had daily services, people wishing to go to individual confession could do so on weekdays. The monasteries that Scott Kenworthy discusses in chapter 4 of the present volume were another possibility.

65. *Nastol'naia kniga*, vol. 4, 244.

66. Ibid., 249. This emphasis on the backward rural population also characterized Khrushchev. See Andrew B. Stone, "'Overcoming Peasant Backwardness': The Khrushchev Antireligious Campaign and the Rural Soviet Union," *Russian Review* 67 (April 2008): 296–320.

67. Nevertheless, based on the apt comments on how to confess children and teenagers, at least some did. Let us not forget that if schools learned that children were getting a religious education, their parents could lose their jobs. Sokolova, *Pod krovom*, 40.

68. Evgeniia Nikolaevna Kuzovenkova, interview by and discussion with the author, Saint Petersburg, 1997.

69. *Nastol'naia kniga*, vol. 4, 252. Prerevolutionary guides, by contrast, included these sins precisely because Imperial-era Russians confessed to them. See Nadieszda Kizenko, "Written Confessions and the Structure of Sacred Narrative," in *Sacred Stories: Religion and Spirituality in Modern Russian Culture*, edited by Mark Steinberg and Heather Coleman (Bloomington: Indiana University Press, 2007), 93–118. One might be tempted to dismiss this simply as imposed Soviet-era prudery, but European counterparts expressed similar squeamishness about similar sins. See "Introduction," in *Medieval Handbooks of Penance: A Translation of the Principal Libri Poenitentiales and Selections from Related Documents*, translated by John Thomas McNeill and Helena M. Gamer (New York: Octagon Books, 1965), 47.

70. *Nastol'naia kniga*, vol. 4, 268.

71. Ibid., 269.

72. Ibid., 275. On this point, Golubtsov had commented in his homily before confession, "Get married in church. Then you won't be discussing whether you should live with your husband or not." Golubtsov, *Besedy pered ispoved'iu*, 58.

73. *Nastol'naia kniga*, vol. 4, 280.

74. Ibid. Archpriest Mikhail Ardov notes that "one paraliturgical *treba* has joined confession and in some cases even replaced it. In common parlance this is called 'the Abortion Prayer,' and in the Trebnik, 'Prayer for a woman when she has cast out a

child.' . . . Our enterprising clerics read it not where they are supposed to (that is, at the bedside of a woman who has suffered a miscarriage), and not to whom they are supposed to (that is, not a woman who has suffered a miscarriage, but a woman who has chosen to have an abortion). For this they usually charge a ruble. This practice, which has spread almost everywhere, brings great harm, for people who are rather far from the Church get the impression that one can pray away an abortion easily and simply: all you have to do is come to church, hear this prayer through, pay your ruble—and your sin is forgiven." Ardov, *Melochi*, 99.

75. See, e.g., Metropolit Antonii (Khrapovitskii), *Uchenie o pastyre, pastyrstve i ob ispovedi* (Warsaw, 1928; New York: Izd. Severo-amerikanskoi i Kanadskoi eparkhii, 1966).

76. *Nastol'naia kniga*, vol. 4, 270.

77. Ardov, *Melochi*, 95.

78. M. V. Korogodina, *Ispoved' v Rossii v XIV–XIX vekakh: Issledovanie i teksty* (Saint Petersburg: Dmitrii Bulanin, 2006), 322–32.

79. Trushin's reports are in Tsentral'nyi gosudarstvennyi arkhiv Moskovskoi oblasti (Central State Archive of Moscow Oblast; hereafter TsGAMO, f. 7383.

80. Tsentral'nyi munitsipal'nyi arkhiv Moskvy, f. 3004; GARF, f. 6911.

81. Edward E. Roslof, "The Orthodox Sacrament of Confession after World War II," paper presented at American Association for the Advancement of Slavic Studies Annual Convention, Toronto, November 21, 2003. I am grateful to Edward Roslof for allowing me to cite this paper.

82. TsGAMO, f. 7383, op. 1, d. 11, ll. 44–45.

83. Ibid., d. 23, ll. 73–76.

84. Ibid., d. 26, l. 173.

85. Ibid., d. 41, l. 96, and d. 44, l. 75 (1957 reports).

86. Ibid., d. 62, l. 37, and op. 3, d. 68, l. 12. I am grateful to Edward Roslof for sharing these citations.

87. The lack of individual, private confession among Bulgarians, and the urge to establish it, e.g., was precisely what prompted Protopresbyter Shavel'skii to write his guide to confession. Shavel'skii, *Pastyrstvo*, 5.

88. McNeill and Gamer, *Medieval Handbooks of Penance*, 22.

89. Father Alexander Schmemann, "Some Reflections on Confession," http://www.schmemann.org/byhim/reflectionsonconfession.html.

## Chapter 7

# A Time and Space of Suffering: Reflections of the Soviet Past in the Memoirs and Narratives of the Evangelical Christians–Baptists

*Olena Panych*

The Evangelical Christians–Baptists constitute one branch of the Baptist faith. Most of their religious communities are located in the republics of the former Soviet Union.[1] As Walter Sawatsky has aptly remarked, these Protestant believers in an Eastern–Slavic Orthodox milieu, "though not expecting to become the dominant Christian culture, nevertheless . . . were behaving as if they belonged, and had a great deal to offer citizens seeking a road that led to a church."[2] Indeed, their religious culture formed in opposition to more powerful ideological systems, the Russian Orthodox Church and Soviet atheism, both of which, in certain historical periods, enjoyed a statewide ideological monopoly.[3] In the Soviet Union, the image of this confession was subjected to conscious distortion by a state-controlled media that treated Evangelicals as real or potential political dissidents and enemies of the regime.[4] At the same time, this religious group received special attention from Western research and missionary centers, which, on the contrary, attempted to represent Soviet Baptists as a totally victimized and persecuted religious community.[5] The demand for literature on Soviet Evangelicals, which had formed in the West by the late Cold War period, created the possibility for members of the Baptist Brotherhood to describe their experiences and personal histories in such a way to create a desirable self-image that might help sustain the group through the suffering they experienced in the Soviet Union and attract attention to their common plight as active believers in a state that professed to endorse atheism. In this chapter, I analyze the key motifs of these memoirs and narrative histories and explain their functional purpose as an adaptive mechanism that helped Evangelical Christians–Baptists earn a respected social status from the suffering they endured. Believers were generally portrayed in their biographical literature as both victims of repression and eventual victors in the struggle against Soviet totalitarianism.

Members of the Council of Churches of Evangelical Christians–Baptists, a radical-reformist wing frequently referred to as the "separated" (*otdelennye*) or "Reform" Baptists, began to produce biographical stories and personal memoirs.[6] The Council of Churches emerged in the 1960s as a separate religious union in response to the protests of believers to the antireligious campaign of Nikita Khrushchev. The council was an underground structure, a form of political dissidence, and an alternative to the legally recognized Union of Evangelical Christians–Baptists.[7] Because the council was a rather new and politically active religious movement, its adherents sought to explain their position by organizing steady informational streams addressed to fellow believers in the Soviet Union, the Soviet authorities, and interested Western organizations. M. Bourdeaux has described their activities as follows:

> An outstanding feature of their life was their organization. So determined were the Soviet authorities to eliminate them that they could have no office premises, no publicly identified administrator, no access to normal post or telephone services (because of KGB interference). Yet they were able to coordinate activities across fifteen republics, document repressions nationwide and send that information systematically out of the Soviet Union over a period of nearly thirty years without ever making a serious factual error.[8]

Accumulating a constant supply of information was an integral part of the Council of Churches' activity and secured it a good deal of symbolic capital among believers. The adherents of the council actively produced biographical and autobiographical stories, which were used as effective tools to construct an image of the "persecuted Church" (a title they assumed in their own writings as a sort of political brand).[9] Reform Baptists set the fashion for both oral and written testimonies for the entire Evangelical Baptist community, which generally accepted their representations of believers as martyrs of the Soviet era.

The first biographical and autobiographical books documenting repression of believers were disseminated through samizdat or in manuscripts. Most probably the first such book was Yuri Grachev's 1970 novel *In the Abyss of Herod*.[10] Grachev was born into a family of believers, and he was subjected to numerous repressions in the years 1934–38, 1940–45, and 1950–54. Later he studied surgery, and in the 1960s he worked as a doctor. In the early 1970s, he was fired because of his church activities, and he died in 1973 at the age of seventy-two. He did not belong to the Reform Baptists, but his book was disseminated among them also in manuscript form until 1994.

A similar case is the 1978–79 trilogy by Nikolai Khrapov, *The Bliss of the Lost Life*. Khrapov was a member of the Council of Churches. He survived five arrests and spent about twenty-eight of his sixty-eight years in various prisons and exile on charges of engaging in "anti-Soviet propaganda" and violating the Soviet legislation on cults. Between imprisonments he organized churches and was busy with preaching and evangelization activities. Today he is perceived by Evangelical Christians–Baptists as one of the most honored martyrs and faith heroes. His trilogy—which consists of the books *Father*, *Fire Ordeal*, and *Life in Death*—is filled with descriptions of actual events, although its heroes bear fictitious names. The main character, Pavel Vladykin, is modeled after the author, but he has a symbolic name that literally means "Lord's Paul" ("a Small One who belongs to the Lord"). The trilogy was printed on a homemade hectograph, or gelatin duplicator, and was disseminated in the 1980s among members of the underground church. It was first published in 1990 and subsequently reprinted at least four times.[11]

Grachev's and Khrapov's stories combine elements of autobiography and fiction. They focus on the period of Stalin's rule and its repression against Baptist believers. Grachev's novel was referred to as "the Christian *Gulag Archipelago*," after the famous novel by Alexandr Solzhenitsyn, reflecting the impact of secular dissident literature, and especially the writings of Solzhenitsyn.

These autobiographies sparked Mikhail Khorev, the leader of the Council of Churches' Evangelization Department, and Georgi Vins, the council's secretary, to also write exemplary memoirs. Khorev was born in 1931 in Leningrad and began to be actively engaged in religious activity in the

Soviet Union during the 1960s. In 1966, 1969, and 1980 he was sentenced for violating Soviet law on cults. He belonged to the editorial board of the underground journal *Vestnik istiny* (Messenger of truth), and he was one of the council's most influential preachers and writers. His writings first appeared in *Vestnik istiny* in 1983–84 when he was imprisoned, under the title "I Write Unto You, Little Children."[12]

Georgi Vins's life story is the most extraordinary. He was the only son of the American missionary Peter Vins, who died in a Stalinist camp. As soon as the Reform Baptist movement appeared, Georgi and his mother, Lidia, became two of its most active members. Lidia was a leader in the Council of Prisoners' Relatives, an underground human rights organization that was part of the Council of Churches. Georgi was sentenced for his religious activities in 1966–69 and again in 1975–79. In 1979, he was deported to the United States. From there, he organized the Foreign Agency of the Council of Churches and the Russian Gospel Ministries in Elkhart, Indiana, in order to provide help for his cobelievers in the Soviet Union. In the eyes of the Western public, Georgi was the true leader of the Reform Baptists.[13] This probably contributed to his excommunication from the Reform Baptist community in the early 1990s. He was the author of numerous poems and stories about believers in the Soviet Union, including those based on himself and his family. His stories were predominantly addressed to an audience abroad. After his arrival in the United States, his writings were rapidly and unofficially disseminated in the Soviet Union.[14]

After the breakup of the Soviet Union, all the writings mentioned here were published by various Christian publishers (some of them with numerous reprints). New historico-biographical stories, collections of eyewitness accounts, and interviews with the members of the Evangelical Christian Brotherhood were also promulgated.[15] They were followed by a great number of memoirs and autobiographies, which have been systematized and expanded.[16]

These stories were usually written by ministers and church leaders—mainly men more than thirty years of age, who actively participated in certain religious activities and were persecuted for this by the Soviet authorities.[17] The authors were of various national origins, but always from within the former Soviet Union, mostly Ukraine or Russia, with some also from Belorussia and the Baltic countries. Many memoirs were written (usually in Russian) by those who migrated to the United States or Germany in the late Soviet or post-Soviet period. In the late 1980s through the 2000s, they were published thanks to financial support from international religious and missionary organizations—such as the Russian Gospel Ministries; the Voice of Peace Christian Mission of Portland; and Friedenstimme, a German missionary organization. Several publishing houses established by members of this religious community in Russia and Ukraine—including "Christian" (Khristianin), the publishing house of the Council of Churches, which was underground until the end of the 1980s—also published a number of memoirs. These memoirs and narratives may be treated as literature that was primarily intended to satisfy the spiritual needs of the Evangelical Christians–Baptists religious community. For a community that insisted on a rather closed and isolated way of life, such narratives were integral to preserving religious integrity.[18] They became widely known among believers, particularly pastors and preachers, who used them frequently in their sermons.[19]

## Making Sense of Suffering: The Biographical Canon in Evangelical Christian–Baptist History

The character of Baptist memoirs and biographical narratives fully confirms the suggestion by Maurice Halbwachs that "the extended group is much more interested in its traditions and ideas than in the event and in what it may have meant for the family or individual who was its witness."[20] This kind of literature plays an exceedingly important role in the culture of Soviet and post-Soviet Evangelicals as "the extended group."[21] They used memories of the repressions of the 1930s as well as persecutions from the 1960s through the 1980s to form and maintain collective memories about the Soviet state. These memories also linked generations of believers and thus helped to maintain the heritage of martyrdom among Russian Baptists that went back to Tsarist Russia and allowed them to incorporate the history of repression into their traditions.[22] That is why such memoirs, which were written mostly by members of the "separated" branch of Baptists, were also popular among other branches of the Evangelical Christians–Baptists.

These texts were intended to reproduce and strengthen cultural myths of martyrdom and sacrifice, which are shared by the larger Christian tradition. Thus, it is appropriate to analyze these texts using an interpretive framework that is also applicable to the literature of other religious minorities and dissidents who have created living hagiography, exploited specific edifying messages, and engaged the theme of martyrdom.[23] The distinctive aspects of Evangelical Christians–Baptists' writings nonetheless resonate with the wider discourse of Soviet political dissidence, which also engages such themes as freedom of conscience, meetings, and media.[24] Authors usually create a peculiar mythologized image of Soviet reality, where the Soviet past is systematically "sifted" through the "sieve" of doctrinal expediency. One can see that the memoirs attempt to construct personalized and authorized versions of sacred narratives following a "master script."[25] Today one can speak of a special canon in the memoir literature of the Evangelical Christians–Baptists, the elements of which are as fixed in the tradition as its distinctive cultural patterns.[26]

There are several functionally important features of these narratives that suggest the existence of a special canon. To begin with, these memoirs are clearly religious literature. God and the sacred are present in the narratives as special agents. The authors are inclined to treat every occasion as a manifestation of God's will and His "voice" as a mystical "message," which they seek to "decipher." This is most evident in situations that involve the Holy Scripture, which is highly sacred to Evangelical believers and was hard to obtain in the Soviet Union. The memoirs of believers are full of descriptions of how "the Lord, responding to their needs, sent them" the Gospel while they were in prison or exile. Quite often such events are portrayed as a miracle, as evidence of God's goodwill toward believers. One example of this is in the testimony of Sergey Golev, a presbyter of the Council of Churches, who was persecuted and imprisoned in the early 1960s for his participation in religiously inspired dissident actions. His memoirs were written in the mid-1970s, more than twenty-five years after he was released from prison in Karelia. He wrote:

> We had no Bible. It was impossible to receive the Gospel since all parcels were searched. However, what is impossible for man is possible for God. I received a parcel from my sister from Pskov with a packet of sugar and something else. Everything was scrutinized carefully, but this packet God forbade the guardian to search; he scarcely touched it and threw it at me. To our common joy and surprise, there was a Gospel inside! In the boiler room, by the light of fire, we were reading the true live Gospel, not the scraps from our memory.[27]

The author reveals that he understands the reality of everyday lives of believers to be an active interpenetration of the mystical into everyday common practices, which is palpable to believers.

Another important feature of Evangelical Baptists' memoir literature is that each particular story is mostly focused on the image of a "faith hero" (*geroi very*) as a persecuted wanderer and fighter for the right to confess his own religious beliefs, in spite of repeated repression by the atheistic authorities. This image is recognizable to the members of the Evangelical Baptist Brotherhood, because it reflects the recollections and informal oral narratives of numerous believers in the Soviet Union. Such a hero is an object of both sympathy and pride. Usually this image is embellished to make him a martyr who always practices his Christian faith despite even the most trying ordeals. If he encounters certain obstacles or "temptations" in his life, this is only to illustrate how to overcome them. This image was developed to serve as an example to follow for future generations of believers and to attract the sympathy and respect of believers in the West.

Among Evangelical Christians–Baptists, the experience of suffering "for the sake of the faith and God's deed" (*za veru i delo Bozhie*) also had a social dimension. Suffering almost automatically granted every faith hero instant recognition and special authority within the community. The experience of suffering thus became a kind of symbolic capital for such heroes and legitimized not only them as religious leaders but also their children. Repression in the camps yielded far greater chances for them to eventually become presbyters and ministers in their communities upon release. In this way, the Soviet state, contrary to its own intentions, was selecting and building the credentials of future Baptist leaders. In the late Soviet period, it was even prestigious to have been "in bonds" (*v uzakh*), especially among the Reform Baptists. Sometimes believers deliberately pleaded to God for such an experience so that they could prove the depth of their faith. Stepan Misiruk, a presbyter, recalled in his autobiographical essay, published in 1996, the period 1966–69 when he prayed to be arrested:

> For four years I performed illegal services, underwent bonds [*uzy*], but I can sincerely say that they are easier to endure than the charges of conspiracy. It was especially hard to endure the reproaches and misunderstandings of believers when other ministers were arrested and I remained free. In my weakness I even prayed: My Lord, why I am not taken?[28]

According to the testimony of eyewitnesses, after the arrest of Yekaterina Gritsenko in 1974 for her work in the underground publishing house "Christian," her father understood this event as a "great honor" to the entire family.[29] However, when she was released after a year of incarceration due to an amnesty, he was rather suspicious. He said: "My baby daughter, why were you released? Maybe you gave some bad promises? Maybe you promised to never print God's Word again?"[30] In other words, Baptists increasingly came to understand that a believer targeted for state-led repression was a public acknowledgement of that person's sincere conviction.

A third important aspect of these biographical narratives is that the faith hero is usually positioned as a physical and spiritual successor to the historical destiny of his parents who also lived as faith heroes and martyrs. The first volume of Nikolai Khrapov's trilogy, nominally devoted to his own childhood, is in fact a narrative about his father, who spent many years in Stalin's concentration camps and died in detention. Eventually, the son followed his father's destiny, often finding himself in similar situations and meeting similar people. The same trend is evident in the memoirs of Georgi Vins, Mikhail Khorev, and many others.

The narratives show that the description of the father's sufferings has a great psychological impact on the main hero and memoir writer. This is especially evident in the situations where the main hero meets his father in prison. Here is a characteristic description of such a meeting by Khorev, who visited his father, Ivan Mikhailovich Khorev, in 1938 after he was arrested and charged with "counterrevolutionary activity" and was serving a five-year sentence:[31]

> Thirty minutes of a visit went quickly, and all visitors reluctantly went out. We children went in last. Our father said to us: "Do you remember where we will meet? By the White Throne!"[32] And, leaning on the barrier with his left hand, he raised his right hand and pointed upward with his forefinger. We didn't know that we would part from our father for good.[33]

The father expresses a kind of spiritual testament for his son, urging him, verbally and nonverbally, to perform the same "feat of faith" (*podvig very*) that he himself has performed. The son feels indebted to his father due to the traumatic experience of parting and because of his compassion for his father's suffering—so much so that the life of the son becomes predestined. Any other choice of the son would qualify as a betrayal of his father's memory. Georgi Vins recalled the moment when he learned about the death of his father in a detention camp:

> Mother shared with me the sad news. "Farewell, father! See you in Heaven! I want to be like you—faithful to God and loving Him!" With such feelings I absorbed the news about the martyr death of my father. By that time I was eighteen and was studying to work in the railway system. I spent all my free time with my friends from church. About that time I delivered my first sermon.[34]

The authors of the memoirs, in their turn, consciously or subconsciously address their narrative histories of their own lives to the next generations of believers. That is why narrators return persistently to the image of children, especially their own. The idea that suffering recurs to successive generations of believers plays a special role in the incorporation of the faith hero into the religious tradition. It testifies to the inherited and inevitable nature of this way of life toward not only one's parents but also other Christians who shared martyrdom for faith, as far back as the Apostles and Christ himself, who became universal archetypes. In the novel by Khrapov, the father of the central hero says to his wife before his last arrest: "We are not those who have started the martyr way of Christians, we are those who complete it."[35] The believers are especially anxious to recall their journey through the same camps and prisons where their fellow believers were imprisoned before them. This gives those imprisoned a mythological feeling of symbolic and spiritual participation in this common and important deed of suffering. Heredity makes the mission of "suffering for the sake of faith" (*stradanie za veru*) important in the context of the so-called "great time" and makes it sacred.[36]

Finally, the fourth distinctive feature of these narratives is the obvious attention the authors give to the *aesthetic design* of their stories. The artistic and rhetorical form contributes to an "aura of factuality" projected onto a depicted reality.[37] To create memoirs and historical narratives, either written or oral, can become a kind of religious service—a feature that actually incorporates these texts into the Evangelical homiletic discourse. This is confirmed by a special lexicon, an active employment of biblical quotations and phrases, and also by the dominance of male authorship. Thus, such memoirs should be considered as distinctive products of the religious elite, who are active memory makers whose writings appeal to a loyal community of memory-consumers within the bounds of this religious tradition.

## Dimensions of Suffering

Pavlenko and Wanner have already analyzed the value of suffering for the community of Evangelical Christians–Baptists who were socialized in Soviet times. They remark that

> in the conditions set by the radically negative attitudes of the society in general toward this social group, the Baptist community had to develop certain values and emotional attitudes so that they could alleviate the feelings of

moral and psychological stress to preserve . . . [the] group. The essence of these attitudes was to present all hardships encountered by each member of the group and all manifestations of negativity as evidence of the strength of one's faith. The apotheosis of this attitude was an understanding of suffering, and even death, for the sake of faith as the highest honor.[38]

Most vividly, the discourse of suffering is reflected in the memoirs and narratives of imprisonment, which was hardly the only means of persecution. Believers were also regularly expelled from work, deprived of access to education, fined, put under surveillance, and subjected to interference in their basic activities. However, the sufferings of prisoners were perceived as requiring the highest level of sympathy, and thus were the most suitable for heroic representation. There are three main dimensions of suffering as depicted by believers in their narratives: torment (physical pain related to repression), sorrow (moral pain caused by separation from families and the miseries of fellow believers), and compassion (regret for a "perishing and fallen world").[39]

The authors of memoirs depict the torment of their life aesthetically, without any details that might cause the reader to doubt the purposefulness of these sufferings and their meaning as a reflection of God's will. Pavel Zakharov, the Council of Churches' evangelist, was convicted in 1945 for "anti-Soviet propaganda." He described his experience during interrogation as follows:

> I said at once that I am a believer and will not answer any questions. For this, I was beaten up two times. In the cell I prayed constantly. The first time the investigator beat my back with a rubber lash. The pain was incredible, but I did not say a word. All my hopes were with the Lord. When I was brought back to the cell, I could not stand, but the other prisoners would not let me fall down. They inspected me and were terrified: my whole back was covered with bloody welts, which made my shirt stick to my back. The prisoners were very troubled—and then I was removed to solitary confinement.
>
> Two weeks later, the investigator beat me again, hitting me in the head three times with something. I regained consciousness and was prostrate on the floor. But God gave me strength. In this trial He hardened me by giving me patience.[40]

More common than testimonies about direct physical violence are recollections about horrific living conditions that believers experienced in prison, exile, and the underground. Extreme hardship was often caused by hard physical labor beyond one's strength, prolonged starvation, exposure to harsh living conditions, and exhaustion due to lack of rest. Also very impressive and engraved in the memories of oppressed believers are the descriptions of unsanitary conditions in prison cells. One such description is provided by Sergey Bublikov, a young believer who was convicted in 1980 for his collaboration in the activities of the "Christian" publishing house:

> When we entered the cell, which was designed for thirty persons, we were struck by the red color of the walls. Our astonishment was soon replaced by horror. When we started to settle on the plank bunk beds, we saw that the walls were covered with great hordes of bedbugs. They crawled upwards, climbing to the ceiling, and fell from there onto the prisoners. Tired, exhausted prisoners made their last efforts to settle in on the bunk beds and fall asleep immediately, while the bedbugs looked for victims. Soon our thirty-person cell was crowded with one hundred and twenty prisoners; there was no room to stand in the passages, not to mention a place to lie down and sleep. Prisoners were lying even on the floor under the bunk beds.[41]

Such hardships made believers sensitive and attentive to every minute detail, which they were inclined to regard either as a special trial or, conversely, as a manifestation of God's care in the form of a "blessing from God." The "small things" that were frequently lacking, but assumed great importance in particular situations, were, for example, that believers did not have a place to be alone for prayer or an opportunity to talk to fellow believers, could not receive letters and parcels from relatives, and sometimes even experienced a temporary inability to satisfy basic subsistence needs of food, warmth, rest, and health care. Maria Tevz, a believer convicted in 1981 for organizing Bible classes for children, recalled her stay in prison with her fellow believer Tamara Bystrova, and her gratitude for the possibility to sooth her sore feet by wearing slippers in summer instead of the usual prison garb:[42]

> Tamara was very resolute. She constantly went [to the authorities] and demanded that they give us our incoming letters. With God's help, she succeeded in receiving the letters of her brother who at the time served in the army. These letters were so full of spiritual nourishment that we awaited them with impatience. She also helped me with my petition to wear slippers in the camp. All prisoners were given shoes in summer and *kirza* [a type of rough artificial leather, similar to pig leather, produced in the Soviet Union, mostly

for soldiers and farmworkers] boots in winter. It was forbidden to wear slippers. Winter in Cheliabinsk is severe, so that the prisoners shivered with cold. I was so grateful to God that because of the petitions of believers and our prayers, I was given permission to wear felt boots in winter and slippers in summer, as this was the only footgear that I could put on my sore feet.[43]

Sorrow is intermingled with physical suffering and compounded by it. Most often, moral sorrow stemmed from the feelings of injustice, disrespect, or humiliation, which believers experienced when they communicated with other people who did not share their religious views. Dramatic recollections of children and relatives, who were involuntarily negatively affected by the suffering of the main heroes, were also frequently cited as sources of moral anguish. Although factual descriptions providing context are rarely accompanied by detailed descriptions of feelings, the anguish of the faith hero is easily understood by the reader because the very logic of narration is designed to evoke moral compassion in the reader. On the other hand, in situations that caused moral suffering, believers were even more inclined to be persistent in defending their way of life and resorting to mystical religious experiences as a coping mechanism to endure suffering. In the memoirs there are many recollections of exhausting fasts, which the believers practiced in prison or in militia stations, and which looked to nonbelievers like political protests. The memoirists mention long prayer sessions that lasted up to six and even ten hours. Such were the recorded recollections of Nadezhda Sloboda, a believer from Belorussia, who was jailed in the early 1960s for religious activity:

> Having crossed the threshold of this gloomy establishment, with a heavy heart after parting with her dear husband and children, Nadezhda Stepanovna found the only consolation in fervent prayer. She occupied a small free place near the wash basin and there, praying, she talked to God. She entrusted to Him the care of her little darlings who had also been taken away and placed in boarding schools far away from their native home. She knew that it was harder for the children to endure the parting. She knew that they were crying inconsolably amidst alien people. She used to pray for her husband who remained boxed up in the house all alone. Enveloped in deep prayer, she did not feel the other prisoners, who had become infuriated, pour water on her, and did not hear them jeering at her. Sometimes, when she kneeled for a long time, they hung sweaters on her, but she prayed and prayed again. Eventually these humiliations ceased.[44]

The ability to persist in confession of faith inspired believers with the feeling of victory, which was especially important given the threats they faced. The belief that God controlled their lives gave them confidence and peace of mind in the face of suffering, and delivered enough "spiritual strength" to adapt to the oppressive conditions and ultimately endure them.[45] This distinctive feature, usually described as "trust in God," is regarded as a great advantage for survival over nonbelievers. Nonbelievers are represented as much more unhappy than believers because they are "deprived of hope," lonely, and weak in the face of the bitterness of "worldly life." Compassion for such people is also reflected and encouraged in the narratives. The afflictions and sufferings of nonbelievers are not depicted through the prism of guilt, but it is implied that all nonbelievers carry "the burden of Original Sin" or "irreconcilability with God," which, in the eyes of believers, makes the distress of nonbelievers much more difficult to bear.

The suffering of people "who perish" is regularly mentioned in the memoirs, but such people are presented only as a part of the context in which the faith hero suffers, which makes the merits and advantages of the believer's devotion to God more visible. One of the letters of Mikhail Khorev, revealing his childhood memories about a meeting with his imprisoned father, depicts an incidental character, a Jew, who, unlike Baptist prisoners, does not appreciate his suffering as a path to martyrdom, but instead assures his wife that all of his suffering is utterly undeserved:

> Near my father, on the right hand, was an elderly Jew. Tears were running from his eyes unceasingly. He was saying something fervently to his wife, and then, all of a sudden, he cried out so that the whole hall could hear: "Hush, comrades!" All people began to speak quieter, and he said louder than others: "Firochka, do you believe me? I am not guilty of anything!" He kept saying something else to his Esther, but the general hubbub of chatter grew again and everything fused into one.[46]

The unusual pathos of the situation is created by an awareness of the futility and senselessness of suffering that may befall a human being. However, in the Baptist discourse of suffering only nonbelievers can suffer for no purpose. The suffering of a believer forcibly imprisoned, repressed, or humiliated always has a certain meaning and final destiny: suffering brings his religious mission to completion because it symbolizes the realization of God's glory throughout the earth, which gives the believer a feeling of consolation and relief.

People "who perish" in memoirs appear less attractive than believers. Yet, nonbelievers give rise to compassion precisely because of their ultimate humiliation, which culminates in their deeper moral and physical collapse. The narrative context often suggests that a believer will be prevented from falling that low and spared a similar fate. One of the memoirs by Georgi Vins makes such a point:

> There are several horses in the camp that are used to cart foodstuffs, firewood, and water from the river. These are terribly emaciated . . . "goners" [*dokhodjagi*], in the camp jargon. When free from work, they are in a pasture on a big ice-coated garbage heap of discarded food that towers in the center of the camp near the dining hall. Hungry horses hoof over the ice heap, tear away the frozen rotten fish and other scraps with their teeth, and gobble them together with the bones and pieces of ice that are frozen to the fish. Often, next to the horses, utterly degraded prisoners are rummaging through the same heap of garbage for food—there are several dozens of them in the camp. Always hungry, unshaven, dirty, lice-ridden, and ragged, they pick rotten fish or pieces of rotten cabbage out of the icy heap with sticks and guzzle it all down. Sometimes they snatch the pieces of rotten fish right from under the hooves of the hungry horses, kicking them away. This is rarely seen in ordinary life outside the camps.[47]

An interesting feature of this story is that its author, in fact, compares humans to beasts by placing them in the same space and depicting their simultaneous engagement in degrading behavior. His intention in this parallel is to suggest to the reader—indirectly, but, as it seems, quite consciously—the idea that during an ordeal, a man by himself, without God's help, is incapable of preserving his full humanity and becomes a brute, a sort of animal. Vins suggests that a person who is not accustomed to food deprivation cannot suppress the feelings of hunger and, like an animal, might well even eat spoiled food that is not suitable for human consumption. From this perspective, a believer's habit of keeping fasts is seen as quite useful in camp conditions that kept prisoners in a state of constant near-starvation.

In the process of recalling suffering, believers always valued not only the very fact of having been tested with physical deprivation, but also the ability to correctly expound on one's suffering and interpret it in the light of instructive and theological patterns that were known to the community of believers and hence to the readers of these memoirs. For this purpose, it was common and even an expedient rhetorical strategy to find appropriate analogies in the Holy Scriptures that show the way of life of believers in a hostile Soviet state as largely reflecting and being in keeping with biblical models. The most remarkable feature here is the existential feeling of approaching death, always present in the narratives, which helps the authors refer to the death of Christ and the suffering of the Apostles as an archetypical situation that anticipates their own living conditions. Khorev described his feeling of closeness to death using the quotation from Saint Paul's First Letter to the Corinthians (15:31), "I die daily."[48] Locutions like "die for oneself," "die for sin," and "die with Christ" are also quite frequent in the memoirs, supplemented by the articulated hope for resurrection, treated as a possible form of worldly and mystical rebirth for an eternal life.[49] The narratives repeatedly emphasize the special God-pleasing virtues of suffering that mirror the biblical story of the death and resurrection of Christ, and thus allow believers to participate in this story by symbolically placing themselves in a dimension of sacred time by reenacting the suffering of the innocent and persecution for one's faith.[50] Participation in sacred time characterizes not only the experiences of the main hero, but also extends to other people who form the social dimension of the narrative and, as such, are worthy of special analysis.

## The Social Space of Suffering

The patterns of suffering experienced by believers in the Soviet Union were realized within a complicated system of interpersonal relationships that formed a peculiar social space. For all the diversity of human characters described in various memoirs, recollections, and biographical stories, the characters beyond the faith hero fall rather easily into four groups. Each has a certain, more or less clear attitude toward the main hero of the story. These groups of people together constitute the social and historical background of the faith hero's life. These four social groups are "cobelievers," "sympathizers," "bystanders," and "enemies."[51] Each of these constructed social types performs a special function in the narrative, not only in their interactions with the main hero-sufferer but with the sacred as well. The people mentioned in the narratives might sometimes move from one category into another. For example, an enemy could become a sympathizer, but the overall essence of the categories remains fixed.

The logic of the unfolding plot in the memoirs is designed to allow the reader to assess the value of each character depending on his/her inclination to share the beliefs and the way of life of the main faith hero. From this point of view, if a character belongs to a group of "cobelievers," this does not automatically guarantee him or her a positive status in the eyes of the narrator. Among cobelievers, there could be people who are portrayed negatively, as well as positive figures who are technically classified as "enemies." However, within the category of cobelievers, for all its variety, the set of available roles is quite limited. In fact, according to the typical logic of this biographical genre, there are just three roles a cobeliever could play in the memoirs. He may be either a copartner in the main hero's suffering, someone who helps and cares for the hero, or a traitor. In most of the cases, the activities of "cobelievers" do not exceed these patterns, rendering the dispositions of cobelievers as rather standard and predictable.

Sergey Golev describes the presence of other believers who function as caregivers in his life:

> Being in the Pskov prison I enjoyed great blessings because believers were praying diligently for my benefit. Each day I received a parcel that fed all my cell—20 people. Prisoners saw how great the love of God's children is to each other.[52]

This story reflects the actual mutual support and assistance that believers provided to one another, which, given the discriminatory state policies and the conditions they created for believers, resulted in the emergence of a quite strong and stable corporate infrastructure of mutual support among the members of the Evangelical Baptist Brotherhood. Such passages suggest that the networks of assistance bequeathed to believers would reliably provide tangible material aid if a believer was repressed for his/her faith.

The image of a "traitor" within the ranks of cobelievers is especially operative in the memoirs of the leaders of Reform Baptists, because it helps them clarify their own political standing. "Traitors" are mostly discovered among senior presbyters and presbyters of communities who turn out to be collaborators with the state authorities—willingly or unwillingly, but in such a way that has the potential to lead to persecution of other community members. The peculiarity of the view toward "cobeliever traitors" is that they are treated not as direct enemies, but as the helpers of direct enemies. This function to serve enemies, often meaning state authorities, is depicted as their sole mission, and repeating it in narratives becomes a way to engrain the presence of cobeliever traitors in the community's historical memory. The experience of communicating with such people, which is usually rendered as being quite traumatic, is described in a mixed tone of sympathy and indignation. The narrator does not seek to discover the views or motivations of a "cobeliever traitor" and does not argue with him, but straight away represents him as the one doomed to spiritual death. However, the details of such characters and communication with them are rare, most probably because the narrators wanted to avoid casting a shadow on their community as a whole and did not want to highlight the possibility of believers turning out to be among the "perishing."

In comparison with traitors, those outside the religious group are portrayed more characteristically with certain emphases on their weaknesses and negative moral characters. They form the main social background for the suffering of the faith hero, and also the referent group that stimulates his missionary drive. Although Baptists in Soviet society were generally treated malevolently, there were different grades or shades of that treatment, which meant that the attitudes of the perpetrators varied and could change. Depending on an assessment of threat level, the narrators discern three additional groups from among those outside the religious group in greater Soviet society: "sympathizers," "bystanders," and "enemies."

The sympathizers are those who, depending on circumstances, are inclined to change their negative attitudes toward believers to a positive one. They are depicted as sensitive to evangelization sermons and willing to learn more about the faith of Evangelical Christians–Baptists. Sympathizers were recruited from the ranks of bystanders or even enemies and had a certain tendency to migrate into the category of cobelievers. Sympathizers are often found among prisoners and even prison personnel. The appearance of sympathizers around the main hero is appraised in the narratives as the hero's personal victory, a token of his spiritual strength and charisma, which is manifest by his power to attract people, group them around himself, and convince them of the righteousness of a faith-based lifestyle.

The sympathizers mostly appear in the narrative in connection with the high moral standards of behavior that believers themselves demonstrated in everyday life and tried to inspire others to follow.[53] However, the appearance of sympathizers (who could eventually become followers) made suffering "for the sake of faith" meaningful and was regarded as a sign that such sufferings were concordant with God's will. Precisely because of the state-led persecutions, there were more and more people who could hear the testimonies of believers in the most crucial moments of their lives. Sympathizers formed a considerable network of support for the imprisoned believers and were regarded as those who might eventually join the Evangelical Baptist community. Sympathizers mostly belonged to marginalized social groups and this seriously affected the social structure of Soviet and post-Soviet Baptist communities and the way in which the greater society perceived these communities.

People who could be characterized as bystanders play only minor roles in the memoirs. The presence of such people is suggested, rather than clearly depicted. However, from the point of view of the narrators, they are not completely neutral and occupy a rather ambivalent position. Usually, bystanders support the persecutions of believers simply because they do not protest against this practice and do not feel any sympathy toward religion or religious people. However, in certain situations bystanders are portrayed as not inclined to consciously harm believers, and some of their actions have clearly positive intentions. Sometimes, openly or anonymously, bystanders incidentally help imprisoned believers in solving their everyday problems, sending and receiving illegal letters, and even safekeeping a forbidden Bible from state authorities.

Most of all, the identity of the narrators as sufferers was clearly shaped by their relationships with those whom they considered enemies and responsible for their sufferings. These enemies were mostly representatives of the state. To be sure, there was always an option to treat persecutors as people who might be subject to evangelization. However, a generalized image emerged of the "Soviet authorities" as a single enemy—an image that combined both mystical and political connotations. The image of the KGB was especially demonized. The KGB was represented as an almost almighty, sinister force, omnipresent and incessantly watching over everyone with a menacing eye.

Within the theological and spiritual framework of this memoir genre, Soviet authorities were portrayed as adherents of the "false gods of atheism" and as idolaters worshiping these false gods. Remarkably, as the grip of communist and atheist ideology became weaker in the late 1960s and 1970s, believers became more daring and confident fighters against this ideology of what they called "dead or dying political gods."[54] This explains the growth in the amount of underground anti-Soviet literature produced in the last years of Soviet power, of which these memoirs are a part, and also the increasingly provocative impertinence of believers during their interrogations and trials in the late 1960s and the 1970s, which is now attributed to their personal moral character and heroism. The ability of believers to resist, and even challenge, Soviet authorities was also inspired by the increasingly visible and tangible forms of support that Western communities offered Soviet Baptists.

Judging by the memoirs, believers, and especially those of the dissident wing, positioned themselves vis-à-vis the authorities as prophets who foresaw the defeat of state-driven policies to promote atheism long before Soviet officials did. This defeat of Soviet atheism unfolded not so much within the actual historical context, but rather within the context of mystical history, within a dimension of "sacred time." Opposition to Soviet authorities was experienced as a symbolic spiritual struggle of good versus evil. As the legitimacy of the Soviet regime began to fade in the last years of the Soviet period, the constructed, invented image of the "enemy" in the narratives of believers became even more scary and threatening. At the same time, the purpose of the narratives was gradually shifting from practical guidance on how to behave in the real conditions of active state repression of believers to an instructive glorification of spiritual heroism in the struggle of all believers against evil.

Memoirs that were written and published in the post-Soviet period often represent believers' struggle with this "enemy" as a personal heroic and romantic story with numerous comical moments, in which the heroes had to display quick-wittedness, inventiveness, and courage, although from a spiritual angle their victory was always predestined. A typical example is from Nikolai Boiko, a presbyter from Odessa. He was convicted four times and spent about thirty years in detention and exile. In his autobiographical essay, he recalled with special fondness his interrogations by the KGB and the speeches he made in the courtroom. Here is a telling excerpt from his recently published memoirs about the exchanges he had with KGB agents, which, according to the author, happened around 1962:

> Boiko! We'll show you!—they kept threatening.
> Would you tell me please, are you Communists?—I asked.
> Yes—they replied. . . .
> And who is Lenin for you?
> A leader.
> And my leader is Jesus Christ, and for Him I am ready to suffer and even die. And you, not yet persecuted, have perverted and broken all regulations of your leader: the Decree [Decree on the freedom of conscience, 1918], the Constitution,—and I started to quote by memory the main theses from the Decree. . . . Two days were spent in such talks.[55]

The author depicts KGB officers as ministers of a sort for an "alternative God and leader." He even reproaches them for "unrighteous service," acting here as an accuser, not as a defendant, and also as a sage and prophet who possesses higher, more divine knowledge than those who claim to have the secular power to interrogate him. He successfully uses logical arguments that are considered legitimate in Soviet society and, in fact, engages his opponents in a polemical exchange that allows him to gain superiority and symbolic domination.[56] His opponents possess physical and legal powers over him, but they are not morally righteous. This virtue belongs to the hero alone. Here, as well as in many other cases, the authors of memoirs depict their enemies as the ones who lose all forms of legitimate (secular) power, although the enemies do not acknowledge this fact.

Overall, the analysis of the memoirs and narratives of persecuted Baptist believers in the late Soviet period leads to the conclusion that Evangelical believers, dealing with the representatives of every other social group, primarily endeavored to build a system of person-to-person relations. Believers were always anxious to recognize various manifestations of humanity amid state-sponsored repressive actions. They observed those actions closely, and interpreted them in a religious context and framework, seeking to use these manifestations to attain for themselves the highest social standing as the mouthpieces for the righteous ideology of their communities.

## Conclusion

The memoirs of Evangelical Christians–Baptists about the Soviet past testify once again to the extent to which history "depends on its social purpose."[57] The memoirs are intended to support the authority of those who are or were among the leaders of this religious group during the Soviet period. They serve to establish the legitimacy and validity of certain patterns of behavior and attitudes that were demonstrated by these leaders and depicted in these narratives. That is why the narratives of personal experiences of suffering at the hands of Soviet authorities are usually presented in a biographical or autobiographical genre, generally describing the typical repressive situations and hardships that believers faced as well as what the appropriate reactions of believers should be to such situations. Thus, one may speak of the existence of a biographical canon, close to that of hagiography, produced by Soviet Baptists and their encounters with an atheist, repressive state apparatus. This literature reflects many elements of Evangelical Baptist theology, which serves as an interpretive framework for a believer who experiences suffering. All depicted events are interpreted as taking place under "God's eye," with an active role given to the spiritual world in this atheist state, which prompts frequent experiences of the sacred for believers even in secular Soviet society. Perceptions of sacred and social time are juxtaposed and combined. This leads to an unusual sort of legitimacy, even glorification, granted by the narrators to the Soviet era, which is interpreted as a special time of ordeal, when believers were challenged to symbolically continue the sufferings of Christ and the Apostles by participating in their own sufferings at the hands of hostile Soviet authorities. The narrators recall this era as an exceptional time when a purposeful life was clearly defined and readily available because their experiences allowed them to pattern their behavior on archetypical biblical examples.

Conversely, both moral and physical suffering can change the emotional and psychological structure of a personality. Recollection, comprehension, and retelling of these traumatic experiences become a cultural norm for Soviet Baptists. There are reasons to argue that the experience of repression, which many Evangelical believers experienced, and certainly the most active among them did, has affected the character of Soviet and post-Soviet Protestantism. The effects of the ever-present threat of repression have been magnified among members of this religious community because the special kind of "martyr habitus" was transmitted over generations with the help of consciously maintained historical memories of the Soviet period, which were standardized and widely circulated in memoirs and became part of a habitual, axiomatic tradition of recalling past sufferings. These elements are visible in many segments of religious practice to the present, such as the widespread custom to make oneself weep during prayer by evoking a feeling of strong emotional stress, the special piety attributed to artistic and picturesque ways of expressing one's religious identity in poetry, lyrics, and music,[58] or the rejection of simplified or more entertainment-driven forms of worship in divine services, which is advocated by many Western missionaries.[59] Uplifting and celebratory expressions of faith are often perceived as a sacrilege and mockery of the sacred forms of worship that have evolved over the years in the Soviet Union and were achieved through much suffering and contribute to the censure in this milieu of all forms of liberalism in theology and divine services. The discourse of suffering, which has crystalized into a genre of memoir writing that seeks to depict the historic and unprecedented encounter between devout Evangelical Christian–Baptist believers and the ideologically hostile Soviet state so as to inspire certain values and practices, is key to explaining many trends in the development of contemporary Eastern–Slavic Protestant culture.

## Notes

1. There are also numerous diasporas in other countries, predominantly in the United States and Germany, that gradually formed during the twentieth century and the beginning of the twenty-first century.

2. Walter W. Sawatsky, "Protestantism in the USSR," in *Religious Policy in the Soviet Union*, edited by Sabrina P. Ramet (Cambridge: Cambridge University Press, 1993), 345.

3. On the origins and earlier history of Evangelical Christians–Baptists in Russia and Ukraine, see Sergei I. Zhuk, *Russia's Lost Reformation: Peasants, Millennialism, and Radical Sects in Southern Russia and Ukraine, 1830–1917* (Washington, D.C., and Baltimore: Woodrow Wilson Center Press and Johns Hopkins University Press, 2004); and Heather J. Coleman, *Russian Baptists and Spiritual Revolution, 1905–1929* (Bloomington: Indiana University Press, 2005).

4. In this chapter, I use "Baptists" and "Evangelicals" as synonyms for the original name "Evangelical Christians–Baptists." See D. E. Powell, *Antireligious Propaganda in the Soviet Union; A Study of Mass Persuasion* (Cambridge, Mass.: MIT Press, 1975).

5. Here I refer to the Keston Institute, which was founded in 1969 by Michael Bourdeaux, and which published numerous works about persecutions of Baptists as well as other believers in the USSR. See, e.g., Michael Bourdeaux, *Faith on Trial in Russia* (London: Holder & Stoughton, 1971); Michael Bourdeaux, *Opium of the People: The Christian Religion in the USSR* (Oxford: Mowbrays, 1977); Michael Bourdeaux, *Religious Liberty in the Soviet Union* (Keston Kend: Keston College, 1976); and Michael Bourdeaux, *Risen Indeed: Lessons in Faith from the USSR* (London: Macmillan, 1983). More information about the interest of the missions and religious centers in the world to the Evangelicals in the Soviet Union is given by Walter W. Sawatsky and Peter F. Penner, eds., *Mission in the Former Soviet Union* (Schwarzenfeld: Neufeld Verlag, 2005).

6. On the history of Evangelical Christians–Baptists in the Soviet Union and the circumstances of the emergence of their Reform movement, see Walter W. Sawatsky, *Soviet Evangelicals since World War II* (Scottsdale, Ariz.: Herald Press, 1981).

7. For more detail, see Michael Bourdeaux, *Religious Ferment in Russia: Protestant Opposition to the Soviet Religious Policy* (London: Macmillan, 1968).

8. Michael Bourdeaux, *Gorbachev, Glasnost, and the Gospel* (London: Hodder & Stoughton, 1990), 120–21.

9. The first autobiographical stories published in the West were written by one of the leaders of the Council of Churches, Georgi Vins. Most probably, the manuscripts were transferred abroad in a clandestine way. See Georgi Vins, *Testament from Prison*, translated by Jane Ellis and edited by Michael Bourdeaux (Elgin, Ill.: D. C. Cook, 1975); Vins, *Three Generations of Suffering: An Autobiography*, translated by Jane Ellis (Toronto: Hodder & Stoughton, 1976); and Vins, *Vernye do kontsa* (Korntal: Licht im Osten, 1976).

10. See Y. V. Grachev, *V Irodovoi bezdne* (Moscow: Blagovestnik, 1994).

11. See N. Krapov, *Schastie poteriannoi zhizni*, 3 vols. (Moscow: Protestant, 1990).

12. Their original title is an allusion to 1 John 2:12. Later they were translated into English. See Mikhail Khorev, *Letters from a Soviet Prison Camp* (London: Monarch, 1988).

13. See Michael Bourdeaux, "Georgi Vins, the Leader," in Bourdeaux, *Faith on Trial*, 60–100.

14. See Georgi Vins, *Gorizonty very* (Elkhart, Ind.: Russian Gospel Ministries, 1994), published in English as Georgi Vins, *Konshaubi: Free on the Inside* (Eastbourne: Kingsway, 1988); Georgi Vins, *Evangelie v uzakh* (Kyiv: Kompass, 1994), published in English as Georgi Vins, *The Gospel in Bonds* (Elkhart, Ind.: Russian Gospel Ministries, 1995); and Georgi Vins, *Tropoiu vernosti* (Elkhart, Ind.: Russian Gospel Ministries, 1990), published in English as Georgi Vins, *Along the Path of Faithfulness* (Elkhart, Ind.: Russian Gospel Ministries, 1990).

15. The collectors and editors of these editions usually also belonged to the Baptist religious community. Frequently, they used their own recollections to enrich these publications. A good example of such a collection is L. E. Kovalenko, *Oblako svidetelej Hristovyh dlja narodov Rossii* (Kyiv: Tsentr Khristianskogo Sotrudnichestva, 2000). The author immigrated to the United States in the 1990s and collected the materials for his book there. Another collection was published by the Council of Churches: Council of Churches, *Podrazhajte vere ih: 40 let probudzhennomu bratstvu* (Moscow: Izdatel'stvo Soveta Tserkvey ECB "Khristianin," 2001). See also the collection of interviews with Soviet Evangelicals who migrated to the United States: K. Prokhorov, ed., *Podvig very: Unikal'nye svidetel'stva o zhizni khristian v SSSR* (Omsk: Nauka, 2010). A set of memoirs and biographies from workers of the underground publishing house "Christian" is given by Margarita Pazych, *Ne hlebom jedinym: Iz istorii izdatel'stva "Hristianin"* (Meinerzhagen: Missionwerk Friedens Bote, 2001). A biography of Galina Rytikova, the second head of the Council of Prisoners' Relatives after Lidia Vins, was published privately in the United States; see Violet Miller, *Never Alone: Galina's Story* (Harrisonburg, Va.: Christian Light, 2007). More than two hundred personal interviews were conducted using oral history methods as part of a special research project supported by the Central Mennonite Committee in the late 1990s; subsequently, these interviews were compiled into Web archives by the Evangelical Research Center in Odessa, which managed the project.

16. The series of personal memoirs and autobiographical essays by the Council of Churches leaders, which had been published as fragments in *Vestnik istiny* in the 1970s and 1980s, appeared in the late 2000s in several books: J. Bondarenko, *Tri prigovora* (Odessa: Bez izdatel'stva, 2006); E. N. Pushkov, *Ty byl vs'udu so mnoiu: Blagovestie* (Portland: Voice of Peace Christian Mission, 2007); I. P. Plett, *Zemnye goda: Predislovie k vechnosti* (Portland: Voice of Peace Christian Mission, 2007); R. Klassen, *Moi mezhy* (Portland: Voice of Peace Christian Mission, 2007); and N. E. Boiko, *Veru v bessmertie* (Moscow: Khristianin, 2007).

17. In some cases, memoirs were published by wives or daughters of ministers, e.g., the remarkable memoirs of Georgi Vins's daughter, Natasha. See Natasha Vins, *Rubezhy detstva* (Elkhart, Ind.: Russian Gospel Ministries, 2000); and, in English, Natasha Vins, *Children of the Storm: The Autobiography of Natasha Vins* (Greenville, S.C.: Bob Jones University Press, 2003).

18. For more detail, see Catherine Wanner, *Communities of the Converted: Ukrainians and Global Evangelism* (Ithaca, N.Y.: Cornell University Press, 2007), 107–8.

19. I draw this conclusion from my personal observations of Evangelical Baptist communities from 2008 to 2010 in the Donetsk region of Ukraine. However, this does not mean that such memoirs are perceived uniformly by all members of today's communities. For a discussion of the collective reception of memory, see W. Kansteiner,

"Finding Meaning in Memory: A Methodological Critique of Collective Memory Studies," *History and Theory* 41 (2002): 179–97.

20. Maurice Halbwachs, *On Collective Memory*, edited and translated and with an introduction by Lewis A. Coser (Chicago: University of Chicago Press, 1992), 102.

21. In exploring the Evangelical Christians–Baptists, it seems fruitful to use Clifford Geertz's concept of religion as a "cultural system." In this context, religious literature can be scrutinized as a tool to strengthen a set of symbols that helps people explain and give meaning to their lives. See Clifford Geertz, *The Interpretation of Cultures* (New York: Basic Books, 1973), 87–125.

22. On how Russian Baptists' sense of martyrdom was formed at the beginning of the twentieth century, see, e.g., Heather J. Coleman, "Tales of Violence against Religious Dissidents in the Orthodox Village," in *Sacred Stories: Religion and Spirituality in Modern Russia*, edited by Mark D. Steinberg and Heather Coleman (Bloomington: Indiana University Press, 2007), 200–221.

23. A model is offered by the research on the Russian Old Believers. See Douglas Rogers, *The Old Faith and the Russian Land: A Historical Ethnography of Ethics in The Urals* (Ithaca, N.Y.: Cornell University Press, 2009); and Robert O. Crummey, "The Miracle of Martyrdom: Reflections on Early Old Believer Hagiography," in *Religion and Culture in Early Modern Russia and Ukraine*, edited by Samuel H. Baron and Nancy Shields Kollmann (DeKalb: Northern Illinois University Press, 1997): 132–45.

24. There is a certain tradition of treating the history of Reform Baptists within the context of the Soviet dissident movement. See Liudmila Alekseeva, *Istorija inakomyslija v SSSR: Noveishiy period* (Vilnus-Moscow: Vest', 1992).

25. The patterns of relations between a "master narrative" and individual "versions of the sacred" are examined in Nadieszda Kizenko, "Written Confessions and the Construction of Sacred Narrative," in *Sacred Stories*, ed. Steinberg and Coleman, 94. However, it is rather difficult to say precisely which original text, beyond the Bible, could be perceived as the master narrative.

26. The formation of the Church's canon, as proceeding from a selection of the Church Fathers' classics, is explored by E. R. Curcuis, *European Literature and the Latin Middle Ages* (Princeton, N.J.: Princeton University Press, 1990), 256–72. In the Baptist milieu, narratives written by such authorities as G. Vins, N. Krapov, and M. Khorev were exemplary models for other Evangelical authors. Judging by how repetitive the plot became within a majority of the memoirs and narratives, one can conclude that these models were perceived as normative and classic literature that constituted a canon of community literature.

27. Council of Churches, *Podrazhajte vere ih*, 29.

28. Misiruk Stepan Nikitovich, "Uzki put': Avtobiograpgicheski ocherk," *Vestnik istiny*, supplement 2 (1996): 26. Later, he was convicted of violating Soviet law on cults and spent about eight years in prison and exile (1969–75 and 1982–85).

29. Pazych, *Ne hlebom jedinym*, 55.

30. These words were documented by Pazych, *Ne hlebom jedinym*, 56.

31. Ivan Mikhailovich Khorev died in prison in 1940. See the collection of documents published by the Council of Churches, *Tserkov dolzhna ostavatsa tserkovju: . . . Dokumentalnyj material ob istorii tserkvy EHB v Rossii* (Moscow: Izdatelstvo Mezhdunarodnogo Soveta Tserkvei, 2008), 387–88.

32. This statement is reminiscent of John 20:11.

33. Mikhail Khorev, "Pishu vam, deti," *Vestnik istiny* 1 (1983): 30.

34. Georgi Vins, *Tropoiu vernosti* (Saint Petersburg: Russkaia missia blagovestia "Biblia dlia vsekh," 2003), 177.

35. Nikolai Khrapov, *Schastje poteryannoj zhizni*, vol. 3 (Gummersbach: Missionwerk Friedensstimme, 2000), 16.

36. See Mircea Eliade, *Mephistopheles and the Androgyne: Studies in Religious Myth and Symbol* (New York: Sheed & Ward, 1965).

37. Geertz, *Interpretation*, 90.

38. V. N. Pavlenko and C. Wanner, "Osobennosti Psikhologii Evangel'skikh Khristian–Baptistov," *Voprosy psikhologii* 5 (2004): 84.

39. This rather short list is an attempt to classify the diverse forms of human experience in order to single out those that made suffering especially valuable for the Baptist community. Such an approach is inspired by Joseph A. Amato, *Victims and Values: A History and a Theory of Suffering* (New York: Greenwood Press, 1990), 2–3.

40. Council of Churches, *Podrazhajte vere ih*, 165.

41. Pazych, *Ne hlebom jedinym*, 112.

42. According to Oleksandr Lakhno, among the Ukrainian adherents of the Council of Churches imprisoned from the the 1960s to the 1980s, about 5 percent were female. See O. P. Lakhno, *Tserkovna opozytsia Evangelskyh Chrystian–Baptystiv Ukrainy (1940–1980-ti roky)* (Poltava: Drukarska majsternya, 2009), 154–62. Women were mostly imprisoned for giving Bible lessons to children, serving in the underground publishing house "Christian," and participating in the Council of Prisoners' Relatives. Memoirs written by women are uncommon; more often, they were interviewed by researchers or described by other memoirists. Stories by women share many similarities with those written by men and follow the same motifs of Baptist biographical literature. The main distinction is that narratives written by women concentrate on typical women's roles (wife and mother) and more often address the emotional experience of the female hero.

43. Pazych, *Ne hlebom jedinym*, 130.

44. Council of Churches, *Podrazhajte vere ih*, 270. The text is based on the hero's memories but written by another person in the style of a biographical narration.

45. On the "divine locus of control," see Pavlenko and Wanner, "Osobennosti psikhologii," 79–80.

46. Khorev, "Pishu vam, deti," 30.

47. Vins, *Gorizonty very*, 44.

48. See Khorev, "Pishu vam, deti," 37–38.

49. These allusions to the New Testament can be found in ibid., 26; and Krapov, *Schastie Poteriannoi Zhizni*, vol. 2, 133, 226.

50. Here I use the term "sacred" as discussed by Émile Durkheim, *The Elementary Forms of Religious Life* (New York: Free Press, 1965), 52–57.

51. In Holocaust studies, there is a tradition of classifying the roles of social actors as victims, perpetrators, and bystanders. See Robert M. Ehrenreich and Tim Cole, "The Perpetrator-Bystander-Victim Constellation: Rethinking Genocidal Relationships," *Human Organization* 64, no. 3 (2005): 213–24. I partially use this framework, regarding it as a productive conceptual approach for the analysis of the culturally constructed social space presented in Baptist memoirs and narratives.

52. Council of Churches, *Podrazhajte vere ih*, 32. The parcels were obviously sent by other members of the Baptist community.

53. Catherine Wanner, "Advocating New Moralities: Conversion to Evangelicalism in Ukraine," *Religion, State & Society* 31, no. 3 (2003): 273–87.

54. On the attitudes of Soviet citizens to communist and atheist ideology in the post-Stalin period, see Vladimir Shlapentokh, *A Normal Totalitarian Society: How the Soviet Union Functioned and How It Collapsed* (Armonk, N.Y.: M. E. Sharpe, 2001), 141–52.

55. N. E. Boiko, *Veru v bessmertie* (Moscow: Khristianin, 2007), 53.

56. I use this term in Bourdieu's meaning. See Pierre Bourdieu, *Language and Symbolic Power* (Cambridge, Mass.: Harvard University Press, 1995), 72–73.

57. Paul Thompson, "History and the Community," in *Oral History. An Interdisciplinary Anthology*, edited by D. K. Dunaway and W. K. Baum (Nashville: Tennessee American Association for State and Local History, 1987), 37–50.

58. Sergey Averintsev remarked that the political practice of torture, so widespread in the Byzantine Empire, influenced the religious consciousness throughout the cultural space of Eastern Europe, giving Orthodox believers more mystical and sensual inclinations. See S. S. Averintsev, *Poetika rannevizantijskoj literatury* (Moscow: Isdatel'stvo Coda, 1997), 62. Perhaps Evangelicals in the USSR experienced repression with similar consequences for their religious culture.

59. See Catherine Wanner, "Missionaries of Faith and Culture: Evangelical Encounters in Ukraine," *Slavic Review* 63, no. 4 (2004): 732–55.

Chapter 8

Preaching the Kingdom Message:
The Jehovah's Witnesses
and Soviet Secularization

*Zoe Knox*

On April 1, 1951, 723 families of Jehovah's Witnesses (808 men, 967 women, and 842 children) were deported from Western Ukraine, western Belorussia, the Baltic states, and Moldavia—territories recently acquired by the Soviet Union—to Tomsk and Irkutsk oblasts in Siberia.[1] The operation, code-named "Sever" (North) and ordered by the Ministry of State Security, was not the first wave of persecution against Witnesses newly resident in the USSR, nor was it the last, but it was the most dramatic move taken by the communist authorities against this small religious community. The deportations and the imprisonment of Witnesses in the gulag system were perceived as positive by the Watch Tower Bible and Tract Society (hereafter, "the Watch Tower Society" or simply "the Society"), the corporate body of the Witnesses, as a golden opportunity to spread its message of salvation. In 1956 an article in *Watchtower* magazine reported: "The Communist government itself has sent them from one end of the country to the other to work in these slave camps; and, as they see it, the government has paid their fare to new territories to preach the Kingdom message."[2] The Soviet regime did not succeed in extinguishing—or even silencing—this community of believers. Indeed, the conflict between the communist authorities and the Jehovah's Witnesses continued until the late 1980s, when the Witnesses, along with other religious groups, were accorded new freedoms as a consequence of Gorbachev's reforms. The Society was permitted to register (and therefore operate legally) in the Ukrainian republic on February 28, 1991, and in the Russian republic on March 27, 1991, not long before the collapse of the Soviet Union in December of the same year. There is clear evidence of the failure of Soviet secularization in the Witnesses' continued efforts to spread Jehovah's word, despite decades of discrimination, persecution, and harassment. The Society counts 162,182 practicing members in 2,339 congregations in Russia today, which is a conservative figure, because it includes only those involved in evangelizing work.[3]

The confrontation between the Jehovah's Witnesses and the Soviet state was multifaceted, and certainly more complex than it initially appears, extending beyond the truism that this was a clash between a militantly atheist state and an illegal religious community. On the face of it, the Witnesses' challenge to secularization was similar to that posed by other Protestant communities, such as the Initsiativniki (Reform Baptists) or Pentecostals, who would not submit to the state-sanctioned All-Union Council of Evangelical Christians–Baptists, and which either refused, or were denied the right, to register with the Council for the Affairs of Religious Cults (from 1965 the Council for Religious Affairs, or CRA[4]), the state body responsible for administering religious life. In other respects, the Jehovah's Witnesses were regarded by the authorities as fundamentally different from—and far more reactionary than—other unregistered Protestant groups. The particular rancor with which Soviet authorities treated those whom they derogatorily termed the "Iegovisty" (Jehovists) suggests that their belief system, organizational structure, and religious literature posed a unique and intractable challenge, one that extended beyond the religious realm.[5] The Society was not only denied the opportunity to register with the state but the organization itself was explicitly banned in 1961. The regime presented it as a threat despite the modest numbers of Jehovah's Witnesses in the Soviet Union—described in 1977 as "insignificant" by Vasilii Konik, a leading Soviet authority on the Witnesses.[6]

Soviet scholars explained the emergence and spread of Protestant *sektantstvo* (sectarianism) through a class-based analysis of socioeconomic structures, which located the roots of religious superstition in the connivances of the bourgeoisie and concomitant powerlessness of the proletariat.[7]

The de-Stalinization policies of the Khrushchev years brought no relief for illegal religious organizations. The state campaign against sectarianism increased markedly in the middle to late 1950s, with a renewed emphasis on eliminating religious superstition and the claim that illegal religious communities were fundamentally anti-Soviet. In sociological studies, antireligious materials, and CRA documents, the Jehovah's Witnesses were usually discussed alongside Pentecostal and unregistered Baptist and Seventh-Day Adventist communities, although the Witnesses were often singled out as posing a particular threat to the Soviet order. Alla Riabus, a villager from Shelekhov in Irkutsk Oblast, echoed official propaganda when she wrote in a letter published in *Vostochno-Sibirskaia pravda* on January 7, 1960: "When a sensible mind compares Orthodoxy, Baptists, and Jehovism, he sees that the sect 'Jehovah's Witnesses' is the most reactionary of all religious sects."[8] The intended audience for such anti-Witness sentiment was not the Witnesses themselves but antireligious activists, students of Marxism and atheism (whether in the university or the factory), and more generally, the readership of print media. The charges leveled against the Witnesses connected with broader themes in Soviet propaganda, particularly those illustrating the need for good communists to be ever vigilant for foreign agents seeking to undermine the Soviet Union from within.

This chapter offers an overview of the historiography of sectarianism in the Soviet Union, the history of the Jehovah's Witnesses, and the peculiarities of Soviet secularization policy, before examining the main Soviet critiques of the Witnesses and the failure of the sustained campaign against this religious community. I argue that the Jehovah's Witnesses acted as a useful foil for the "new Soviet man," the archetypical citizen that the Communist Party set out to fashion. The new Soviet man would be replete in the qualities required for wholehearted participation in the construction of communism and bound to fellow citizens through loyalty to the party, the state, and the collective. The Jehovah's Witnesses were presented in stark contrast to this model citizen. They embodied broader threats to Soviet society, evident in accusations that the Witnesses were American spies, warmongers, imperialists, reactionaries, and prone to shirk their duties as citizens, particularly when it came to raising children. To be sure, the American origins of the movement and the location of the worldwide headquarters in Brooklyn, New York, meant that Soviet Witnesses were perceived to be aligned with a hostile political camp. The threat also lay in the Society's teachings (interpreted as explicitly political), the refusal of Witnesses to carry out fundamental duties of Soviet citizenship, and the circulation of illegal religious literature. The Witnesses occupied a prominent place in the canon of harmful influences, even when compared with other illegal sectarian groups.

## Religious History and Sectarianism in the Soviet Union

During the past twenty years, religion in the countries of the former Soviet Union has been the subject of balanced and informed historical analyses, a result of the end of the limits on intellectual inquiry for historians in these countries, the archival revolution that followed the demise of Soviet-style communism, and the increased interest in religious history, a trend that is particularly noticeable in studies of the modern era.[9] One might speak of a "recovery of Russian religious history," in an echo of Henry F. May's 1964 essay heralding a new era for historians of the United States.[10] As a result of these developments, the study of religion in the Soviet Union has undergone a significant change, evident in a move away from ecclesiastical history and toward a firmer focus on religious culture and practice, an approach that has facilitated the study of religious communities which lacked a formal, institutional relationship with the state.[11] There have been only a few studies of Jehovah's Witnesses in the Soviet Union, which is surprising given their status as exemplars of "reactionary sectarians." In the Soviet period, if Western scholars of religion did mention the Witnesses—and most did not—they invariably recognized the hostility with which the Communist authorities regarded them and their intractable opposition to the regime. In 1961, for example, Walter Kolarz wrote that the Witnesses formed "the most efficient and widespread illegal organisation that has ever existed under Soviet rule."[12] Almost twenty years later, Christel Lane observed: "The faith of the Witnesses must be considered one of the most clearly articulated and comprehensive counterideologies in the Soviet Union, possessing strong political overtones."[13] Despite this extraordinary level of intransigence, in the post-Soviet period scholars have paid very little attention to Jehovah's Witnesses.[14]

Soviet studies of the Jehovah's Witnesses rarely addressed the movement across the USSR but usually focused on its activity and followers in particular republics and regions, not surprisingly those in which the concentration of Witnesses was greatest.[15] In Russian-language studies, the movement is generally understood to be "a late current in Protestantism."[16] In 1981, Konik argued that the Witnesses should be regarded as a church (*tserkov'*), not as a sect (*sekta*), because of the Watch Tower Society's longevity, worldwide presence, consistent organizational structure, and distinctiveness from other Christian groups.[17] In 2002, Mikhail Odintsov, an expert on religion, identified the Jehovah's Witnesses as one of the largest Protestant churches in Russia.[18] In the post-Soviet period, the Russian language literature on the Witnesses has been written by anticult activists or by scholars of religious studies. Neither approach is balanced; the former is entirely critical, the latter is curiously uncritical, and both rely heavily on the Society's own publications when recounting Witness history in Russia.[19] These binary positions leave little room for detached and critical scholarly analysis (as argued elsewhere, the English-language literature on the Witnesses is hardly more nuanced[20]).

This chapter represents the first attempt to redress this imbalance in the scholarly literature by placing the Jehovah's Witnesses in the landscape of Soviet religious history. It draws on material in the files of the Council for the Affairs of Religious Cults and the CRA in the State Archive of the Russian Federation. It also draws on Soviet-era sociological and historical analyses of the Witnesses as well as antireligious propaganda. To a lesser extent, literature produced by the Watch Tower Society is considered. The Society discourages members from offering independent accounts of their own experiences, which denies historians of the Witnesses the rich bank of biographical and autobiographical material at the fingertips of scholars of evangelical Christian churches (see Olena Panych's analysis of Baptist literature in chapter 7 of the present volume), and more broadly the insights of those writing from within a religious tradition (such as the work of Mormon historians on the Church of Jesus Christ of Latter-Day Saints[21]). Instead, the Watch Tower Society tells the story of the trials suffered by Soviet Witnesses on behalf of its members; indeed, the communist experience holds a special place in the narrative of Witness persecution.

## Historical Context

The movement today known as the Jehovah's Witnesses was founded by Charles Taze Russell, born in 1852, the son of a draper from Allegheny City, which is now a part of Pittsburgh. Russell began to question Christianity when he was unable to defend traditional tenets of Protestantism when challenged by nonbelievers. In 1870, Russell wandered into a sermon given by Jonas Wendell, a Second Adventist preacher, where, he later wrote, "I first had my attention called to the second coming of our Lord."²² The chance encounter renewed his interest in studying the Bible, which led in turn to revelations about prophecy, based on biblical chronology.²³ Russell's mission was to seek the truth in scripture and advertise this to all, principally through the printed word. Guided by Russell's own tracts, groups of men began meeting to study scripture; they became known as the Bible Students. In 1877, fifty thousand copies of the booklet *The Object and Manner of Our Lord's Return* were produced, funded by Russell from proceeds of the family business. This marked the beginning of a prolific publishing venture. Russell began financing periodicals, most notably *Zion's Watch Tower and Herald of Christ's Presence* (known since 1939 as *The Watchtower*). In 1884, a legal corporation was established: Zion's Watch Tower and Tract Society. Russell became very well known in his day. He had regular syndicated columns in a number of U.S. newspapers. He also traveled extensively, across North America and Europe and to Japan and Russia, accompanied by small groups of supporters. This international activity was guided by the belief that the "Second Presence" would come once His word was ministered to the ends of the Earth.²⁴ This is the same strategy guiding the Watch Tower Society's worldwide activities today.

The Watch Tower Society reports that Russell traveled to Kishinev (Chișinău in present-day Moldova) in 1891.²⁵ The section "Some Interesting Letters" in the December 1, 1911, issue of *Zion's Watch Tower and Herald of Christ's Presence* included a report from "R. H. Oleszynski—Russia." Oleszynski wrote: "The truth is spread considerably over the country in many different ways" and noted that Jews were especially eager, and Roman Catholic Poles relatively reluctant, to engage with Russell's teachings.²⁶ Also in 1911, the Herkendells, a German couple, chose to honeymoon by witnessing to the German-speaking population in Russia.²⁷ Still, there were only an estimated one hundred Jehovah's Witnesses in the Soviet Union before World War II, although this number increased when communities in Western Ukraine and Belorussia became subject to Soviet rule after the annexation of these territories from Poland in 1939, and again when Latvia, Lithuania, and Moldavia were annexed in 1940. The number of Witnesses also increased as a result of incarcerated Jehovah's Witnesses converting Russian prisoners in Nazi concentration camps.²⁸ In Ravensbrück alone, 300 female prisoners from Russia became Jehovah's Witnesses.²⁹ The Watch Tower Society counted 4,797 Witnesses across the Soviet Union in 1946;³⁰ of this number, "more than 1,600" were in Russia.³¹

The differences between the teachings of the Watch Tower Society and mainstream Christian churches are significant, chief among them the interpretation of scripture, the nature of the second coming, and belief in the existence of hell. In the Soviet Union, the Society's doctrines contradicted the state socialism espoused by the Communist Party, which regarded belief in a future theocratic paradise as harmful sublimation and procrastination with no scientific basis. But it was the Jehovah's Witnesses' disparagement of the Soviet state that earned them the most enmity. Soon after the close of World War II communist authorities recognized the challenge to their authority posed by the communities of Witnesses then resident on Soviet soil. An article in the February 1, 1946, issue of *Watchtower* reported that more than a thousand Witnesses had been "transferred into the depths of Russia" from eastern Poland.[32] There was more to come, however; Odintsov wrote: "In the postwar history of Russian Jehovah's Witnesses there are two especially sorrowful dates—1949 and 1951."[33] In these years, there were mass exiles under operations codenamed "Iug" (South) and "Sever" (North), respectively, to Siberia, Kazakhstan, and the Far East. The regime did not succeed in silencing the Witnesses through exile, however. A. S. Gerasimets—who wrote numerous studies of sectarianism in the 1950s, 1960s, and 1970s—noted in 1973 that, compared with other Protestant groups, there were small numbers of Jehovah's Witnesses across the Soviet Union, but there were more Witnesses in Irkutsk Oblast than Baptists, Adventists, and Pentecostals combined.[34]

The Watch Tower Society's position on the Soviet Union was defined by scripture. It viewed the Cold War divide between communist East and capitalist West as evidence that Armageddon was approaching, the final confrontation between good and evil that would mark the return of Jehovah and the eternal salvation of those "living in the Truth," to use the Society's vocabulary. The Society did not, however, side with one or the other of the superpowers, as they represented twin evils because of the conviction that all earthly governments are controlled by Satan. Instead, the Society interpreted the conflict as the clash between the king of the north and the king of the south described in the Book of Daniel, from which neither monarch would emerge victorious.[35] This position on the Cold War separated American Jehovah's Witnesses from evangelical Christians in the United States, which was understood by the latter to be the conflict between democratic, Christian America and the godless, communist Soviet state. The condemnation of all earthly governments was not lost on the Soviet authorities: a lengthy report by the Council for the Affairs of Religious Cults on the activities of religious associations across the Soviet Union in 1961 included just six short sentences on the Iegovisty, the last of these stating: "Soviet rule is considered the rule of Satan."[36]

## Secularization

Paul Froese has called the Soviet secularization project a "plot to kill God," highlighting the aim to create an atheist society rather than a secular one.[37] The campaign was made urgent by the conviction that religious belief diverted the attention of the workers away from the real sources of division, conflict, and inequality in society. Furthermore, believers were thought to be sabotaging the construction of communism by interposing a supernatural realm. In the immediate aftermath of the Bolshevik Revolution there was some relief for Protestant communities, whose members understood that the end of the Orthodox Church's privileges also signaled an end to their own persecution. This was to change under Stalin, however. Sergei Zhuk has noted that the harsh religious law of 1929 marked "the end of collaboration between religious and political radicals in Russian history."[38] The enthusiasm of the nineteenth-century populists for the socialist aspects of some religious movements was finally lost to Soviet ideologues with the drive for the collectivization of agriculture. Collectivization targeted rural areas, where sectarian movements were strongest, and, as Alexander Etkind noted, the policy "produced an aggressive anti-sectarian literature."[39]

Within this broad antireligious and atheist campaign, *sektantstvo* (sectarianism) came to occupy a prominent position in the canon of harmful bourgeois influences. All sectarian groups were out of step with Soviet society, and some more so than others.[40] Soviet authorities repeatedly claimed that legitimate churches were registered with the state and enjoyed the freedoms guaranteed by the Soviet Constitution and by religious legislation. This was repeated in propaganda designed for both domestic and foreign consumption. The Legal Department of the CRA prepared educational material outlining which provisions of the Constitution and of religious legislation met the statutes on freedom of conscience in the Helsinki Accords of 1975.[41] In *Church and Religion in the USSR* (1977), Vladimir Kuroedov, then head of the CRA, wrote: "Certain people try to circumvent the law pursuing aims that are usually careerist and dictated by self-interest, under the guise of religion: This generally occurs in sectarian groups (e.g., Jehovah's witnesses [sic; see note 42], Pentecostalists, and a few others)."[42] It is a truism that religious organizations registered with the CRA could more easily be monitored and controlled by the regime. For example, the Moscow Patriarchate, the administrative body of the Russian Orthodox Church, which cooperated with the state and so maintained its institutional integrity, was used by the regime when the Church could prove useful (an obvious example is Stalin's concessions to the Church in 1943). Some Protestant churches were permitted to register; their activities were closely controlled by the CRA.[43] Unregistered organizations could not be readily monitored, controlled, or utilized in the same manner, and herein lay the challenge of the Jehovah's Witnesses, as well as unregistered Pentecostalists, Baptists, and other "underground" or "catacomb" churches, as the Western scholarly literature of the day dubbed these communities. An additional challenge to the regime's effort to control communities of Witnesses was that there were no bishops, priests, or pastors to influence, undermine, or remove: the Society regards all Witnesses as ministers, because all are required to spread Jehovah's word.

The first material explicitly addressing the Jehovah's Witnesses appeared in 1956.[44] Soviet-era studies of the Witnesses—and other sectarian groups—invariably began with quotations on the dangers of religious belief from the work of Marx, Engels, and Lenin. Statements about the extensive guarantees of religious freedom in the Soviet Union followed. Such works generally included extracts from resolutions at recent congresses of the Communist Party of the Soviet Union on combating religious superstition. If not explicitly stated, the implication was that there persisted some troublemakers who used religious adherence as a front for subversive activities. These studies usually closed with recommendations on how diligent antireligious workers and good Soviet citizens might counter their pernicious influence.[45] The Witnesses' literal interpretation of scripture led to an emphasis in Soviet antireligious handbooks on turning to the Bible to prove the falsehood of their teachings.[46] Authors advised readers to counter them with logic, by, for example, pointing out the scientific impossibility of the creation story in the Book of Genesis or of claims that Moses was two hundred years old. Antireligious experts hoped this would be enough to undermine the entire foundation of Witness belief.[47] Testimonies from those who had "seen the light" also featured heavily in Soviet-era propaganda (in common with materials produced by the anticult movement that emerged in the United States in the 1970s).[48] The way Jehovah's Witnesses were presented in antireligious publications and in official documents drew explicitly on broader propaganda tropes, extending beyond the usual methods of stigmatizing, marginalizing, and criminalizing illegal religious groups. The broader threats to Soviet society that the Witnesses seemed to encapsulate are discussed in the next section.

## Soviet Critiques of the Witnesses

Protestant communities were regarded as outsiders in the Russian Empire, as studies of the Shalaputs and Shtundists by Sergei Zhuk and the Baptists by Heather Coleman have shown.[49] The departure from the official Orthodox Church led adherents of Protestantism to be regarded as foreign (typically German), even if they were Russian or Ukrainian. In the communist era, any connection between sectarians and Western capitalist countries, however tenuous, was enough for believers to be regarded with suspicion. The location of the worldwide headquarters meant that the Jehovah's Witnesses were regarded as loyal to the United States. The title of the opening chapter of *Religioznaia sekta Iegovistov* (1959), one of the earliest Soviet publications dedicated to the Witnesses, was unambiguous: "The motherland of Jehovism is located in America."[50]

Soviet scholars described the sect as "American in origin and in essence."[51] They located the very foundations of the Jehovah's Witnesses in a bourgeois enterprise; it was interpreted as a plot designed by Russell (a merchant) to divert the attention of American workers away from class struggle.[52] According to A. S. Gerasimets, it was conceived "on the base of bourgeois interests and bourgeois ideology for the sake of saving and safeguarding moribund capitalism."[53] The Jehovah's Witnesses were portrayed as "obedient tools in the hands of American imperialism."[54] A number of Soviet scholars claimed that the Society was funded by the Rockefellers, themselves Baptists, in order to profit from the increased arms production that would accompany Armageddon.[55] Laura Engelstein observed that nineteenth-century opponents of the Skoptsy emphasized their greed and materiality because "explaining the sect's appeal in material terms made the community seem sinister and mercenary, while relieving converts of responsibility for their choice."[56] In the communist era, avariciousness was a grave sin. The inherently capitalist nature of the Witnesses was supposedly revealed in the practice of tithing of 10 percent (in fact, both donating and the size of the contribution are voluntary); one antireligious author alleged that "the lion's share of this goes into the pocket of various rogues, acting in the role of Jehovist members,"[57] and another said that it more generally benefited "the reactionary power America and other capitalist countries."⁵⁸ For propagandists, the connection with the United States made the capitalist impulses of the Iegovisty all the more evident. In 1977, E. G. Filimonov explained the ideological threat posed by sectarians with foreign links: "The social views and political persuasions of believers are defined by their loyalty to the political orientation of the main sectarian organization."⁵⁹

The distinctive door-to-door ministry conducted by the Witnesses worldwide was presented by Soviet scholars as a product of their American origins. Konik explained that Finnish Witnesses posing as tourists spread religious literature at a Black Sea resort in the 1920s and 1930s, which demonstrated that Witnesses "employ methods . . . that cannot be distinguished from the methods activated by the intelligence services of capitalist governments."⁶⁰ It was presented as a cover for gathering information on residents to report back to Brooklyn.⁶¹ One presumes that the parallels with the surveillance and reporting carried out by Soviet security agencies would not have been lost on readers. The Witnesses were presented as agents of American intelligence services and these activities as evidence of, to quote the title of one early publication, "'Jehovah's Witnesses' in the Service of Imperialism."⁶²

In the 1940s, the Jehovah's Witnesses in the United States were persecuted for their refusal to enact the rituals of citizenship, such as saluting the flag and performing military service. Ironically, some interpreted this as evidence of communist sympathies, prompting the Society to produce a brochure titled "Jehovah's Witnesses: Communists or Christians?" The title was answered with another question: "If Communists, why outlawed in Russia?"⁶³ Witnesses were also the target of vigilante attacks and mob violence by those believing them to be part of a Nazi fifth column, prompting the American Civil Liberties Union to publish a report on the persecution subtitled *The Record of Violence against a Religious Organization Unparalleled in America since the Attacks on the Mormons* (1941).⁶⁴ In both the United States and the Soviet Union, the Witnesses were understood to be undermining the state from within. There was, of course, no civil liberties watchdog operating legally and openly in the USSR to draw attention to these violations, and no recourse to a legal system, which resulted in landmark rulings and assured the Witnesses a prominent place in legal history.⁶⁵ The Society's teaching on secular authority and earthly governments brought them into sharp conflict with states across the world in both the twentieth and twenty-first centuries.

The Watch Tower Society's theology was quite unique among Protestant-related bodies for its unequivocal hostility toward all earthly governments, not just the Soviet regime. Filimonov argued that it was necessary for antireligious workers to adopt different methods according to the type of sectarian to be approached. He divided them into three groups: those who were loyal to Soviet power, those who were disloyal, and those who were openly hostile and negative. The third category included the Jehovah's Witnesses, Pentecostals, Mennonites, and others.[66] Filimonov's understanding of the Witnesses as openly hostile toward Soviet power derived from his interpretation of Watch Tower theology as politically partisan, a claim almost invariably made in anti-Witness literature. Fedor Boiarskii, for example, refused to accept the profession of neutrality: "Anti-Soviet slander, praising the American style of life, justifying the aggressive activities of imperialist governments against peaceful peoples—is this really not political!"[67] The Jehovah's Witnesses were presented in explicitly political terms: their hierarchical and centralized organization as a political structure, their literature as "exaggerating the personality cult of the [Society's] leaders,"[68] their ongoing activity as clandestine and conspiratorial, their missionizing as surveillance for the United States, their central task as espionage, and the circulation of *Watchtower* and *Awake!* as evidence of a "vast propaganda apparatus."[69] The evidence drawn from the Watch Tower Society's own publications—articles in seized magazines that called Soviet communism a "totalitarian system"—was, perhaps understandably, cited by the CRA authorities as evidence of a political orientation.[70] Although analyses such as Filimonov's portrayed the Jehovah's Witnesses as determined enemies of the Soviet Union, scholars were forced to admit that the Society criticized American imperialism, Soviet communism, Nazism, and fascism alike.[71]

The image of the Jehovah's Witnesses as the most reactionary sectarians in the USSR was cemented by their refusal to carry out the most fundamental duties of Soviet citizenship. There were frequent reports in government documents that they were not familiar with the organs of power and would not vote in elections at any level.[72] The refusal to bear arms was a key indicator of their lack of loyalty to the state, as it was in many other countries in the twentieth century. Much was also made of the contrast between the warmongering theocracy of the Watch Tower Society and the peace-loving democracy of Soviet socialism. A propaganda poster printed in 1981 depicts a shabby-looking but suited man standing on top of a brick tower, which is protruding from a top hat worn by a rudimentarily drawn head in profile; the only facial features are a hook nose, a golden coin for an eye, and a dollar sign on the cheek. The man atop the tower has a copy of *Watchtower* tucked under one arm and at the end of the other swings an atom bomb. He shouts, "Anti-Sovietism, anticommunism, lies, slander!" In the background is a stylized city skyline, presumably Manhattan.[73] In addition to refusal to perform military service and alleged warmongering, anti-Witness propaganda also condemned their lack of participation in aspects of life central to the daily rituals of a good Soviet citizen, such as going to the cinema and the theatre[74] and visiting sanatoriums.[75] As a result, the inability of atheist workers to reach Iegovisty through the usual channels—such as lectures, films, and magazines—was a frustration for them, leading to calls by authorities for more individual work. The need for individual work with Witnesses was duly emphasized by regional CRA plenipotentiaries in reports to the headquarters in Moscow and to republican officials on how they planned to counter the influence of the Witnesses in the cities, towns, and villages under their jurisdiction.

Soviet propagandists labeled the Jehovah's Witnesses "cosmopolitans" and accused them of refusing to recognize the Soviet Union as their motherland.[76] The failure to participate in the collective rituals of communism, such as celebrating revolutionary holidays, was a particularly grave crime in a country that demanded the involvement of all citizens in a struggle that defined the state, and the failure of Witnesses to fulfill the duties of citizenship was frequently noted in reports from regional CRA plenipotentiaries. It was also highlighted in propaganda that sought to give this behavior a resonance beyond the religious sphere and take these tales of sedition to a broader audience. A typical article appeared in the magazine *Znamia* (Banner), which was published in Maloiaroslavets in Kaluga Oblast, on July 27, 1983, titled "Two Lessons in Vigilance." One lesson related to A. E. Boltnev, a forestry worker who refused to perform military service on the grounds of his religious beliefs. He copied *Watchtower* magazines received from abroad by hand and by machine and, armed with this literature, "conducted religious agitation" among his fellow workers in the *leskhoz* (forestry enterprise).[77] The lesson is for ordinary citizens to be vigilant against potential advances from those calling themselves believers but seeking to spread anti-Soviet views under the guise of spiritual enlightenment.

Although the Watch Tower Society's doctrines loomed large in analyses of the faith, anti-Witness propaganda was not limited to its teachings. The potential for the Iegovisty to inflict harm on broader society was a recurring theme. In his study of the denunciations of sectarians in the Moscow region in the latter half of the nineteenth century, Jeffrey Burds found that these were rarely motivated by religious deviance alone, but "the language of the confrontations suggests that the denunciations were often a kind of popular theater that overlay tensions that were far more profound."[78] Likewise, the charges leveled at the Jehovah's Witnesses focused not on their departure from legal Protestant churches or indeed from scientific atheism but instead on the deviant lifestyle and corrupted moral code that arose from their religious beliefs. These were presented as profoundly incompatible with the ways of the celebrated new Soviet man. For example, according to V. V. Klochkov, a lack of commitment to the construction of communism led one Witness to the ultimate crime: stealing from the collective. He recounted the story of a Witness who, when caught stealing watermelons from the fields in the *kolkhoz* (collective farm), declared that his faith permitted him to commit this criminal act.[79] This kind of crime, and the justification for it, was typical in anti-Witness propaganda. The failure to fully participate in the Soviet project was presented as inflicting social harm and as extending beyond mere superstition to threaten the basic building blocks of communist society.

The antireligious campaign of the Khrushchev era emphasized countering religious belief among children and youth. The classroom became a key arena for the transmission of atheist propaganda as Soviet achievements in space travel and technology were lauded as evidence of the triumph of science over faith.[80] According to Soviet ideologues, the development of a scientific worldview in children was jeopardized by parents who chose to eschew socialist enlightenment and raise their offspring in ignorance and darkness. CRA plenipotentiaries observed a low level of culture and a high level of illiteracy in adult Jehovah's Witnesses; presumably this contempt for education and civilized society would be passed on to the younger generation.[81] In addition, the children of sectarians were particularly vulnerable to "becoming clouded" by the beliefs of their parents,[82] in part due to the markedly different lifestyle resulting from their religious convictions.[83] The CRA authorities reported that Witness children were denied permission to participate in activities that were a vital part of a communist upbringing, such as singing, participation in *fizkul'tura* (sports and culture), and membership in the communist youth organizations, Komsomol and the Young Pioneers.[84] The cruel treatment of children was also a frequent accusation against Soviet Witnesses.[85] In some respects, this echoed Western anti-Witness literature of the same era, which focused on the strictures placed on children by Witness parents and reported on the legal battles over parental rights, state authority, and consent in adolescence, particularly in relation to the use of blood in medicine.

Children had a particularly prominent role in building a communist utopia and the protection from harmful influences—even their own parents—was the duty of the state. This was a major part of the prosecution's case against Maria Fedorovna Kushnirchuk, a woman who lived in the Ivano-Frankivska Oblast in Ukraine who had been a Witness since 1978 and hosted group Bible study meetings in her apartment. Kushnirchuk would not allow her young daughter, Galina, to attend morning school, go on excursions or cultural outings, watch television or go to the cinema, or join communist organizations for children. Instead, Galina was allegedly forced to read the Bible and to learn psalms and prayers by heart. Kushnirchuk was sentenced to two and half years in a corrective labor colony.[86] Secularization was of course part of a much broader, and very ambitious, social program that aimed to create a cultured, emancipated, enlightened, and radiant (atheist) Soviet citizenry. The idea that children might be denied access to this worldview through parental neglect was a frequent accusation against those of various political, religious, and social stripes who fell afoul of the communist authorities. The message of the trial was about citizenship, loyalty, and duty toward the state rather than about religious education or belief.

## The Impact of Anti-Iegovisty Propaganda

The publication of Bible tracts and other educational literature has been central to the Society since the earliest days of the movement (even today, Witnesses who engage in house-to-house ministry are known as publishers, and figures on membership are considered publishing statistics). The limits on independent publishing in the Soviet Union necessitated alternate routes for the production, duplication, and circulation of the Society's material. Literature was smuggled into the country from abroad in false-bottomed suitcases, sewn into hats, and hidden inside machinery.[87] It was then reproduced using a variety of methods.[88] CRA officials reported that copies of magazines and pamphlets were transferred from one region and republic to another, suggesting a sophisticated distribution network for fiercely anti-Soviet illegal material, which the authorities could do little to stop.[89] When Konik embarked on one of his studies, he was able to draw on books, brochures, journals, reference works, and pamphlets circulating in the original and facsimile versions, in a variety of European languages, including (but not limited to) Russian, Ukrainian, Polish, English, and German.[90]

This literature even permeated the gulag system. Helene Celmina, who was imprisoned in a women's camp east of Kazan from 1962 to 1966, published an account of prison life after her expulsion from the Soviet Union. She wrote that Witness literature (e.g., *Watchtower*) "arrived regularly, in good shape and in large quantities," to the puzzlement of the guards, because "no one has discovered how it gets into the camp."[91] It is impossible to determine the frequency of contact between Soviet Witnesses and the Brooklyn headquarters and how closely the former were able to follow the latter's teachings.

The identification of local communities of Iegovisty as either "Russellites" or "Rutherfordites" in numerous CRA reports suggests that some Soviet Witnesses rejected the Society's leadership.[92] This division arose in 1917 following controversy over Joseph Franklin Rutherford's elevation to the presidency after Russell's death; some Witnesses (the Russellites) saw Rutherford's leadership as illegitimate and rejected the subsequent doctrinal changes. This division was apparently maintained in the Soviet Union. The opaque nature of the Witnesses' organizational structure led two authors to refer to their network as the "holy *okhrana*," a reference to the covert activities of the political police in late Imperial Russia.[93] The "archreactionary literature" circulated by Witnesses became no less confrontational despite sustained persecution.[94] The authorities were well aware of the ongoing refusal of Witnesses to accept the authority of the Soviet regime; a CRA report from Ukraine in 1983 cited passages in *Watchtower* and *Awake!* and also from brochures that explicitly denounced communism, criticized the October Revolution, and condemned the Moscow Patriarchate for its accommodation of the regime.[95]

The confiscation of illegal literature as well as printers, tape recorders, and typographical equipment was described in detail by the CRA authorities. During the trial of Vasilii Gavrish in 1983, a Krasnodarsk regional court established that the convicted man had "systematically received through illegal channels publications from the Jehovist center in the city of Brooklyn, and illegally reproduced in quantity in the USSR in the printed form of religious books, brochures, journals, and other literature, which maintained deliberately false, slanderous concoctions against the Soviet government and social system, and spread among members of the sect living in the territory of Dinsk and other regions of Krasnodarsk Krai."[96] Gavrish was sentenced to three years in a corrective labor colony. The authorities closely watched those suspected of disseminating such literature; documents in the CRA files suggest a high level of surveillance of individuals and families in some areas.[97] On the night of November 13–14, 1977, pamphlets and fliers were seized from the homes of Witnesses in the city of Krasnodar in southern Russia. Among the confiscated items was a single-page, typed flier urging Soviet citizens to reject atheism and turn to the Bible for answers.[98] The circulation of such literature highlighted the failure of Soviet secularization policy and the tenacity of religious belief and made a mockery of the claim that the communist regime was creating a new, postreligious society.

It was not only the continued existence of communities of Jehovah's Witnesses but also their growth that troubled the Soviet authorities. A recurring metaphor in antireligious propaganda was of a sticky web spun by sectarians to entrap the naive, as in one book on Baptists and Witnesses in Northern Ossetia: "Sectarian ideology and practice is like a spider's web. It stretches to hidden corners and lies in wait for its prey. [The spider] waits for it to entangle itself; if it doesn't tear itself away from its tenacious embrace, it faces severe trials."[99] The dangers of being drawn into such circles were many; as one propagandist warned, "It is possible to offer many examples of severe psychiatric illnesses of people falling into various unregistered sectarian organizations" (as though it is the fact of not being registered which drove them insane).[100] The sectarians, those "hunters of misfortunes and failures," targeted the grief-stricken, vulnerable, and confused in particular.[101] Vigilance was essential, because Witnesses might try to spread their beliefs in the enterprise, in the field, on the journey to work, during travel for seasonal labor—and even in the *bania* (bathhouse).[102] Although Western accounts suggested that the harshness of the climactic conditions,[103] or of life under the communist regime,[104] attracted Soviet citizens to the Witnesses, Soviet scholars explained their appeal in terms of delusion, ignorance, or vulnerability. It was no longer the oppressor class that fostered workers' beliefs in the supernatural—class was no longer meant to exist in the Soviet Union—but instead the active efforts of Witnesses to entrap the naïve, directed by capitalist powers.

The CRA report, "Basic Data on the State of Religion in the USSR for 1975," gave firm figures for the number of registered (11,662) and unregistered religious associations (4,189). Of the latter, 401 were Iegovisty; only Muslim (713), Evangelical Christians–Baptists (968), and Pentecostal (862) associations were more numerous.[105] The numbers of Jehovah's Witnesses across the country cannot be determined. Although the Watch Tower

Society keeps detailed records of membership around the world, it does not give figures for countries in which it is forced to operate underground (it does not wish to aid governments that seek to eliminate its presence). The bureaucratic behemoth that was the Soviet state meant CRA representatives at the republican and regional levels regularly relayed membership figures back to the CRA office on Smolenskii Bul'var in Moscow. Some of these reports offer a high level of detail, not only about the number of Witnesses in a certain region, town, or village, but also age range, nationality, place of birth, educational level, and social class.[106] Reports from CRA plenipotentiaries in the regions frequently noted an increase in the number of Witnesses across their territory despite efforts to eliminate their activities. In Zaporizh'ka Oblast in Ukraine, the number of Witnesses increased from around 20 to 169 in the five years from 1968 to 1973. G. Kazakov, a CRA plenipotentiary in the region, called for renewed efforts to counter their continued activities and growth, a common call in reports in the 1970s and 1980s.[107] A comprehensive plan presented by V. F. Korostelev from Irkutsk Oblast on eliminating the activities of Iegovisty in the region over the course of the year 1980–81 reveals the concerted efforts of religious authorities to halt the growth of Witness communities.[108] Irkutsk Oblast, one of the major destinations for deportees, had developed into one of the most active regions in the Soviet Union for Witness activity.

Aleksandr Klibanov wrote in the closing chapter of *History of Religious Sectarianism in Russia* (1965): "During the existence of Soviet society, the absolute number of followers of sectarianism has markedly declined."[109] A study by Klochkov published the same year pointed specifically to the falling membership of Jehovah's Witnesses.[110] In 1977, Filimonov suggested that sectarian organizations were not able to replenish their numbers in socialist societies, citing the sociodemographic profile of sectarians (pensioners between fifty and sixty years of age, who were poorly educated and barely literate) as evidence that they would soon disappear altogether.[111] The following year, Konik wrote that, along with other confessions, the Jehovah's Witnesses organization was "suffering a crisis," with low numbers and few recruits chiefly because of Soviet influence on their activities.[112] Regional CRA returns from the early 1980s regularly reported that the only Witness communities in some regions were family groups, many members of which were elderly, and suggested that soon the groups would disappear entirely.[113]

In the late Soviet period, the communist authorities remained concerned about the continued existence and growth of communities of Jehovah's

Witnesses. Despite the claims above, the assessments by atheist workers and the CRA authorities were not uniformly positive. Documents in the CRA archives also reveal that representatives in a number of regions and republics reported that local measures to eliminate Witness communities were failing. Examples can be found from across the Soviet Union, and in each postwar decade. A report from Zaporizh'ka Oblast called for greater legal powers for regional CRA authorities to counter the Witnesses' influence and further expansion in the region.[114] The failure of Soviet policy to eliminate the presence of Jehovah's Witnesses across its territory was clearly demonstrated the year after the collapse of Soviet-style communism. From June 26 to 28, 1992, an international convention was held in the (recently renamed) city of Saint Petersburg, the first ever on the territory of the former Soviet Union. A total of 29,000 Witnesses from the newly independent post-Soviet states attended. They were joined by 17,000 foreign delegates, 10,000 of them from neighboring Finland.[115]

The CRA authorities across the Soviet Union never came to properly understand the Jehovah's Witnesses, despite frequent appeals by Soviet scholars for antireligious activists to become better acquainted with their beliefs and practices, in order to better fight them.[116] The lack of understanding is not unique to the Witnesses. Felix Corley observed, "Few if any of the bureaucrats who came into contact with religious believers in the course of their work seemed to have any understanding of or respect for religious faith."[117] This is hardly surprising given that as late as December 1955, the European Department of the Ministry of Foreign Affairs wrote to the Council for the Affairs of Religious Cults thanking the body for sending a book on Russian sectarianism published over forty years earlier in 1911.[118] The failure of regional authorities to understand the Witnesses is demonstrated in a letter sent to central CRA authorities from a plenipotentiary in Voroshilovgrad in Ukraine in November 1983, which described the confiscation of "antisocial, wild Il'inskoi literature" from the apartment of one V. I. Beskrovnyy. Beskrovnyy, born in 1918, is described throughout as one of the Jehovist-Ilintsevs, although the literature clearly emanates from the Watch Tower Society.[119] It is also notable that, in a highly centralized bureaucracy, the CRA authorities reported on the Jehovah's Witnesses using a variety of different names and spellings.[120]

The prominence of the Iegovisty in antisectarian propaganda and in CRA documents on harmful religious groups was out of proportion to their actual numbers. The closing paragraph of a letter from Vasilii Babiichuk, from the Irkutsk Oblast, to a local newspaper in 1959 explained how his release from the clutches of Jehovah's Witnesses allowed his reintegration into Soviet society: "How good it is not to believe in god, to be in step with all Soviet people, to bring benefit to society."[121] By presenting the Witnesses as "out of step" with Soviet society, their presence was given a resonance beyond the religious realm. The regime sought to portray them as the ultimate foil to the archetypical new Soviet man. The picture presented was of a highly politicized, fanatically anti-Soviet, bellicose (*voinstvennyi*), misanthropic (*chelovekonenavistnicheskii*), conspiratorial religious organization directed from Brooklyn and set on swelling its ranks with unsuspecting citizens in the guise of spiritual enlightenment, leading them to reject their responsibilities and become crazed fanatics. Given that the intended audience for these caricatures was the broader Soviet population (not the Witnesses), it is hardly surprising that this propaganda failed to eliminate this religious community. It was woven into broader themes of Soviet propaganda and aimed not to convert the Witnesses to Soviet atheism but instead to caution citizens to be ever wary of the enemy within.

## Notes

1. The author is very grateful to the Nuffield Foundation for financial support, which made archival research for this chapter possible. Here, see Mikhail I. Odintsov, *Sovet ministrov SSSR postanovliaet: "Vyselit' navechno!"* (Moscow: Art-Biznes-Tsentr, 2002), 20–21. Official documents relating to the deportations can be found in *Sovet ministrov SSSR postanovliaet*. For accounts by Jehovah's Witnesses, see the many stories in Watch Tower Bible and Tract Society, *2008 Yearbook of Jehovah's Witnesses* (New York: Watch Tower Bible and Tract Society, 2008).

2. "Communist Leaders Fear Bible Truth," *Watchtower*, April 1, 1956, 209–18. This is not to suggest that the Watch Tower Society did nothing to aid Jehovah's Witnesses in the USSR; on the contrary, in the same year this article was published the Society coordinated a campaign for the annual General Assemblies across the world to send petitions to Soviet Premier Nikolai Bulganin protesting against the arrest, incarceration, and deportation of Witnesses across the Soviet Union and appealing for permission to establish a national Branch Office to distribute literature in the USSR, and for Soviet Witnesses to maintain contact with the international headquarters. A letter dated March 2, 1957 from the Ministry of Foreign Affairs to the Council for the Affairs of Religious Cults, which accompanies a copy of a petition from Lahore, includes only one brief statement about the group: "The leadership of this reactionary sect is located in the USA." Gosudarstvennyi arkhiv Rossiiskoi Federatsii (State Archive of the Russian Federation; hereafter GARF, f. 6991 (Sovet po delam religii pri Sovete Ministrov CCCP), op. 4, d. 79, l. 43. Copies of the petition can be found in GARF, f. 6991, op. 4, d. 77, ll. 7–26.

3. Watch Tower Bible and Tract Society, "Statistics: 2010 Report of Jehovah's Witnesses Worldwide," http://www.watchtower.org/e/statistics/worldwide_report.htm.

Scholars generally accept the Society's own statistics on membership. For further discussion, see Zoe Knox, "Writing Witness History: The Historiography of the Jehovah's Witnesses and the Watch Tower Bible and Tract Society of Pennsylvania," *Journal of Religious History* 35, no. 2 (2011): 166.

4. The Council for the Affairs of the Russian Orthodox Church and the CARC merged to become the CRA in 1965.

5. Although it was, and still is, widely used, the term "Iegovisty" is derogatory and has been recognized as such in both Soviet and post-Soviet studies of the Jehovah's Witnesses. V. V. Konik, *"Istiny" svidetelei Iegovy* (Moscow: Politizdat, 1978), 101; and L. N. Mitrokhina, ed., *Khristianstvo: Slovar'* (Moscow: Respublika, 1994), 156.

6. V. V. Konik, *Kakogo boga oni svideteli?* (Kyiv: Znanie, 1977), 5. Konik notes that the number of Jehovah's Witnesses in the USSR fell after 1975, when the onset of Armageddon failed to materialize, as anticipated by millions of Witnesses worldwide. This observation is interesting for two reasons: first, it echoes claims by Western sociologists that the scale of disillusionment with the Watch Tower Society after 1975 was such that it would not recover, and second, Konik's assessment accepts that Witnesses in the USSR were firmly linked into the broader international movement.

7. According to A. I. Klibanov, an eminent Soviet scholar of sectarianism, Adventism was born "from the despair of the middle strata of American society in the period of the Industrial Revolution—the patriarchal farmers and the urban petty bourgeoisie, expropriated in the course of capitalist development." Klibanov, *History of Religious Sectarianism in Russia (1860s–1917)* (Oxford: Pergamon Press, 1982), 375. The Russian-language original was published in 1965.

8. Reprinted as Alla Riabus, "Rvite s religiei smelo i bespovorotno," in *Nam ne po puti s iegovistami'*, edited by A. S. Gerasimets (Irkutsk: Irkutskoe otdelenie obshestva po raspostraneniiu politicheskikh i nauchnykh znanii RSFSR, 1960), 32.

9. For more on these broader historiographical trends, see A. L. Litvin, *Writing History in Twentieth-Century Russia: A View from Within* (Basingstoke: Palgrave, 2001); Donald J. Raleigh, "Doing Soviet History: The Impact of the Archival Revolution," *Russian Review* 61, no. 1 (January 2002): 16–24; and Robert B. Townsend, "A New Found Religion? The Field Surges among AHA Members," *Perspectives on History* (December 2009), http://www.historians.org/perspectives/issues/2009/0912/0912new3.cfm. For an enlightening discussion of the struggle by the editors of one journal to move away from publishing articles on strictly ecclesiastical history to publishing on religious practice, symbolism, culture, and other topics that extend beyond the institutional context, see John Gascoigne, "The *Journal of Religious History* 1960–2010: The Changing Face of Religious History over Fifty Years," *Journal of Religious History* 34, no. 3 (September 2010): 262–71.

10. "For the study and understanding of American culture and history, the recovery of American religious history may well be the most important achievement of the last thirty years." Henry F. May, "The Recovery of American Religious History," *American Historical Review* 70, no. 1 (1964): 79.

11. Notable contributions include those by Heather J. Coleman, *Russian Baptists and Spiritual Revolution, 1905–1929* (Bloomington: Indiana University Press, 2005); Laura Engelstein, *Castration and the Heavenly Kingdom: A Russian Folktale* (Ithaca, N.Y.: Cornell University Press, 1999); Roy R. Robson, *Old Believers in Modern Russia* (DeKalb: Northern Illinois University Press, 1995); Catherine Wanner, *Communities of the Converted: Ukrainians and Global Evangelism* (Ithaca, N.Y.: Cornell University

Press, 2007); and Sergei I. Zhuk, *Russia's Lost Reformation: Peasants, Millennialism and Radical Sects In Southern Russia and Ukraine, 1830–1917* (Washington, D.C., and Baltimore: Woodrow Wilson Center Press and Johns Hopkins University Press, 2004).

12. Walter Kolarz, *Religion in the Soviet Union* (London: Macmillan, 1961), 341–42.

13. Christel Lane, *Christian Religion in the Soviet Union: A Sociological Study* (London: George Allen and Unwin, 1978), 189.

14. Notable exceptions are E. B. Baran, "Contested Victims: Jehovah's Witnesses and the Russian Orthodox Church, 1990–2004," *Religion, State and Society* 35, no. 3 (2007): 261–78; and Zoe Knox, "Religious Freedom in Russia: The Putin Years," in *Religion, Morality, and Community in Post-Soviet Societies*, edited by Mark D. Steinberg and Catherine Wanner (Washington, D.C., and Bloomington: Woodrow Wilson Center Press and Indiana University Press, 2008), 298–302.

15. See, e.g., E. S. Prokoshina, "Vozniknovenie obshchin svidetelei Iegovy i rasprostranenie ikh v Belorussii," in *Iegovizm*, edited by M. Ia. Lensu (Minsk: Nauka i tekhnika, 1981), 5–19 (on Belorussia); V. F. Gazhos, *Osobennosti ideologii iegovizma i religioznoe soznanie sektantov: Na materialakh Moldavskoi SSR* (Kishinev: Redaktsionno-izdatel'skii otdel Akademii nauk Moldavskoi SSR, 1969) (on Moldova); A. K. Khachirov and B. Zh. Vidzhelov, *Pautina* (Ordzhonikidze: Ir, 1979) (on North Ossetia); and A. S. Gerasimets, ed., *Nam ne po puti s iegovistami'* (Irkutsk: Irkutskoe otdelenie obshestva po rasposraneniiu politicheskikh i nauchnykh znanii RSFSR, 1960) (on Irkutsk Oblast).

16. Mitrokhina, *Khristianstvo*, 411. This is true of the literature published in both the Soviet and post-Soviet periods; see the discussion by N. S. Gordienko, *Rossiiskie Svideteli Iegovy: Istoriia i sovremennost'* (Saint Petersburg: Tipografiia Pravda, 2002), 11–12; and V. Konik, *Illiuzii Svidetelei Iegovy* (Moscow: Sovetskaia Rossiia, 1981), 7. Characterizing the Witnesses in this way represents a departure from the position taken in most English-language studies of this group in which they are often presented as barely Christian in some ways, or at least outside mainstream Protestant currents. In this sense, the origins and development of the Witnesses are understood by religious scholars in Russia better than their counterparts in the West, who frequently overlook the Adventist origins of the organization.

17. Konik, *Illiuzii Svidetelei Iegovy*, 160–61. Gordienko observed: "Even in Soviet times, when Jehovah's Witnesses were small in number, serious religious scholars did not consider it correct to call them 'sectarians.'" Gordienko, *Rossiiskie Svideteli Iegovy*, 10. Sergei Ivanenko goes so far as to argue that Jehovah's Witnesses are traditional for Russia, identifying features typical of Russian religious organizations in the emergence and theology of the Witnesses. See Sergei Ivanenko, *Svideteli Iegovy: Traditsionnaia dlia Rossii religioznaia organizatsiia* (Moscow: Art-Biznes-Tsentr, 2002); and Sergei Ivanenko, *O liudiakh, nikogda ne rasstaiushchikhsia s Bibliei* (Moscow: Art-Biznes-Tsentr, 1999), 86.

18. Odintsov, *Sovet ministrov SSSR postanovliaet*, 39.

19. An exemplar of the first category is Aleksandr Dvorkin, *Psevdokhristianskaia sekta "svideteli Iegovy": O liudiakh, nikogda ne rasstaiushchikhsia so "storozhevoi Bashnei"* (Saint Petersburg: Formika, 2002). Typical of the second are Ivanenko, *Svideteli Iegovy*; Ivanenko, *O liudiakh*; and Gordienko, *Rossiiskie Svideteli Iegovy'*. Ivanenko's *Svideteli Iegovy* and Gordienko's *Rossiiskie Svideteli Iegovy* are so uncritical that they have been given to visitors at Kingdom Halls in Russia.

20. Knox, "Writing Witness History," 157–80.

21. Kevin M. Schultz and Paul Harvey, "Everywhere and Nowhere: Recent Trends in American Religious History and Historiography," *Journal of the American Academy of Religion* 78, no. 1 (March 2010): 138.

22. Charles Taze Russell, "Supplement," *Zion's Watch Tower, and Herald of Christ's Presence* 1, no. 1 (July 1, 1879).

23. The chronology uncovered by Russell centered on the overthrow of Jerusalem by Babylon, which marked the end of Jehovah's theocratic governance and the beginning of man's, an era called the Gentile Times. The mathematical underpinning of this chronology was detailed in the seven volumes in Russell's *Millennial Dawn* series, which was later renamed *Studies in the Scriptures*.

24. Jehovah's Witnesses refer to the "Second Presence" rather than "Second Coming" because they adhere to the Adventist belief in a visible, bodily return to Earth.

25. Watch Tower Bible and Tract Society of Pennsylvania, *Jehovah's Witnesses: Proclaimers of God's Kingdom* (New York: Watch Tower Bible and Tract Society, 1993), 406.

26. "'Die Stimme' Stirring Up Jews in Russia," *Zion's Watch Tower and Herald of Christ's Presence* 32, no. 23 (December 1, 1911): 451.

27. Watch Tower Bible and Tract Society of Pennsylvania, *Jehovah's Witnesses*, 411.

28. Hans Hermann Dirksen, "Jehovah's Witnesses under Communist Regimes," *Religion, State and Society* 30, no. 3 (September 2002): 231–32.

29. "Reconstructive and Relief Work in Europe," *Watchtower*, February 1, 1946, 47. These figures are accepted by scholars. See, e.g., Odintsov, *Sovet ministrov SSSR postanovliaet*, 13.

30. Watch Tower Bible and Tract Society of Pennsylvania, *Jehovah's Witnesses*, 508.

31. "Reconstructive and Relief Work in Europe," 47.

32. Ibid. For more on the mass migrations during and immediately after World War II, see Pavel Polian, *Against Their Will: The History and Geography of Forced Migrations in the USSR* (Budapest: Central European University Press, 2004), 115–80.

33. Odintsov, *Sovet ministrov SSSR postanovliaet*, 17. On Operation Iug, see the report on a conference addressing the exile of Jehovah's Witnesses from Moldavia to Chita Oblast in southeastern Siberia, which includes official documents on the deportations, as given by N. S. Gordienko, *Neizvestnye stranitsy istorii (Po materialoi konferentsii Uroki repressii g. Chita, 15 dekabria 1999 goda)* (Saint Petersburg: Otpechatano v AOOT Tipografiia Pravda, 2000).

34. A. S. Gerasimets, *Osobennosti ideologii i kul'ta "svidetelie Iegovy" v SSSR* (Irkutsk: Znanie, 1973), 3. See also the concern with Witnesses in a 1969 report from a CRA plenipotentiary in Irkutsk, in GARF, f. 6991, op. 6, d. 227, ll. 36–39.

35. Watch Tower Society, *Pay Attention to Daniel's Prophecy!* (New York: Watch Tower Bible and Tract Society, 1999), 280–81.

36. GARF, f. 6991, op. 4, d. 428, l. 39.

37. Paul Froese, *The Plot to Kill God: Findings from the Soviet Experiment in Secularization* (Berkeley: University of California Press, 2008).

38. Zhuk, *Russia's Lost Reformation*, 402.

39. Alexander Etkind, "Russian Sects Still Seem Obscure," *Kritika: Explorations in Russian and Eurasian History* 2, no. 1 (2001): 169. This continued past the initial collectivization push and into the Khrushchev era, as noted by Andrew B. Stone, "'Overcoming Peasant Backwardness': The Khrushchev Antireligious Campaign and the Rural Soviet Union," *Russian Review* 67, no. 2 (2008): 296–320.

40. The definition of *sektantstvo* offered by V. I. Kalugin makes this clear. V. I. Kalugin, *Sovremennoe religioznoe sektantstvo, ego raznovidnosti i ideologiia* (Moscow: Vysshaia shkola, 1962), 5.

41. GARF, f. 6991, o.6, d. 1121, ll. 8–14.

42. Kuroyedov, *Church and Religion in the USSR* (1977; Moscow: Novosti Press Agency, 1982), 51. He continues: "Such lawbreakers, naturally, are brought to justice" (p. 51). Note the use of the lowercase "w" for "Witnesses," which follows an outdated convention. The Watch Tower Society switched to the uppercase "W" in 1976.

43. See, e.g., the minutes of a CARC meeting in 1955 at which an application from an archbishop of the Lutheran Church in Estonia to publish a religious journal was considered. The Council determined that one issue could be published annually, of no more than ten pages, in a print run limited to 4,000. GARF, f. 6991, op. 4, d. 36, l. 19.

44. Gerasimets, *Osobennosti ideologii*, 6.

45. For an early study of the Witnesses that follows this template, see E. A. Pritchina, *"Svideteli iegovy" na sluzhbe imperializma* (Moscow: Obshchestvo po rasprostraneniiu politicheskikh i nauchnykh znanii RSFSR, 1959). A typical example focused on unregistered Baptists, Jehovah's Witnesses, and other illegal religious groups: V. V. Klochkov, *Pod vidom religioznykh obriadov* . . . (Moscow: Znanie, 1965).

46. See, e.g., Konik, *Illiuzii Svidetelei Iegovy*, 155.

47. Khachirov and Vidzhelov, *Pautina*, 122; Konik, *Kakogo boga oni svideteli?* 15, 24.

48. See, e.g., a booklet published by the Irkutsk branch of the Knowledge Society, which reproduced an open letter from three former leaders of the Witnesses in Siberia renouncing their faith, first published in *Vostochno-Sibirskaia Pravda* on January 25, 1963: N. Rogozniak, N. Khamei, and V. Pron', *My ne mozhem molchat' (otkrytoe pis'mo chlenam organizatsii 'svidetelei Iegovy')* (Irkutsk: Znanie, 1963). See also the account by a former member involved in the circulation of Witness literature, which finishes: "The only way to a bright future is with communism!" Grigorii Dodu, *Ia ushel ot sektantov* (Chita: Chitanskoe knizhnoe izdatel'stvo, 1959), 1–19; and the account by former member M. V. Andibur, *Pered sudom naroda* (Abakan: Khakasskoe knizhnoe izdatel'stvo, 1963).

49. Coleman, *Russian Baptists and Spiritual Revolution*; and Zhuk, *Russia's Lost Reformation*.

50. A. Gerasimets and N. Reshetnikov, *Religioznaia sekta Iegovistov* (Irkutsk: Irkutskoe otdelenie vserossiiskogo obshchestvo po rasprostraneniiu politicheskikh i nauchnykh znanii, 1959), 4.

51. V. Varavka and S. Meshavkin, *Pravda o sektantakh* (Sverdlovsk: Knizhnoe izdatel'stvo, 1960), 21.

52. Fedor Boiarskii, *Proroki: Ocherk* (Alma Ata: Kazakhskoe gosudarstvennoe izdatel'stvo khudozhestvennoi literatury, 1960), 7. Russell and the subsequent presidents of the Watch Tower Society were invariably described as having bourgeois backgrounds and immense wealth.

53. A. S. Gerasimets, "Redislovie," in *Nam ne po puti s iegovistami'*, edited by A. S. Gerasimets (Irkutsk: Irkutskoe otdelenie obshestva po raspostraneniiu politicheskikh i nauchnykh znanii RSFSR, 1960), 3.

54. Klochkov, *Pod vidom religioznykh obriadov*, 57.

55. Gerasimets and Reshetnikov, *Religioznaia sekta Iegovistov*, 5–6, 27; Dodu, *Ia ushel ot sektantov'stvo*, 21; Boiarskii, *Proroki*, 9. The Watch Tower Society was also

described as an organ of J. P. Morgan, the American financier. Varavka and Meshavkin, *Pravda o sektantakh*, 23.

56. Engelstein, *Castration*, 67; see also the excerpts from a Geographical Society report on Skoptsy in Siberian exile on 126.

57. Klochkov, *Pod vidom religioznykh obriadov*, 53.

58. Gerasimets and Reshetnikov, *Religioznaia sekta Iegovistov*, 25.

59. E. G. Filimonov, "Novye tendentsii v ideologii i deiatel'nosti sovremenno sektantstva," *Seriia nauchnyi ateizii*, no. 11/77 (1977): 9.

60. Konik, *Illiuzii Svidetelei Iegovy*, 16.

61. Khachirov and Vidzhelov, *Pautina*, 82–83, and also 150.

62. Pritchina, *"Svideteli iegovy" na sluzhbe imperializma*.

63. Watch Tower Bible and Tract Society, "Jehovah's Witnesses: Communists or Christians?" brochure, 1951.

64. American Civil Liberties Union, *The Persecution of Jehovah's Witnesses: The Record of Violence against a Religious Organization Unparalleled in America since the Attacks on the Mormons* (New York: American Civil Liberties Union, 1941).

65. S. F. Peters, *Judging Jehovah's Witnesses: Religious Persecution and the Dawn of the Rights Revolution* (Lawrence: University Press of Kansas, 2000).

66. Filimonov, "Novye tendentsii v ideologii," 57.

67. Boiarskii, *Proroki*, 8. For a similar view, see Gerasimets, "Redislovie," 3.

68. Gerasimets and Reshetnikov, *Religioznaia sekta Iegovistov*, 19.

69. Khachirov and Vidzhelov, *Pautina*, 85.

70. GARF, f. 6991, op. 6, d. 2578, l. 12.

71. Khachirov and Vidzhelov, *Pautina*, 145; Konik, *"Istiny" svidetelei Iegovy*, 71.

72. Document 60 in Odintsov, *Sovet ministrov SSSR postanovliaet*, 186. From GARF, f. 6991, op. 6, d. 3011, l. 7. The governing body does not proscribe voting in elections, teaching that it is a matter of conscience, but in practice most Witnesses abstain from voting.

73. A poem printed on the poster titled "Jehovah's Witnesses" reads: "Having covered the Soviet Union with slander / He's forecasting a world war. . . . / Watch out for this persistent sect / It's dangerous to play war games with them!" The crude imagery and doggerel are typical of Soviet antireligious propaganda. Soviet Poster, ID 06keston-pos-00028, Izdatelstvo Plakat, 1981, Keston Archive and Library, Baylor University, Waco, Tex.

74. Khachirov and Vidzhelov, *Pautina*, 119.

75. Klochkov, *Pod vidom religioznykh obriadov*, 49.

76. Gerasimets and Reshetnikov, *Religioznaia sekta Iegovistov*, 35; Khachirov and Vidzhelov, *Pautina*, 163; Klochkov, *Pod vidom religioznykh obriadov*, 45, 59; Konik, *"Istiny" svidetelei Iegovy*, 74–75.

77. GARF, f. 6991, op. 6, d. 2579, ll. 3–13. The documents in the file include CRA communications about publishing the details of these cases as well as a copy of the eventual article. Iu. Solianikov and A. Shcheglov, "Dva uroka bditel'nosti'," *Znamia* (July 27, 1983): 3.

78. Jeffrey Burds, "A Culture of Denunciation: Peasant Labor Migration and Religious Anathematization in Rural Russia, 1860–1905," *Journal of Modern History* 68, no. 3 (1996): 811. Engelstein made a similar observation at the official level in her study of the Skoptsy. In Imperial Russia, decrees against the Skoptsy focused on their ability to inflict "social harm" rather than their religious deviance. It was therefore the

behavior of the sectarians that was emphasized, not their religious beliefs. Engelstein, *Castration*, 45–88.

79. Klochkov, *Pod vidom religioznykh obriadov*, 42.

80. Michael Froggatt, "Renouncing Dogma, Teaching Utopia: Science in Schools under Khrushchev," in *The Dilemmas of De-Stalinization: Negotiating Cultural and Social Change in the Khrushchev Era*, edited by Polly Jones (London: Routledge, 2006), 257–63. For Soviet propagandists, the Society's emphasis on Armageddon was presented as particularly unscientific and as demonstrating its opposition to progress.

81. GARF, f. 6991, op. 6, d. 227, l. 37.

82. Khachirov and Vidzhelov, *Pautina*, 156. The cruel treatment of children in Jehovah's Witness families was a frequent theme in the literature. Open letters and testimonies from children and youth appear in Gerasimets, *Nam ne po puti s iegovistami'*, 35–36. See also Gerasimets and Reshetnikov, *Religioznaia sekta Iegovistov*, 3.

83. Konik, *"Istiny" svidetelei Iegovy*, 93. The authorities were particularly troubled by unregistered Seventh-Day Adventists, who refused to send their children to school on Saturdays. GARF, f. 6991, op. 6, d. 2588, l. 2.

84. Typical is a report dated October 20, 1973, from I. Paterilo, a CRA plenipotentiary, on the various Jehovist groups in villages and towns across Kirovograd Oblast in central Ukraine: GARF, f. 6991, op. 6, d. 553, ll. 48–52.

85. The treatment of children was a theme in anti-Witness propaganda across the Soviet Union, from Central Asia to the Baltics. E.g., in 1961, *Sovetskaia Kirgizia* ran a story about a girl in Sokuluk who was removed from the care of her parents after she complained that they had forbidden her to participate in communist activities and had beaten her for not learning her prayers. Central Asian Research Centre, "Christian Churches and Sects in Central Asia and Kazakhstan," *Central Asian Review* 11, no. 4 (1963): 352.

86. GARF, f. 6991, op. 6, d. 2619, ll. 30–33.

87. Photographs of confiscated literature as well as the machinery that produced it and the nooks which concealed it appear in E. Erofteeva and I. Doru, *Taina 'svidetelei Iegovy'* (Stavropol: Knizhnoe izdatel'stvo, 1968). U.S. currency is also shown among the accoutrements hidden by Jehovah's Witnesses. See also the photographs in Dodu, *Ia ushel ot sektantov'*.

88. See, e.g., a list of materials and machinery seized in Crimea in 1972 in GARF, f. 6991, op. 6, d. 553, l. 54.

89. GARF, f. 6991, op. 6, d. 553, l. 37.

90. Konik, *Illiuzii Svidetelei Iegovy*, 6.

91. Helene Celmina, *Women in Soviet Prisons* (New York: Paragon Publishers, 1985), 125–26. Many of the case studies in the *2008 Yearbook* recount the production and distribution of literature by Witnesses incarcerated in labor camps; Watch Tower Bible and Tract Society, *2008 Yearbook of Jehovah's Witnesses*, 109, 112–13, 144, 152.

92. This contradicts the claim in one of the most widely cited studies of Witnesses in the USSR that although a small group, they were "well organized and unified." Gordienko, *Rossiiskie Svideteli Iegovy'*, 24. A discussion of a split in the early 1960s is given by Konik, *"Istiny" svidetelei Iegovy'*, 8, and in a 1981 report on a group of seventeen Jehovists in Zakarpatskoi Oblast who did not recognize the authority of Brooklyn. GARF, f. 6991, op. 6, d. 2201, l. 16.

93. E. M. Bartoshevich and E. I. Borisoglebskii, *Svideteli Iegovy* (Moscow: Politizdat, 1969), 159. Interestingly, in the post-Soviet period, Aleksandr Dvorkin, a

high-profile, anticult activist, compared the Witnesses' organizational structure to that of the Communist Party of the Soviet Union in *Sektovedenie: Totalitarnye sekty (opyt sistematicheskogo issledovaniia)* (Nizhnii Novgorod: Izdatel'stvo "Khristianskaia" biblioteka, 2008), 148.

94. Klochkov, *Pod vidom religioznykh obriadov*, 57.

95. GARF, f. 6991, op. 6, d. 2578, ll. 10–18.

96. GARF, f. 6991, op. 6, d. 2783, l. 10.

97. See, e.g., the reports in GARF, f. 6991, op. 6, d. 2578, ll. 10–18 (which shows the use of photographs to identify people in the Witness community); and GARF, f. 6991, op. 6, d. 2619, ll. 20–21 (on the commemoration of the memorial of Christ's death in Ivanov-Frankovskaia Oblast in March 1983).

98. GARF, f. 6991, op. 6, d. 1165, ll. 140–42.

99. Khachirov and Vidzhelov, *Pautina*, 6. The open comparison appears elsewhere, such as the section "O lipkoi pautine Iegovistov" [On the sticky spider's web of Jehovists], in *Pravda o sektantakh*, by Varavka and Meshavkin, 20–31, and in the image of a spider in its web wearing a black top hat (in the style of an American banker) bearing a dollar sign on the cover of Dodu, *Ia ushel ot sektantov'*. It was used by Soviet authorities to describe other sectarian groups; see, e.g., the comments of the president of the Saratov People's Court on the trap of the 'clingy spider's web' spun by Skoptsy leaders in Engelstein, *Castration*, 211.

100. Klochkov, *Pod vidom religioznykh obriadov*, 14; see the tragic story of the Jehovist "Mariia K." recounted on 13–14.

101. Ibid., 62–67.

102. Konik calls this "by chance witnessing." Konik, *"Istiny" svidetelei Iegovy*, 85. See also Gerasimets and Reshetnikov, *Religioznaia sekta Iegovistov*, 31.

103. With reference to the Jehovah's Witnesses, among other sects, a report in *Central Asian Review* noted that "the deportation of sect leaders from European Russia to Siberia and Kazakhstan assisted the spread of the sects whose more extreme teachings seem to have considerable appeal for some people in the harsh climate of those parts." Central Asian Research Centre, "Christian Churches and Sects in Central Asia and Kazakhstan," 343.

104. Kolarz explained that the Jehovah's Witnesses "thrive in the grim circumstances created by the Soviet régime, especially in the newly annexed territories of the Soviet Union." Kolarz, *Religion in the Soviet Union*, 339.

105. GARF, f. 6991, op. 6, d. 912, l. 34.

106. See, e.g., a report from Krasnoiarsk Krai of August 5, 1976. GARF, f. 6991, op. 6, d. 959, ll. 63–64. Such detailed information was occasionally reproduced in books on the Jehovah's Witnesses in a particular area, such as this volume on Witnesses in Irkutsk: Gerasimets, "Redislovie," 6, which gives the number of Witnesses in the region as 100 and provides short profiles of believers (name, age, level of literacy).

107. There were forty members in the city of Zaporozh, sixty-one in the village of Konstantinovka, thirty-three in Voznesenka in the Melitopolsky district, and thirty-five in Tokmak in the district of Molochansk. GARF, f. 6991, op. 6, d. 553, ll. 43–45.

108. GARF, f. 6991, op. 6, d. 2201, ll. 2–4.

109. Klibanov, *History of Religious Sectarianism*, 408. The size of the various sectarian communities in the Russian Empire and later the Soviet Union are difficult to determine and the figures for both periods remain contested; see, e.g., the discussion of the number of Shtundists in Kherson Province in 1890 given by Zhuk, *Russia's Lost*

*Reformation*; and a corrective by Heather Coleman, "Review of Zhuk," *Slavic Review* 64, no. 4 (2005): 907. One scholar has clearly found the task too difficult and thus has simply referred to the "rather decent" membership of catacomb churches in the Soviet period; see Nickolas Lupinin, "The Russian Orthodox Church," in *Eastern Christianity and the Cold War, 1945–91*, edited by Lucian Leustean (London: Routledge, 2010), 26.

110. Klochkov, *Pod vidom religioznykh obriadov*, 47.

111. Filimonov, "Novye tendentsii v ideologii," 15, 18. Requests from the regional CRA authorities in the late 1970s and early 1980s to strike groups of Jehovah's Witnesses in their region off the register of illegal groups frequently cited the infirmity, illness, or the death of aged members as the reason that a particular group was not longer active. GARF, f. 6991, op. 6, d. 2626, l. 66.

112. Konik, *"Istiny" svidetelei Iegovy*, 8. It was reported that in Moldova there was from 1960 a mass defection of members, which would lead to the demise of the Witnesses in the republic. V. F. Gazhos, *Evoliutsiia religioznogo sektantstva v Moldavii* (Kishinev: Shtiintsa, 1975), 83.

113. See, e.g., the following reports from various regions in Odessa Oblast: GARF, f. 6991, op. 6, d. 2626, l. 55; l. 66; l. 70; l. 77.

114. GARF, f. 6991, op. 6, d. 553, ll. 43–44.

115. "Russia's First International Convention of Jehovah's Witnesses," *Awake!* December 22, 1992, 23–28.

116. Filimonov, "Novye tendentsii v ideologii," 62; Khachirov and Vidzhelov, *Pautina*, 174.

117. Felix Corley, *Religion in the Soviet Union: An Archival Reader* (New York: New York University Press, 1996), 2.

118. GARF, f. 6991, op. 4, d. 43, ll. 40–41.

119. GARF, f. 6991, op. 6, d. 2613, ll. 81–82. CRA plenipotentiaries in the regions often reported the presence of several types of Jehovists in their territories. GARF, f. 6991, op. 6, d. 553, ll. 48–49. For a discussion of "Iegovisty Il'intsy," see Khachirov and Vidzhelov, *Pautina*, 71–76. For a discussion of the differences between the two, see Konik, *"Istiny" svidetelei Iegovy*, 29–31. See also Kalugin, *Sovremennoe religioznoe sektantstvo*, 29–33.

120. The CRA reports from Moldova on the number of Witnesses refer to these communities in a number of ways, among them Iegovisty, sekta Iegovistov, sekta svidetelei Iegova, and Egovisty. GARF, f. 6991, op. 4, d. 299, ll. 84, 110, 115, 133.

121. Vasilii Babiichuk, "Kak khorosho b'et' neveryiushchii," in *Nam ne po puti s iegovistami'*, edited by A. S. Gerasimets (Irkutsk: Irkutskoe otdelenie obshestva po raspostraneniiu politicheskikh i nauchnykh znanii RSFSR, 1960), 53.

## Chapter 9

# A Multireligious Region in an Atheist State: Unionwide Policies Meet Communal Distinctions in the Postwar Mari Republic

*Sonja Luehrmann*

In many parts of the Soviet Union, the struggle against *religion* (imagined as a single phenomenon with a predictable set of causes and socially harmful effects) inevitably concerned *religions* in the plural. Regional religious landscapes contained such diversity that people who followed their own practices and traditions knew well that their neighbors in the next village did things differently. In places as ethnically and religiously diverse as the Middle Volga region, religion was not a discrete body of doctrines and practices under the auspices of a single institution. Rather, it constituted a shifting field of diverse allegiances and shared sensibilities with intimate connections to a person's place of residence and ethnolinguistic identity.[1] Local officials and cultural professionals often struggled to implement Unionwide policies that were designed to target particular groups and practices. The challenges of carrying out secularizing policies in a multireligious region, such as the Mari ASSR, one of the autonomous national republics in the Volga region, offer a particularly clear view of the tensions between specific understandings of religion held by policymakers in Moscow and the many roles that relationships with the sacred played in the lives of Soviet citizens. Although the disconnect was never bridged, encounters with actually existing religious landscapes also left their mark on atheist theories and policies.

In the Volga region, Soviet communists set out to transform the centuries-old coexistence of indigenous, land-based religions, Islam, and Christianity. The region's cities had been dominated by the official church of the Russian empire, Orthodox Christianity, since Tsar Ivan IV's conquest of the area in the sixteenth century, with some concessions to Muslim Tatar merchant populations.[2] In the countryside, a radius of a few miles might contain a Tatar village with a mosque, a community of Russian Old Believers, and a Mari or Udmurt village whose residents were officially Russian Orthodox, but more likely to visit their local sacred grove than the far-off parish church. In groves of fir, oak, or birch trees, often located on hilltops, such villagers made offerings of farm animals, waterfowl, homemade cheese, and pancakes to agricultural deities as part of ceremonies to mark important events in the rural cycle, most notably spring sowing, midsummer haymaking, and the harvest in the fall.

Religious distinctions were reinforced by linguistic ones. Tatars speak a Turkic language, and Maris and Udmurts Finno-Ugric ones, all of which are quite distinct from Slavic languages. But numerous linguistic borrowings and shared ways of engaging the sacred also demonstrate the frequent back-and-forth between neighbors. The Arab formula *bismillah* (in the name of Allah) has been part of Mari prayers since at least the nineteenth century, and the Mari term for a sacrifice acceptable to the gods, *alal*, is derived from the Arabic *halal* (permitted, acceptable). Before and even during the Soviet era, pilgrimages to sacred springs and graves of Sufi saints in the region drew participants from a variety of ethnoreligious communities. Outside of such pilgrimage sites, people might not visit the place of worship of another village or religious tradition, but they still held shared assumptions about how to approach a sacred place and what to do there: a layperson came "to pray," bringing some sort of offering, be it money, food, or candles; and a dress code applied that involved special attention to head coverings.[3] Christian, Muslim, and pagan women wore headscarves at all sacred sites. Men prayed with covered heads in mosques and sacred groves, while removing their hats in churches. Rather than the indiscriminate mixing of religious traditions often implied by the term "syncretism," being a Christian, Muslim, or pagan on the Middle Volga meant participating in a set of distinct, but mutually intelligible practices that were tied to community membership as much as to particular beliefs.[4]

Soviet officials charged with combating religion in this setting confronted a number of difficult questions: How should one carry out Union-wide campaigns against religious phenomena that did not exist in all parts of the region? What might persuade people that religion was incompatible with socialist society when it was such an integral part of their own understandings of communal identity? To complicate matters even more, atheist activists in the period after World War II were increasingly conscious of ongoing religious innovation, both in terms of the emergence of new religious communities and of old ritual practices adapting to Soviet realities. How would superiors in Moscow react to such challenges to established narratives that cast religion as a survival of the past?

Given the long-established religious diversity in many parts of the Soviet Union, the effects of antireligious policy were at once particularizing—requiring and often imposing well-defined boundaries between religious groups—and diffuse—priorities were set in Moscow, creating a one-size-fits-all approach to religious life that rarely gave local activists much room to engage the diversity of religious expression in their region. To fully appreciate the mechanisms and consequences of Soviet secularization, one has to go beyond the homogenizing vision of policymakers themselves, and look at the extent to which standardized policies affected communal practices that did not fit the standard atheist understandings of religion.

## Centralized Campaigns, Peripheral Realities

In October 1959, articles in the Russian- and Mari-language versions of a district newspaper in the Mari ASSR informed readers about the dangers of "sects." The initiative was in line with rising concern over forms of religious expression that evaded the regulatory authority of "socialist legality" throughout Nikita Khrushchev's Soviet Union. The law on religious associations of 1929, which restricted religious worship to registered cult buildings and prohibited religious groups from social outreach of any kind, was more stringently enforced again after a period of relaxed control during World War II and its immediate aftermath.[5] However, like many parts of northern and eastern Russia outside of urban centers, the remote, heavily wooded Morki district lacked the Protestant groups who were the primary targets of Khrushchev's campaign against sects. In this region of Mari villages interspersed with Tatar, Chuvash, and some Russian settlements, the editorial team's search for a local example of dangerous sectarianism came up with a target that no bureaucrat in Moscow would have anticipated: the indigenous Mari religion.

Under the heading "How I Broke with a Pagan Sect," a collective farm worker and war veteran tells of his involvement and disillusionment with Mari ritualism.[6] This journalistic reworking of Communist Party mandates to secularize Soviet society demonstrates the challenges of implementing antireligious policy in a religiously diverse state, where policies designed to combat particular religious communities could have unintended effects on others.

The news article carries some of the canonical features of Khrushchev's antisectarian campaign, yet there are also sharp departures from standard Soviet rhetoric. Although religious actors depicted in atheist propaganda since the 1920s and 1930s were often portrayed as members of old, pre-revolutionary elites,[7] the author of the article, V. Kirillov, grew up in a family of Soviet collective farm workers. His parents were religious believers, "but did not take part in religious pagan rituals, did not visit the sacred grove."[8] World War II tore the author from this relatively normative Soviet life: he was mobilized and injured at the front, and returned to his home village as an invalid unable to care for his ageing mother and six children. Adding to his suffering, two of his children died of an illness. Kirillov was "in despair," and in this state was approached by "people who followed the old pagan cult":

> They advised me to participate in a prayer ceremony, to offer a sacrifice to the pagan god in order to bring back the health that I lost during the war. After talking to me daily, they finally managed to win me over to their side [*sklonit' menia na svoiu storonu*].[9]

As in many official attempts to explain the persistence and spread of religious commitments in postwar Soviet society, war, injury, and suffering were posited as making this citizen vulnerable to religious convictions that had not been a part of his upbringing.[10] In the logic of atheist narratives, it was particularly scandalous that those religious groups that managed to thrive under socialism did so because they preyed upon people at such vulnerable moments by using Soviet tools of persuasion and peer influence to turn them away from the this-worldly goals of collectivized production. Through their daily efforts, members of the pagan "sect" were able to convince Kirillov to sacrifice a goose at a ceremony, which was then eagerly consumed by the "'sisters' and 'brothers' at the prayer meeting, [all of them] eager to have a good meal." Although Kirillov's health worsened as a result of his involvement with pagan believers, the "organizers" of the ceremony continued to visit him with "the sweetest of speeches" intended to "pull me again into their swamp." They finally made him "the treasurer of the sect, that is, the collector of money."[11]

The article uses the language of antisectarian campaigns to describe religious activity in Mari sacred groves when it highlights the group's efforts to attract "old people and women, who easily fell under the influence of our agitation," and the author's decision to "turn away" from the "deceptive path." When Khrushchev-era atheists discussed Protestant groups, such as Baptists and Pentecostals, they often noted the uncanny affinity of these "sects" with Soviet forms of organization. In 1959, a report on Baptists from the Kirov region focused on their misuse of the tune of the Soviet national anthem for the purpose of singing religious texts;[12] and a presenter at a conference on atheist propaganda in Moscow noted that "each sectarian is a propagandist by the book, [as] he is obliged to find and recruit [*vyiavliat' i verbovat'*] members for the community."[13] The sectarians of the Soviet atheist imagination were people who refused to frequent Soviet cinemas and libraries, but expanded their own support base through parallel offerings of entertainment, mutual aid funds, and ideological information through fliers and unsanctioned assemblies. The references to "recruitment" and "agitation" in the article evoke such organized efforts at keeping members active and engaged.

In Soviet parlance, the term "sect" was usually reserved for Christian groups of Protestant (Baptist, Adventist, Pentecostal, etc.) or Orthodox (Old Believer and other religious dissenters) derivation. In this respect, Soviet atheists borrowed from the prerevolutionary terminology in which only Russian Orthodox communities loyal to the Holy Synod were considered worthy of the designation "church."[14] In their quest to document their participation in the campaign against sects accused of violating Soviet laws and taking advantage of Soviet citizens, the editorial team of the district newspaper had to make indigenous ritualists conform to the image of proselytizing groups that insisted on individual commitment and strict discipline among their members. This represented quite a stretch from the ways in which religious adherence had long been understood in the Volga region, showing the mental leaps that local communist activists had to make in order to demonstrate the advance of secularization in their communities.

Kirillov's remark that his parents were "believers," but did not participate in rituals, points toward a form of religious community that differed from the groups that the antisectarian campaign was designed to eliminate, but was arguably more widespread in rural Russia. Instead of being considered a matter of individual conviction, religious adherence in the Volga region had long been associated with communal, ethnolinguistic identity. First the Muslim Tatar khans, and then, from the sixteenth century onward, the conquering Muscovites imposed tax regimes that differentiated between adherents of the dominant religious faith groups, be it Islam or Orthodoxy, and those of other religions. In the khanate, only Muslims could be part of the tax-collecting nobility. Under the tsars, Muslims and members of other tolerated minority religions were exempt from serving in the army, and converts to Christianity transferred from paying in-kind tribute to the monetary tax and labor obligations of Orthodox peasants.[15] For the Finno-Ugric speaking villagers who had long been caught in between the two states with written and institutionalized religions, conversion to Christianity or Islam contained an element of converting to "Russianness" or "Tatarness." Nineteenth-century Maris, for example, called Orthodox Christianity the "Russian faith" (Mari *rushla vera*), and villagers accused of apostasy from Orthodoxy during periodic revivals of Mari rituals defended themselves by arguing that God had created seventy-seven peoples, and wanted each to worship in its own way.[16]

This sense of parallel engagement with the divine within distinct, but comparable communities fit well within the Imperial government's approach to allocating rights and obligations based on "differentiated collectivity."[17] The Bolsheviks, however, came to the Volga region with the dual and sometimes conflicting aims of cultural emancipation and equality. In the 1920s, a number of Finno-Ugric and Turkic groups received a measure of political recognition with the creation of autonomous Soviet socialist republics (ASSRs) for the Maris, Mordvins, Udmurts, Bashkirs, Chuvash, and Tatars. In most of these, the titular nationality represented less than half the population, a percentage that decreased even further through the influx of ethnic Russians that came with industrialization and wartime relocations. Throughout the second half of the twentieth century, Maris made up about 43 percent of the population of the Mari ASSR, compared with Russians, at 47 percent, and Tatars, 6 percent.[18]

Despite shifting demographics and inconsistent political backing and funding, opportunities for schooling in the native language of the titular nationality existed in each republic throughout the Soviet period, as did native-language print and broadcast media. Ethnic culture was celebrated, but only within a common folkloric framework in which love and knowledge of one's own folktales, dances, and traditional foods did not stand in the way of working together with colleagues of other ethnicities and allowing one's children to find marriage partners of different ethnic origins.[19]

For Soviet culture builders, one of the obstacles to creating a harmonious society, in which ethnic boundaries would not stand in the way of the greater good of building communism, was the longstanding association of religious and ethnic loyalties in Russia's multiethnic regions. Early on, initiatives to integrate rural populations into secular Soviet culture through folkloric celebrations sought to eliminate markers that audiences and performers might consider to have religious connotations. For example, the costumes used by Mari dance troupes from the 1920s onward were decorated with new forms of large, floral embroidery, avoiding the cross-stitch designs of Mari peasant dress that had the magical function of protecting the hems from penetration by evil spirits.[20] More broadly, lists of Soviet ethnicities that had initially included groups distinguished only by their religious affiliation (such as the Tatar-speaking, but Christian Kräshen) were revised in the late 1930s to reflect linguistic and economic distinctions and disregard religious ones.[21]

Despite these early attempts to decouple religion and ethnicity, the association remained unchallenged in the 1959 article—the only religious option the Mari author considers for his parents, had they felt the urge to act on their "beliefs," was to visit the sacred grove, rather than a mosque or an Old Believer house of prayer. Within the logic of the article, the most effective critique of rural religiosity was to make it appear as something it was not—the outcome of efforts at persuasion and recruitment analogous to those of communist propaganda. Early Khrushchev-era policies treated religion as dangerous precisely because it offered a parallel universe to the kind of mobilized society that Stalin's successor was trying to create. The focus on groups of highly motivated believers did little to help provincial officials address the more embedded relationships between everyday rural life and adherence to traditional, nonproselytizing religions in many parts of the Soviet Union.[22] But the Mari example shows that the antisectarian campaign directed official attention to unsanctioned and fluid forms of religious practice, sometimes forcing atheist activists to address some of the blind spots of their approach to secularization.

## Looking for Sects among the Unconverted

At first glance, the label "sect" seems an odd choice for the sort of traditional, ethnically based religiosity that is represented by Mari sacrificial ceremonies. But from the point of view of local activists struggling to implement religious policy emanating from Moscow, "sect" may have represented a convenient label for groups that defied the instruments of registration and surveillance through which the Soviet government sought to control the ongoing religious practice in socialist society.

The creation of the Council for the Affairs of the Russian Orthodox Church and its twin Council for Religious Cult Affairs during the war against the Nazi invasion signaled the Stalinist government's recognition that religious institutions would remain present in Soviet life for the foreseeable future, and that properly managed relations with them could be a source of legitimacy.[23] Through a network of local commissioners, both councils sought to control religious life by offering religious communities legal registration in return for compliance with the restrictions of Soviet law: for example, a mosque, church, synagogue, or temple had to refrain from carrying out educational and charitable activities, and it had to keep detailed records of rituals conducted and of its income and expenses. Although still committed to the eventual annihilation of religion through atheist propaganda, the Soviet Union began to behave more like other modern states, whose bureaucratic interfaces with religious institutions distinguished between acceptable forms of religiosity and those deemed deviant.[24] As a general label for religious deviancy, "sect" could be made to refer to people gathered for open-air grove rituals as well as to underground evangelists.

From the point of view of officials in charge of monitoring religious groups through registration and bureaucratic auditing, any religious phenomenon that persisted without clear submission to denominational structures was particularly troubling, especially if it seemed capable of adapting to modern Soviet life. The deviance of "sects" thus lay in the way they resisted the retreat to liturgical piety divorced from social life that the Soviet model of secularization required of religious organizations. In the western republics such as Belorussia and Ukraine as well as in central and southern Russia, sectarianism was exemplified by non-Orthodox Christian denominations, which spread rapidly after the lifting of Imperial-era restrictions in the 1920s and then again during World War II. The war was also the time when Baptist and Seventh-Day Adventist communities first appeared in the Mari ASSR, possibly introduced by evacuees from cities farther west.[25]

But in the Volga region, Christian dissenters were just a small part of a larger phenomenon of unsanctioned religiosity that followed the evolving contours of Soviet life and yet evaded registration and state control. In the late 1940s and early 1950s, the ASSR's commissioner for Religious Cult Affairs, Aleksandr Nabatov, found that the largest religious community outside the Russian Orthodox Church consisted of Maris who participated in large sacrificial ceremonies in the spring and fall.[26] These ceremonies sometimes attracted participants from across the region, but the boundaries of the sponsoring communities increasingly coincided with those of collective farms, and farm chairmen were among the people asking for permission to conduct these rituals, which they found helpful for maintaining workers' morale. Nabatov's request for permission to register groups of adherents of the "Mari cult" was denied by the Council's board in Moscow, with the reasoning that to legalize these rituals would be to encourage a return to "backward" forms of religiosity among a population that should properly be considered Orthodox Christian.[27] For bureaucrats schooled in Marxist views of historical evolution, being Christian was one step closer to atheist modernity than being "pagan."

Regular services in Orthodox churches were easier for Soviet bureaucrats to monitor and report on than seasonal open-air rituals, but the dynamism of unregistered groups of various denominations proved difficult to ignore. Nabatov's successor, Viktor Savel'ev, who served in the 1960s and 1970s as commissioner of the then-united Council for Religious Affairs, found that unsanctioned religious practice was especially common in the settlements along the railroad line that linked the republic's capital, Ioshkar-Ola, to Kazan' and Moscow. These multiethnic settlements had been founded as Soviet towns without any houses of worship, depriving religion of a traditional, local institutional base. But far from becoming staunch atheists, citizens availed themselves of the services of unregistered clerics ranging from itinerant mullahs to self-described priests and nuns who claimed to represent the underground "True Orthodox Church" (Istinnaia Pravoslavnaia Tserkov') or various concords of Old Believers. Private apartments and sometimes cemeteries served as gathering places for Muslim, Orthodox Christian, and Protestant prayer.[28] The persistence of religious rituals in communities designed to be thoroughly secular confounded expectations of the natural disappearance of religion under socialism, but also challenged narratives about the conservative nature of religious convictions that purportedly made them incompatible with socialist progress. Tellingly, all of these forms of religious practice that evaded socialist legality were included in the commissioner's report under the heading of "sectarianism" (*sektantstvo*).

In addition to their uncanny capacity to evolve along with Soviet society, a common feature that united the diverse phenomena that Soviet authorities labeled "sects" was that membership in these groups was difficult to define because of what Nabatov called the "ad hoc character" (*iavochnyi poriadok*) of their gatherings.[29] In the absence of a registered "cult building" and a fixed list of members, it was unclear if someone present at a ritual site or known to have enlisted the services of an unlicensed cleric should be considered a "religious believer." This called to question the distinction between religion and ethnic folklore that was important to Soviet ideas of an ethnically diverse but secular society, and suggested that religiosity was not exclusively the domain of old people and social outcasts, but rather persisted in the mainstream of Soviet life.

The railroad settlements exemplify how Soviet law created its own religious deviancy, because inhabitants of towns without officially recognized houses of worship had no choice but to conduct collective rituals in an ad-hoc, unsanctioned fashion. For example, only one mosque officially reopened in the postwar Mari ASSR, compared with twenty-three that had been closed down in the 1920s and 1930s. The reopened mosque was in the Morki district, where Tatar villages were dispersed among those of other ethnicities, while most of the republic's Tatar population lived farther northeast.[30] Deprived of the opportunity to worship legally, Muslims gathered in private apartments for Friday prayers and celebrated holidays at village graveyards,[31] a choice of location that may have been prompted by an ambiguity in Soviet law that exempted graveyards from the prohibition on open-air rituals. A letter from the Commissioner of Religious Affairs in the Tatar ASSR asked his superiors in 1972 to clarify the status of graveyards as sites of religious ritual. Although he assumed that the law was intended to reserve the right to hold religious ceremonies at graveyards for officially registered religious communities, the commissioner claimed that local officials often interpreted it in a broader fashion and permitted unregistered groups to conduct a variety of ceremonies there.[32]

When the newspaper from the Morki district reported on participants in ancestral village rituals as constituting a "sect," it referred to a familiar understanding of "sect" as an unsanctioned religious community that gathered within the shadows of Soviet law, often with the tacit permission of local authorities. The label provided a script for how to eliminate the phenomenon described: identify the leaders responsible for drawing others into the organization and persuade rank-and-file members to denounce the leaders' evil intentions. However, a closer look at the Russian and Mari versions of the article shows that it was not easy to describe rural religiosity in the language of a campaign against organizations that were based on uniformity of belief among a selected, loyal membership. Even within the logic of the article, it becomes apparent that not all forms of religious deviancy were the same, nor would they respond to the same political measures.

The terminology in which the Russian version of the article describes Mari village rituals borrows from descriptions of Protestant groups and other so-called sects in atheist literature; the grove worshipers have a structured leadership that "organizes" ceremonies and monitors participants. But when it comes to describing the "sect's" activity in terms that local Mari speakers would recognize, the analogy becomes more tenuous. In the title of the Mari version of the article, the appellation "pagan sect" is rendered in a phrase derived from Russian—*iazycheskii sekt*—although presumably what is being described is a longstanding part of Mari village life. The text of the article also uses the word *sekt*, derived from Russian *sekta*, minus the feminine ending to reflect the lack of grammatical gender in Finno-Ugric languages. Where the Russian text speaks of "adherents of the old pagan cult,"[33] the Mari version more colloquially describes them as *otyshko lektyn kumalshe eng-vlak*—literally, "people who go out to the grove and pray."[34] In Mari, it was apparently more difficult to describe the group in terms that suggested an organization with a clearly defined membership and doctrine.

In the end, the editorial team resorted to elements of atheist critique that had little to do with sects, but seemed to better fit the topic at hand. One element is generic anticlerical rhetoric that might have been wielded against any form of religiosity: the donations of believers were used by the treasurer to buy alcohol, and all ritual gatherings "ended in a drinking spree."[35] Drunken clergy and duped believers were stock images of atheist mockery against such established religious groups as the Russian Orthodox Church, showing that in some way it was easier to portray Mari ritualists as analogous to village priests than evangelical missionaries.[36] Shifting perspective again, the article takes care to name the place where the "sect" holds its ceremonies, thereby evoking another Unionwide campaign that was more closely targeted to rural religiosity: the struggle against sacred sites, which did indeed touch on the practices of an almost unlimited number of groups across the Soviet Union.

## "May They Forget the Road to Kuryk Chongga"

The attempt to address traditional rural religiosity under the heading of the struggle against sects seems to have been unusual. At least from the

Mari ASSR, no evidence other than the news article from the Morki district points in this direction. Throughout the 1960s and 1970s, atheist writing on "sects" in the republic increasingly focused on Protestant groups that were internally split over how to act toward Soviet power, such as Baptists, Seventh-Day Adventists, and Pentecostals. The dissenting wings of these denominations kept commissioners of religious affairs across the Soviet Union busy by defying laws on registration and the participation of minors in worship.[37] Where Mari ritual practice was mentioned as an object of secularizing policy, it more commonly appeared as part of the campaign against sacred sites, which the 1959 article alludes to when it defines the purported sect in terms of its gathering place.

The narrator, Kirillov, is identified as the "former treasurer of the pagan sect at Shor"ial village's grove 'Kuryk Chongga.'" The grove's name (a Mari phrase meaning "hilly place") also appears in the article's final paragraph, where Kirillov appeals to readers with a lesson to be learned from his own past mistakes:

> There is no use in waiting for help from god, one has to work for oneself, fight for the real idea of building communism. I say with certainty: Not only will I not start to pray again, but I will also work to expose the dark works of the "*kart* elders" [Mari priests]. May all people who are stuck in ignorance and belief in god, and who cannot give up old survivals, forget the road to Kuryk Chongga.[38]

In spite of its efforts to portray religious practice in Shor"ial as sect-like, the article ultimately defines adherence to religious traditions as a function of visiting a particular place, so that ceasing to go there and acknowledge its sacred connotations becomes synonymous with abandoning religious traditions.

This was in line with the struggle against pilgrimages to "sacred sites," initiated in November 1958 by a Central Committee resolution as a new way of combating unsanctioned religiosity. Not unlike the campaign against sects, the campaign against popular pilgrimages, as described by Stella Rock in this volume, initially targeted aspects of Christian practice in central Russia and the western republics of the Soviet Union, such as mass visits to springs and other bodies of water associated with icons of the Virgin Mary or Saint Nicholas. Although carried out by Orthodox Christians and often accompanied by church services, these manifestations of popular religiosity had long been regarded with suspicion by the Church hierarchy: before the Revolution, local bishops and the Holy Synod strove to control the proliferation of sacred sites outside the confines of Church property and to safeguard the Church's monopoly on legitimizing or rejecting narratives of miraculous occurrences.[39]

Under Soviet power, and especially considering Khrushchev's renewed emphasis on enforcing legal restrictions on religious life, a priest's support for open-air observances could result in his replacement or even the closing of his church, jeopardizing the already precarious existence of the congregation.[40] Shortly after the Central Committee passed its resolution, the Council for Orthodox Church Affairs secured a statement from the Moscow Patriarchate condemning pilgrimages to "so-called sacred sites" as pagan customs and calling on all priests to take measures against them.[41] Again, the Soviet state and the Orthodox Church were using a common language to describe a deviant religiosity that they primarily imagined as internal to Christianity. But this time, the Church's support may have been somewhat more forced than in the struggle against sects, and the state soon realized that this particular struggle could be extended far beyond Christian populations.

Unlike the concept of sect, which forced atheist activists to find specific organizational structures that often did not exist in settings of rural religiosity, the struggle against sacred sites simply required local officials to compile lists of place names and monitor gatherings there.[42] For this reason, the campaign transferred easily to areas where Christianity was not the dominant religion, such as Muslim Central Asia, or to areas where Christianity was just one religious tradition among many, as was the case in the Volga region.[43]

In the Mari ASSR, mass pilgrimages to sacred springs had already attracted the attention of Commissioner Nabatov in the early 1950s, and he had written to the regional party committee with the suggestion to increase propaganda work in adjacent villages and collective farms. He also pointed out the troubling phenomenon of local officials trying to profit by claiming the offerings brought by pilgrims for their institutional coffers.[44]

In comparison with Orthodox pilgrimages in central Russia, gatherings at sacred sites in the Mari ASSR presented the additional problem that no religious institution could be held responsible for organizing or preventing them. The dates of the pilgrimages were often determined by saints' days from the calendar of the Orthodox Church, but unbaptized Maris attended alongside Orthodox Christians, Muslims, and Old Believers.[45] These gatherings without clergy, where order was maintained by self-appointed guardians of the site and by local collective farm and rural council authorities, are another example of how Soviet campaigns created religious deviance by restricting the contexts of permitted religious practice. In the effort to eradicate religion, restrictions on traditional religious institutions almost forced ritual practitioners into tight interdependence with the structures of Soviet society and thereby more firmly embedded these religious practices in everyday life.

In an ethnically diverse region, where the boundaries between religious communities were softened by shared assumptions about how to engage sacred powers, the idea that popular religiosity could be effectively combated by declaring particular places off limits, rather than by eliminating beliefs, worked to the advantage of atheist activists. The focus on monitoring and destroying religious sites allowed officials to sidestep the difficult question of who should be considered a member of a religious organization and if the practitioners actually subscribed to religious beliefs. Although some sites—such as Tatar graveyards or Mari sacred groves—were strictly associated with particular ethnic communities and their religious rites, others, such as sacred springs, drew visitors of all ethnicities and religious persuasions. Although the dates of pilgrimages were often determined by the calendar of the Russian Orthodox Church, they also resonated with the yearly cycle of agricultural work that was common to all communities. Outdoor religious observances intensified in the interval between summer haymaking and the harvest, and between the harvest and winter snow. All gatherings could be dealt with by a common spectrum of official responses—either tacitly ignore the ceremony if it did not fall on a day of urgent agricultural work, or send in the police to disperse the worshipers, tear out water spouts, and overturn kettles with sacrificial foods. There were also initiatives to cut down sacred groves, ostensibly to gain agricultural land or make room for road construction.

Independent of the precise nature of the site, local stories portray all these acts of destruction by state agents as sacrilegious and bringing about similar consequences. I heard many stories of calamities that befell policemen who kicked the spouts of sacred springs, forestry workers who cut down trees in sacred groves, and district officials who overturned gravestones: either they themselves became lame or blind, or lightning struck their house, or their loved ones were killed in accidents, all of which suggested that even agents of the atheist state were not immune to the power invested in the sacred site. The campaign against sacred sites presents an example of a successful match between the diffuseness of secularizing policy and the diffuse boundaries of rural religious practice, where following common rhythms and knowing where to find help in personal or communal crises was more important than assenting to the teachings of a particular religious institution. If nothing else, the struggle against manifestations of the sacred in the natural world hit the multitude of religious traditions in Russia at a point where they were all equally outside of the bounds of Soviet law.

## Grappling with Religious Diversity

The campaigns against sects and sacred sites represent two Khrushchev-era attempts to oppose those religious practices that took place outside the bounds of established institutions. But ultimately, Soviet secularization policies aimed not just at keeping religion within legal bounds, but sought to eliminate it and build an atheist society. In the postwar Soviet Union, the task of conducting atheist propaganda passed from the League of the Militant Godless, a creation of the 1920s that ceased to operate during World War II, to the Society for the Dissemination of Political and Scientific Knowledge, founded in 1947. The latter (renamed the Knowledge Society, Obshchestvo Znanie, in 1963) was an association of intellectuals with a broad mandate to popularize scientific discoveries. It treated atheism as a logical consequence of adopting a "scientific worldview" and abandoning supernatural explanations for human behavior and natural phenomena.[46] But the scholars and teachers active in the Knowledge Society were also among the first to realize that neither the promotion of science nor the renewed antireligious assaults of the late 1950s and early 1960s were enough to make religion disappear. Coercive restrictions alone did not immediately produce a secular society, and neither did broad access to basic scientific education.

Atheist scholars in the late Khrushchev and early Brezhnev years began to acknowledge the limited successes of previous secularizing policies, and increasingly focused their efforts on creating a positive social role for atheism. The Knowledge Society disseminated scenarios for new, secular rituals, and sociologists of religion theorized their impact on society.[47] In this process, many emphasized the need to account for the religious and ethnic diversity of Russia's regions and make atheism relevant to members of specific religious groups. As a speaker at a training seminar for teachers in the North Caucasus noted, telling a Muslim or Orthodox Christian audience that the pope worked for the U.S. Central Intelligence Agency was not likely to make anyone abandon their religious beliefs.[48] In the Mari republic, telling villagers with pagan sympathies that the Orthodox Church had been an agent of Russian Imperial expansion was equally ineffective.

Starting in the mid-1960s, expertise in specific religious traditions was among the desired qualities of Knowledge Society lecturers, and there were some efforts to offer training for such specialists in the Volga region. But it is doubtful how much effect these sessions had on the overall conduct of propaganda.[49] Most lecture topics continued to oppose a generic "religion" to values of Soviet modernity, focusing on "scientific prediction and religious prophecy" or "medicine and religion."[50] There was also a problem with finding people who were knowledgeable about local religions and languages and willing to stand up as atheists in front of their own communities. A report from the Udmurt ASSR, the Mari republic's neighbor to the north, noted that there was very little atheist propaganda among the republic's Muslim minority, because many Tatar lecturers offered to "conduct atheist work among believers of any denomination, only not among Muslims," fearing the "nonatheist public opinion" of their fellow Tatars.[51] The equation of religious affiliation with community membership, shared among all ethnic groups in the Volga region, remained a problem for Soviet atheists, especially in the context of a broader cultural policy that aimed to respect and foster ethnic cultures while integrating them in a heavily centralized state.[52]

One way in which atheist policy sought to show what a secular society might look like for people who followed particular ethnic traditions was through the organization of ethnic festivals to replace religious holidays. This idea went back to the indigenization policies of the 1920s, but it had fallen into disfavor during the Stalinist repression of "bourgeois nationalism," and was only revived in the 1960s.[53] Instituting these new festivals involved deciding whether to create a totally new holiday or "secularize" one that already existed. These choices were made based on the organizers' understanding of the present religious commitments of an ethnic group. In the 1920s, for Muslim Tatars festival planners secularized an existing plowing festival named Sabantui, eliminating the prayers for fertility, but retaining the spectacular elements of horse racing and wrestling, and encouraging the performance of Tatar song and dance. In the postwar era, Sabantui continued to be celebrated by collective farms at the end of spring plowing, and official recognition was reaffirmed during a new Unionwide campaign for secular holidays in the years 1963–66. The rationale for supporting Sabantui was that it was a pre-Islamic custom expressing the Tatar folk spirit, and that its Soviet version returned the festival to its original state before Islamic clerics appropriated it and imposed their own restrictions by condemning dance and music during the celebrations.[54]

The Maris had an analogous spring plowing festival known as Agavairem, a meatless sacrifice in special birch groves close to a village's fields.[55] But in designing a Mari festival, Soviet planners ignored Agavairem, instead inventing the completely new (Ioshkar) Peledysh Pairem, the Festival of (Red) Flowers, which was first instituted in 1921 and was revived in 1965. The artificially created festival was revived, although Commissioner Nabatov had suggested secularizing "Aga Pairem" as a Mari national festival in 1951.[56] One reason why Agavairem was not treated on a par with Sabantui may have been the split this would have caused between villages where Orthodox Christianity was more entrenched and villages that celebrated Mari rituals. But the different treatment of Sabantui and Agavairem also suggests that the Soviet government's oft-noted willingness to promote "paganism" as a set of positive folk values only extended to settings where such traditions could safely be ascribed to a folkloric past that had been superseded by the advent of monotheism.[57] Mari ritual seemed too alive to be integrated into secular life as folk culture; it was combated because it constituted a real attempt to invoke powerful spirits.

Political decisions about promoting or condemning certain folk customs thus grew out of a diagnosis of the steps a group of rural dwellers needed to take in order to become full participants in Soviet modernity. Among Muslims and Christians, reviving memories of a premonotheistic past could be a way to stimulate the kind of optimistic commitment to the material world that clerical religion supposedly suppressed. Among groups where faith in spirits and deities was still a part of everyday life, the path to secularity involved attempts to disenchant the material world. In this effort, even monotheism could be treated as a helpful intermediate stage—recall the Council for Religious Cult Affair's conclusion that it was better to consider Maris Russian Orthodox than to legalize grove rituals.

Such contradictory policies show that Soviet atheists never quite came to terms with the difficult nexus between religion and communal identities. But it was in grappling with this connection that activists came closest to explaining what a secular society had to offer to an ethnically diverse population.

## Local Religious Landscapes and New Atheist Critiques

When the report on the Udmurt ASSR notes that the popular equation between religion and ethnicity made atheist propaganda among coethnics seem like a betrayal of one's own nationality, it alludes to a narrative about the harm of religion that increasingly gained ground among postwar atheists in the Volga region: religion was both a product of exclusionary social boundaries and a factor in their perpetuation. A secular society, on the other hand, would be free of distinctions of gender, age, or place of residence. Present in rudimentary form in the reports of early postwar officials, this view of religion and secularity was elaborated by Brezhnev-era sociologists, and its unintended consequences continue into the post-Soviet era.

When promoting atheism, activists had to explain how exactly religious practice impeded the construction of socialism. A popular materialist argument was that it detracted labor power and economic resources from the state economy. This critique had long been leveled against many forms of indigenous ritual in Russia and Siberia, and it was present in the campaign against sacred sites, where pilgrimages and communal rituals were often represented as mere excuses for drunkenness and wanton wasting of time.[58] But the more thoughtful observers of local religious life also realized the shortcomings of this explanation. As Commissioner Nabatov noted early on, collective farm chairmen themselves often found religious rituals helpful for motivating their workers to fulfill state demands. In later decades, the emphasis on communist legality under Khrushchev and Brezhnev implied the recognition that some religious believers could very well be exemplary workers and loyal citizens. Nabatov's successor Savel'ev, for example, received and investigated complaints from religious believers about employment discrimination, reflecting at least an official expectation that state officials should oppose general equations between religious belief and bad work habits.[59] If the economic harmfulness of religion was hard to demonstrate, a more powerful critique in this multiethnic region asserted that religious commitments sustained old boundaries, hierarchies, and enmities.

Commissioner Nabatov already noted that religion could serve as a boundary marker both within and between ethnic groups when he reported on Muslim life in the Paran'ga district, an area of relatively compact Tatar settlement in the Mari ASSR. In 1949, he found that the district party leadership opposed the idea of reopening one of the mosques that had been closed before the war, reasoning that the existence of a legally operating mosque in one village would result in a flood of petitions from other villages. Local Tatars, the district chairman explained, would never go to pray in another village, but only in their own village mosque.[60] In addition to intensifying small-scale communal loyalties, Islam served as a marker of ethnic distinction in relation to non-Muslims, as shown by an incident that occurred in 1951 in the school of the district center:

> One pupil, son of a party worker, was not circumcised. His peers found out about this and started to taunt him: "*Urus* [Russian]! Uncircumcised!" . . . The boy complained about this to his mother. The mother, in the absence of the father, had the student circumcised by Akhmatulin. The boy spent a week in bed and then returned to school. [There], the child could not bear the persistent taunts and exposed his penis by taking off his pants during recess.[61]

The incident, which came to Nabatov's attention during an investigation of said Akhmatulin for conducting illegal circumcisions "without observing the elementary rules of hygiene," was interpreted by him as evidence of "national enmity between Tatars and Russians." The passage drew the attention of his Moscow superiors, who marked it with a red pencil.[62] Nabatov's account shows some of the gendered assumptions about religious practice that are well-documented elsewhere in the Soviet Union: the mother takes the child to be circumcised, holding the father blameless, who could have faced severe consequences as a party official.[63] It also shows how atheist critiques of religion helped mitigate the contradictions of the Soviet government's carefully managed recognition and celebration of ethnic identities. As opposed to "good" ethnicity that expressed itself in folkloric customs within a union of essentially similar cultures, religiously infused ethnicity could result in children's taunts and disruptions of public decency and, by implication, provoke more serious quarrels among adults.

This capacity for religion to attach itself to other distinctions and give them a dangerous edge became the focus of attention for Brezhnev-era sociologists who sought to explain the tenacious survival of religion under socialism. In the late 1960s, Viktor Pivovarov of the Institute of Scientific Atheism in Moscow's Academy of Social Sciences began to conduct large-scale surveys on atheism and religious belief in several regions and autonomous republics of the RSFSR, as well as in the Tadzhik and Moldovan Union Republics. One of Pivovarov's students, Viktor Solov'ev, returned to his native Mari ASSR in 1971 and organized a survey there. Like his mentor, Solov'ev had the full support of local political and cultural infrastructures: respondents were chosen by random sampling and interviewed by activists from district party cells, and the Knowledge Society helped vet the questionnaire and popularize the results among its members.[64] But Pivovarov's and Solov'ev's publications also challenged widespread assumptions about religion as either naturally dying out or surviving only thanks to the gullibility of simple-minded believers. Instead, they proposed a more complex analysis of the causes and consequences of religious persistence under socialism, one that was directly tied to the religiously and ethnically diverse nature of many of the regions where the surveys were carried out.

In Solov'ev's 1972 study, questions about religious belief, confession, and participation in ritual came at the end of a long list of more than 300 items. In interpreting the results of this survey and a follow-up study conducted in 1985, the sociologist looked for statistical correlations between professed religious belief, ethnic adherence, and attitudes toward interethnic relations. He also paid attention to indicators of participation in modern Soviet life that had no immediate ethnic connotations, such as trade union membership, volunteer work, and visits to cinemas and libraries.[65] The results allowed him to argue for the "positive role of atheism" in creating good Soviet citizens. In the 1985 study, 10.5 percent of religious believers disapproved of interethnic marriage, compared with 3.2 percent of atheists, and Mari and Tatar atheists were more likely to speak Russian at home than believers of the same nationalities.[66] In 1972, religious believers were found to be less likely to put the interests of society before their personal interests and to participate in community service (*obshchestvennaia rabota*).[67] Even after controlling for differences in age and urban or rural residence, the follow-up study still indicated that religious believers read fewer books per month and watched fewer films, two crucial signs of connection to a wider Soviet public sphere with its specific ideals of cultured personhood.[68]

While thus criticizing religion for holding people back from full engagement in Soviet social life, Solov'ev avoided demonizing either religious believers in general or believers of specific ethnic backgrounds. Both versions of the study showed some of the highest percentages of religious believers among Tatar residents of the Mari ASSR, who also had greater reservations against interethnic marriage and friendships than had Maris or Russians.[69] Solov'ev pointed out that compared with the neighboring Tatar ASSR, Tatars in the Mari ASSR had both a higher percentage of actual intermarriage with other ethnicities *and* were more likely to be critical of such unions. He concluded that it was their position as members of an ethnic minority that made them "more cautious."[70] Atheist propaganda in the Volga region, Solov'ev argued, had to take into account the history of competition among paganism, Christianity, and Islam, a confrontation that "created distrust of people of other faiths, sowed enmity between adherents of different religions and representatives of different nations, [and] distracted the workers from the struggle against their exploiters."[71]

Because religion bore the traces of the region's colonial history, it was among the "survivals of the past" that strengthened the authority of old people over young and men over women, in addition to reinforcing ethnic enmity.[72] The solution suggested by Solov'ev and Knowledge Society activists who cited his study was to improve the provision of social and cultural services to rural residents, housewives, and pensioners, in order to break the vicious circle of isolation from Soviet modernity and allegiance to outdated authorities.[73]

Whereas the veracity of Solov'ev's statistics may be open to debate, he and his fellow sociologists proposed a critique of religion that was explicitly grounded in the multireligious nature of many regions of the Soviet Union. Religion as the embodiment and reinforcement of everything old (although most threatening when it took on new forms, as the anxiety about "sects" has shown) was especially problematic in regions where the "old" involved many longstanding enmities between neighbors who were divided by faith, language, and customs.[74] Solov'ev, himself an ethnic Mari raised in the northeast of the republic, where Maris, Tatars, and ethnic Russian Old Believers lived in close proximity, writes with understanding about the fact that members of minority groups may not have "complete certainty that people of other nationalities will not see in their habits elements of unculturedness, backwardness, and ignorance . . . will not offend the religious sensibilities of believers or suspect unbelievers of religiosity."[75] In an ethnically diverse republic, the argument goes, actually existing religious sensibilities create potential zones of interethnic misunderstandings and offense, while reputations for religiosity become part of ethnic stereotypes and reinforce boundaries. Atheism, by contrast, connects citizens more tightly to a Unionwide public sphere in which the ideal of solidarity counteracts the narrow pursuit of personal, regional, and ethnic interests.

## Conclusion: Atheism and Religion in a Diverse Region

To atheists in the Mari ASSR, religion embodied the uncanny power of the old to survive and reappear in new guises. It took the shape of sects that conducted their own "propaganda" to mirror Communist Party tactics, of sacred sites whose ritual communities adapted their scope to the changing sizes of collective farms, and of age-old ethnic divisions that erupted in Soviet schools. Marxist-Leninist theory with its affirmation of progress and denial of everything "backward" is one reason why Soviet attempts to manage religious expression went beyond privatization, which many other modern states demanded. Instead, a more antagonistic process of "domestication" occurred, where the intimate spaces of home and face-to-face relations into which religion withdrew were themselves targeted for transformation.[76] Multiethnic regions in particular were treated as areas where the intricate divisions between small-scale communities diminished people's capacity to relate to one another as fellow citizens. Religion could not be tolerated even in intimate spaces, because it helped to restrict intimacy to coethnics and fellow believers. But even as atheist scholars elaborated their critique of religion as a bulwark of social boundaries, other shifts were occurring in Soviet attitudes toward past social relations. These shifts helped pave the way for a new public role for religion in post-Soviet Russia.

During the final decades of Soviet rule, images of "the old" changed from something powerful that needed to be overcome to something quaint and vanishing that needed to be preserved. The change is palpable in literary and political trends of the Brezhnev era, but also in Solov'ev's changing descriptions of rural life in the Volga region.[77] In 1977, the sociologist still denounces the tendency of old people to assert their authority over the young—by upholding religious rules, for instance—as an obstacle to socialist development that often began as "well-meant advice" but could end with "open violence."[78] In the publication of the follow-up study ten years later, he writes more nostalgically about old ethics and old knowledge, and more critically about members of the younger generations. Citing the "question of generational continuity" that had been raised by writers such as Chingis Aitmatov and Dmitrii Likhachev, he notes that in older villages, people had cared in common for wells, bridges, and dams. By contrast, residents of the new consolidated settlements that were created in the 1970s had lost this sense of communal responsibility: "Today, when the bridge has collapsed, people at best take their demand to the rural council, if they don't write to Moscow."[79] As local pride and ethnic consciousness appeared to be disintegrating too rapidly and problems of alcoholism and rural flight attracted attention, religion—predefined as an upholder of old boundaries—began to look more like a possible ally for politicians and cultural professionals attempting to build and preserve cohesive communities.

In light of this ongoing reevaluation of older traditions, it seems less surprising that religion was relatively seamlessly reintegrated into public life in the Volga region after the collapse of Soviet socialism—at least those religious traditions with links to established ethnic communities. As elsewhere in the former Soviet Union, celebrations of ethnic culture in the Mari republic inevitably included religious dignitaries by the mid-1990s. The official equation of Mari paganism, Russian Orthodoxy, and Islam with the three main ethnic groups of the republic was enshrined in the representation of these three denominations on the republican advisory council for religious affairs. The council excluded newer Protestant groups, but also those with a much longer history in the republic, such as Old Believers.[80] When I interviewed Solov'ev in 2005, the sociologist remained a committed atheist, but considered the tendency to underestimate the link between religious traditions and ethnic loyalties to have been the core mistake of atheist propaganda. And the last Commissioner of Religious Affairs, who had served in the republic from 1984 to 1990, cited Lenin's dictum that there is within every society "an amalgamation of the old, the present-day, and the future." He noted that the present state of Russian society was shaped by the speed with which nationalism and religion had reunited after the end of Soviet secularizing policies.

The commissioner's post-Soviet equivalent, an adviser on religious affairs within the republic's presidential administration, took the unity of religion and ethnicity for granted and considered it the government's job to make sure that every ethnic group had access to its proper forms of worship, thereby maintaining equality and civic peace.[81] In her view, religion still had divisive potential if one denomination was left unsatisfied or if aggressive proselytizing of the sort practiced by evangelical groups was allowed. However, if effectively managed, a shared pride in religious tolerance could help counteract efforts by any one ethnic group to gain dominance.

Quite in line with Lenin's insight about the ways in which forces from the past, present, and future can influence a society simultaneously, reviving and preserving old religious traditions after socialism often meant reshaping them in an image much closer to the expectations of one-time secularizing opponents. At the beginning of the twenty-first century, there was a movement under way to codify and standardize folk religious practice, such as coming up with curricula presenting the core teachings and values of Mari ritual.[82] As elsewhere in the world, educated Muslims eager to adopt correct Islamic practice were critical of the traditional practices in Tatar villages, which they saw as tainted by Christian and pagan influences. Orthodox clergy and lay activists interested in reconnecting to Byzantine spirituality leveled analogous critiques against the well-intentioned but ill-informed "faith of the grandmothers."[83] The fuzzy dogmatic boundaries that had made it difficult for Soviet officials to either register rural worshipers as religious organizations or combat them as sects were now becoming a problem for religious activists themselves. And some of the Protestant groups that continued to be reviled as foreign "sects" once again demonstrated their adaptability by appealing to old roots, translating Biblical and liturgical texts into Mari and sponsoring concerts of Finno-Ugric spiritual song. In claiming local legitimacy for their faith, they tacitly subscribed to the paradigm that religiosity should reflect and overlap with ethnicity.

The pervasive equation between religious and ethnic boundaries belies the continuing fluidity and diversity of religious practice and nonpractice in the republic, and thus attests both to the failure and the success of Soviet attempts to discipline religion. Efforts to exclude religion from the markers of communal identity failed because the meanings and functions of religion in local life eluded attempts to conceptualize them adequately, let alone eliminate them. But after seven decades of Soviet rule, the secular ethnic identities within a larger national whole that Soviet planners sought to promote are as firmly a part of life in the Volga region as the religious boundaries they were meant to replace. What is more, post-Soviet religious practitioners of all denominations are more self-reflective about their actions than previous generations because they suddenly gained access to formal religious knowledge after having had little exposure to it as children. Government officials and other observers can now be more confident in identifying discrete religious communities with claims to dogmatic unity and distinct practices. Herein lies a paradoxical triumph of Soviet atheism even as it recedes into the past.

## Notes

1. The regions for which this was true included the Crimean Peninsula and the North Caucasus, among others. See Boris Kolymagin, *Krymskaia ekumena: Religioznaia zhizn' poslevoennogo Kryma* (Saint Petersburg: Aleteiia, 2004); and Sergei A. Shtyrkov, "Prakticheskoe religiovedenie vremen Nikity Khrushcheva: respublikanskaia gazeta v bor'be s 'religioznymi perezhitkami' (na primere Severo-Osetinskoi ASSR)," in *Traditsii narodov Kavkaza v meniaiushchemsia mire: Preemstvennost' i razryvy v sotsiokul'turnykh praktikakh*, edited by Iu. Karpov (Saint Petersburg: Peterburgskoe Vostokovedenie, 2010), 306–43.

2. Robert Geraci, *Window on the East: National and Imperial Identities in Late Tsarist Russia* (Ithaca, N.Y.: Cornell University Press, 2001).

3. On linguistic borrowings, see Rifkat Akhmet'ianov, *Obshchaia leksika dukhovnoi kul'tury narodov srednego Povolzh'ia* (Moscow: Nauka, 1981). On shared religious sites and regional sensibilities for engaging the sacred, see Allen Frank, "The Veneration of Muslim Saints among the Maris of Russia," *Eurasian Studies Yearbook*

70 (1988): 79–84; and Sonja Luehrmann, "A Dual Quarrel of Images on the Middle Volga: Icon Veneration in the Face of Protestant and Pagan Critique," in *Eastern Christians in Anthropological Perspective*, edited by Chris Hann and Hermann Goltz (Berkeley: University of California Press, 2010), 56–78.

4. This emphasis on parallel, mutually intelligible practices rather than religious mixing resonates with the findings of anthropologists in other multireligious regions, such as the Balkans and North India. See Glenn Bowman, "Orthodox–Muslim Interactions at 'Mixed Shrines' in Macedonia," in *Eastern Christians in Anthropological Perspective*, ed. Hann and Goltz, 195–219; Peter van der Veer, "Playing or Praying: A Sufi Saint's Day in Surat," *Journal of Asian Studies* 51, no. 3 (1992): 545–65.

5. Tatiana A. Chumachenko, *Church and State in Soviet Russia: Russian Orthodoxy from World War II to the Khrushchev Years*, edited and translated by Edward Roslof (Armonk, N.Y.: M. E. Sharpe, 2002), 161; Kolymagin, *Krymskaia ekumena*, 133–35.

6. V. Kirillov, "Kak ia porval s iazycheskoi sektoi," *Za kommunizm*, October 27, 1959; also published in Mari as "Kuze myi iazycheskii sekt dech iörshyn korangynam," *Kommunizm verch*, October 27, 1959.

7. Daniel Peris, *Storming the Heavens: The Soviet League of the Militant Godless* (Ithaca, N.Y.: Cornell University Press, 1998); William Husband, *"Godless Communists": Atheism and Society in Soviet Russia, 1917–1932* (DeKalb: Northern Illinois University Press, 2000).

8. Kirillov, "Kak ia porval," 4.

9. Ibid.

10. On common antireligious narratives of the time, see David Powell, *Antireligious Propaganda in the Soviet Union: A Study of Mass Persuasion* (Cambridge, Mass.: MIT Press, 1975); and Bernd Groth, S.J., *Sowjetischer Atheismus und Theologie im Gespräch* (Frankfurt: Josef Knecht, 1986).

11. Kirillov, "Kak ia porval," 4.

12. Nikolai Iarygin, *Evangel'skoe dvizhenie v Volgo-Viatskom regione* (Moscow: Akademicheskii proekt, 2004), 154. The text of a Baptist hymn to the tune of the national anthem is also recorded in Council of Religious Cult Affairs Chairman Puzin's speech to a Unionwide gatherings of commissioners, April 18, 1961, Gosudarstvennyi arkhiv Rossiiskoi Federatsii (State Archive of the Russian Federation; hereafter GARF), f. R-6991, op. 3, d. 1360, l. 23v.

13. Stenographic transcript of a theoretical conference of the atheist section of the All-Russia Society for the Dissemination of Political and Scientific Knowledge, May 29–30, 1959, GARF, f. A-561, op. 1, d. 282, l. 27. On similar discomfort with perceived similarities between "sectarian" and Soviet structures in the 1920s, see Heather Coleman, *Russian Baptists and Spiritual Revolution, 1905–1929* (Bloomington: Indiana University Press, 2005).

14. On the continuities and breaks in Imperial Russian and Soviet thinking about "sects," see Laura Engelstein, *Castration and the Heavenly Kingdom: A Russian Folktale* (Ithaca, N.Y.: Cornell University Press, 1999); chapter 1, by Gregory L. Freeze, in the present volume; Catherine Wanner, *Communities of the Converted: Ukrainians and Global Evangelism* (Ithaca, N.Y.: Cornell University Press, 2007), chap. 1.

15. Andreas Kappeler, *Rußlands erste Nationalitäten: Das Zarenreich und die Völker der Mittleren Volga vom 16, bis 19, Jahrhundert* (Vienna: Böhlau, 1982).

16. Nikandr Popov, "Na Mariiskom iazycheskom molenii," *Etnograficheskoe obozrenie* 3 (1996): 130–45; Paul Werth, *At the Margins of Orthodoxy: Mission, Governance,*

and *Confessional Politics in Russia's Volga-Kama Region, 1827–1905* (Ithaca, N.Y.: Cornell University Press, 2002), 30.

17. Jane Burbank, "An Imperial Rights Regime: Law and Citizenship in the Russian Empire," *Kritika*, n.s., 7, no. 3 (2006): 397–431, at 406. On the skill with which the Russian Imperial government used religious difference as a tool for governance, see also Nicholas Breyfogle, *Heretics and Colonizers: Forging Russia's Empire in the South Caucasus* (Ithaca, N.Y.: Cornell University Press, 2005).

18. Seppo Lalukka, *Vostochno-Finskie narody Rossii: Analiz etnodemograficheskikh protsessov* (Saint Petersburg: Evropeiskii dom, 1997), 122.

19. Terry Martin, *The Affirmative Action Empire: Nations and Nationalism in the Soviet Union, 1923–1939* (Ithaca, N.Y.: Cornell University Press, 2001), 183; Yuri Slezkine, "The USSR as a Communal Apartment, or How a Socialist State Promoted Ethnic Particularism," *Slavic Review* 53, no. 2 (1994): 414–52. Survey questions about attitudes to ethnically mixed work collectives and interethnic marriage were among the staples of late Soviet empirical sociology and ethnography. For an influential work, see Iulian Bromlei, *Etnos i etnografiia* (Moscow: Nauka, 1973).

20. Tamara Molotova, *Mariiskii narodnyi kostium* (Ioshkar-Ola: Mariiskoe knizhnoe izdatel'stvo, 1992).

21. Francine Hirsch, *Empire of Nations: Ethnographic Knowledge and the Making of the Soviet Union* (Ithaca, N.Y.: Cornell University Press, 2005), 304; Paul Werth, "From 'Pagan' Muslims to 'Baptized' Communists: Religious Conversion and Ethnic Particularity in Russia's Eastern Provinces," *Comparative Studies in Society and History* 42, no. 3 (2000): 497–523.

22. On the aims and ironies of Khrushchev-era atheist campaigns in rural regions, see Shtyrkov, "Prakticheskoe religiovedenie"; and Andrew B. Stone, "Overcoming Peasant Backwardness: The Khrushchev Anti-Religious Campaign and the Rural Soviet Union," *Russian Review* 67, no. 2 (2008): 296–320.

23. Chumachenko, *Church and State in Soviet Russia*; Mikhail V. Shkarovskii, *Russkaia pravoslavnaia tserkov' i sovetskoe gosudarstvo v 1943–1964 gg.: Ot peremiriia k novoi voine* (Saint Petersburg: DEAN-ADIA-M, 1995).

24. Compare, for instance, the ways in which French state policies on secular schooling and, more recently, head scarves in schools have caused Catholic and Islamic communities to debate and redefine issues of religious orthodoxy and deviancy. See Jean Baubérot, *Laïcité 1905–2005: Entre passion et raison* (Paris: Seuil, 2004); and John R. Bowen, *Why the French Don't Like Headscarves: Islam, the State, and Public Space* (Princeton, N.J.: Princeton University Press, 2007).

25. Quarterly report of Commissioner for Religious Cult Affairs Nabatov from the Mari ASSR, January 22, 1946, GARF, f. R-6991, op. 3, d. 569, l. 2; Report from Commissioner Savel'ev to the First Secretary of the Ioshkar-Ola City Committee, April 9, 1968, GARF, f. R-6991, op. 6, d. 156, l. 29.

26. For an English-language study of Soviet-era Mari ritualism (based on interviews with an émigré from the Bashkir ASSR), see Thomas A. Sebeok and Frances J. Ingemann, *Studies in Cheremis: The Supernatural* (New York: Wenner-Gren Foundation, 1956). For a study based on Soviet published sources, see Allen Frank, "Mari-Language Sources on Mari Religious Practices in the Soviet Period," *Eurasian Studies Yearbook* 66 (1994): 77–87.

27. Letter from Council Chairman Polianskii to Nabatov, July 31, 1947, GARF, f. R-6991, op. 3, d. 569, l. 64.

28. Report from Commissioner Savel'ev on a visit to Zvenigovo district, August 8, 1967, GARF, f. R-6991, op. 6, d. 80, ll. 224–28; Savel'ev's report on a conversation with Pentecostal leaders in Krasnogorsk, December 13, 1977, Gosudarstvennyi arkhiv Respubliki Marii El (State Archive of the Mari El Republic; (hereafter GARME), f. R-836, op. 2, d. 21, l.18.

29. Draft circular from Nabatov to the district executive committees of the Mari ASSR, January 1950, GARF, f. R-6991, op. 3, d. 570, l. 78.

30. Nabatov's quarterly report for the fourth quarter of 1950, GARF, f. R-6991, op. 3, d. 570, l. 134.

31. Report from the Mari ASSR submitted as part of the Unionwide census of religious communities, January 1, 1962, GARF, f. R-6991, op. 4, d. 308.

32. Letter from Commissioner Mikhalev to Council Chairman Kuroedov, October 10, 1972, GARF, f. R-6991, op. 6, d. 470, ll. 236–38.

33. Kirillov, "Kak ia porval," 4.

34. Kirillov, "Kuze myi iazycheskii sekt dech," 4. On the difficulty of translating the terminology of Soviet campaigns into the languages of minority nationalities, see Caroline Humphrey, "Janus-Faced Signs: The Political Language of a Soviet Minority before Glasnost," in *Social Anthropology and the Politics of Language*, edited by Ralph Grillo (London: Routledge, 1989), 145–75.

35. Kirillov, "Kak ia porval," 4.

36. On Soviet attitudes toward alcohol use during rural festivals, see Malte Rolf, *Das sowjetische Massenfest* (Hamburg: Hamburger Edition, 2006), 243–46.

37. In 1974, e.g., Commissioner Savel'ev reports on the number of "factually existing religious congregations" in the republic that he has persuaded to register since 1968. Among those in the process of registering was a congregation of the Council of Churches of the Evangelical Christians-Baptists, a group that had resisted registration since its founding in 1961. Report from Savel'ev to Council Chairman Kuroedov, October 21, 1974, GARF, f. R-6991, op. 6, d. 634, l. 99. See also Olena Panych, this volume.

38. Kirillov, "Kuze myi iazycheskii sekt dech," 4.

39. Vera Shevzov, *Russian Orthodoxy on the Eve of Revolution* (Oxford: Oxford University Press, 2004), 196.

40. Shtyrkov, "Prakticheskoe religiovedenie," 324–26.

41. Chumachenko, *Church and State in Soviet Russia*, 155.

42. Such a list is included, for instance, in the 1962 census of religious organizations in the Mari ASSR, cited in n. 24.

43. Report on compliance with the CC resolution "On Measures to End Pilgrimages to So-Called Sacred Sites" in the republics of Central Asia and Kazakhstan, March 28, 1963, GARF, f. R-6991, op. 3, d. 1423, ll. 33–44.

44. "On Sacred Sites," Memorandum from Nabatov to the Mari Regional Committee, July 4, 1952, GARF, f. R-6991, op. 3, d. 571, ll. 30–32.

45. Nabatov's report for the second quarter of 1952, July 4, 1952, GARF, f. R-6991, op. 3, d. 571, ll. 18–19, and for the third quarter, October 7, 1952, ibid., l. 41.

46. Peris, *Storming the Heavens*, 222; Powell, *Antireligious Propaganda*, 48–51.

47. Viktoriia Smolkin, "Sviato mesto pusto ne byvaet: Ateisticheskoe vospitanie v Sovetskom Soiuze, 1964–1968," *Neprikosnovennyi zapas* 65 (2009): 36–52.

48. Z. S. Akhmerov, "Problemy nauchno-ateisticheskogo vospitaniia v natsional'noi shkole," in *Tezisy dokladov na nauchno-pedagogicheskoi konferentsii po*

*voprosam kommunisticheskogo vospitaniia v natsional'noi shkole* (Maikop: Nauchno-issledovatel'skii institut natsional'nykh shkol APN RSFSR, 1965), 22–24.

49. A list of model lecturers for 1965 from the papers of the atheist section of the Mari division of the Knowledge Society lists them as specialists in Orthodoxy, Paganism, or Islam. GARME, f. R-737, op. 2, d. 161, l. 24v. In 1969, a seminar on the critique of Islam was held in Kazan' for lecturers from the Tatar ASSR and neighboring regions: Commissioner I. Mikhalev to Council for Religious Affairs Chairman Kuroedov, June 17, 1969, GARF, f. R-6991, op. 6, d. 220, ll. 354–55v.

50. List of recommended lecture topics, Mari Division of the Knowledge Society, 1961, GARME, f. R-737, op. 2, d. 98, l. 166. This list does include two locally specific topics: "the origin and essence of paganism" and "contemporary religious organizations and their activities in the Mari ASSR."

51. Draft resolution of the Council for Religious Affairs, "On Shortcomings in the Control over Implementing Legislation on Religious Cults in the Udmurt ASSR," December 1969, GARF, f. R-6991, op. 6, d. 293, l. 89a. On the precarious position of activists conducting pro-Soviet propaganda in their own communities in early Soviet Central Asia, see Marianne Kamp, *The New Woman in Uzbekistan: Islam, Modernity, and Unveiling under Communism* (Seattle: University of Washington Press, 2006).

52. Slezkine, "The USSR as a Communal Apartment."

53. Ksenofont Sanukov, *Iz istorii Marii El: Tragediia 30x godov* (Ioshkar-Ola: Mariiskii gosudarstvennyi universitet, 2000), 36. On indigenization, see Martin, *Affirmative Action Empire*, chaps. 3 and 4.

54. "Sotsialisticheskoe pereustroistvo byta i bor'ba za novye traditsii" (All-Union Knowledge Society, 1963, mimeographed lecture text on file in the Russian State Library, Moscow), 22–23.

55. "Agavairem (Prazdnik pashni)," in *Kalendarnye prazdniki i obriady mariitsev*, edited by Ol'ga Kalinina (Ioshkar-Ola: Mariiskii nauchno-issledovatel'skii institut iazyka, literatury i istorii im. V. M. Vasil'eva, 2003), 43–77.

56. Sonja Luehrmann, *Secularism Soviet Style: Teaching Atheism and Religion in a Volga Republic* (Bloomington: Indiana University Press, 2011), 47.

57. Eve Levin, "*Dvoeverie* and Popular Religion," in *Seeking God: The Recovery of Religious Identity in Orthodox Russia, Ukraine, and Georgia*, edited by S. K. Batalden (DeKalb: Northern Illinois University Press, 1993), 31–52; Natalya Sadomskaya, "Soviet Anthropology and Contemporary Rituals," *Cahiers du monde russe et soviétique* 31, nos. 2–3 (1990): 245–54.

58. Yuri Slezkine, *Arctic Mirrors: Russia and the Small Peoples of the North* (Ithaca, N.Y.: Cornell University Press, 1994), 227.

59. Report from Savel'ev to the Council for Religious Affairs, January 16, 1980, and related documents, GARME, f. R-836, op. 2, d. 21, ll. 24–25, 28. In this case, Savel'ev investigated a complaint from a member of an unregistered Pentecostal church in the railroad settlement of Krasnogorsk that he was fired from his job as a watchman because he was a religious believer. Although Savel'ev initially arranged for the believer to be hired again, he was transferred to an outlying sawmill three months later, ostensibly because his position had been eliminated as a budgetary measure. It may well be that both agencies tacitly agreed that this was the best way to prevent religious proselytizing in the town while satisfying the requirements of communist legality. See also Wanner, *Communities of the Converted*, 86.

60. Report from Nabatov for the second quarter of 1949, July 16, 1949, GARF, f. R-6991, op. 3, d. 570, ll. 26–27.

61. Report from Nabatov on the third quarter of 1951, October 11, 1951, ibid, l. 162.

62. Ibid.

63. Douglas Northrop, *Veiled Empire: Gender and Power in Stalinist Central Asia* (Ithaca, N.Y.: Cornell University Press, 2004), 176; Irina Paert, "Demystifying the Heavens: Women, Religion, and Khrushchev's Anti-Religious Campaign, 1954–64," in *Women in the Khrushchev Era*, edited by Melanie Ilič, Susan E. Reid, and Lynne Attwood (Basingstoke: Palgrave Macmillan, 2004), 203–21.

64. Viktor Grigor'evich Pivovarov, *Byt, kul'tura, natsional'nye traditsii i verovaniia naseleniia Checheno-ingushskoi ASSR: Osnovnye zadachi, instrumentarii, protsedury i nauchno-organizatsionnyi plan konkretno-sotsiologicheskogo issledovaniia* (Groznyi: Checheno-ingushskoe knizhnoe izdatel'stvo, 1971); Smolkin, "Sviato mesto pusto ne byvaet"; Minutes of the meeting of the bureau of the Mari regional party committee, May 10, 1972, GARME, f. P-1, op. 37, d. 29, l. 6.

65. Viktor Stepanovich Solov'ev, *Sotsiologicheskie issledovaniia—v praktiku ideologicheskoi raboty: Nekotorye itogi izucheniia problem byta, kul'tury, traditsii i verovanii naseleniia Mariiskoi ASSR* (Ioshkar-Ola: Mariiskoe knizhnoe izdatel'stvo, 1977); Solov'ev, *Po puti dukhovnogo progressa: Nekotorye itogi povtornogo sotsiologicheskogo issledovaniia problem byta, kul'tury, natsional'nykh traditsii, ateizma i verovanii naseleniia Mariiskoi ASSR* (Ioshkar-Ola: Mariiskoe knizhnoe izdatel'stvo, 1987).

66. Solov'ev, *Po puti dukhovnogo progressa*, 144.

67. Solov'ev, *Sotsiologicheskie issledovaniia*, 100.

68. Solov'ev, *Po puti dukhovnogo progressa*, 116.

69. Solov'ev, *Sotsiologicheskie issledovaniia*, 93; Solov'ev, *Po puti dukhovnogo progressa*, 91.

70. Solov'ev, *Sotsiologicheskie issledovaniia*, 73–74.

71. Ibid., 95.

72. Ibid., 99.

73. Nikolai Sofronov, *Ateisticheskoe vospitanie kolkhoznogo krest'ianstva* (Ioshkar-Ola: Mariiskoe knizhnoe izdatel'stvo, 1973).

74. Bruce Grant, *The Captive and the Gift: Cultural Histories of Sovereignty in Russia and the Caucasus* (Ithaca, N.Y.: Cornell University Press, 2009).

75. Solov'ev, *Po puti dukhovnogo progressa*, 91.

76. Tamara Dragadze, "The Domestication of Religion under Soviet Communism," in *Socialism: Ideals, Ideologies, and Local Practice*, edited by C. M. Hann (London: Routledge, 1993), 148–56.

77. John and Carol Garrard, *Russian Orthodoxy Resurgent: Faith and Power in the New Russia* (Princeton, N.J.: Princeton University Press, 2008), 93–97; Nikolai Mitrokhin, "Ethno Nationalist Mythology in the Soviet Party-State Apparatus," *The Harriman Review* 15, no. 1 (2004): 20–29.

78. Solov'ev, *Sotsiologicheskie issledovaniia*, 99.

79. Solov'ev, *Po puti dukhovnogo progressa*, 46.

80. Sonja Luehrmann, "Recycling Cultural Construction: Desecularisation in Postsoviet Mari El," *Religion, State and Society* 33, no. 1 (2005): 35–56. For comparative views of tendencies to equate religion and ethnicity in other regions, see Marjorie Mandelstam Balzer, "Whose Steeple Is Higher? Religious Competition in Siberia," ibid.,

57–69; and Matthijs Pelkmans, *Defending the Border: Identity, Religion, and Modernity in the Republic of Georgia* (Ithaca, N.Y.: Cornell University Press, 2006).

81. Both interviews were conducted in June and July 2003.

82. Luehrmann, *Secularism Soviet Style*, chapter 4. See also Ludek Broz, "Conversion to Religion? Negotiating Continuity and Discontinuity in Contemporary Altai," in *Conversions after Socialism: Disruptions, Modernisms, and Technologies of Faith in the Former Soviet Union*, edited by Matthijs Pelkmans (New York: Berghahn, 2009), 17–38.

83. For an analysis of neo-orthodox Islam in the postsocialist world, see Kristen Ghodsee, *Muslim Lives in Eastern Europe: Gender, Ethnicity, and the Transformation of Islam in Postsocialist Bulgaria* (Princeton, N.J.: Princeton University Press, 2010). On Orthodox Christianity and the "faith of the grandmothers," see Luehrmann, "Dual Quarrel," 69.

## Chapter 10

## The Revival before the Revival: Popular and Institutionalized Religion in Ukraine on the Eve of the Collapse of Communism

*Viktor Yelensky*

When present-day observers and historians refer to the phenomenon of "religious revival" in Ukraine and Russia, they usually mean the outburst of religion in the former Soviet Union after the collapse of communism. However, twentieth-century Ukraine witnessed a steady growth of interest in religion, which has not yet been comprehensively explored by scholars. The ongoing enthusiasm for religion challenged the very foundation of official ideology and was perceived by the authorities as a real threat that needed to be eliminated. Yet, by the 1970s and 1980s the failure of antireligious policies became obvious even to party officials charged with realizing these goals. They could no longer ignore the rise of popular religiosity and religious seeking among Soviet intellectuals and professionals. Spiritual and mystical-religious aspirations engaged broad circles of intellectuals by the 1970s and found expression in poetry and the arts.[1] Despite the endless stream of reports on the consistent decline of popular religiosity, religion in everyday life became ever more present in the late Soviet period. Moreover, in spite of substantial resources invested in fighting "illegal sectarian activity," the so-called religious underground persisted and became even more active. Using archival data, interviews with clergy Communist Party officials, and Soviet propagandists, as well as a variety of published sources, in this chapter I explore the peculiarities of the turn to religion in the 1970s and 1980s against the background of the regime's continuing efforts to eliminate religion.

## Soviet Antireligious Policy: The Last Round

Several themes have dominated the scholarship on religious revivals in twentieth-century Ukraine. Nikolai Berdyaev, one of the most energetic proponents of the religious renaissance in the early twentieth century, argued that "this was nevertheless a movement [among the cultural elite], estranged not only from the processes occurring among the masses of the people, but also from the processes occurring in the wider circles of the intelligentsia."[2] Some scholars have analyzed the conversion of Marxists to Eastern Orthodoxy, which is described by Nikolai Zernov in his book, *The Russian Religious Renaissance of the Twentieth Century*.[3] Converted Marxists were figures of great importance and tremendous intellectual power, but they comprised a tiny group within the prerevolutionary intelligentsia.

A second theme of key importance, and in sharp counterdistinction to Berdyaev's emphasis on the intelligentsia, was the renewal of popular religious life in Ukrainian territories occupied by the Nazis in the 1941–44 period.[4] The renaissance in the occupied areas was a purely spontaneous embrace of religion without intellectual and theological foundations, but often with considerable political implications, as reflected in chapter 3 in this volume, by John-Paul Himka. Religious affiliation in Ukraine often reinforced national allegiance and in some instances became an expression of anti-Soviet views. Wartime religious upheaval was also propelled by the horrors of war and the need for spiritual retreat in the midst of everyday threats and tragedies. However, both of these processes, the wartime popular resurgence of religion and the embrace of religiosity among the intelligentsia, generally occurred with the benevolent neutrality of the authorities and sometimes even with their official support.

In contrast, the religious revival of the 1970s and 1980s occurred against the backdrop of a weakening, but still active, campaign to eliminate religion. Religious policies somewhat changed again after Nikita Khrushchev's dismissal in 1964. Party officials reconsidered the most odious elements of the former first secretary's approach to religion, which focused on the attainment of comprehensive control over religious institutions, the eradication of clandestine religious activity, the elimination of the "religious underground," and the creation of a mammoth scientific-atheistic education system.

Despite the fact that the religious situation was becoming increasingly explosive and effectively undermining the reputation of the USSR on the international scene, during the Brezhnev period the government did not make any radical changes. Brezhnev's policies were based on the ideal of a police state superpower with strong military arsenals, a developed economy, a relatively high standard of living, nonexistent official opposition, and the "moral-political" unity of the nation. The regime's religious policies were driven by two factors: the political elite's desire to maintain stability by undercutting the roots of instability and the need to create a relative balance between the needs of the ideological apparatus and foreign policy imperatives.

The ideological apparatus aimed at overcoming religiosity by taking actions to limit the number of religious communities and the number of faithful, and by devaluing the significance of religious ceremonies. The party's ideological cadres used Lenin's dogma of an uncompromising attitude of all communists toward "religious prejudice" as well as a widespread propaganda network to achieve these goals. Certain aspects of the ideological doctrine became sacred, resulting in their unconditional implementation even when they ran contrary to the state's interests and sometimes even to common sense.

At the same time, the Ministry of Foreign Affairs, some KGB services, and journalists stationed abroad were assigned the task of creating a beneficial environment for reaching Soviet foreign policy goals. Hence, they were interested in somewhat liberalizing religious regulations, softening restrictions on religious activity, and limiting atheist education to its less militant forms. Given ongoing worldwide human rights campaigns and the growing attention of Western governments (as well as Western societies in general) to the problem of religious freedom in the USSR, these Communist Party officials were aware that discrimination against the faithful would have international repercussions. In addition, the restrictions on church activities were fueling religious opposition and contributing to the cooperation of religious activists with political dissident movements, all of which were utterly undesirable to the KGB.

The legal basis for restricting the activity of religious organizations in Soviet Ukraine was defined by the "Regulations Concerning Religious

Organizations in the Ukrainian SSR."[5] Although these regulations were written in 1976, in large part they reproduced the Stalinist legislation of 1929. In 1929, the government revoked the right of registered religions to spread "religious propaganda" and outlawed any external activity of religious organizations, thereby containing religious communities within then-existing church walls.

In contrast, the state had unrestricted freedom to spread atheist propaganda. In addition, a large number of special decrees and regulations led to even more severe restrictions of religious activity than was prescribed by the 1929 basic law. Thus, the violation of the minimal set of rights granted to believers was a common occurrence.

The eighteen years of Brezhnev's tenure represented a crisis in orientation for religious policy. Officials in the central party and government apparatus were becoming increasingly aware that total suppression of religious activity was impossible. Yet they were not in a position to articulate an alternative policy that was compatible with Leninist-Stalinist postulates propagated over the course of decades. Among certain younger party functionaries (the ideological predecessors of the Communist Party of the Russian Federation), projects circulated incorporating the Russian Orthodox Church into the ideological apparatus of the party, which in turn was supposed to fundamentally blend the Russian Orthodox Church with Russian nationalism and reduce the Church's flirtation with the national republics and its use of internationalist rhetoric. The church-state model they proposed ultimately gave birth to right-wing, anti-Semitic nationalists such as Chivilikhin, Belov,[6] and Prokhanov,[7] and to Vasilyev's "Pamyat."[8] While aware of the demise of the traditional Soviet ideological integrators, the old party cadre at all levels were unprepared to pursue such radical changes in church-state policies.[9]

The ideological departments and sections within party central and regional committees still possessed a solid organizational infrastructure and considerable financing. Suffice it to say that in the early 1980s about 1 million lectures to promote atheism and "dethrone religious myths" were given in the USSR every year, in comparison with 760,000 in 1966.[10] However, when Mikhail Gorbachev launched the policy of glasnost, those responsible for atheist propaganda, when questioned by the Institute for Scientific Atheism attached to the Academy of Social Sciences, acknowledged that the "effectiveness of atheist propaganda was low or even of no significance."[11] The almost sacred attitude of stalwart communists, led by the chief party ideologist Mikhail Suslov, toward certain aspects of Lenin's doctrine produced antireligious fervor even when such zeal expressly contradicted common sense and even national interests.[12] Disagreements over the limits of religious liberties, which may have existed between pragmatically disposed foreign service officials, including the KGB's externally oriented departments and the propaganda departments and local party organizations, were usually solved in favor of the group that advocated an uncompromising limitation on all religious activity that could in any way contribute to national and religious distinctiveness. In the end, the farther from Moscow and the closer to the provinces, the more intense the atheist propaganda became.

## "For the Same Misdeed in Moscow Nails Are Trimmed, While in Kyiv the Hand Is Cut": Ukrainian Versions of Soviet Antireligious Policy

Historically, the religious and national policies of Ukrainian Communists were under particularly strict surveillance by the Kremlin. The geopolitical significance of Ukraine, its resources, and a suspiciousness among Moscow officials of Ukrainian "separatism" and "bourgeois nationalism," led to rapid and sharp responses by Lenin and later Stalin upon the slightest demonstration of autonomy by Ukrainian leaders.[13] Accordingly, Moscow sent "leading figures" to Ukraine who were able to unconditionally implement policies prescribed by the Kremlin. A notorious "political tradition" emerged from an ongoing, uncompromising struggle against national and religious aspirations, cultural novelties, and freethinking intelligentsia that became quite harsh, especially when compared with how similar dynamics played out in Moscow. In Ukraine there were prohibitions against even mentioning the Christian roots of Ukrainian culture, and efforts were made to eliminate all visible traces of religion in the public sphere, which sometimes assumed ridiculous proportions. For instance, in the late 1970s a Ukrainian opera prima donna, Evgeniya Myroshnichenko, was prohibited from appearing on television for several months as a punishment for wearing a cross during a concert performance.

Volodymyr Shcherbytsky, who headed the Communist Party of Ukraine from 1972 until 1989, took uncompromising stands on religious issues. Archival documents and reminiscences of party officials from that period disprove the memoirs of Shcherbytsky's associate, Valeryi Vrublevskyi, who claimed that Shcherbytsky was very tolerant toward religion and did his best to protect and respect the religious sentiments of Ukrainians from the attacks of "Moscovite boyars." In actual fact, the party's first secretary in Ukraine showed his obvious displeasure with the disproportionately high number of religious communities in Ukraine and expressed his unyielding determination to change this state of affairs. Indeed, on the eve of Gorbachev's reforms in Ukraine, there were over 6,000 officially functioning religious communities in Ukraine, or one-third of the total number of religious organizations in the USSR. This number included 4,000 Orthodox parishes, which constituted 65 percent of the religious communities in Ukraine; more than 1,100 communities of Evangelical Christians–Baptists; about 100 communities of Roman Catholics; and 80 communities of the Church of Reformation, which served Transcarpathian Hungarians and others.[14] However, the number of official church institutions in no way reflected the real religious needs of the Ukrainian population and yet the authorities refused to permit an increase in the number of church institutions.

Vladimir Kuroedov, head of the Council for Religious Affairs (CRA) attached to the USSR Council of Ministers, recalled:

> I have heard (although I cannot present documented evidence for this) that the extremely fierce attitude [toward religion and churches] came personally from V. Shcherbytsky. He believed that there were too many churches in Ukraine, and that there was a need to "put an end to this shame." They liked to close churches in Ukraine. It often happened that they [Ukrainians] brought packs of proposals to close churches in Ukraine to a session of the Council for Religious Affairs [only the Moscow Council was authorized to make the final decision to close or to open a church]. I did come across [Valentyn] Malanchuk and [Yuryi] Yelchenko, secretaries of the Central Committee of the Communist Party of Ukraine on ideology in the 1970s. Yelchenko seemed to be a sincere, interesting man, but his line on the church was very tough. He even wanted to close Florovsky and Pokrovsky monasteries in Kyiv. Monasteries, he said, disgrace us.[15]

The policy toward religious communities of national minorities (e.g., Jews, Poles, and Hungarians) was based on three goals: separating national and religious components, preventing the consolidation of ethnic groups on religious grounds, and neutralizing the influence of foreign religious centers. Such a policy had an obvious antinationalist connotation because, for instance, neither Jewish nor Polish minorities had secular national or cultural institutions and they expressed their ethnic identities through religious institutions. Shcherbytsky's regime in Ukraine did not leave any space for the public expression of unofficial views, not to mention opposition opinions. It was impossible to form clubs of intellectuals, institutionalize any type of non-Marxist social or cultural movement, to establish a media enterprise that did not glorify the regime, or to create nongovernmental organizations, like Solidarity or the Lutheran Church, which played significant roles in "the mobilization of conscience" in Poland and East Germany, respectively. It was also impossible to express national communism, which took quite eloquent forms in the Trans-Caucasian Soviet republics.[16] In spite of routine appeals from Moscow to eliminate "the remnants of bourgeois nationalism" and to suppress anticommunist sentiments, the leaders of Soviet Armenia and Georgia strengthened their respective nationalisms by granting the Armenian Apostolic Church and the Georgian Orthodox Church a prominent role in the forging of national identities on the republic level. Until the late 1970s, foreign observers spoke of "the second baptism of Georgia."[17]

All these indulgences were absolutely not feasible in Ukraine. A phenomenon such as the Russian Pochvennichestvo (Return to the Soil) with its pathos of resistance to the denationalization of the Russian people was not allowed. Such pathos against supporting one's own nation and Ukrainian historical, cultural, and spiritual heritage meant that Ukrainian intellectuals were not only confined to a prescribed ideological framework, but crossing the limits of the permissible was particularly dangerous, as dissident intellectuals and writers, such as Yevgen Sverstyuk, Ivan Dzyuba, and others learned in the 1960s.

## "A Country of Mass Atheism": Calculations, Miscalculations, and Distortions

During the period of stagnation under Brezhnev, religion was firmly considered by the thinking public as an alternative value system that could uncompromisingly stand up to official ideology and slogans, the untenability of which became more and more obvious. Noting the increase of adult baptism, the intelligentsia's fascination with religious literature, the growing popularity of religious broadcasting by foreign radio stations, and the outspoken disregard for atheist propaganda and other materials, party officials expressed anxiety over the anticommunist trends in the country that these developments represented. Communist ideologists increasingly realized that the USSR could no longer pretend to call itself "a country of mass atheism." Beginning in the mid-1970s, party officials more or less openly confessed that religious activists become more and more aggressive in spreading their beliefs and views. At the same time, to obscure the growing interest in religion, new euphemisms were coined and introduced into semiofficial discourse. In an interview with the author in 1993, the head of the Religious Affairs Section attached to the Odessa region's state administration said:

> Attending the advanced training program in Moscow in 1979 for the first time ever, I learned about the "rising religious brazenness" of the Soviet people, which meant the rise in attendance at churches and the growth in the number of baptisms and funerals conducted by priests. The [Communist Party of the Soviet Union] Central Committee's officials emphasized that religion had come into fashion among youth and "rotten" intelligentsia. They warned that the servants of religious cults were trying to take advantage of the policy of détente to crucially strengthen their positions. However, they said, the party and Soviet cadres would not "spread panic" and therefore could not admit to all these facts publicly.[18]

Echoing these views, the former first deputy head of the CRA in Kyiv said in 1993,

> Having been instructed by the Central Committee of the Communist Party of Ukraine before my assignment to Kyiv's Council for Religious Affairs, I was forewarned of the changing religious landscape in comparison with the early 1960s. Religion, I had been told, had ceased to be the exclusive domain of old women.[19]

Moreover, many party officials realized that the achievements of the communist administration's efforts to substitute some secular ersatz-religion for religiosity was much more flawed than was officially declared. In closed meetings, communist leaders admitted the fact of a religious resurgence and sometimes expressed cautious doubts about the existing system of atheist education and the party's attitude toward religion, churches, and believers. The commissioner for the Donetsk region to the CRA attached to the Ukraine Republic Council of Ministers even said, "In frank talks with some of my colleagues, we reasoned that sixty years of struggling against religion devoured enormous resources [and] embittered millions of our compatriots but finally led to nothing."[20]

Unfortunately, no reliable data are available to characterize the religious identities of the Ukrainian population in the 1970s and 1980s. Several factors render the sociological research from that period problematic, such as lack of unbiased data accumulated by Soviet sociologists of religion; peculiarities of the Marxist-Leninist view of religion, which is sometimes extensively described in the empirical material; the self-imposed isolation of Soviet society; the inclination of many believers in the USSR, particularly highly educated persons who held respected positions, to practice covertly, which presumably would mean that religious practice was more extensive than reported, and especially among this group; subordination of research on religion to the aim of overcoming religion, which meant that sociologists had to manipulate empirical data to prove that Soviet society was one of "victorious atheism"; and the outspoken ideologically motivated "understatements" in the interpretation of data that documented a persistence in religious belief and practice among Ukrainians.[21]

Moreover, to list the number of religious institutions and even to speculate in print about the approximate number of believers in the country was strictly prohibited. It was highly problematic to try to argue about the actual level of religiosity with the Glavlit (General Directorate for the Protection of State Secrets in the Press, the main nonmilitary censorship establishment). Censors ruthlessly deleted the numbers and any other evidence of the persistence of religion, not to mention indicators of a religious revival. Data from some surveys conducted in various regions of the USSR, such as North Caucasia, Central Asia, and Western Ukraine, for example, were not only left unpublished, but no attempts were made to interpret them because they so heavily contradicted the official discourse.[22] Even in 1986, the relatively "innocent" statement that "religions and churches have existed for thousands of years and will exist for a long time in the future, having significant impact on social consciousness and the political life of different states and nations"[23] became a subject of furious criticism from ideological "purists" after it was published.[24]

Significantly, scholars not only avoided estimating the level of religiosity throughout the USSR, but also failed to report on the principal results of their research when they conflicted with ideological mandates. For instance, a survey and detailed study of the sociodemographic structure of a "religious" population was conducted in Belorussia in 1967 in which 10,000 people were surveyed in five or six regions of the republic. However, thanks to the censors, there are no reports pertaining to the percentage of believers or their activities in this population in a single file of 10,000 cases. The findings of other studies that were conducted in the regions of Sumy, Ternopil', Ivano-Frankivsk, Zakarpatia, Chernihiv, and elsewhere in Ukraine suffered a similar fate.[25] Based on this evidence, one might assume that the research findings were dissonant with the prevailing ideology and challenged the assertion that the USSR was a country of "mass atheism."

Analyzing the fragments of empirical data that were collected and reported in sociological research of religion in the USSR from the middle 1960s to the early 1980s, William Fletcher comes to the conclusion that 45 percent of the population of the USSR were believers and that, although Soviet sociologists claimed religion was a phenomenon of the past and since the Revolution it had been weakening and dying out, a lot of evidence contradicted these claims.[26] Nevertheless, as Fletcher points out, his index of religiosity is only an "average" for the entire Soviet Union. For regions where Russians predominate, this average is high; but for areas where Islam is widespread, as well as for Lithuania and Western Ukraine, it is low.[27]

Fletcher's assertions are somewhat abstract and imprecise mainly because of the limited empirical data that were available at the time. Nonetheless, Fletcher's conclusions are much more realistic than official declarations asserting that the vast majority of Soviet people were neither influenced by nor members of any religious group.[28]

The report of the CRA under the Council of Ministers of the USSR stressed that in 1984 in Ukraine, 178,000 persons were baptized. Also in 1984, in the Ukrainian regions of Ivano-Frankivsk, L'viv, Sumy, and Ternopil', a church funeral service was performed, respectively, for more than 69.6, 65.7, 64.8, and 62.9 percent of those who died.[29] Another report noted that in the Khmelnits'k region approximately 20 percent of adults participated in church services on the most important holy days.[30]

Secret reports submitted by party officials reveal that in 1985, the first year of Gorbachev's reforms, 26 percent of newborns in Ukraine were baptized. Nearly 3 percent of marriages were consecrated in a church, and more than 40 percent of the dead were buried with the assistance of a church. Notably, the figures on baptism and funerals performed by the Catholic Church in the Netherlands that same year did not essentially differ from the figures in Ukraine.[31] After studying the available data of the percentage of baptisms performed in the Russian Orthodox Church during the 1960s, Christel Lane concluded that the rate of baptism was not much lower than infant baptisms in the Church of England: "Viewed against the background of strong pressure against the baptism from the official side and of the practical obstacles of obtaining one in churchless areas these figures are impressive."[32] Undoubtedly, the Ukrainian figures are underestimated. They do not include baptisms and funerals conducted by underground or unregistered religious institutions or those conducted by clergy in private. These practices were common, especially in the big cities.

The Soviet literature consistently insisted that the absolute majority of Soviet youth did not have religious beliefs and were not practicing believers. But even the accessible empirical data allow us to cast doubt on such assertions. For example, a survey conducted in the Smolensk region in 1970 showed that about 10 percent of survey participants openly expressed their religious convictions.[33] Among 3,123 young respondents polled by Ukrainian sociologists in the Donetsk, Cherkassy, Transcarpathia, and Poltava regions in 1981, only 8 percent appeared to be nonbelievers.[34]

The Russian intellectual Sergei Averintsev told a very revealing anecdote. In the 1970s, his wife was stopped in the street by an elderly woman and was asked to name the exact beginning date of Lent. "You are young," she explained, "you should know."[35] In the 1970s and 1980s, Western observers almost unanimously proclaimed a significant rise in interest in religion among Soviet youth, particularly in the large cities. Relatively consistent observations in "public" urban churches, which were open to foreigners, have convinced experts that official statements alleging that only 3 percent of Soviet youth were religious were open to criticism.[36] A young theologian from Paris who had been told that the churches in the USSR were attended exclusively by grandmothers, visited the country and observed that approximately one-third of these "grandmothers" were younger than twenty-five years of age.[37]

A survey of Soviet youth involvement in religious practices conducted by H. L. Biddulph in 1976 showed that one-third of the parishioners of three Orthodox churches in Kyiv, Moscow, and Tbilisi were under thirty years of age.[38] At Easter in 1970, half the worshippers in the patriarchal cathedral in Moscow were said to have been under thirty. Gerhard Simon, referring to a letter by the Orthodox dissident Anatolyi Levitin-Krasnov (1915–91) to Pope Paul VI, wrote about a small group experiencing religious revival and increasing interest among young intellectuals in religious questions.[39] In sum, not only was a religious renaissance sparked in the 1970s in Ukraine, but it was largely among urban, educated youth—both phenomena were in direct contradiction to the intended outcome of antireligious propaganda of the period.

## Popular Religiosity in the 1970s and 1980s in Ukraine

Reports by commissioners of the CRA, memos of party functionaries, and testimonies of clergy and laypeople testify to the fact that popular religiosity in those times not only persisted but expressed itself in an increasingly active and visible manner. The leitmotif of a tremendous corpus of secret memoranda written by high-level Communist Party officials responsible for atheist education was that ordinary people were indifferent to atheism, inclined to religion, and that local party committees were not very enthusiastic about atheist education. Auditors from the party's Central Committee in Ukraine also complained that local Soviet administrations were not zealous enough in controlling the activity of religious communities and, especially, the activities of clandestine sects, for which they relied exclusively on the KGB. According to a Ukrainian businessman who served as a party official in the 1980s:

> The most outspoken Soviet administrators responsible for the observance of legislation on religious cults frankly told me that religion was just one among dozens of their duties. They couldn't exercise effective supervision over industry, transport, municipal economy, and so on along with keeping religious communities under surveillance. Naturally, their performance was evaluated in terms of achievements in industrial and agricultural production. Religion for them was a secondary issue, not to mention that a great number of Soviet administrators and "captains of industry" did not have atheist convictions. Many friends of mine from these strata quietly invited priests to baptize their children and secretly brought soil from their grandparents' graves to churches.[40]

In an interview with the author, a Ukrainian diplomat added:

> I was absolutely sure that in Galicia and Volyn' in the 1970s and 1980s—as well as before and after this period—that the rate of baptism among newborn children approached 100 percent. Party officials were not excluded. Even if they did not respect the Church's rituals, their parents and relatives did.[41]

According to an archpriest of the Ukrainian Orthodox Church–Moscow Patriarchate in Kyiv:

> In the early 1980s, our church was filled with a lot of people not well-informed about Orthodoxy. Most of them studied at universities but some were middle-aged men and women absolutely deprived of a religious tradition. They wished to be baptized and to join my parish. Some of these new converts held prestigious positions and avoided publicity—everyone realized that in Kyiv the KGB had informers in every parish. Very often I performed sacraments at home. After 1988, it seemed like the dam burst: I baptized up to thirty adults every day.[42]

In the face of this religious activity, the chief ideological organs demanded "a real decrease in the number of the faithful and in the overall volume of religious rituals." The local authorities responded by regularly doctoring the numbers. Occasionally, the central Communist Party authorities in Moscow and Kyiv were fed clearly falsified reports, validated neither by their authors nor by their superiors. For instance, the party leadership in Ternopil' region in 1975 officially pegged the number of baptized newborns at 36 percent. In the same year, the leaders of Donetsk oblast, with a much smaller number of churches and much less religious activity, reported that 34.8 percent of all newborns were baptized. The Ternopil' region was under much closer surveillance than were religious communities in Donetsk. Western Ukraine was pressured by party officials from Moscow and Kyiv to radically get rid of "the relapse into Ukrainian bourgeois nationalism," and the vestiges of religious rituals, for which there was documented evidence. Therefore, as late as 1980 the oblast reported a much lower number of baptisms, 21.2 percent of the overall number of newborns, than the Donetsk oblast, which was under less pressure from above and therefore could afford to come up with a less "satisfactory" number, which in 1980 was 21.7 percent.

By 1985 the official numbers of recorded baptisms had completely parted ways with reality. For example, it was asserted that only 12.2 percent of newborns were baptized in the Ternopil' region, whereas the proportion in the Donetsk region was 15.2 percent. As an inspector of the Council of Religious Affairs in Ukraine said, "Without a doubt, the number of so-called main religious rituals (baptisms, weddings, and funerals) was substantially underreported. In some regions, officials sent to Kyiv statistics that were two to three times lower than the figures they knew to exist. Additionally, no one counted the number of rituals conducted in underground churches and in churches located in resort areas where people from churchless Siberia, the Urals, and the Far East brought children to be baptized during the vacation season."[43]

Mikhail Koltun, a bishop in the Ukrainian Greek Catholic Church, which was outlawed in 1946 and functioned underground until 1989, recalled: "How many children I have baptized secretly! I baptized the kids of party members, police, and other officials. They strived for spirituality too."[44]

The desire of the local party committees and authorities to embellish the level of atheist achievement and "to color the truth" to be in line with expectations of the ideological apparatus were not the only reasons to substantially doctor the statistics of religiosity. They also sought to hide the widespread practice of unofficially performing religious rites, that is, activities that were not registered by any church. Yet, even under such circumstances and despite the pressure to reduce numbers of religious participants on an annual basis, the official number of those who attended Easter services at Orthodox churches in Ukraine in 1978 totaled around 1.2 million people.[45]

It is worth recalling that Khrushchev's antireligious campaign met serious obstacles in Western and, to a lesser extent, in Right Bank Ukraine.[46] According to the directive from Moscow during this campaign, Ukrainian authorities had to close half of all Orthodox Church buildings. In fact, during the late 1950s and early 1960s they almost achieved this task: In Crimea, 70 percent of all churches were closed; in the eastern region of Zaporizhzhia, 91 percent were closed; in Transcarpathia, because of the resistance of local authorities, they managed to close "only" 17 percent; and in Ternopil', 36 percent were closed.[47] Sometimes, buildings were closed only on paper. During the 1970s and 1980s, in many instances the Orthodox faithful demanded permission to recommence religious services in buildings that were closed during Khrushchev's rule. Hundreds of such appeals were sent to the CRA in Kyiv and Moscow, the Central Committee of the Communist Party of the Soviet Union, and the Supreme Councils of the USSR and Soviet Ukraine. In 1985, a total of 173 Ukrainian settlements filed such petitions. However, none of the petitions were granted. In response, in dozens of Ukrainian towns and villages, the faithful revived religious life in officially deregistered communities and opened closed church buildings without the permission of the authorities. For example, there was a case in the village of Broshniv in the Rozhnyativsky district of the Ivano-Frankivsk region when, in 1977, after the authorities refused to register the Orthodox congregation and closed it down, the faithful ripped off the padlock, repaired it, and recommenced collective prayers without a priest. According to the secretary of the local district executive committee, "Sometimes it came to open clashes. People gathered by ringing bells. Peasants wouldn't go to work for a few days because of the conflict. People said that they might kill anyone who tried to prevent the opening of a local church. I personally was threatened for this reason."[48]

After the Ukrainian Council for Religions refused to register the church in Rostock in the Ternopil' region, the faithful took over the church building. According to an inspector of the CRA, believers provided twenty-four-hour protection to the church from the local authorities. When the inspection was conducted, they quickly informed one another and announced that they were ready to protect the church in any way necessary. The Orthodox community in Volyn' kept not only the keys to most of the unregistered churches but ritual objects from fifty-five closed churches in the region as well. And yet, according to the notes of the Central Committee's propaganda department in 1979, only in the Ternopil' region was worship regularly held in unregistered churches in sixty-five towns.[49]

A turning point came during official preparations for celebrating the Millennium of Christianity in Rus', which was celebrated in 1988. This event is critical to understanding the true state of religiosity in Ukraine. Preparations for the event made the faithful even more active in their desire to regain access to confiscated buildings and property. As CRA head Vladimir Kuroedov stated in an interview, the very first time that the Patriarch of Moscow and All Rus' Pimen (1910–90) raised the issue of the celebration on the governmental level was in 1977. The patriarch asked Kuroedov to help return Novodevichy Convent in Moscow to the Russian Orthodox Church under the auspices of preparations.[50] Such a request disturbed the party's ideologists who realized that the Church and believers might use the occasion to ask authorities to return confiscated churches all over the country. The Communist Party of the Soviet Union's Central Committee designed a widescale program of counterpropaganda measures to prevent use of the commemoration for anti-Soviet aims and for spurring a religious revival in connection with the 1988 event.[51]

The main objectives of the counterpropaganda campaign launched by the ideological department of the Communist Party of Ukraine were to minimize the impact of the commemoration on the republic's population and to preclude any significant attempts at religious revival; to block Ukrainian national aspirations and the strengthening of the movement for legalizing the Greek Catholic Church; to neutralize the influence of Western Ukrainian and Ukrainian émigré institutions on other religious organizations and believers elsewhere in Soviet Ukraine by presenting "ideologically correct" interpretations of all issues concerning religion; and to use the commemoration for improving the image abroad of the USSR and Soviet Ukraine.[52] At the same time, as far back as 1981, the party Central Committee in Ukraine passed a secret resolution directed to local party committees and to executive committees of regional councils to prevent believers from petitioning for the return of confiscated church buildings and properties. Local authorities were instructed to occupy uninhabited buildings of deregistered communities with social institutions, art galleries, museums, and the like, even if these ramshackle church buildings were in a precarious state. This campaign was called the "exploration of uninhabited buildings" and was put under the strict control of the Central Committee of the Communist Party of the Soviet Union. Until the end of 1986, as many as 893 church buildings were "explored" in this manner.[53] Sometimes the conversion of church buildings to secular aims caused civil disobedience. Dairy workers at times refused to milk collective farm cows and tractor drivers hampered the sowing season because they chose to protect the churches from being taken over and used for secular purposes instead.

By the late 1980s, a deeply respectful attitude toward church-related values, religious holidays, and symbols became relatively common in Ukraine. Growing numbers of people became more open in celebrating religious holy days and more courageous in refusing to participate in the numerous sports, cultural, and propaganda events that were imposed by the party's activists on religious holy days. People began to refuse to work on the most important holy days when they did not coincide with weekends in regions where traditional religious culture—and anti-Soviet sentiment—was preserved to the greatest degree, such as in Transcarpathia, Volyn', Galicia, and Podilia. The authorities' response was to introduce new proposals "to reinforce atheistic education." Yet this very education was facing growing resistance and even hostility. As Soviet values eroded, anticlericalism and atheism became increasingly unpopular, especially among the intelligentsia. Some members of the cultural elite, such as the worldwide acclaimed tenor Ivan Kozlovskyi (1900–93), demonstrated their aversion to atheism in a public and even aggressive manner by interrupting lecturers on atheism.[54] Lecturers on scientific atheism received a cool reception in scientific and research institutions. Often scholars and scientists openly refused to attend the semicompulsory lectures.[55]

In a paradoxical manner, antiatheism combined, especially in Western Ukraine, with ironic and even wary attitudes toward Orthodox priests. On the one hand, the Church was perceived as an effective oppositional force to the regime's ideology. On the other hand, the idea of a hidden but close relationship between the Orthodox clergy and the party bureaucracy was very popular among many ordinary people. This notion was frequently reflected in popular culture where the priests or bishops were portrayed as figures equal to party and state officials in the social hierarchy.[56] The belief that "all 'holy joes' [*popy*] are communists" was widespread. This view was echoed by a professor of the Kyiv Pedogogical Institute who was responsible for providing lectures on atheism to workers and farmers in the different regions of Ukraine. He claimed that "when delivering a lecture to industrial workers or collective farmers I always insisted that a religious outlook was incompatible with membership in the Communist Party. However, almost every time someone in the audience would claim that his or her friend, relative, or neighbor personally met a priest with a Communist Party card." Such moments left him with little recourse and he usually responded to such situations by stating that the Soviet Union's party statutes demand that each communist fight against religious prejudice. Therefore, he added, the mission of clergymen is incompatible by definition with membership in the Communist Party.[57]

Commitment to uproot institutional religiosity began to soften in the early Brezhnev years, when the state closed forty-eight Orthodox churches on average annually from 1965 to 1974. From 1974 to 1987, it closed only twenty-two churches on average annually. The ever-decreasing number of open churches enormously complicated the opportunities that individuals had for normal catechization and regular religious practice, community life, and so on. Therefore, all manner of occult and esoteric study groups also found fertile ground, creating a favorable environment for exotic teachings that allowed nonconfessional forms of mysticism to flourish at the same time that traditional religiosity thrived.

Xenia Kasyanova, a human rights activist and sociologist, who, on her own initiative, conducted provocative (although dangerous in those times) surveys.[58] A time had arrived, she concluded, when people could afford to develop a state of mind different from that prescribed by "the party, the government and Leonid Illyich personally." As she explained:

> A friend of mine, who was recently ordained, tried to convince me that all his friends who came to the faith did so in 1975. All as one. It can be discounted as a coincidence. Yet, 1975 truly did seem to be a breakthrough year. Both the intelligentsia and the youth turned to religion. . . . Our spirit was finally allowed to shrug off the shackles of reality . . . and it flew up. Yoga teachers, "bio-polarists," clairvoyants, astrologists, teachers, and barefoot prophets became strikingly popular. The prohibition on miracles, the transcendant, and supernatural forces was lifted and people suddenly realized that many unusual and amazing things exist right next to them. They started listening. They started following those things.[59]

## Dissent and Religion: The About-Face

The middle 1970s and early 1980s saw the rise of such diverse religious phenomena as Orthodox Christian dissidence, mass baptisms of the urban intelligentsia, conversion to Orthodoxy of Jewish intellectuals and students, and the emergence of a new generation of Ukrainian Greek Catholic Church members: This Church's young priests and parishioners challenged the Soviet prohibition of it. In 1973, Volodymyr Prokopiv, a Ukrainian Catholic priest from Lithuania, came to L'viv Oblast and collected 12,000 signatures for a petition urging the state to lift the ban on the Greek Catholic Church in Ukraine and then traveled to Moscow with the petition. The role of the Greek Catholic enclave can hardly be overestimated in the overall religious revival in the 1970s and 1980s.[60] On the heels of Khrushchev's antireligious campaign, Galicia had became the most active hub of Orthodox communities that still embodied elements of national identity, which was instrumental in the formation of resistance against Soviet religious-national policies. Galician Orthodox communities also played an important role in the alliance of priests, monks, and nuns who refused to repudiate Catholicism and join the Russian Orthodox Church. They also made a critical contribution to the "quiet Ukrainization" of the Orthodox clergy. The proportion of Western Ukrainian students in Russian Orthodox theological schools was extremely high.[61] During the Brezhnev era, bishops who were ethnic Ukrainians became the largest ethnic group within the Russian Orthodox Church.[62] At the Russian Orthodox Church's Local Council in 1990 two Ukrainians, Metropolitan Filaret (Denysenko) and Volodymyr (Sabodan), would become real contenders for the Moscow patriarchal see.

Although the authorities continued to claim that Galicia's "debris of Uniatism" (Ukrainian Catholicism) was approaching its demise, classified documents dating from the period warned that much of the "debris" had been resurrected. They pointed out that the underground church was not decaying and even continued to attract new young priests. Notably, in the 1970s almost a quarter of all antireligious publications in the Soviet Ukraine press criticized a "nonexistent" Uniatism, and in the L'viv region Uniate criticism comprised one-half of all antireligious publications.[63] Local authorities were urged to closely survey underground monks and nuns and to prevent them from renting apartments to young people because it turned out that a number of such "tenants" took monastic vows.

In an effort to disentangle religion from nationality/ethnicity, and specifically to extricate the Ukrainian Greek Catholic Church from anti-Soviet Ukrainian nationalism, the Orthodox clergy as well as the commissioners of the CRA demanded the abolition of all traces of Eastern-Rite Catholicism in the western oblasts of Ukraine, including architectural elements and liturgical and other ritual practices. Through the second half of the

1980s, the authorities were still confiscating liturgy books blessed by Andrei Sheptytsky and icons with burning hearts, which is a purely Catholic symbol not found in the Eastern Orthodox icon tradition. The Latin-rite crucifixes with Jesus' body hanging on three nails were exchanged for traditional Orthodox ones with four nails and a straight-handed figure of the Savior. In some Galician villages, such as the Dolynskyi district in the Ivano-Frankivsk region, people who had been forcibly resettled from Poland or their descendants refused to attend services that "didn't mention the Pope." Thirty years after the 1946 L'viv Pseudo-Sobor—during which the 1596 Union of Brest agreement (which created the Ukrainian Greek Catholic Church) was renounced and the property of the Ukrainian Greek Catholic Church was transferred to the Russian Orthodox Church, with the intention of liquidating the Greek Catholic Church—the Orthodox dissident Anatoliy Krasnov-Levitin stated that "Uniatism in Western Ukraine is a mass movement. Persecution of this movement means not only religious oppression, but also restrictions on the ethnic rights of Western Ukrainians."[64] Ukrainian dissident Valentyn Moroz was more categorical:

> The Uniate movement has grown into the spiritual body of Ukraine and has become a national symbol. . . . The [Uniate] Church is interwoven into cultural life so deeply that it is impossible to touch it without damaging the spiritual structure of the nation. . . . One must understand that a struggle against the Church means a struggle against national culture.[65]

By the mid-1980s, such views were widely held in Western Ukraine.

Another complication for party and KBG officials in Ukraine was the religious upheaval among Protestants. Secret reports emphasized the growth of Baptist, Pentecostal, and Adventist congregations. The proportion of young people in these congregations was also increasing. In large urban communities, youngsters made up no fewer than 30 percent of participants. Most Pentecostals, Jehovah's Witnesses, followers of the Council of Evangelical Baptist Churches, and Adventist-Reformist communities in Ukraine existed unofficially and their members faced unrelenting repression. Although there were obvious substantial theological differences among them, these religious groups were united by their common opposition to the existing legislation that regulated religious activities in the USSR, as well as by their conscious rejection of any form of cooperation with the government and their readiness to endure suffering for their convictions.

Because many religious communities of these denominations remained unregistered, the authorities continued to shut down their prayer gatherings and fine organizers under the provisions of the March 26, 1966, *ukaz* (decree) of the republic's Supreme Council, "On the Administrative Responsibility for the Violation of Legislation on Religious Cults." This decree was passed in response to rallies of dissident Baptists and, at least initially, was directed against them. Consequently, a substantial portion of the Protestants from unregistered communities (accounting for many thousands of people) were under surveillance by local authorities and KGB regional and district departments. The local party and civic organizations were assigned to "reeducate" them via public condemnations at specially convened village gatherings, parent-teacher conferences at schools, and so on. Their children were subjected to forced atheism, and the opposition to Soviet schools among Protestant families in general became heated and exhausting for the authorities. In response to massive and state-sponsored attacks, Evangelicals tried to build an emotional-psychological network that would be impenetrable by outsiders. Members of this network easily recognized one other by behavior, appearance, and even greetings. A family, normally an extended family, with three or more children was the core of this network, constituting a "home church," which proved to be a reliable foundation for a persecuted church in especially hard times. Dissident Evangelicals, Reformed Adventists, and Jehovah's Witnesses paid a high price for their unwillingness to yield, as is documented elsewhere in this volume. Practically all leaders of the dissident Baptist and Pentecostal groups, with very few exceptions, were repeatedly charged under the criminal code. Every year dozens of Jehovah's Witnesses were imprisoned as conscientious objectors. Some believers were tried more than once for the same transgression. Six out of seven leaders of the Jehovah's Witnesses Council, all ethnic Ukrainians, were sentenced to long prison terms: S. Burak died in Kyiv's Lukyanivska Prison in 1946; M. Tsyba was imprisoned from 1946 to 1956, and again from 1960 to 1970; M. Dubovinskyi was imprisoned from 1944 to 1950, and again from 1957 to 1967; P. Zyatek was imprisoned from 1945 to 1955, and from 1960 to 1970; I. Pashkovskyi was imprisoned from 1947 to 1956; and M. Dasevych was imprisoned from 1944 to 1950.[66]

D. Kovalewsky, who analyzed ninety-nine cases of religiously motivated protests by Soviet citizens, discovered that the majority of protests known to the West originated in three republics—Lithuania (33.3 percent), Russia (29.3 percent), and Ukraine (24.4 percent). Unregistered Baptists were responsible for 40 percent of the protests, Lithuanian Catholics for 34.3 percent, and Ukrainian Greek Catholics for 8.1 percent.[67] Evangelicals produced unique, sometimes even desperate, forms of resistance to the "godless state," including samizdat memoirs of suffering (which Olena Panych analyzes in chapter 7 of this volume), mass demonstrations, defiant public meetings of youth, prayer gatherings for prisoners, and the Pentecostal movement for emigration from the USSR, which was the most unexpected event for KGB and party officials.[68]

The long-standing and exhausting oppositional stance to the secular world that was upheld by these religious communities and used as a justification for trying to destroy them and to prove the futility of a Christian way of life, contributed to the formation of many common features among Baptists, Pentecostals, Adventists, and Jehovah's Witnesses. All had a specific organizational model of communal life that included a strictly fixed and demanding understanding of membership upheld by severe sanctions for violating communal rules, unshakable confidence in the truthfulness and righteousness of their chosen way of life, the exercise of strict community control over all areas of a believer's life, binding orders for all members to maintain a "critical distance" from the profane world, a very pronounced group self-awareness, deliberate fostering of a group psychology and collective memories to forge unity, and sincere efforts to save a fallen world and bring salvation by spreading Protestant beliefs and converting dissidents and nonbelievers. This sectarian model of communal life (in the sociological sense, not that of Soviet propaganda) was formed by and large in response to secularizing pressures imposed by the Soviet state.[69] The regime's aspiration to put an end to the religious underground and, at the same time, the stiff resistance of these underground communities to the regime was a dramatic, albeit sometimes tragic, page in the history of those times.

In the meantime, the Soviet intelligentsia underwent a generational change. The "men of the sixties" who had been inspired by the Twentieth Party Congress of the Communist Party of the Soviet Union and Khrushchev's "thaw" and were mainly indifferent to religion, began to have less of a voice.[70] They still believed in the advantages of socialism, although they recognized that it had been distorted, violated, and crushed by Stalinists. Those who followed in their footsteps no longer believed in the ideals of "the commissars in dusty helmets."[71]

A Ukrainian human rights activist and teacher of literature, Valerii Marchenko (1947–84), who perished in a Soviet prison, shrewdly described the mood of those who took the place of the "men of the 1960s":[72]

The realm of the spirit is a phenomenon that until recently remained unknown and mysterious to us. . . . And as for conscious Ukrainians, it is a generous gift that will surely bear fruit, once we invest all our spirited devotion to it.[73]

The Ukrainian human rights activists Oksana Meshko, Oles' Berdnyk, Ivan Kandyba, and other members of the Ukrainian Helsinki Group pointed out in their 1976 manifesto that they aspired "to familiarize the Ukrainian and global community with the facts of violations of . . . religious rights." From its very beginning, the Ukrainian human rights movement was inspired by figures with deep religious convictions, such as Father Vasyl' Romanyuk (1925–95); Patriarch Volodymyr of Kyiv and All Ukraine-Rus', who served from 1993 to 1995; Georgi Vins, secretary of the Council of Evangelical Baptist Churches; Myroslav Marynovich, the current vice rector of the Ukrainian Catholic University; and Zynovyi Antonyuk, a prominent figure in the Ukrainian Orthodox revival of the late 1980s.

In February 1977, Levko Lukyanenko, a member of the Ukrainian Helsinki Group, published his "Christmas Appeal to Engaged Atheists," in which he claimed that religion was for Ukrainian activists a battlefield for human rights and freedoms:

> Have you ever come to church? Not with hammers to smash crucifixes, not with the keys to lock out parishioners, not with hate, but with an open heart? No, you most certainly haven't. Because if you had, you would have at least once stepped in front of the high dome over the iconostasis and looked to the One, who instead of the heathen moral justice maxim, "An eye for an eye and a tooth for a tooth," gave people the principle of magnanimity, who urged people not to respond to evil with evil, but to forgive. You would have understood how strongly Christianity contributed to softening human habits and how considerably it forwarded people from initial barbarism to humanity![74]

## Conclusion

The revival of religion in Ukraine reflected serious shifts, if not tectonic dislocations, within the entire Soviet Union. Toward the end of the 1970s, the eschatological prospect of communism with its kingdom of heaven on earth was finally desacralized. Ironically, this quasireligious surrogate appeared to be "secularized" by modernization, rationalization and, especially, by globalization, "which destroyed all closed borders and destroyed communism before our very eyes," as Fr. Vladimir Zelinskii said.[75] The Soviet "gospel" had been discredited. Technocratic enthusiasm waned in spite of the breakthroughs of Soviet science and especially the cosmic odyssey of the first Soviet astronauts who had to prove that "heaven is empty." As Victoria Smolkin-Rothrock argues, "The story of the conquest of the cosmos in Soviet atheism lays bare the paradox of the attempt to invest scientific materialism with a spiritual center. Not only did Soviet space achievements fail to produce mass religious disbelief, they also revealed the ideological pitfalls of the utopia promised by Marxism-Leninism."[76] The Soviet people increasingly perceived the furious attacks on religion as senseless and counterproductive—they were not only attacks against human dignity and human rights but against social stability as well.[77] It was this very perception in the late 1980s that led to the rapid cessation of the system of atheist education and advocacy of antireligious policies as well as to an acknowledged and widespread consensus of the significance of religion, a consensus that was rarely heard in Soviet society at that time in many other types of discussions of the country's future.

## Notes

1. Eloquent biblical themes and spiritual motifs appear in the poetry of prominent Ukrainian dissidents, e.g., Vasyl' Stus (1938–85), who spent half of his life in prison, and Yevgen Sverstyuk (b. 1928), and in the poetry of Ukrainian poets Lina Kostenko (b. 1930) and Iryna Zhylenko (b. 1941). See, e.g., R. R. Halytska, "Religious-Spiritual Discourse of Feminine Poetry of the 1960s (On the Works of Emma Andievska, Anna-Maria Holod, Iryna Zhylenko, Zoreslava Koval, Lina Kostenko and Marta Melnychuk-Oberraukh)," Ph.D. diss., Vasyl Stefanyk Transcarpathian National University, 2008.

2. Nikolai Berdyaev, "Russkii dukhovnyi renesans nachala XX v. i Zhurnal *Put'*" [The Russian spiritual renaissance of the early XX century and the journal *Put*], *Put'* 49 (1935), 12–13, http://www.chebucto.ns.ca/Philosophy/Sui-Generis/Berdyaev/essays/rsr.htm.

3. Nicolas Zernov, *The Russian Religious Renaissance of the Twentieth Century* (New York: Harper & Row, 1963).

4. Karel Berghoff, "Chi bulo religiyne vidrodzhennya v Ukraini pid chas natsistskoi okupatsii?" *Ukrainskyi istorychnyi zhurnal* 3 (2005): 16–36.

5. N. A. Kolesnik, ed., "Regulations Concerning the Religious Organizations in the Ukrainian SSR (for Official Use Only), Collection of Documents and Data on Religion and the Church (Kyiv: Redaktsionno-izdatel'skii otdel MVD USSR, 1983), 75–88.

6. Vladimir Chivilikhin (1928–84) and Vasilii Belov (b. 1932) are both prominent Soviet and Russian novelists, eloquent antiliberals and anti-Westernists, and proponents of an exclusively Russian historical pathway and world mission.

7. Alexander Prokhanov (b. 1938) is a Soviet and Russian journalist, novelist, and political figure, and one of the most consistent supporters of the idea of a Russian

imperial future. For his rapturous essays about the USSR's military power and Soviet military action in Afghanistan, he was nicknamed by political opponents as the "nightingale of the [Soviet Army] General Staff."

8. Vasilyev's "Pamyat" (Memory) is a national patriotic organization led by Dmitrii Vasilyev (1945–93). During the 1980s, it was Russia's best-known Russian nationalist organization.

9. Hegumen Innokentyi (Pavlov) considered the possible attitudes of the high-ranking Orthodox hierarchy toward such political evolution, and quoted the most prominent and energetic among them in the 1960s and 1970s, Metropolitan Nikodim (Rotov, 1929–78). In a trusted circle of confidants, he admitted, "Wait a while. We will reach a time when the Politburo [of the Communist Party's Central Committee] will begin [meetings] by singing the 'Heavenly Father.'" Hegumen Innokentyi (Pavlov), "Outgoing Epoch," *Russkaya mysl'* 4313 (2000). See also Vladimir Bondarenko, "'Russkii orden' v TsK partii: Mifi i real'nost'—Beseda s predsedatelem Soiuza pisatelei Rossii Valeriem Ganichevim" ["Russian order" in Party's Central Committee: Myths and reality—Conversation with the chairman of the Union of Writers of Russia Valeryi Ganichev], *Russkoe Voskresenie. Pravoslavie, samoderzhavie, narodnost'*, no. 109 (July 18, 2002).

10. David E. Powell, *Antireligious Propaganda in the Soviet Union* (Cambridge, Mass.: MIT Press, 1975), 105.

11. V. V. Melnikov and T. O. Tserbaev, "Opinion Poll on the Jubilee," *1000-Year Anniversary of the Baptism of Rus'* (Moscow: Academy of Social Sciences of CC CPSU, 1989), 88–89.

12. "My colleagues and I personally could not convince our commanders in Moscow to allow us to put a stop to traditional antireligious rhetoric while conducting political propaganda among Afghan militants. Old generals from the Political Command of the Soviet Army and Navy assessed the rejection of antireligious agitation as a revision of the foundations of Marxism-Leninism. They insisted that we never would be successful in our goals as long as the Afghan people were under the influence of the 'reactionary teachings of Islam.' For that antireligious propaganda, which had an eloquent anti-Islamic character, we paid with our soldiers' lives." P.D., staff member of the commissioner for human rights of Ukraine from 1979 to 1982 and political adviser to the Soviet military contingent in Afghanistan, interview by the author, September 1999.

13. At the Eleventh Congress of the Russian Communist Party (Bolsheviks) in 1922, Vladimir Lenin made the following revealing statement: "Ukraine is an independent republic, and this is very good. However, . . . there lie cunning people and the Central Committee [of the Communist Party of Ukraine] cannot claim that they fool us, but somehow they move aside us." V. I. Lenin, *Polnoe Sobranie Sochinenii*, vol. 45, 105–6.

14. For more detail, see Viktor Yelensky, *Derzhavno-Tserkovni vidnosini na Ukraini, 1917–1990* [Church and State in Ukraine, 1917–1990] (Kyiv: Znannya, 1991).

15. Vladimir Kuroedov (1906–94) headed the Council for Russian Orthodox Affairs from 1960 until its merger with the Council for Religious Cult Affairs into the Council for Religious Affairs attached to the Soviet Council of Ministers in 1965. He then headed the combined Council from 1965 to 1984. For a 2,200-word fragment of his only interview to the press (excluding several "parade" interviews in support of official propaganda on the "triumph of Socialist freedom of conscience"), see Vladimir Kuroedov, "Chleni Politbiuro ne buli dobrimi christianami . . ." [Members of Politbiuro Were Not Good Christians . . .], *Lyudyna i Svit* 1 (1992), 16–22.

16. The best-known concession of Soviet power to Georgian nationalism was reinstatement of the constitutional status of the Georgian language as Georgia's official state language after mass street demonstrations in Tbilisi on April 14, 1978. The Communist Party of Georgia, and even its leader Edward Shevardnadze, supported the demonstrators. The Trans-Caucasian republics were the only republics within the USSR where national languages had an official status written into their respective constitutions.

17. See, e.g., C. I. Peters, "The Georgian Orthodox Church," in *Eastern Christianity and Politics in the Twentieth Century*, edited by Petro Ramet (Durham, N.C.: Duke University Press, 1988), 307.

18. V.K., head of the Section for Religious Affairs attached to Odessa region administration, former commissioner of Council for Religious Affairs attached to Soviet Ukraine's Council of Ministers for the Odessa region from the late 1970s through the 1980s, interview with the author, in Puscha-Voditsa, near Kyiv, November 1993.

19. P.P., retired state official, first deputy head of Council for Religious Affairs attached to the Council of Ministers of Soviet Ukraine in the 1970s and 1980s, interview by the author, Kyiv, September 11–13, 1993.

20. L.S., retiree, former head of the Shahtarsk City Council's Executive Committee in 1970s, and commissioner of the Council for Religious Affairs attached to the Council of Ministers of Soviet Ukraine for the Donetsk region in the 1980s, interview by the author, Donetsk, August 1997.

21. See James Thrower, *Marxist-Leninist "Scientific Atheism" and the Study of Religion and Atheism in the USSR* (Berlin: Mouton de Gruyter, 1983), esp. chap. 7, "'Scientific Atheism' and the 'Concrete' Sociological Study of Religion and Atheism in the USSR."

22. E.F., deputy director of the Institute for Scientific Atheism attached to Academy of Social Sciences of the Communist Party's Central Committee in 1980s, interview by the author, Moscow, May 1991.

23. Aleksandr Belov, ed., *Ateism i religiia: Voprosy i otvety* [Atheism and religion: Questions and answers] (Moscow: Politizdat, 1986), 34.

24. O.B., head of Department of Atheist Literature of Politizdat SSSR, interview by the author, Moscow, August 1988.

25. *Konkretnye Issledovaniia Sovremennykh Religioznykh Verovanii: Metodika, Organizatsiia, Rezul'taty* [Specific Surveys of Contemporary Religious Believers] (Moscow: Mysl', 1967), 63–83.

26. William C. Fletcher, *Soviet Believers: The Religious Sector of the Population* (Lawrence: Regents Press of Kansas, 1981), 14–15, 211–13.

27. Ibid., 69–70.

28. Ibid., 211–13.

29. "Document 173, Council for Religious Affairs, Moscow, No. 134S, May 7, 1985, Copy No. 1," in *Religion in the Soviet Union: An Archival Reader*, edited by Felix Corley (New York: New York University Press, 1996), 299–300, 302.

30. Olexander Bazchan and Yuri Danylyuk, *Viprobuvannya viroyu* [The trial by faith] (Kyiv: Institut Istorii Ukraini, 2000), 273.

31. See Lilian Voye and Karel Dobbelaere, "Roman Catholicism: Universalism at Stake," in *Religions sans Frontières? Present and Future Trends of Migration, Culture, and Communication*, edited by Roberto Cipriani (Rome: Presidenza del Consiglio dei Ministri, Dipartimento per l'Informazione e l'Editoria, 1994), 83, 92.

32. Cristel Lane, *Christian Religion in the Soviet Union: A Sociological Study* (Albany: State University of New York Press, 1978), 44.

33. L. A. Prokovschenkov, *Osobennosti proiavleniia i sotsial'no-psikhologicheskie faktory sokhraneniia religioznosti sredi rabotaiushchei molodezhi* [The peculiarities of expression and social-psychological factors of preserving religiosity among young workers), dissertation abstract, candidate in the philosophical sciences, AON pri TSK KPSS, Moscow, 1979.

34. E. A. Filimonov, ed., *Aktual'nie Problemy Nauchno-Ateisticheskogo Vospitaniia Molodezhi* (Moscow: Molodaia gvardiia, 1983), 68.

35. Sergei Averintsev, "Mi i nashi ierarkhi" [Our hierarchies and us], in *Sophia-Logos*, edited by Sergei Averintsev (Kyiv: Dukh i Litera, 1999), 350.

36. Paul A. Lucey, "The Soviet Press on Religion and Youth," *Religion in Communist Lands* 10, no. 2 (1982): 206–9, citing *Molodoi Kommunist* [Young Communist], no. 8 (1975): 193.

37. Ieromonah Nikon, "Vpechatleniia ochevidtsa" [An eyewitness's impression], *Vestnik RKhD* no. 132 (1980): 206–7.

38. H. L. Biddulph, "Religious Participation of Youth in the USSR," *Soviet Studies* 31, no. 3 (1979): 417–33.

39. Gerhard Simon, *Church, State and Opposition in the USSR* (Berkeley: University of California Press, 1974), 107.

40. Y.C., businessman, instructor to Kherson regional committee of the Ukrainian Communist Party in the 1980s, interview by the author, Moscow, May 1993.

41. I.B., Ukrainian diplomat, who in 1980 was an instructor in the Rivne Regional Committee of the Ukrainian Communist Party, interview by the author, Kyiv, September 1995.

42. Fr. A.Z., archpriest of the Ukrainian Orthodox Church–Moscow Patriarchate in the 1980s, who was a priest at Saint Makarious Church in Kyiv, interview by the author, Kyiv, January 1998.

43. V.S., staff member of the Ukrainian Parliamentary Commission for Spirituality and Culture, inspector for the Council for Religious Affairs attached to the Ukraine Republic Council of Ministers, and occasional lecturer at the Tovaristvo Znania (Knowledge Society) in the 1980s, interview by the author, Kyiv, February 1997.

44. "Ya viris u Tserkvi . . ." [I grew up in the Church . . .], *Lyudyna i Svit* 1 (1998): 34. From Mikhail Koltun, bishop of Zboriv Diocese, Ukrainian Greek Catholic Church, interview by the author, 1998.

45. Petro Bondarchuk, "Religiyna povedinka pravoslavnih viruyuchih v Ukraini: Osoblivosti i tendetsii zmin (seredina 1940-h—seredina 1980-h rr" [Religious behavior of Orthodox faithful in Ukraine: Peculiarities and tendencies of change, mid-1940s to mid-1980s], *Ukrainskyi istorichnyi zhurnal* no. 3 (2007): 143.

46. In the mid-1980s, 56 percent of all religious organizations in Ukraine were located in seven western regions that were not part of the USSR before the World War II, compared with less than 2 percent in the most populous Donbass region. One of the most crucial factors explaining this disparity is that the Greek Catholic and Orthodox Churches played a salient role in the process of national identity formation for Ukrainians under Habsburg, Polish, Czech, and Hungarian rule, whereas the Orthodox Church in the Russian Empire, as a pillar of a common Ukrainian-Russian identity, could not play such a role. Comparative surveys of religiosity in Central and Eastern Ukraine show

direct correlations between the role of religious institutions in nation building and religious behavior. The more salient this role is, the more consistent religious behavior is.

47. Central State Archives of Supreme Bodies of Power and Government of Ukraine (Tsentral'nyi derzhavnyi arkhiv vyshchykh orhaniv vlady ta upravlinnia Ukrainy, known as TsDAVO), f 4648, op. 1, sprava 433, ark. 1.

48. Nadezhda Beliakova, "Iz istorii registratsii religioznykh ob'edinenii v Ukraine i Belorussii v 1976–1986 godakh" [On the history of registration of religious communities in Ukraine and Belorussia in 1976–1986], *Neprikosnovennyi zapas* 3 (2008): 120–34.

49. Ibid., 129.

50. Novodevichy Convent was returned to the Moscow Eparchy of the Russian Orthodox Church in 2010.

51. Vladimir Kuroedov, head of the Council for Religious Affairs attached to the USSR Council of Ministers, interview by the author, Moscow, December 1991.

52. See *Aktual'nye problemy ateisticheskoi kontrpropagandy, DSP* [Current problems of atheist counterpropaganda, for service use only], no. 3 (Kyiv: Politizdat Ukrainy, 1985), 5–32; *Aktual'nye problemy ateisticheskoi kontrpropagandy, DSP* [Current problems of atheist counterpropaganda, for service use only), no. 4 (Kyiv: Politizdat Ukrainy, 1987), 5–28.

53. *Aktual'nye problemy ateisticheskoi kontrpropagandy*, no. 4, 7.

54. O.B., interview.

55. V.S., interview.

56. Here is an example of the type of joke that was inspired by such paradoxical perspectives: An Orthodox bishop and the secretary of the regional committee of Communist Party shared the compartment of a railway carriage. Both had a meal. Surprised that the bishop's meal was more expensive and less common than his, the secretary asked the bishop how he had managed to get hold of such rare commodities. It would be easy for you also, the bishop replied, if your Communist Party had managed to separate itself from the state.

57. Yu.E., associate professor at the Kyiv Pedagogical University in the 1970s and 1980s, interview by the author, Kyiv, December 1994.

58. "Xenia Kasyanova" is a pseudonym for the prominent Russian sociologist Valentina Chesnokova (1934–2010). The political circumstances of the 1970s forced her to conduct her survey on Russian national psychology secretly. However, some young, and now well-known, sociologists and mathematicians voluntarily helped her with the processing of questionnaires that contained hundreds of questions.

59. Xenia Kasyanova, *Osobennosti russkogo natsional'nogo kharaktera* [The peculiarities of the Russian national character] (Moscow: Institute of the National Model of Economics, 1994), 238.

60. "Khronika Katolicheskoi Tserkvi na Ukraine" [Chronicle of the Catholic Church in Ukraine], *Radio Liberty*, January 3, 1985.

61. E.g., in the mid-1980s Western Ukrainians constituted more than a half of all students of Leningrad Theological seminary. See S. N. Pavlov, "O sovremennom sostoianii Russkoi Pravoslavnoi Tserkvi" [On the current state of the Russian Orthodox Church], *Sotsiologicheskie issledovaniia* 4 (1987): 42. The same author noted that numerous Western Ukrainian students came almost exclusivly from rural areas and argued that in Western Ukrainian cities, especially among the intelligentsia, people were

more devoted to the Greek Catholic Church. Hegumen Innokentyi Pavlov, "Prisutstvie Moskovskoi Patriarkhii v Galitsii: Istoriia i itogi" (The presence of Moscow Patriarchate in Galicia: History and outcome), in *Ukrainskaia Greko-Katolicheskaia Tserkov': Preodolenie mifa* [The Ukrainian Greek Catholic Church: The overcoming of myths] (Moscow: Institut izuchenia religii v stranakh SNG i Baltii, 2002), 69.

62. Nikolai Mitrokhin and Sofia Timofeeva, *Episkopy i eparkhii Russkoi pravoslavnoi Tserkvi* [The bishops and dioceses of the Russian Orthodox Church] (Moscow: Panorama, 1997), 15–19.

63. See *Stanovlennya i rozvitok masovoho ateizmu v zahidnih oblastyah Ukrains'koi SSR* (Formation and development of mass atheism in the western regions of the Ukrainian Soviet Socialist Republic) (Kyiv: Naukova Dymka, 1981), 183–84.

64. Anatolii Levitin-Krasnov, "V oboroni Ukrainskoyi Katolitskoi Tserkvi" [Defending the Ukrainian Catholic Church], *Suchasnist'*, no. 1 (1975): 108.

65. Valentyn Moroz, *A Chronicle of Resistance in Ukraine* (Baltimore: Smoloskyp, 1970), 2, 5.

66. Sergei Ivanenko, *O liudyakh, nikogda ne rasstaiushchikhsia s Bibliei* [On people who never part with the Bible] (Moscow: Respublika, 1999), 242–48.

67. D. Kovalewsky, "Religious Belief in the Brezhnev Era: Renaissance, Resistance and Realpolitik," *Journal for the Scientific Study of Religion* 19, no. 3 (September 1980): 284.

68. See "Open Letter to the President of the USA, Mr. Jimmy Carter, from the Christians of Evangelical Faith, Pentecostals and Baptists Whom Soviet Officials Refuse the Right to Emigrate," September 1979, http://www.memo.ru/history/diss/carter/files/14-eng.doc. See also Catherine Wanner, *Communities of the Converted: Ukrainians and Global Evangelism* (Ithaca, N.Y.: Cornell University Press, 2007), 1, 90–94.

69. Even during perestroika, Protestant leaders admitted the presence of sectarian features in their congregations. "Nowadays, the days of blessed opportunities and changes, it is especially hurtful to realize that certain sectarian manifestations in our church hinder it from accomplishing its ministry to the fullest," wrote an Adventist, O. Senin, in "Sekta ili Tserkov'?" (Sect or Church?), *Tserkov' ostatka*, no. 2 (1988). These sentiments were echoed by a Baptist, who wrote, "It is evident we will need a great deal of time before we are ready to admit that the traditions formed in the local churches and the spirit of evangelical teaching are not identical concepts, as a Baptist theologian thinks. No Christian denomination has escaped various traditional developments. Sad faces, secluded lives, neglected ethics, the rejection of cultural heritage—all of this is a serious obstacle for many truth seekers." G. Serhienko, "Vy budete mne svideteliami" [You shall be my witnesses], *Bratskii vestnik* 6 (1988): 65.

70. The Twentieth Congress of the Communist Party of the Soviet Union, February 14–26, 1956, is famous for Nikita Krushchev's "Secret Speech," which denounced Joseph Stalin and his "cult of personality" and condemned the repressions of the 1930s and 1940s. The Khrushchev Thaw is the period from the middle 1950s to the early 1960s when repression in the Soviet Union was reversed. Millions of Soviet political prisoners were released due to Khrushchev's policies of de-Stalinization.

71. The line is from Bulat Okudzhava's lyrics for "Sentimental March." The idealization of "the Commissars in Dusty Helmets" as true Leninists, as knights without fear and above reproach, who later became victims of Stalinist repression, became a necessary element in the mythology of the liberal wing of the Soviet intelligentsia in the

late 1950s and 1960s. See, e.g., Andrei Piontkowsky, "The Russian Sphinx: Hope and Despair," in *Spring in Winter: The 1989 Revolutions*, edited by Gwyn Prins (Manchester: Manchester University Press, 1990), 174.

72. Valerii Marchenko was first arrested in 1973 and was sentenced to six years imprisonment and two years exile. He was arrested for a second time in 1983.

73. Valerii Marchenko, *Listi materi z nevoli* [Letters to mother from captivity] (Kyiv: Olzhich Foundation, 1994), 374.

74. Levko Lukyanenko, "Marksists'ka teoriya nespromozchna vytysnity viry v Boga, zayavlyae Luk'yanenko u Zvernenni do ateistiv" [Marxist theory is incapable of banishing faith in God, states Lukyanenko in his appeal to atheists], *Svoboda*, September 20, 1977, 8.

75. Fr. Vladimir Zelinskii, "Pravoslavie i Globalizatsiia: Vzgliad iz zapada" [Orthodoxy and globalization: The view from the West], 2001, http://www.Kyiv-orthodox.org/culture/modern/zelinsky_global.htm.

76. Victoria Smolkin-Rothrock, "Cosmic Enlightenment: Cosmonauts and the Conquest of Space in Soviet Atheist Education," in *Into the Cosmos: Space Exploration and Soviet Culture*, edited by James T. Andrews and Asif A. Siddiqi (Pittsburgh: University of Pittsburgh Press, 2011).

77. "In the mid-1980s, I was routinely asked during my lectures, 'Why can't the state leave believers in peace? Why must the Communist Party try to reeducate people who are good citizens and productive in their workplace? Why is trust in communism incompatible with trust in God?'" From V.S., interview.

# Contributors

**Gregory L. Freeze** is the Victor and Gwendolyn Beinfield Professor of History at Brandeis University. He is the author of many books and articles on Russian social history and Russian Orthodoxy, including *The Parish Clergy in Nineteenth-Century Russia: Crisis, Reform, Counter-Reform* (1983); *Description of the Clergy in Rural Russia: The Memoir of a Nineteenth-Century Parish Priest* (1985); and, most recently, *Russia: A History* (2009).

**John-Paul Himka** is professor of Ukrainian history in the Department of History and Classics at the University of Alberta. He is the author of many books and articles on Eastern European history, including *Last Judgment Iconography in the Carpathians* (2009), and *Religion and Nationality in Western Ukraine: The Greek Catholic Church and the Ruthenian National Movement in Galicia* (1999). He is coeditor of *Letters from Heaven: Popular Religion in Russia and Ukraine* (2006).

**Scott Kenworthy** is an associate professor in the Department of History and the Department of Religious Studies at Miami University of Ohio. He is the author of *The Heart of Russia: Trinity-Sergius, Monasticism, and Society after 1825* (2010).

**Nadieszda Kizenko** is an associate professor of history at the State University of New York at Albany and the author of *A Prodigal Saint: Father John Kronstadt and the Russian People* (2000), which won the Heldt Prize in 2000. She also translated and edited *Ten Homilies on the Beatitudes of St. John of Kronstadt* (2003).

**Zoe Knox** is a lecturer in modern Russian history at the University of Leicester. She is the author of *Russian Society and the Orthodox Church: Religion in Russia after Communism* (2009). She is currently completing a book titled *Watchtower Theology and Soviet Ideology: Jehovah's Witnesses in the USSR, 1939–1991*.

**Sonja Luehrmann** is an assistant professor of cultural anthropology at Simon Fraser University. She is the author of *Secularism Soviet Style: Teaching Atheism and Religion in a Volga Republic* (2011), and *Alutiiq Villages under Russian and U.S. Rule* (2008). She is currently writing a book on the problems of studying religious practice through the militantly secularist lens of Soviet-era archival documents.

**Olena Panych** is the vice rector for research at the Donetsk Christian University in Donetsk, Ukraine. As a historian of Ukrainian religious history, she has written many articles on religious minorities in Ukraine.

**Stella Rock** is a senior research fellow at the Keston Center for Religion, Politics, and Society at Baylor University. She is a historian of lived religion in Russia and its relationship to national identity. She is the author of *Popular Religion in Russia: "Double-Belief" and the Making of an Academic Myth* (2007).

**Anna Shternshis** is the Al and Malka Green Associate Professor of Yiddish in the German Department and the Center for Diaspora and Transnational Studies at the University of Toronto. She is the author of *Soviet and Kosher: Jewish Popular Culture in the Soviet Union, 1923–1939* (2006). She is currently working on two book projects. One is devoted to Jewish daily life in the Soviet Union from the 1930s to the 1980s, and the other is about the evacuation of Soviet Jews during World War II.

**Catherine Wanner** is a professor of history and cultural anthropology at Pennsylvania State University. She is the author of *Communities of the Converted: Ukrainians and Global Evangelism* (2007), and *Burden of Dreams*: *History and Identity in Post-Soviet Ukraine* (1998), as well as coeditor of *Religion, Morality, and Community after Communism* (2008). She is completing a book on secularization in postwar Western Ukraine.

**Viktor Yelensky** is a senior researcher at the Institute of Philosophy of the Ukrainian Academy of Sciences. He was formerly the Kyiv bureau chief of Radio Free Europe / Radio Liberty and has written numerous articles on religion in Ukraine. His most recent book is *Religion after Communism* (2009).

# Index

abortions, 208, 209, 216–17n74
Abramowitch, Alexander (Mendele Moykher Sforim), 74
Academy of Social Sciences, 305
Adventism. *See* Seventh-Day Adventists
Afghan people, religious influences of, 325n12
Agavairem (plowing festival), 288
Agitprop Bureau (Ukrainian Communist Party), 39
Aitmatov, Chingis, 293
Aksenfeld, Israel, 74
alcohol use, 282, 289, 293
Aleksander-Nevskii brotherhood, 127
Aleksandra, Bishop (Ereshchenko), 47
Aleksii, Metropolitan (Hromadsky), 105
Aleksii I, 117, 124–27, 129, 133–34, 138–39, 146
Aleksii II, 144
All-Union Council of Evangelical Christians–Baptists, 245
Altshuler, Mordechai, 75, 83
Amato, Joseph A., 242
American Civil Liberties Union, 254
anticlericalism, 28–30, 50–51n8
Anticosmopolitan Campaign, 16
antireligious campaigns, 12–13, 27–62; and clergy, social revolution in, 28–30; and Orthodox Church disestablishment, 30–35; and politics of piety, 44–48; and religious policy, 12–13, 35–40, 48–49; and religious revival, 40–44; and repression and retreat, 28–35; and secularization, 3–7. *See also* Khrushchev's antireligious campaigns; religious revivals
Anti-Religious Commission, 38, 41, 47, 58n67, 61n124
anti-Semitism, 74–75, 81, 90
Antonyuk, Zynovyi, 323
Ardov, Mikhail, 209, 216–17n74
Armageddon, 269n80
Armenian Apostolic Church, 308
Arsenii, Hieromonk (Romashchenko), 141, 142
Asad, Talal, 8–9, 190–91
ASSRs (autonomous Soviet Socialist republics), 277
atheism: and critiques of religion, 288–92; Marx on, 25n9; and piety, forms of, 4; and propaganda, 34–35, 305; and religious diversity, 286–87, 292–95; and religious revival, 313, 317–18; and sacred sites, 285; and sects, 276, 283
autocephalous church movements, 34, 37, 46–48, 61–62n128, 62n133
Autonomous Orthodox clergy, 111
autonomous Soviet socialist republics (ASSRs), 277

Averintsev, Sergey, 243n58, 312
*Awake!* magazine, 255, 259

Babii, Ivan, 97
Babiichuk, Vasilii, 262–63
Bainbridge, W., 25n13
Balyberdin, A., 174
Bandera, Stepan, 96, 107
Bandera movement, 96, 98–102, 107, 109, 110–12
baptisms, 311, 313–14
Baptists. *See* Evangelical Christians–Baptists
"Basic Data on the State of Religion in the USSR for 1975" (CRA), 260
*batraki* (landless agricultural workers), 43
*bedniaki* (poor peasants), 43
Beglov, Aleksei, 173, 183–84n33, 184n35
believer–versus–Soviet citizen dichotomy, 160
Belov, Vasilii, 305, 324n16
Berdnyk, Oles', 323
Berdyaev, Nikolai, 303
Beskrovnyy, V. I., 262
Beyzer, Mikhail, 75
*Bezbozhnik* on antireligious propaganda, 39
Bible Students (Jehovah's Witness group), 249
Biddulph, H. L., 312
*The Bliss of the Lost Life* (Khrapov), 220
Boiarskii, Fedor, 255
Boiko, Nikolai, 236
Bolsheviks: antireligious campaign of, 117–18; and church disestablishment, 31; and clergy, social revolution in, 28–30; and relics, 124; and religious revival, 43, 44–45, 48; and Russian Orthodox Church, 10–11, 161
Boltnev, A. E., 256
Book of Daniel, 250
Bourdeaux, Michael, 219, 239n5
Bourdieu, Pierre, 243n56
Brezhnev, Leonid, 289, 304–5, 318

Bublikov, Sergey, 228
Bulgakov, S. V., 216n60
Bulganin, Nikolai, 263n2
Burak, S., 321
Burds, Jeffrey, 257
bystanders as narrative category, 235
Bystrova, Tamara, 228–29

calendar reforms, 34, 35–36, 57n61
Celmina, Helene, 259
censorship, 310
*Central Asian Review* on Jehovah's Witnesses, 270n103
Chaves, Mark, 25n13
Cheka. *See* secret police
Chesnokova, Valentina, 328n58
children: illegitimate, 73, 83; and Jehovah's Witnesses, 257–58, 269n85; in Jewish family life, 65–72, 89; religious education of, 57n66; and sacramental confession, 198, 207, 216n67
Chivilikhin, Vladimir, 305, 324n6
"Christian" (Khristianin) (publishing house), 222, 224, 228, 242n42
"Christmas Appeal to Engaged Atheists" (Lukyanenko), 323
Chukov, Grigorii, 200
*Church and Religion in the USSR* (Kuroedov), 251
church closures: and antireligious campaigns, 315–16; in Brezhnev years, 318; in Great Terror, 119; illegal, 37–38; and sacramental confessions, 198–99; and Trinity-Sergius Lavra, 118
church desecration, 176–80
church property, confiscation of, 31–32, 52–53nn23–25, 53n30, 53–54nn34–35
Church Slavonic, 34
circumcisions, 290
clergy: and politics of piety, 45–46; social revolution in, 28–30
clerical estate, 29
closings of churches. *See* church closures
clothes as offerings, 171–72

cobelievers as narrative category, 233–34
Code on Marriage, the Family, and Guardianship of 1918 (Soviet Union), 72–73
Coleman, Heather, 253
collectivization of agriculture, 194–95, 251, 266$n$39
Communist Party, 35–36, 146, 165, 250
concentration camps, 225–26, 231, 249
confession. *See* sacramental confession
confessional seal, 213$n$11
conscientious objectors, 321
consistories, closing of, 192
Corley, Felix, 262
Council of Churches of Evangelical Christians–Baptists, 219–22, 298$n$37, 320
Council of 1917–18, 196
Council of Prisoners' Relatives, 221, 242$n$42
Council for Religious Affairs (CRA): and Jehovah's Witness history, 248; and Kuroedov, 307; and propaganda, 258, 259–62; and religious revival, 309, 311, 312, 315–16, 319; and sectarianism, 246, 251–52, 255; and Soviet critique, 256, 257
Council for Religious Cult Affairs, 245, 248, 250–51, 279, 280, 288
Council for Russian Orthodox Church Affairs: and antireligious campaigns, 144; creation of, 120, 279; personnel changes in, 143; and pilgrimages, 164, 166, 169–70, 284; role of, 131, 137; and Trinity-Sergius Lavra, 120–21, 125, 126, 138, 142, 148
courtship practices, 72–81, 89–90
CRA. *See* Council for Religious Affairs

Dasevych, M., 321
Davie, Grace, 178
Dennen, Leon, 71
denunciations, 155$n$78, 193, 213$n$10
deportations of Jehovah's Witnesses, 244–45, 250, 263$n$2, 266$n$33, 270$n$103

desecration of churches, 176–80
de-Stalinization campaigns, 143, 151
Dikarev, B. T., 55$n$41
divorces, 73, 207–8, 209
Dormition Cathedral of the Holy Trinity–Saint Sergius Lavra. *See* Trinity-Sergius Lavra
Dubovinskyi, M., 321
Dudin, Andrei, 168, 172
Dudko, Dimitry, 203
Durkheim, Émile, 242$n$50
Dvorkin, Aleksandr, 269–70$n$93
Dzyuba, Ivan, 308

"Economic and Philosophic Manuscripts of 1844" (Marx), 25$n$9
education, gender differences in, 67–70, 89
elderly people: and pilgrimages, 178, 179–80; and sacramental confession, 206
elders, spiritual, 195–200
Engels, Friedrich, 252
Engelstein, Laura, 253, 268–69$n$78
Etkind, Alexander, 251
"European exceptionalism," 7
Evangelical Christian Brotherhood, 221, 224, 233
Evangelical Christians–Baptists, 20–21, 218–43; and Banderites, 111, 116$n$70; and biographical canon, 222–26; in Mari Republic, 279; numbers of, 13; and religious revival, 320–22; and Soviet national anthem, 276, 296$n$12; and suffering, dimensions of, 226–32; and suffering, social space of, 232–37
Evangelical Research Center, 240
"exploration of uninhabited buildings" campaigns, 316–17

faith heroes (*geroi very*), 223–26, 229–30, 233, 234
family life, Jewish. *See* Jewish family life
famines, 90, 162
*Father* (Khrapov), 220

Federal Security Service of the Russian Federation (Federal'naya sluzhba bezopasnosti Rossiyskoy Federatsii, FSB), 194, 195
Feodosii, Bishop (Sergeev), 54–55n41
Filaret, Metropolitan, 144
Filaret, Metropolitan (Denysenko), 319
Filimonov, E. G., 254, 255, 261
Filipovich, Leonty, 213n6
*Fire Ordeal* (Khrapov), 220
First Five-Year Plan (1928–32), 194, 195
First Letter to the Corinthians, 232
Fishman, David, 68
Flerin, Dimitrii, 193
Fletcher, William, 311
folklore, 277–78
Foreign Agency of the Council of Churches and the Russian Gospel Ministries, 221
freedom of religion, 149–50
Freeze, ChaeRan, 82
Freeze, Gregory L., 10, 12–13, 14, 27, 331
Friedenstimme (missionary organization), 222
Froese, Paul, 251
Frolova, Nadezhda Nikitichna, 202
Fudel', Sergei Iosifovich, 202

Galicia: Orthodox communities in, 319; Ukrainians in, 95–96, 102–3
Gamer, Helena, 211–12
Gavrish, Vasilii, 259
Geertz, Clifford, 241n21
gender socialization, 65–72, 89. *See also* women
Gentile Times era, 266n23
Georgia, nationalism in, 308
Georgian Orthodox Church, 308
Gerasimets, A. S., 250
Germany, Bandera movement and, 96
Gitelman, Zvi, 17, 90n1
glasnost, 305
Glavlit (General Directorate for the Protection of State Secrets in the Press), 310

"Glory to Ukraine!" greeting, 101
Golev, Sergey, 223, 233
*Golos* (newspaper) on pilgrimage processions, 168
Golubtsov, Aleksandr P., 200, 213n8
Golubtsov, Nikolai, 200–3, 215n48, 216n72
Gorbachev, Mikhail, 149, 245, 305, 307
Gordienko, N. S., 265n17, 266n33
Gorsuch, Anne, 67
Gosudarstvennoye politicheskoye upravlenie (GPU, state political directorate), 33, 38, 41, 42, 44–46, 48
*govenie* (preparation for confession), 191
GPU. *See* Gosudarstvennoye politicheskoye upravlenie
Grachev, Yuri, 220
graveyards, religious rituals at, 281, 285
Great Terror of 1937–38, 14, 73, 118–19
"great turn" (*velikii perelom*), 27, 28, 49
Greek Catholic Church: legal status of, 314, 316; members in, 319; and national identity, 327–28n46; property of, 320; and Sheptytsky, 93–95, 106, 110
Greene, Robert H., 163, 165
Gregorian calendar, 34
Gritsenko, Vasilii, 213n10
Gritsenko, Yekaterina, 224
groves, sacred. *See* sacred groves
Gruzdev, Pavel, 198, 203, 214n29
*Gulag Archipelago* (Solzhenitsyn), 220
gulags, 119, 244, 259
Gurii, Archimandrite (Viacheslav Egorov), 127–28, 153n34, 153n38

Halbwachs, Maurice, 222
head coverings, 273, 297n24
Helsinki Accords of 1975, 251
Helsinki Group, 323
Hentosh, Liliana, 113n12
Himka, John-Paul, 15–16, 93, 303, 331
*History of Religious Sectarianism in Russia* (Klibanov), 261
Holocaust, 81, 242n51

Holodomor (Ukrainian Famine of 1932–33), 90
Holy Communion, 212
Holy Synod, 121, 166
Holy Trinity–Saint Sergius Lavra. *See* Trinity-Sergius Lavra
holy water, 146, 150
"home churches," 321
homilies, 201–2, 203, 205
homosexuality, 142
"How I Broke with a Pagan Sect" (Kirillov), 275
Hryniokh, Ivan, 98
human rights, 304, 323, 324
Husband, William, 4

"icon renewals," 40–41, 59$n$85
icons, pilgrimages and, 162, 166–73
"Iegovisty" (Jehovists), 245, 251, 256, 258–63, 264$n$5. *See also* Jehovah's Witnesses
Initsiativniki (Reform Baptists), 245
Innokentyi, Hegumen (Pavlov), 325$n$9
Institute for Scientific Atheism, 305
intermarriages, 64, 74–81, 89, 90, 278, 291, 297$n$19. *See also* marriage partners, choice of
internationalism, 71–72, 74–75, 80
*In the Abyss of Herod* (Grachev), 220
Intourist, 147
Ioann, Archimandrite (Dmitrii Razumov), 128–29, 134, 135, 137–39
Ioann, Bishop, 174, 175
Iosif, Archimandrite (Evseenok), 136, 141, 142, 144
Iosif, Hegumen (Iatsuk), 194
Islam, 277, 289–90, 294
Iurchenko, Varsonofii, 197
"I Write Unto You, Little Children" (Khorev), 221

Jehovah's Witnesses, 20–21, 244–71; and anti-Ieogvisty propaganda, 258–63, 270$n$99; as conscientious objectors, 321; deportations of, 244–45, 250, 263$n$2, 266$n$33, 270$n$103; historical context for, 247–51; membership base of, 13; and religious revival, 320; and sectarianism, 247–48; and secularization, 246, 251–53; Soviet critiques of, 253–58; U.S. headquarters of, 246, 253–54
Jewish family life, 13–14, 63–92; boys and girls in, 65–72, 89; courtship and marriage partners in, 72–81, 89–90; interviews on, 65, 66 (table 2.1); modesty in, 69–70, 89; wedding ceremonies in, 81–88, 89–90. *See also* Jews
Jews, 99, 102, 103, 111. *See also* Jewish family life
J. M. Dawson Institute of Church-State Studies, 181$n$4
John of Kronstadt, 203
John Paul II, 113$n$23
Joseph II, 94
*Journal of the Moscow Patriarchate*, publication of, 120

Kalinin, Mikhail, 30–31
Kalugin, V. I., 267$n$40
Kandyba, Ivan, 323
Karpov, Georgii: and antireligious campaigns, 146; and church restoration, 133; and Council for Russian Orthodox Church Affairs, 120, 137; and monasteries, 121, 123, 126–27, 128–29, 141, 142
Kasyanova, Xenia, 318, 328$n$58
Kazakov, G., 261
Kenworthy, Scott, 17–18, 117, 197, 216$n$64, 332
Keston Institute, 181$n$4, 239$n$5
KGB (Komitet gosudarstvennoy bezopasnosti): and antireligious campaigns, 144, 313; depiction of, 235, 236; and religious activists, 304; and Russian Orthodox Church, 149; surveillance by, 321
*khadorim* (Jewish primary schools), 68, 89
*kheyder* (Jewish single-class schools), 68

Khomiak, Mykhailo, 114$n$28
Khorev, Ivan Mikhailovich, 225, 241$n$31
Khorev, Mikhail, 220–21, 225, 230, 232, 241$n$26
Khrapov, Nikolai, 220, 225, 226
Khrushchev, Nikita, 151, 219, 246, 274–75, 303, 322, 329$n$70. *See also* Khrushchev's antireligious campaigns
Khrushchev's antireligious campaigns: and children and youth, 257; and communist ideology, 210, 289; failure of, 17; and monasteries, 18, 118, 137, 142–50; and pilgrims, 177, 284; and religious revival, 315; repression under, 166; and rural population, 216$n$66
Khukhrianskii, Melkhizedek, 194
*khupa* (ceremonial canopies), 86–87, 88
Kirillov, V., 275–76, 283
*Kirovskaia Pravda* (periodical) on pilgrimages, 165, 170
Kizenko, Nadieszda, 19, 190, 332
klezmer music, 86, 87, 89
Klibanov, Aleksandr, 261, 264$n$7
Klochkov, V. V., 257, 261
Knowledge Society (Obshchestvo Znanie), 286–87, 290, 292, 299$n$49
Knox, Zoe, 13, 20–21, 244, 332
Kolarz, Walter, 247
Koltun, Mikhail, 314
Komsomol (Young Communist League), 35, 37, 56$n$55, 64, 80, 162, 257
Konik, Vasilii, 245, 247–48, 254, 258–59
Kormina, Jeanne, 177
Korogodina, Maria, 209
Korostelev, V. F., 261
Kostenko, Lina, 324$n$1
Kovalenko, L. E., 240
Kovalewsky, D., 321
Kovch, Emyliian, 100, 113$n$23, 114$n$41
Kozlovskyi, Ivan, 317
Krapov, N., 241$n$26
Krasnov-Levitin, Anatoliy, 320
Krechkov, Tikhon, 194
kulaks (prosperous peasants), 12, 33, 43, 48–49

Kuroedov, Vladimir, 251, 267$n$42, 307, 316, 325$n$15
Kursk Korennaia procession, 170
Kushnirchuk, Maria Fedorovna, 258
Kuzovenkova, Evgeniia Nikolaevna, 207

Lake Svetloyar, pilgrimages at, 165
Lakhno, Oleksandr, 242$n$42
Lane, Christel, 247, 311
Law on Religious Associations of 1929 (Soviet Union), 164
League of Atheists, 39, 40
League of the Militant Godless, 4, 286
leisure activities, 71, 72
Lenin, Vladimir: and antireligious campaigns, 305–6; and church disestablishment, 31; on religion and state power, 11–12; and religious belief, 252, 304; and socialism, 5; on societal structure, 294; and Trinity-Sergius Lavra, 124; and Ukrainian autonomy, 306; on Ukrainian communists, 325$n$13
Lenkavsky, Stepan, 110
Levitin-Krasnov, Anatolyi, 312
*Life in Death* (Khrapov), 220
Likhachev, Dmitrii, 293
Lipkovshchina (Ukrainian Autocephalous Church), 47
Living Church, 32–33, 37, 46, 55$n$45, 56$n$49, 199
love, romantic, 73, 74
Luehrmann, Sonja, 21–22, 272, 332
Lukyanenko, Levko, 323
Lutheran Church, 308
L'viv (Ukraine): historical background on, 94; OUN in, 98; pogrom in, 99, 114$n$28

Maeva, Rogneda Vladimirovna, 202
"magic of the state," 25$n$17
Malanchuk, Valentyn, 307
Malenkov, Georgy Maximilianovich, 138
Malyi Donskoi Cathedral, 199
*mamzerim* (illegitimate children), 83
Marchenko, Valeriy, 322–23, 330$n$72
Maria Theresa (Habsburg empress), 94

Mari Republic, 21–22, 272–301; and atheist critiques, 288–92; campaigns and realities in, 274–78; religious diversity in, 286–88, 292–95; and sacred sites, 282–86; and sects, 274–76, 278–83, 294–95

marriage partners: choice of, 72–81, 89–90; nationalities of, 76–81, 89. *See also* intermarriages

Martel, René, 103

Martin, David, 25*n*14

martyrdom, Evangelical Christians–Baptists and, 222, 238

Marx, Karl, 5, 25*n*9, 252

Marxism-Leninism, 310, 324

Marxists, conversion of, 303

Marynovich, Myroslav, 323

"master narratives," 223, 241*n*25

matchmakers (*shadkhan*) and matchmaking, 63–64, 74, 77, 82, 89, 90

May, Henry F., 247

McNeill, John, 211–12

Mechev, Sergei, 197

Melnyk, Andrii, 97–99, 102, 107, 110

memoirs and personal narratives, 160, 181*n*3, 219–38, 322

men: and autocephalous church movement, 46; and religious revival, 43

Men', Alexander, 203

Meshko, Oksana, 323

Mikhei, Hieromonk (Alykov), 141, 142

Millennium of Christianity in Rus', 149, 316

Mil'tonov, Aleksandr, 194

Miner, Steven Merritt, 184*n*

"miracles," 40–41

miraculous healings, 172

Misiruk, Stepan, 224, 241*n*28

misogyny, 208–9

Mitrokhin, Nikolai, 128, 153*n*38, 155*n*75

Moldova, monasteries in, 122

*moleben* (prayer services), 167, 168–69, 173–74, 176, 199, 210

Molotov, Vyacheslav Mikhailovich, 126

monasticism, 121–24, 163, 197. *See also* Trinity–Sergius Lavra

Moroz, Valentyn, 320

Moscow Central Municipal Archive, 209

Moscow Patriarchate, 133–34, 137, 138, 144

Moses, 252

mosques, 281, 289

Mother of God. *See* Virgin Mary

museums, 132–33, 163, 183*n*27

Muslims. *See* Islam

Myroshnichenko, Evgeniya, 306

Nabatov, Aleksandr, 280–81, 284, 288, 289–90

*namolennye* (power from veneration), 177

Narkompros (People's Commissariat of Enlightenment), 40

Narodnyi Komissariat Iustitsii (People's Commissariat of Justice), 183*n*27

Narodnyy Komissariat Vnutrennikh Del (People's Commissariat for Internal Affairs, NKVD), 30, 38, 49, 57*n*66, 118, 181–82*n*9, 193–95

*Nastol'nye knigi* (priests' guides), 204–6, 207–9, 216*n*60

nationalism, 47, 93, 95–112

nationalities, marriage choices and, 76–81, 89

National Unity Day, 182*n*13

Nazis, 119–20

New Economic Policy (NEP), 27, 48

"new Soviet man," 2, 10, 246, 257, 263

Nicholas II, 191

Nicholas the Wonderworker: and church closures, 198; and desecration of churches, 176; and pilgrimages, 159, 165–73, 283

Nikon, Hieromonk (Preobrazhenskii), 141–42, 145

NKVD. *See* Narodnyy Komissariat Vnutrennikh Del

Nuffield Foundation, 263*n*1

obediences (monastic work assignments), 128

*The Object and Manner of Our Lord's Return* (Bible Students), 249

Odintsov, Mikhail, 248, 250
OGPU. *See* secret police
Okopnyi, Borys Petrovich, 198
Okudzhava, Bulat, 329–30n71
Old Believers, 280
Oleszynski, R. H., 249
"On Measures for Stopping Pilgrimages to So-Called Holy Sites" (1958 Soviet resolution), 146, 166, 174
"On the Administrative Responsibility for the Violation of Legislation on Religious Cults" (Ukrainian Supreme Council), 321
"On the Transfer to the Moscow Patriarchate of Buildings Located on the Territory of the Trinity–Sergius Lavra" (Soviet of Ministers), 138
Operation Iug (South), 250, 266n33
Operation Sever (North), 244, 250
"opiate of the people," religion as, 5
Organization of Ukrainian Nationalists (OUN), 96–102, 109–10, 114n41
Orthodox Christianity and Church: and church-state relations, 147, 149; disestablishment of, 30–35; in Mari Republic, 273, 277; and pilgrimages, 159–63; and sacramental confession, 190–91, 195–96, 203, 207, 211, 212; and sectarianism, 279; and secularization, 7; and Stalin, 120; and Trinity–Sergius Lavra, 117, 125–27; and Ukrainian national identity, 315, 327–28n46. *See also* Greek Catholic Church
Orthodox Church of America, 212
Ostal'skii, Arkadii Iosifovich, 53n25
Ottoman Empire, 213n8
OUN. *See* Organization of Ukrainian Nationalists

paganism, 185n59, 275–76, 280, 282, 284, 288, 294
"Pamyat" (Memory), 305, 325n8
Panchenko, A. A., 184n33, 186n88
Pankivsky, Kost, 116n70
Panteleimon, Saint, 198

Panych, Olena, 13, 20–21, 218, 332
Pashkovskyi, I., 321
Paul VI (pope), 312
Pavlenko, V. N., 226–27
Pavlov, S. N., 328–29n61
"Peace in the Lord!" (On the Murder of Priests) (Sheptytsky), 109
Peledysh Pairem (Festival of (Red) Flowers), 288
Pelikh, Tikhon, 200
penance, notions of, 204–9, 211–12
Pentecostals, 245, 320, 321
Peris, Daniel, 4, 15
personal narratives. *See* memoirs and personal narratives
Peter the Great, 150, 191, 192
pilgrimages, 18–19, 159–89; and antireligious campaigns, 145–47; and desecration of churches, 176–80; and early Soviet practice, 168–69; improvisation of, 169–73; and late imperial practice, 167–68; nature of, 160–64; restriction of, 173–76, 180, 283–84; and secularization, 164–66, 180; Velikoretskoe procession of the cross, 159, 160, 165, 166–80
Pimen, Archimandrite (Izvekov), 138, 140–41, 144, 146–47
Pimen, Archimandrite (Khmelevskii), 144, 147–49
pine trees, veneration at, 172–73, 176. *See also* sacred groves
Pivovarov, Viktor, 290–91
Plokhy, Serhii, 26n21
Plyshevskaia, Maria Sil'vestrovna, 204
Plyshevskaia, Tamara, 198–99
Pochaev Lavra, 122, 144
Pochvennichestvo (Return to the Soil), 308
Poizdnyk, Inna, 95, 104
Pokrovskii, I.V., 121–23, 152n11
Poles, mass murder of, 102–8, 114n41
Polikarp, Bishop, 174, 175
Polikarpov, Vasilii, 33
political protests, 161–62
Poselianin, Evgenii, 196

Pospielovsky, Dimitry, 3
poverty, 84–85
Powell, David, 3–4
"A Prayer to Ukraine" (Banderite movement), 110
*Priests' Tableside Companions*, 204–9, 216*n*60
Prokhanov, Alexander, 305, 324–25*n*7
Prokopiv, Volodymyr, 319
propaganda: antireligious, 12, 38–40, 58*n*75; and anti-Semitism, 74–75; atheist, 34–35, 305; and Jehovah's Witnesses, 255–63, 270*n*99
punishments, gender socialization and, 65, 67, 69, 72

Rabinowitch, Sholem (Sholem Aleichm), 74
Radio Free Europe, 200
Ransel, David, 85
*The Record of Violence against a Religious Organization Unparalleled in America since the Attacks on the Mormons* (American Civil Liberties Union), 254
Red Army, 161, 199
Redlich, Shimon, 108–9
"Regulations Concerning Religious Organizations in the Ukrainian SSR" (1976), 304–5
relics, 124–26, 131, 136, 150, 163, 183*n*27
religious revivals, 22, 302–30; and antireligious campaigns, 40–44; and dissent, 318–23; and mass atheism, challenges to, 308–12; and popular religiosity, 312–18; and secularization, 1–2; and Soviet antireligious policy, 303–6; and Soviet antireligious policy, Ukrainian versions of, 306–8
*Religioznaia sekta Iegovistov* (Gerasimets and Reshetnikov), 253
Renovationists, 32–34, 54*n*38, 54–55*nn*40–41, 55*n*45, 55*nn*48–49, 121, 168–69

revivals, religious. *See* religious revivals
Revolution of 1848 (Ukraine), 94
Riabus, Alla, 246
ritual baths (*mikvah*), 82
Rock, Stella, 18–19, 159, 283, 332
Rockefeller family, 253
Roman Catholic Church, 94, 106, 111, 212
Romanov, Aleksei Mihailovich, 192
romantic love, 73, 74
Romanyuk, Vasyl', 323
Roosevelt, Elliot, 139
Roslof, Edward E., 209–10
rural areas: backwardness of, 216*n*66; religious revival in, 42–43
Russell, Charles Taze, 248–49, 253, 259, 266*n*23, 267*n*52
"Russellites," 259
Russian Gospel Ministries, 222
Russian Orthodox Church. *See* Orthodox Christianity and Church
*The Russian Religious Renaissance of the Twentieth Century* (Zernov), 303
Ruthenian people, 94–95
Rutherford, Joseph Franklin, 259
"Rutherfordites," 259
Rytikova, Galina, 240

Sabantui (plowing festival), 287–88
sacramental confession, 19–20, 190–217; background on, 190–92; increase in, 43; in postwar era, 200–204; and secret police, 193–95; and sin and penance, 204–9, 211–12; and spiritual elders, 195–200; statistics on, 209–10
sacred groves, 273, 276, 278, 283, 285
sacred sites, 164, 166, 282–86, 289. *See also* springs as sacred sites
sacred time, 232, 236, 238
samizdat, 160, 179, 220, 322
Sarov monastery, 177
Savel'ev, Viktor, 280, 289, 299*n*59
Savva, Hieromonk (Ostapenko), 145
Sawatsky, Walter, 218
Schmemann, Alexander, 200, 212, 215*n*37

"seating the bride" ceremonies, 82
"Second Presence," 249, 266n24
secret police (Obyedinyonnoye gosudarstvennoye politicheskoye upravleniye, OGPU), 43, 45, 47–48, 193–95
sectarianism (*sektantstvo*), 48, 245–48, 251
sects, Mari Republic and, 274–76, 278–83, 294–95
secularization: and antireligious campaigns, 3–7; and Jehovah's Witnesses, 246, 251–53; and pilgrimages, 164–66, 180; and religious change, 10–23; and religious revival, 1–2; rethinking, 7–10; and sacramental confession, 197; and Soviet Jews, 64
*Seekers of Happiness* (film), 74
seminaries, 29
Senin, O., 329
"Sentimental March" (Okudzhava), 329–30n71
Separation Decree (1918), 11
separation of church and state, 11, 30, 31, 161, 166
Serafim, Archimandrite (Shinkarev), 145
Seraphim, Saint, 163, 171, 177
Serebrennikov, Vasilii, 200
*seredniaki* (middle peasants), 43
Sergeevna, Ol'ga, 200
Sergiev, John, 196
Sergii, Metropolitan (Stragorodskii), 119, 120, 121, 128, 135, 204
Sergius of Radonezh: relics of, 124, 125–26, 131, 136, 145, 150; and Trinity–Sergius Lavra, 117
"Sermon to Ukrainian Youth" (Sheptytsky), 97
Seventh-Day Adventists, 265n16, 279, 320
Shcherbitsky, Volodymyr, 306–8
Sheptytsky, Andrei, 15–16, 93–116; and Bandera movement, 96, 98–102, 107, 109, 110–12; biographical details on, 94–95; and liturgy books, 320; and Melnyk faction, 97–99, 102, 107; and Poles, mass murder of, 102–8; and Ukrainian national movement, 95–112
Sheptytsky, Klymentii, 106
Shevardnadze, Edward, 326n16
Shkarovskii, M. V., 131
Shpiller, Vsevolod, 200, 203
Shternshis, Anna, 10, 13, 63, 332–33
*shtetlekh* (small villages), 85–88
Sich Sharpshooters, 96
Simanskii, Aleksii, 120
Simeon of Verkhotur'e, 161
Simon, Gerhard, 312
sin, notions of, 204–9, 211–12
Sivers, Sampson, 203–4
Skoptsy, 253, 268–69n78
Sloboda, Nadezhda, 229
Smirnov, Ioann, 196
Smolkin-Rothrock, Victoria, 324
social revolution in clergy, 28–30
Society for the Dissemination of Political and Scientific Knowledge, 286
"soft line" on religion, 36, 46
Sohor, Lev, 100–101
Solidarity (nongovernmental organization), 308
Solov'ev, Aleksii, 200, 215n40
Solov'ev, Viktor, 290–92, 293, 294
Solzhenitsyn, Alexandr, 220
souvenirs from shrines, 171, 186n88
Soviet of Ministers, 120, 123, 133, 138, 144
Soviet Union, rethinking religion in, 10–23. *See also specific bodies of believers (e.g.,* Jehovah's Witnesses*)*
Soviet Writers Union, 16
spiritual elders, 195–200
Spiritual Regulation of 1722 (Russia), 191, 192, 193
springs as sacred sites, 146, 151, 164, 166, 171, 183–84n33
Stalin, Joseph: and church recognition, 199; and church tolerance, 118, 119–20, 123–24; and concentration camps, 225; and "cult of personality," 329n70; religious laws under,

251; and "religious propaganda," 305; and Trinity-Sergius Lavra, 124, 126, 131, 134, 136, 149; and Ukrainian autonomy, 306
Stark, Rodney, 25n13
State Archive of the Russian Federation, 209
State Security Ministry (Soviet Union), 244
Stepanovna, Nadezhda, 229
Stetsko, Yaroslav, 98, 110–11
Stolbenskii, Nil, 163
Stone, Andrew, 26n23, 266n39
Stus, Vasyl', 324n1
suffering: and biographical canon, 222–26; dimensions of, 226–32, 238; social space of, 232–37
Suslov, Mikhail, 305–6
Sventsitskii, Valentin, 197
Sverstyuk, Yevgen, 308, 324n1
Symeon the New Theologian, 201
sympathizers as narrative category, 234–35
Szeptycki, Roman. *See* Sheptytsky, Andrei

Talantov, Boris, 176
Tarasii, Hegumen (Mishin), 145
Tarnavsky, Manuil, 116n61
Tatars, 273, 277, 287, 291
Taussig, Michael, 25n17
"The Ten Commandments of a Ukrainian Nationalist" (Lenkavsky), 110
Terror of 1937–38. *See* Great Terror of 1937–38
Tevz, Maria, 228–29
Theological Academy, 133–34, 135, 144
Tikhon, Patriarch, 30–31, 183n26
Tikhonites, 32–33, 41, 43, 46, 48, 55n45, 61n124, 168
Timofievich, A. P., 183n24
Tolgskii, Aleksandr, 200
torture, practice of, 243n58
traitors as narrative category, 233–34
Transfiguration Church, 167, 169–70, 176

Trinity-Sergius Lavra, 17–18, 117–58; background on, 119–21; brotherhood, reestablishing of, 118, 127–30; and Khrushchev's antireligious campaign, 118, 143–50; and late Stalin period, 1946–53, 131–36, 149; in middle 1950s, 137–43; and monasticism during and after World War II, 121–24; reopening of, 118, 124–27
Trotsky, Leon, 31
True Orthodox Church (Istinnaia Pravoslavnaia Tserkov'), 170, 280
Trushin, Aleksei Alekseevich: and antireligious campaigns, 144–45, 146–49, 150; and church restoration, 134; and Council for Russian Orthodox Church Affairs, 120; and monastery's influence, 135–36; and monastic brotherhood, 140, 141–42; reports of, 154n46, 209–10; and Trinity-Sergius Lavra, 128, 131–32
*The Truth About Religion in Russia* (Moscow Patriarchate), 199
*tserkovniki* (unordained clergy), 12, 28, 48–49, 50n5
Tsyba, M., 321
Twardowski, Bolesław, 105, 106–7, 108, 109, 115n48

Udmurts, 273
Ukraine, antireligious campaigns in. *See* antireligious campaigns
Ukraine, religious revivals in. *See* religious revivals
Ukrainian Autocephalous Orthodox Church, 47
Ukrainian Greek Catholic Church. *See* Greek Catholic Church
Ukrainian Insurgent Army (Ukrayins'ka Povstans'ka Armiya, UPA), 96, 102–3, 104, 109–10, 111, 115–16n61
Ukrainian National Democratic Union (UNDO), 112n7
*Ukrains'ki shchodenni visti* (newspaper) and Bandera movement, 99–100
Uniates, 94, 319, 320

Union of Brest agreement (1596), 320
Union of Evangelical Christians–Baptists, 219
Union of Militant Atheists, 15
United Nations, 144
urban areas, religious revival in, 42, 43–44

Varnava, Schemamonk-Hierodeacon (Zaitsev), 145
Vasilevskaia, Vera, 164, 180–81
Vasilyev, Dmitrii, 305, 325$n$8
Velikoretskoe Church, 170, 174
Velikoretskoe procession of the cross, 159, 160, 165, 166–80
Vendland, Ioann, 128, 131
Veniamin, Archimandrite (Viktor Milov), 129–30, 136, 137, 154$n$42
*Vestnik istiny* (journal), Khorev on editorial board of, 221
Viatka Cathedral, 169
Viatka Diocese, 169, 185$n$65
Vins, Georgi, 220–21, 225, 231, 239$n$9, 241$n$26, 323
Vins, Lidia, 221, 240
Vins, Natasha, 240$n$17
Vins, Peter, 221
Virgin Mary, 171, 283
"virtuosi," religious, 197, 202–3, 211, 215$n$39
Vladykin, Pavel, 220
Voice of Peace Christian Mission of Portland, 222
Volksdeutsche, 107
Volodymyr, Metropolitan (Sabodan), 319
Volodymyr, Patriarch, 323
Voskresenskii, Aleksandr, 200
*Vostochno-Sibirskaia pravda* (periodical) on Jehovah's Witnesses, 246
Vrublevskyi, Valeryi, 306–7
Vvedenskii, Aleksandr, 40

Waffen-SS, 102
Wanner, Catherine, 1, 190–91, 226–27, 333
Watch Tower Bible and Tract Society: and deportations, 244, 263$n$2; and Jehovah's Witness history, 248, 249–50; membership records of, 260–61; registration of, 245; and Soviet critique, 256; theology of, 255
*Watchtower* magazine: circulation of, 255; and communism, 259; on deportations, 244, 250; and Soviet critique, 256
Weber, Max, 5, 7, 197
wedding ceremonies, 81–88, 89–90
Wendell, Jonas, 248–49
"White-guardist" emigré press, 39
women: and abortion, 208; gender socialization of, 65–72, 89; imprisoned for religious beliefs, 242$n$42; and marriage, 72–81; and misogyny, 208–9; and pilgrimages, 161–62, 179–80; in religious groups, 42–43; and religious traditions, 72; and sacramental confession, 202, 204, 208–11
World Council of Churches, 144

Yelchenko, Yuryi, 307
Yelensky, Viktor, 8, 22, 302, 333
Yiddish language, 69–70, 74
Young, Glennys, 4, 162
Young Pioneers, 61$n$116, 65, 257

ZAGS (Otdel Zapisi aktov grazhdanskogo sostoyaniia, Civil Registry Office), 73, 76, 83–84, 87–88
Zakharov, Pavel, 227
Zelinskii, Vladimir, 323
Zernov, Nikolai, 303
Zheltova, Nina Fedorovna, 202
Zhuk, Sergei, 251, 253
Zhylenko, Iryna, 324$n$1
Zinov'ev, Grigorii, 57$n$61
Zionism, 17
*Zion's Watch Tower and Herald of Christ's Presence* (periodical), 249
Zion's Watch Tower and Tract Society, 249. *See also* Watch Tower Bible and Tract Society
*Znamia* (Banner) on Jehovah's Witnesses, 256
Zyatek, P., 321